VLSI 87

VLSI Design of Digital Systems

IFIP TC 10/WG 10.5 International Conference on
Very Large Scale Integration
Vancouver, Canada, 10–12 August 1987

NORTH-HOLLAND
AMSTERDAM • NEW YORK • OXFORD • TOKYO

VLSI 87

VLSI Design of Digital Systems

Proceedings of the IFIP TC 10/WG 10.5 International Conference on
Very Large Scale Integration
Vancouver, Canada, 10–12 August 1987

edited by

Carlo H. SÉQUIN

University of California
Berkeley, CA
U.S.A.

1988

NORTH-HOLLAND
AMSTERDAM ● NEW YORK ● OXFORD ● TOKYO

ISBN: 0 444 70370 5

Published by:
ELSEVIER SCIENCE PUBLISHERS B.V.
P.O. Box 1991
1000 BZ Amsterdam
The Netherlands

Sole distributors for the U.S.A. and Canada:
ELSEVIER SCIENCE PUBLISHING COMPANY, INC.
52 Vanderbilt Avenue
New York, N.Y. 10017
U.S.A.

PRINTED IN THE NETHERLANDS

VLSI '87

international conference

August 10, 11, 12, 1987
Vancouver, Canada

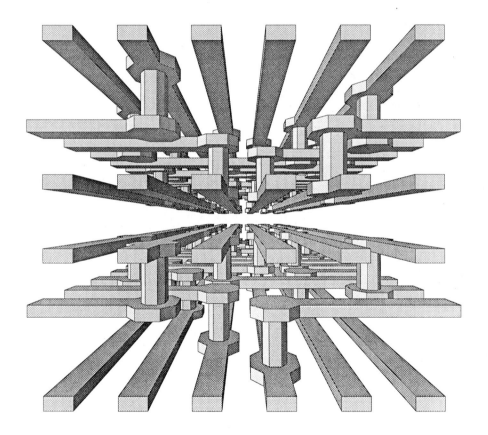

PREFACE

VLSI — The Last 10 Years — The Next 10 Years

VLSI'87 is the fourth in a series of bi-annual international conferences on Very Large Scale Integration. All but the first one have been organized by the working group WG 10.5 (VLSI), of the IFIP Technical Committee TC 10. Good VLSI systems result from an intergration of expertise in fabrication technology, circuit design, system architecture, and CAD tools. Thus a key concern of this working group and of the conference organizers is to maintain representation throughout the range of disciplines related to the field of VLSI. We would also like to ensure that this conference remains relevant to both the industrial and academic community.

It is about ten years ago that Lynn Conway and Carver Mead started a "movement" that rapidly spread through the academic community and eventually also changed the way of industrial VLSI design. Their computer-science point of view and their vertically-integrated approach to systems design have shaped the nature of most of the periodic VLSI conferences. It opened the emerging field of VLSI to a whole new community of disciples with varied backgrounds. Because of the impact of the ideas that started to emerge from Xerox PARC in 1977, I set the birth date of VLSI in that period. This would make VLSI ten years old today! At such round birthdays it is customary to take stock and look at some of the important developments.

In 1977 the pattern of exponential improvements in technology was already established. Exceeding a million transistors on a single silicon chip was just a matter of time, and the possibility of integrating one billion devices had at least been mentioned, even though most people probably were skeptical.

Circuit design remains an ongoing strong activity. This is crucial for the full exploitation of the technological advances. A lot of activity is concentrated on making ever more dense and effective memory cells or more powerful driver circuits using combinations of CMOS and bipolar technologies. The success of this year's VLSI Circuit Symposium in Karuizawa, Japan attests to this fact.

A dramatic change has occurred in the area of computer-aided design tools. Circuit analysis tools such as SPICE were widely accepted a decade ago, but each company had its own in-house plotting and design-rule-checking tools. Synthesis tools were virtually unknown in 1977. Since then a significant change in attitude has occurred. The number of workers building CAD tools has increased dramatically. A large number of CAD tools now exists in the public domain and interface standards are being developed. More and more of the chip and systems design tasks will be automated.

The fourth branch of VLSI is architecture. The available (simple) design tools have shaped the architectures being implemented in VLSI today, strongly favoring regular structures and reduced instruction sets. But the real revolution is still ahead of us. Multicomputers, systolic arrays, transputers, connection machines, and neural networks explore many interesting avenues. But no approach has been able to achieve any kind of maturity or dominance. The need to solve the generic problem of parallel and distributed computing still lies ahead as one of the crucial challenges for the 1990's.

Thus of the four branches mentioned above, the biggest change has occurred in the area of computer-aided design tools. The central role of CAD is reflected in the theme for this year's conference: "Matching Technology and Architecture with the help of Computer Aided Design", as well as by the submitted papers. The submissions were even more heavily dominated by CAD papers than expected. We received only enough manuscripts for one good architecture session, and not a single technology paper.

Our goal was to keep this conference interdisciplinary. The cross-fertilization between the various disciplines must continue. So the conference committee made a big effort to put together a session on technology that should be of relevance to CAD tool builders and system architects. We brought together a group of experienced people with special knowledge in different technologies that might be crucial for the future of VLSI. We hope that the session on high-performance technologies and the subsequent panel discussion will provide some insight into the bewildering variety of competing technologies and will tell us which ones need to be watched.

Because distributed processing is an issue that we cannot ignore much longer, we also organized the paper submission and reviewing process in a distributed manner. Each paper was reviewed separately in all three geographical domains: Asia and Australia, Europe and Africa, and the Americas. Typically we got six reviews on each paper with a world-wide balance of reviewers. I would like to thank the program committee members and all the reviewers for their effort and dedication.

Finally a word about the frontispiece of these proceedings. The graphic design, executed with the Berkeley UNIGRAFIX system, tries to symbolize several important trends in VLSI.

Firstly, it is a schematic picture of the wiring in a channel between two macro blocks employing six levels of interconnects. Practical programs that can complete channel routing for three or more layers of interconnects are now emerging. Thus the graphic design symbolizes the importance of CAD tools.

Secondly, the figure serves as a reminder that VLSI becomes more and more wire-dominated. An escape into the third dimension will be our only hope to build ever more complex systems on a single chip of silicon.

Lastly, the strongly perspective view is somewhat reminiscent of the opening scene of "Star Wars". This may be taken as a statement that I believe that the field of VLSI remains future-oriented, exciting, and adventurous.

Carlo H. Séquin, Berkeley   *June 1, 1987*

ORGANIZATION

GENERAL CHAIRMAN

D.R. Colton, *Canadian Microelectronics Corporation*

PROGRAM COMMITTEE

C.H. Séquin (Chair), *University of California, Berkeley*
S. Asai, *Hitachi Corporation*
D. Ditzel, *AT & T Bell Laboratories*
S. Goto, *NEC Corporation*
A. Halaas, *University of Trondheim*
H. Hiraishi, *Kyoto University*
K. Horninger, *Siemens AG*
U. Lauther, *Siemens AG*
J. Meindl, *Rensselaer Polytechnic Institute*
S. Murai, *Mitsubishi Corporation*
M. Newman, *Commission of the European Communities*
A.R. Newton, *University of California, Berkeley*
A. Steckl, *Rensselaer Polytechnic Institute*

CONTENTS

Session 3: SPECIFICATION AND VERIFICATION

Session 4: PLACEMENT AND ROUTING

Session 5: PLACEMENT REFINEMENT

Session 6: HIGH-PERFORMANCE TECHNOLOGIES

Session 1
KEYNOTE SPEAKERS

VLSI '87, C.H. Séquin (editor)
Elsevier Science Publishers B.V. (North-Holland)
© IFIP, 1988

DEVELOPMENT OF THREE DIMENSIONAL INTEGRATION TECHNOLOGIES IN JAPAN

Seijiro FURUKAWA

Tokyo Institute of Technology
Dept. of Applied Electronics, Graduate School of Sci. & Eng.
4259 Nagatsuda, Midoriku, Yokohama 227, Japan

It can be said because of physical limits in microfabrication, ULSI
will be reaching the limit in 1990's. As a break-through of such
problems, the vertical integration, that is,3D integration will be
promising. In this paper, the features of 3D integration are considered by comparing with the conventional (2D) LSI,at first. Then, SOI
technology by which crystalline silicon films on insulators are fabricated will be discussed as one of the most important basic technologies
for 3D-IC. After that,the state of the art of 3D-IC and architectual
study concerning with 3D-IC in Japan will be reviewed. Finally, expected problems in 3D-IC will be discussed.

1. INTRODUCTION

As the information society becomes more and more reality, the volume of informations which are processed with high speed will be further increased, resulting
in great need for progress in large scale integrated and high speed system
using solid state devices. Therefore, we could still expect the trend toward
ever-increasing levels of integration and speed in integrated circuits (IC) in
future |1|,|2|.

In the conventional LSI (i.e. two dimensional LSI), however, there would be many
problems,in future, such as 1) difficulties in large area fine patterning, 2)
the increase of signal delay time in the interconnections in a chip and/or
between chips to decrease the speed of the systems, 3) difficulties in integration having more and more functions placed on a chip, and so on. There is a
possible solution for the break-through of such problems. That is to adopt three
dimensional (3D) structure, either partially- or completely-stacked active layers
for the integration of devices. An application of a partial 3D structure has
been tried for cell structures of the very high density dynamic memory (DRAM)
as a trench cell or stacked load resistance. Such 3D integration will be used
broadly in actual productions within a few years. From the view point of the
3D integration, the complete-stacked layer, especially multi-layer can be said
more important for signal processing,since it has such advantages as 1) high
speed operation, 2) parallel processing, 3) multi-function operation and 4)high
packing density.

In this paper, the author will review the features of 3D-IC, SOI and other basic
technologies for 3D-IC, the state of the art of 3D-IC to show the feasibility
of such structure in Japan and so on.

2. FEATURES OF 3D-IC

The general idea about 3D-IC will be obtained by Fig. 1 which shows a complete
3D-IC consisting of monolithic multi-layers. The advantages expected of 3D-IC
can be summarizd as follows;

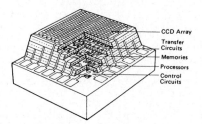

Fig.1 A conceptional view of
an example of 3D-IC's

1) <u>High packing density and/or ultra-large scale integration</u>: This could be
   achieved without havingthe serious problem about power dissipation and the
   sacrifice of signal processing speed, if CMOS or Bi-CMOS circuits were
   employed.

2) <u>High speed for signal processing</u>: This advantage is associated with shorter interconnection delay time and the decrease of parasitic capacitance due
   to SOI structure. Moreover, many engineers seem to have such opinion that
   parallel signal processing can be easily achieved by 3D-IC, because this
   structure could transfer widely different large number of information
   signals from upper to bottom layers or vice-versa through via-holes with
   short interconnections and/or optical signal transmitting methods.

3) <u>Integration of multi-function</u>: Each layer or a set of several layers in
   3D-IC can be assigned for each own functional performance, so that, so
   called " a smart sensor" which has a signal processor as well as a sensors
   can be easily realized as shown in Fig.1. Of course, each layer can be
   adopted for each different type of devices,i.e. MOS and Bipolar transistors.

3.   SOI AND OTHER BASIC TECHNOLOGIES FOR 3D-IC FABRICATION

In order to fabricate 3D-IC successfully, the following basic technologies are
at least necessary:

   1) SOI (Silicon on Insulator) technologies ⌉
   2) Planarization technologies |
   3) Interconnection technologies |-Low Temperature Processes
   4) Via-holes technologies   ⌋

All above technologies have to be consisted with the low temperature processes.
Especially, the effective temperature raised during the crystallization of the
active layers must be kept low enough not to change the performance of the
devices fabricated in the underneath layers for obtaining SOI structures.

3.1   SOI TECHNOLOGIES

There are so many kind of SOI technologies which are classified   in Table 1.
In general speaking, the active layers should have well defined crystalline
orientation as well as good crystallinity. More in detail, if the crystalline
orientation of the layer is not defined, the thickness of gate oxide film will
have a large standard deviation to cause a large standard deviation of the
threshold voltage in MOS inverters. This will cause a drastic decrease in the
production yield. From the view point of crystalline control, the seeding
methods in which the crystalline orientations are defined by those of the Si
substrates will be useful. From the view point of crystallinity, melting and
recrystallization methods give a fairly good result. From the point of effective
low process temperature, laser-beam or electron-beam recrystallization methods
are suitable.

For such reason, laser- or electron beam recrystallization methods have been successfully developed for 3D-IC applications. The beams are scanned along the partially restricted active layer. This means that the effective process temperature is relatively low, though the polycrystalline silicon layer is melted. (The melting temperature of silicon is 1430°C) The basic concept of these methods is control the temperature profile in the poly-silcon layer like twin peaks, as shown in Fig.2. This is the key issue of this methods. If the minimum point of the temperature profile in the melted layer is on the center line between the edges of the restricted layer, the recrystallization of the layer originates on that line to yield a single crystalline layer. On the other hand, if the temperature profile had a single peak, the recrystallization of the melted layer originates at the both sides or random sites to yield poly-crystal or single-crystal having sub-boundaries in the active area. Anyway, it is noted that these beam methods have such a shortcoming as the single crystalline film is obtained only in the restricted area, like stripes.

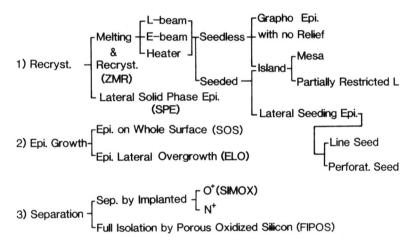

4) Direct Bonding

Table 1. Classification of SOI technologies.

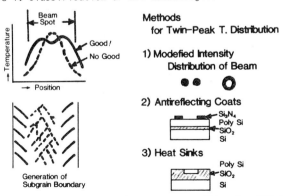

Fig.2 Key issues of Melting and Recrystallization SOI technologies and methods for realizing twin-peak temperature distribution.

Several kinds of methods as shown in Fig.2 have been studied to realize the twin peak temperature distribution. The author think**s** that it is not necessary to explain details about all of the methods, except one. Recently, a crystalline - orientation-controlled,single crystal area has been obtained in chip size level having seeded structure as shown in Fig.3 by laser-beam recrystallization technology. The film by this technology is defect free and the controlled subgrain-boundary is only observed at the deposited anti-reflecting film for laser-beam. Figure 4 shows an optical micrograph of recrystallized silicon film |3|. Many small square patterns show the etched patterns which have been made intentionally to check crystalline orientation. These patterns show that the film is well orientation-controlled.

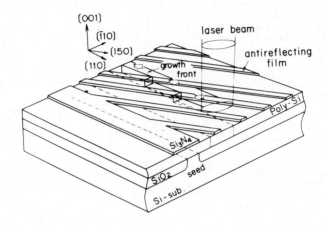

Fig.3   Structure of seed and anti-reflecting film which has
        been developed recently, for laser-beam recrystallization.

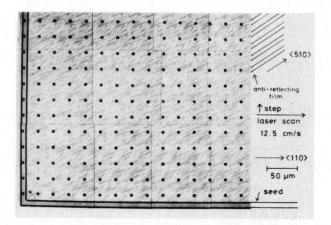

Fig.4   Optical micrograph of laser beam recrystallized Si.

Recent progresses in electron-beam recrystallization methods are 1) Amplitude
Modulation Scanning |4| and Perforation Seed |5| methods. The latter method can
make a fairely good recrystallized silicon film which has no subgrain-boundary
and no void near the seeds. The voids near the seeds were usually obseeved for
the case of the conventional,i.e., line seed. Considering such progresses, the
melting and recrystallization methods by laser- and electron-beam would be more
appreciated as SOI technology for 3D-IC fabrication in future.

Lateral solid phase epitaxy (LSPE) of amorphous Si layers is one of a   promising methods to realize SOI structure for 3D-IC, since it is a low temperature
process (about 600°C). In this method, however, the LSPE growth is essentially
limited by random crystallization or poly-crystallization with randomly nucleat-
ed grains in the layers, and the maximum LSPE length is determined by the competition between LSPE growth rate and the random crystallization. For the non-
doped amorphous Si layer, the maximum LSPE length is shorter than $10 \mu m$ of which
value is almost independent on the annealing temperature. But, if the amorphous
Si layer is heavily doped by phosphorous atoms,the maximum length becomes as
long as $45 \mu m$|6|. The crystallinity in LSPE layer has been checked by MOSFETs
by the other groups|7|. The electron mobility has found to reach as high as 600
cm^2/Vs. This suggests that the crystallinity in LSPE layer is good enough for
device fabrication, at least, at the region near the seed.

Epitaxial growth methods for SOI are now fundamental stage except SOS. But the
author believes that the epitaxial lateral overgrowth (ELO) will become very
useful in future. The separation methods become now a practical level. Separation by Implanted Oxygen (SIMOX) , however, is suitable for 2D-IC rather than
3D-IC, since the furnace heat process as high as 1000°C is necessary for decreas-
ing the defects induced by the high dose implantation|8|. Full Isolation by
Porous Oxidized Silicon (FIPOS) is also just for 2D-IC. Very recently, the direct
bonding of Si wafer on SiO_2/Si wafer has been shown possible |9|. But it can be
said this method is also for 2D-IC application.

3.2   PLANARIZATION TECHNOLOGIES

In 3D-IC fabrication, the planarization technologies are more important than
2D-IC having multi-level interconnections. For this reason, many efforts have
been made. Generally speaking, the technologies are consisted of organic or inorganic material deposition followed by back-etching. Figure 6 shows an example
of the recent works developed |10|. The figure (a) shows the result without
using the planarization technology. The figure (b) shows with using the
technology which is consisted of such processes as 1) dummy patterns are fabricated in the bottom area, 2) organic layer is coated by the spinning method and
3) etching back by the plasma assisted etching method.

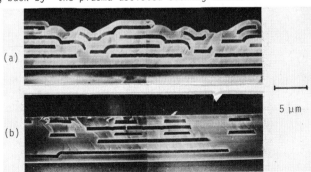

Fig.6. Cross-sectional views of 5 layers interconnections (a) without (b)
       with the planarization technology.

3.3   INTERCONNECTION AND VIA-HOLES TECHNOLOGIES

These technologies have bee developed also for multi-level interconnections in
2D-IC. It is worthwhile to note that via-holes having 1 μm diameter for 1 μm
thick SiO_2 film are now available.

4.   THE STATE OF THE ART OF 3D-IC

4.1   DEVICE PERFORMANCE IN MULTI-LAYER STRUCTURE

A lot of basic studies on device performance in SOI structures by various methods
has been made. The principal interesting properties of devices in multi-layers
are the carrier mobility and threshold voltage of MOS transistors. The experiments made for MOS transistors in 3 layers show that average mobilities of
the transistors fabricated in 2nd and 3rd SOI layers are slightly small compared
with those of bulk Si, though SOI films are observed to be single-crystalline.
Moreover, the divergence(standard deviation/average value) of threshold voltage
of MOS transistors of the 3rd layer is worse than that of the 2nd layer. Table
2 shows an example of carrier mobility statistics in 4" wafer measured from
the transistors in 3 layers, the 2nd and 3rd ones of which were formed by the
laser-beam recrystallization method with seedless structure |10|. Such large
divergences are considered due to crystalline defects and also difference of
the crystalline orientation in SOI films. It is reported recently that the divergences have become lower than 10 % by using crystalline orientation control
by the seeded structure as shown in Fig.3.

Layer	L/W (μm)	Mobility (cm^2/Vs) Average $\bar{\mu}$	Deviation σ	SiO_2 Thickness(A)
1st	1.9/10.3	753.1	70	400
2nd	2.9/6.9	528.4	96.3	590
3rd	2.6/7.4	549.9	266.2	735

Table 2.

Concerning with leakage currents of dynamic memory cells, 3D-dynamic memory configurations have been studied as shown in Fig.7. Four types of the configuration
are experimentally studied as shown in the left insets of the figure. It is con-
cluded that any configuration type except type (d) has almost same performance.
In this experiment, the 2nd and 3rd layers were formed by twin laser-beam, called
"M-shaped beam", which was transformed from Gaussian beam through Fresnel bi-
prisms|11|.

4.2   3D-IC MODELS

Several small scale functional models of 3D-IC have been fabricated to show the
feasibility and to make the image of 3D-IC clear. Figure 8 shows a 256 bit static
RAM in 2 active layers |12|. Address access time at 5V was 120 nsec and power
consumption was 100 mW. This test device was understood to confirm 1) the basic
function of 3D-IC, 2) feasibility of internal signal transfer in a layer as
well as inter-layer signal transfer and 3) usefulness of the laser-beam recrystallization method. An image sensing devices integrated with signal processor in 3D structure is very attractive, since only sensing devices can be
fabricated on the top active layer to have a large area for the light detecting
and a high sensitivity. Such a model tested was consited of 3 layers, 1st layer
of which was bulk Si and adopted for logic circuits, 2nd layer was SOI and adopted for digitizers, and 3rd layer was amorphous one and adopted for photo-detect-
ors |13|. Very recently, a new version of the image sensor with signal processor
has been tested , in which 2nd and 3rd layers are both SOI structures.

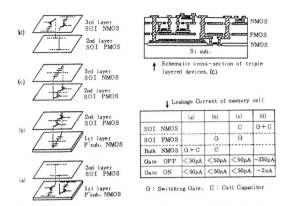

Fig.7 Study on 3D-dynamic memory configurations, schematic cross-section of 3 layered devices and leakage currents of cells.

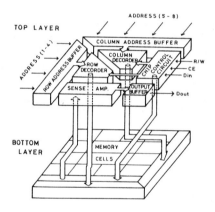

Fig.8 Block diagram of 256 bit Static RAM fabricated in double active layers.

5. PROBLEMS OF 3D-IC'S

It is necessary to make comments regarding to the problems of 3D-IC's.
1) The first one is low production yield. In order to decrease the production cost, the number of layers should not be larger than 3 or 4 layers. If 3D-IC with 10 active layers, for example, is needed, 3 monolithic 3D-IC's having 3,3,4 active layers respectively are recommended to be stacked by using high temperature-resist organic or inorganic materials.
2) The second one is high power dissipation for the case of super-ultra large scale integration. Of course, CMOS and Bi-CMOS circuits must be employed to sove such problems, at least. An innovation, however, of cooling method would be necessary as well as packaging technology.
3) The third one is the signal cross-talk between active layers. This problem can be easily understood from the oscilloscope traces as shown in Fig.9. A ring oscillator buit in the 2nd layer was coupled with circuits in the 1st layer. The wave forms and frequencies of the ring oscillator were

affected by the signal of the circuit in the 1st layer (Ex-Signal). It can
be found that the output signal of the ring oscillator changes showing
disturbance, lock-in and modulation phenomena occurence, if the ex-signal
is large. This problem could be solved by insertingshielding layers between
upper and lower active layers. However, this method will cause to increase
signal dealy time due to the capacitive loading. The other solution is to
manage the layout of the circuit. Anyway, the cross talk will restrict
structual flexibility of the 3D-IC, if layout design does not improve.

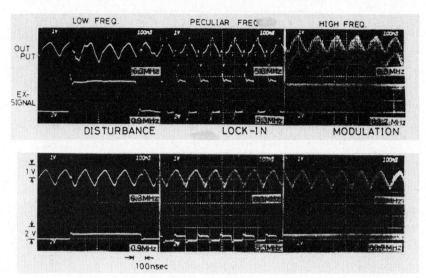

Fig.9 Dependence of the waveform of the ring oscillator in the
       2nd layer on the external signal given from the underlying
       active layer.

6.   ARCHITECTUAL STUDY CONCERNING WITH 3D-IC

A few architectual studies concerning with 3D-IC have been made in Japan. All
of them are in level of ideas. In other words, they have been proposed just
showing possible use of the structual merits of 3D-IC, as follows:
       1) 3D-Programmable Logic Array (T.Nanya, Tokyo Inst. of Technology)
       2) 3D-Content Addressable Memory (T.Ogura, NTT-Atsugi)
       3) 3D-Optical Coupled Shared Memory (T.Abe & Y.Hirose, Hiroshima U.)
       4) Flow Through Concept applied to 3D-IC (H.Terada, Oosaka U.)
Figure 10 shows an idea of 3D-PLA. It can be understood that if upper and lower
layers could be interconnected through via-holes at any places, various configurations for PLA's could be easily realized.

7.   RESEARCH ACTIVITIES IN JAPAN

It might be useful to give a brief explain about the research activities related
to 3D-IC in Japan. Many laboratories have interests to study on this subject.
They are ones belong to electric companies such as Fujitsu, Hitachi, Matsushita
Mitsubishi,, NEC, NTT, Oki, Sanyo, Sharp, Toshiba and so on. The Electro-Tehnical
Laboratory which belongs to the Japanese government,and universities such as
KyotoU., Oosaka U., Tokyo Inst. of Technology and Waseda U. are also concerned
with 3D-IC study (rather fundamental).

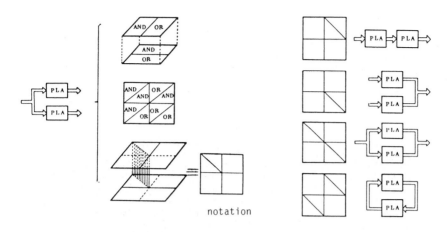

(a)   (b)

Fig.10 A realization of a 2D-PLA circuit by means of a 3D-PLA (a)
and examples of 2 layers 3D-PLA(b).

In 1981, the future electron device project started as a part of the R&D project
of basic technology for future industries by Agency of Industrial Science and
Technology, MITI. Concerning to 3D-IC,the basic research is undertaken by ETL,
and basic technology development is performed by companies (Matsushita, Mitsubishi, NEC, Oki, Sanyo, Sharp and Toshiba) through the aadoministration of the
Research and Development Association for Future Electron Devices. The general
idea about the research plans of this project can be understood by Table 3, in
which the revised budgets in Yen for 3D-IC program in the association are shown.
It is noted that the budgets were not so big.

	Phase I				Phase I			Phase III		
Year	'81	'82	'83	'84	'85	'86	'87	'88	'89	'90
Revised Budget (Yen)	3.2E8	4.4E8	5.5E8	5.6E8	6.0E8	–	–	–	–	–
Scope	Multi-layered SOI				Chip Technology			3D IC Design Feasibility on 3D-IC'		

Table 3 R&D program and budgets for 3D-devices administrated
by the R&D Association for Future Electron Devices.

8.   CONCLUSION

The concept and features of 3D-IC are demonstrated. The 3D-IC is now in the
early stage of fundamental research. From the view point of hardware, SOI
technologies for 3D-structure are the most important basic technologies which
we have still to develop. However, the feasibility of 3D-IC has been shown.
The state of the art of 3D-IC confirmed the predicted merits. From the view
point of software, we still need the extensive works from architectual design
of chip and system for realizing smart or sophisticated 3D-IC's. We have
learned that progress of the integrated circuit can be expected, if such circuit

are used practically. In this meaning, the author has a opinion that multi-
functional 3D-IC, for example, so called " smart sensor"etc. will make a brak-
through in the development of 3D-IC's.

ACKNOWLEDGEMENT

The author would like to thank the R&D Association for Future Electron Devices
and the personnel related to the Association.

REFERENCES

|1|.   T.Tsurushima, Extended Abstracts of the 2nd Int. Workshop on Future Elec
      Electron devices, SOI Technology and 3D integration, pp.1-4 (1985)
|2|.   Y.Akasaka and T.Nishimura, Tech. Digest of Int. Electron Devices Meeting
      #18.6, pp.488-491 (1986)
|3|.   K.Sugahara et al., Extended Abstract of the Int.Conf. on Solid State
      Devices and Materials, #B11-1, pp.565-568 (1986)
|4|.   T.Hamasaki et al., J.Appl.Phys. **59**,2971 (1986)
|5|.   S.Horita and H.Ishiwara, Appl.Phys.Lett., **50**(12) 748 (1987)
|6|.   H.Ishiwara et al., Appl.Phys.Lett. **49**(20) 1363 (1986)
|7|.   K.Kusukawa et al., Extended Abstracts of the 19th conf. on Solid State
      Devices and Materials,#C1-2, pp.179-182 (1987)
|8|.   K.Izumi et al., Jpn.J.Appl.Phys., **Suppl1. 19-1**, pp.151-154 (1980)
|9|.   J.B.Lasky et al., Tech. Digest of Int. Electron Devices Meeting #28.4,
      pp.684-687 (1985)
|10|. T.Nishimura et al., Extended Abstracts of the 16th (Int.) Conf. on Solid
      State Devices and Materials, #B10.4, pp.527-530 (1984)
|11|. M.Maekawa, Proc. of 5th Symposium on Future Electron Devices, #III-9,
      pp.215-230 (1986)
|12|. Y.Inoue et al., IEEE Electron Devices Lett., **EDL-7**,5, pp.327-329 (1986)
|13|. S.Hirose et al.,Tech.Digests of '85 Symposium on VLSI Technology, IV-8,
      pp.34-35 (1985)

VLSI '87, C.H. Séquin (editor)
Elsevier Science Publishers B.V. (North-Holland)
© IFIP, 1988

EUROPEAN APPROACHES TO ASICs

Joseph BOREL
I.C. R and D Vice President

THOMSON SEMICONDUCTEURS
BP 217
38019 GRENOBLE CEDEX - FRANCE

1. INTRODUCTION

The ASICs business is becoming more and more similar to the one of the other
segments of application, that is to say requiring :
- high expertise in silicon processing (advanced process, manufacturing
   skills)
- good product ranges (in semicustoms applications) or appropriate CAD and
   libraries (in custom applications)
- adequate packaging capabilities (both in terms of packages types and cycle
   times).

The success is based on high quality services, and this can be achieved with
the help of efficient CAD software packages and libraries available to the
customer .

Most of these constraints are similar to what is needed in the standard
products business. This explains why the market at first covered by small
companies (LSI Logic, VLSI Technology, Gould Semiconductor ...) is now
shifting towards larger semiconductor companies :
. in the U.S.   : T.I., MOTOROLA, NATIONAL SEMICONDUCTOR, INTEL
. in JAPAN   : NEC, HITACHI, FUJITSU, TOSHIBA
. in EUROPE   : PHILIPS, SGS/THOMSON, SIEMENS

We will review in this presentation :
- the European market situation
- the present European solutions
- the preparation of the future with the I.D.P.S. (Integrated Design and
   Production system), a major program within ESPRIT 2.

2. THE EUROPEAN MARKET SITUATION

The general forecasted evolution of the worldwide market for ASICs is given
in Table 1.

The split of the ASICs market is done in terms of :
- SEMICUSTOM versus CUSTOM
- MOS versus BIPOLAR

It can be seen that :
. Semicustom market evolution is at a high 24% CAGR* over the considered
   period.

. MOS is gaining market shares and bipolar will stay agressive and keep
   a 17% CAGR which is significantly above the CAGR of total ICs which is
   evaluated at 13%.
_____
* CAGR : Compound Average Growth Rate

14   *J. Borel*

TAM ($M)	86	87	88	89	90	91	CAGR
SEMI CUSTOM (PLA AND GATE ARRAY)	1,700	2,100	2,800	3,500	3,800	5,000	24%
CUSTOM (STAND. CELLS AND FULL CUSTOM)	1,700	1,900	2,400	2,800	3,100	3,800	19%
TOTAL ASICs	3,400	4,000	5,200	6,300	6,900	8,800	21%
MOS	2,100	2,500	3,400	4,200	4,600	6,000	23%
BIPOLAR	1,300	1,500	1,800	2,100	2,300	2,800	17%

AVERAGE ANNUAL GROWTH OF 13% FOR TOTAL ICs
AVERAGE ANNUAL GROWTH OF 21% FOR ASICs

WORLDWIDE TOTAL AVAILABLE MARKET
FORECASTED EVOLUTION

Table 1

In summary, ASIC market evolution is well above ICs market evolution and Semicustom CMOS products will be mainly developed in the coming years.

These figures explain clearly why major ICs manufacturers cannot ignore such a market. When comparing the market share evolution of ASICs (Figure 1) and standards, ASICs are gaining 4% market share over the 1986-1990 period.

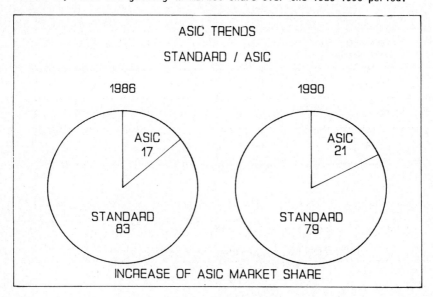

Figure 1

The ASIC market TAM evaluation in EUROPE is given in Table 2 in comparison with the total IC market evaluation.

TAM ($M) EUROPE	86	87	88	89	90	91	CAGR
TOTAL IC	5,400	6,200	7,200	8,000	8,500	9,400	12%
TOTAL ASICs	800	1,000	1,200	1,600	1,800	2,200	22.5%

THE ASIC MARKET TAM EVALUATION IN EUROPE

Table 2

The CAGR difference is still more pronounced than in the case of the world-wide market. Europe will remain a strong customer in the ASIC world : Table 3

MARKET VALUES $M (1990 FORECAST)	IC's	ASICs	RATIO $\frac{ASICs}{IC's}$
WORLDWIDE	37,800	6,900	18 %
EUROPE	8,500	1,800	21 %
RATIO $\frac{EUR}{WW}$	22.5 %	26 %	

EUROPE VERSUS THE WORLDWIDE MARKET
(1990 forecasted situation)

Table 3

The components of the European ASICs market in terms of design methodology are given in Figure 2 and do not change significantly in relative magnitude from 1986 to 1990 ; half of the market is covered by full custom and cell based designs and half is covered by semicustoms (that is to say PLA and G.A. solutions).

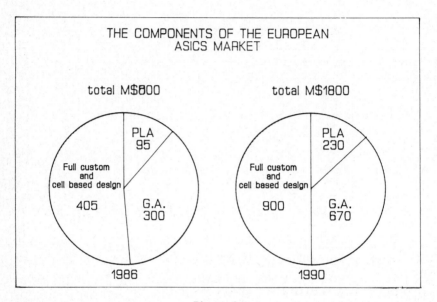

Figure 2

These figures represent the merchant market evolution though it is always difficult to make a sharp boundary between full customs and dedicated products ; besides it is not easy to know what amount of gate arrays business is involved in intracompany shipments.

An estimation of the European ASICs market by country can be obtained from the semiconductor TAM (assuming that the ASICs business will follow the semi-conductor business evolution in each country).

This would give the following ranking (in 92) :
  - Germany : 34 %
  - U.K.   : 20 %
  - France : 14 %
  - Italy   : 10 %

3. THE EUROPEAN CAPABILITIES

In terms of gate arrays Europe presently has a level of sales which approaches 50% of its consumption (expressed in dollars value) ; there is room for European companies to gain market shares :
- market increases faster than average worldwide value
- there is no European semicustom manufacturer in the top ten
- Europe has a high technical expertise in technology and CAD
- Most of the companies are vertically integrated (allowing intracompany business).

This has led the major European companies to increase their commitments in the ASICs business.

Figure 3 gives the European ASICs manufacturing capabilities in terms of production, engineering and developments of advanced technologies both in CMOS and bipolar.

MANUFACTURER	TECHNOLOGY	3 uм	2 uм	1.5 uм	1.2 uм	MAX NB OF LEVEL OF METAL INTERC.
PHILIPS	CMOS	P	P	E	D	
	BIP	P	P	E	D	
THOMSON/SGS	CMOS	P	P	E	E	2
	BIP	P	P	E	D	3
SIEMENS	CMOS	P	P	E	E	2
	BIP	P	P	E	D	3
PLESSEY	CMOS	P	P	E	D	2
	BIP	P	P	E	D	2-3
MEDL (GEC)	CMOS	P	P	D	D	2
MHS	CMOS	P	P	E	D	2
ES2	CMOS		E			2

P : PRODUCTION - E : ENGINEERING - D : DEVELOPMENT -

EUROPEAN ASIC MANUFACTURING CAPABILITIES

Figure 3

It can be seen from this figure that most of the companies have the 2 um CD's generations at the production level and some begin to manufacture in limited quantities products at the 1.2 um level.

The next step will be considering what are the priorities in terms of services. Figure 4 represents the percentage of users considering a given criterion as important when selecting an ASICs vendor.

Short turn around time to prototype appears to be ranked very high and well above production price per part. This specific point has been taken into consideration for defining priorities in programs within ESPRIT 2 framework and has led to the definition of the I.D.P.S. program that we will describe briefly in section 5.

	PERCENTAGE OF USERS CONSIDERING THIS CRITERION AS IMPORTANT WHEN SELECTING AN IC VENDOR
1. SHORT TURNAROUND TIME TO PROTOTYPE	93 %
2. AVAILABILITY OF PREPRODUCTION PARTS IN DESIRED QUALITY	88 %
3. AVAILABILITY OF QUALITY AND RELIABILITY DATA	86 %
4. REPUTATION	86 %
5. PRODUCTION PRICE PER PART	81 %
6. TEST SUPPORT	81 %
7. WORKSTATION SUPPORT	76 %
8. LOCAL DESIGN SUPPORT	76 %
9. LARGE CELL LIBRARY	76 %
10. TECHNOLOGY LEADER	75 %

DATA COMPUTED FROM 1986 CUSTOM AND SEMICUSTOM IC INDUSTRY STUDY ELECTRONIC ENGINEERING TIMES

THE NEEDS FOR FAST PROTOTYPING

Figure 4

Reputation is also of importance to customers who want to be sure of finding the same manufacturer when they need the same parts two or three years later. This may be an other advantage for large companies that are supposed to have a longer lifetime than start ups.

Coming back to the cycle time problem, it is well understood that major improvements have to be done (and can be done), both at the design and manufacturing levels. Within a time frame of 4 to 5 years, the objectives given in Table 4 can be obtained on a regular basis ; in fact, today in "rush processing" such cycle times are already feasible, but on a case by case basis.

			1 9 8 7 (AVERAGE)	FUTURE
GATE ARRAY	:	DESIGN	7 - 13 WEEKS	2 WEEKS
		MANUFACTURING	5 WEEKS	1 WEEK
		TOTAL	12 - 18 WEEKS	3 WEEKS
CELL BASED DESIGN	:	DESIGN	7 - 13 WEEKS	2 WEEKS
		MANUFACTURING	9 WEEKS	2 WEEKS
		TOTAL	16 - 22 WEEKS	4 WEEKS

CYCLE TIMES IMPROVEMENTS
THROUGH FAST PROTOTYPING

Table 4

This evolution, shown in Figure 5, asks some comments :
- the traditional gate array approach will evolve towards the sea of gates approach using in a first generation soft macroblocks, and then hard macroblocks (structured arrays)
- the custom designs will be made starting from a higher level of description (structural or behavioural description) and will use in the physical implementation cells and macrocells obtained through software tools (called generators) allowing technology independence.

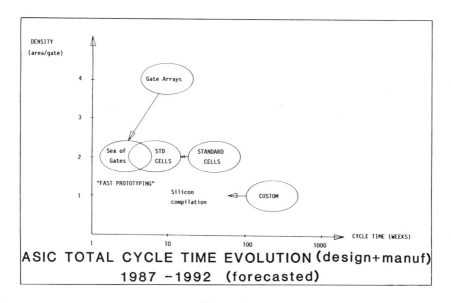

Figure 5

The significant expected decrease in design time through this new methodology will make the traditional standard cell approach very questionable (both in terms of NRE* cost and density performances of the product).

4. EXAMPLES OF EUROPEAN ACHIEVEMENTS

At the European level several major companies have made a significant effort to cover the ASIC business either semicustom or custom.

---

* NRE : Non Recursive Expenses

SIEMENS through a common program with TOSHIBA and General ELectric is developing the ADVANCELL concept which is aimed at setting up an international SC standard, compatible with a sea of gate implementation.

The ADVANCELL library composition is given in Table 5.

Cell Type	Cell Quantity		Features
	end 86	end 87	
Primitive Cells	163	163	Basic Logic Functions
I/O Cells	25	300	CMOS and TTL Interfaces
Megacells	10	23	2900 Series, other
Soft Cells	-	108	7400 Series Compatible
Compiled Modules	-	3 Functions	ROM, RAM, PLA
Analog Cells	-	20	Basic Analog Functions

Table 5

ADVANCELL ^{TM} Library from SIEMENS - TOSHIBA - G.E.

Together with the Advancell approach, Siemens has developed a "compatible" sea of gates approach for first design validation, prototyping, or small series. This sea of gate has a complexity ranging from 3K (area : 6 mm2) to 160K RAW gates (area : 340 mm2) and will be fully qualified in 1988.

PLESSEY in a similar way has developed the MEGACELL approach which allows with a cell based design to reach complexities of 100K gates and more, with a dimensionless implementation (covering the range 2 u, 1.5 um, 1.2 um of CD's).

The designer (using the software package called SHADE) can choose the best trade off for his application between :
- design time
- chip size
- performances

Associated with the design is available a test methodology with the corresponding supporting software.

Larger cells can be used and are parameterisable (they are called PARACELLS). The table below gives a summary of the main PARACELLS available.

RAM	8 - 64 bits	32 - 2048 words	16Kbits max
ROM	4 - 32 bits	64 - 2048 words	64Kbits max
PLA	2 - 32 i/ps	2 - 32 o/ps	8-128 prod.terms
ALU	4 - 32 bits	16 functions	
ADDER	4 - 32 bits		
COMPARATOR	4 - 32 bits		
CAM	4 - 24 bits	4 - 16 words	
REG.FILE	4 - 32 bits	4 - 16 words	

Table 6

Summary of PARACELLS

This system is already being used over a range of applications :
- multipliers
- FFT butterfly
- complex floating point arithmetic chip
- edge detector for real time imaging applications ...
Clock ranges extend from 10 to 20 MHZ and complexities up to 20K gates in 2 um CMOS technology.

PHILIPS has a broad range of internal applications and is aiming at covering all these applications with different compromises between performance, cost, short design times ... etc ...

Customer priorities seem to be oriented towards :
- representativeness (prototypes representative for larger manufacturing quantities)
- minimum die area
- advanced performances
- just in time availability

The design system is based on a hierarchical approach using the VLDL language as the hardware description language.

THOMSON and SGS , through their recent merging have defined a very agressive strategy to cover custom and semicustom needs both in the analog and digital fields and using their available advanced technologies :
- CMOS   : 2 u - 1,5 um - 1,2 um CD's (digital and analog, EPROM and E2PROM capabilities)
- BIPOLAR : 3 um - 2 um digital and analog
- BICMOS : 2 um

The CAD system is an "OPEN" system allowing to capitalize on the best commercially available or internally developed tools. The libraries are based on the extensive use of "software generators" allowing technology independence.

This system allows custom and semicustom designs :
- common CAD "front end"
- specific "back end" depending on the implementation strategy

An example of semicustom development is the sea of gate approach ; the characteristics of the base design are given in the following tables (Tables 7 and 8).

. <u>PRODUCT DESCRIPTION</u>

    - VERY HIGH DENSITY LOGIC ARRAY
    - CHANNELLESS ARCHITECTURE
    - UP TO 128,000 AVAILABLE GATES
    - 60,000 USABLE GATES (EST.)
    - 320 SIGNAL I/O

. <u>TECHNOLOGY PERFORMANCE</u>

    - 1.2 UM DRAWN GATE LENGTH (0.9 UM EFF)
    - DOUBLE METAL HCMOS
    - 2 INPUT NAND TPD = 0.44 NS (TYP ; FO = 2, DOUBLE DRIVE)
    - OUTPUT DRIVE : 2-16 MA

. <u>T.CAD 2</u> (THOMSON CAD SYSTEM) CAPABILITY

    - VERIFICATION - SIMULATION - TEST GENERATION - LAYOUT
    - AUTO HIERARCHICAL CELL PLACEMENT
    - HARD MACRO GENERATION

SEA OF GATE SERIES FEATURES

Table 7

. EXTENSIVE LIBRARY OF SSI FUNCTIONS
    - 150 SSI (SINGLE DRIVE AND DOUBLE DRIVE)

. LSI FUNCTIONS
    - AMD 2900 FAMILY
    - MULTIPLIERS, ALUS, REGISTER FILES ...

. MEMORY
    - RAM GENERATORS   (SINGLE PORT - DUAL PORT)
    - FIFO GENERATOR   (SINGLE PORT - DUAL PORT)
    - ROM GENERATOR

SEA OF GATES LIBRARY

Table 8

5. The I.D.P.S. project

The I.D.P.S. (Integrated Design and Production System) is a project that has been included at the European Economic Community level in the ESPRIT 2 program and it is presently interesting most of the major European semi-conductor companies.

It is one of the large Technology Information Packages (TIP) of ESPRIT 2 with a scheduled amount of resources above 1000 (human x year) over a 5 years timescale.

The main characteristics of the program are given below :
- objectives :
  . fast prototyping service for the ASIC market
- technology
  . fast manufacturing of ASICs
    - 1.2 and 0.8 um CMOS
    - direct writing on wafers by Ebeam
    - 14 days from PG tapes to 25 assembled and tested prototypes
- design
  . 1.2 and 0.8 um CMOS library
    - block generators (ROM - RAM - PLA - Data path - I/Os ...)
    - microprocessor core family (ie 16 to the 32 bits risc)
    - analog library
- CAD
  . integrated system
    - synthesis tools
    - silicon compilation
    - technology independence
    - aided then automated tests generation
    - 14 days from design start to PG tapes

and the milestones are shown in Figure 6.

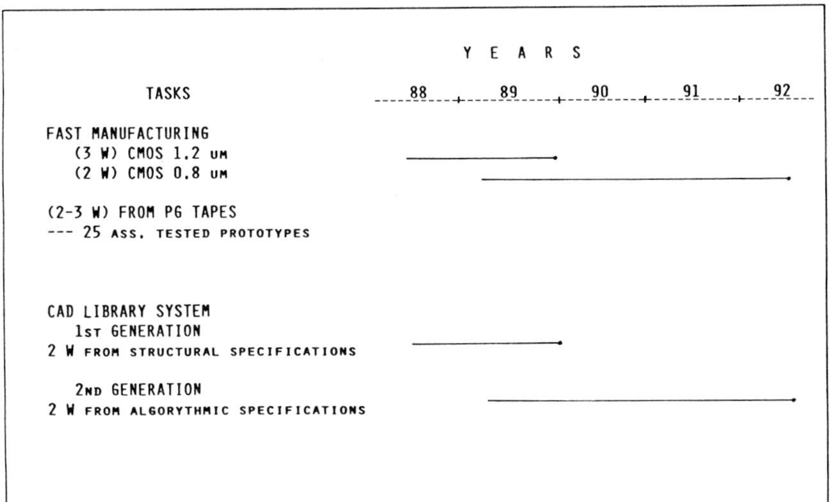

MAIN TASKS AND MILESTONES OF I.D.P.S.

Figure 6

6. CONCLUSION

European companies have been traditionnally developing their semicustom and custom circuits internally because of their vertically integrated structure. So they have been very sensitive to technology and CAD evolution and right now they are well prepared to increase their activities on the merchant market either through agreements with foreign companies (Siemens) or through merging their activities (Thomson and SGS). This is mandatory if they want to survive in a very competitive market where only large companies have the capability of developing very complex and expensive silicon processes or CAD systems that can pay back only if they are used in larger fields of applications (standard or dedicated products).

The development of fast prototyping, which is one of the priorities of the ESPRIT 2 program, will help them at least on two major points :
- first they will work together and share their experience and resources
- second they will have with the fast prototyping capabilities a very power-full marketing tool to gain market shares.

But again this will become reality only if the manufacturing science of the European companies reaches a worldwide level, which is necessary to be competitive at the product level, including the case of ASICs which are becoming more and more under the control of large companies with a large investment capability in a fast moving market requiring a lot of R and D investment.

REFERENCES

Market figures are mainly from the THOMSON SEMICONDUCTEURS economist Jean Philippe DAUVIN.

References on the European data are derived partly from the proceedings of the Grenoble I.F.I.P. Workshop on Fast Prototyping, 17-19 March 1987.

VLSI '87, C.H. Séquin (editor)
Elsevier Science Publishers B.V. (North-Holland)
© IFIP, 1988

SYSTEM DEMANDS VS OPPORTUNITIES:
THE ROLES OF TECHNOLOGY AND DESIGN

William R. Heller
International Business Machines Corporation
Poughkeepsie, NY 12602

There is some purpose in taking stock of the situation in the human use of
computing systems. A view on the run is better than not looking where one is
going. In this talk I shall start with an outline of subtopics to be covered:
realities of current systems; system demands; technology opportunities; design
challenges; and some interesting future possibilities.

Very impressive facts of the present period are the new hardware and new
software available to system users. Work stations have compuational and graphic
capabilities which pack into a reasonable fraction of an office and its
occupant's income, the power which only ten or fifteen years ago required a
large and special room and millions of dollars. To help or supplement these
work stations, special hardware to enhance logic simulation and layout is now
available.

A growing trend is the development and use of a variety of parallel processing
machines. These range from the use of a relatively small number of processors
with a shared or partially shared memory through message-passing configurations
with hundreds of processors to the Connection Machine with 65,000 processors.
These offer competition to supercomputers, which are themselves advancing in
speed and capability.

With all this new hardware, we are also, necessarily, seeing the development of
new software. Especially for the new work stations and for personal computers,
the spread sheet and its numerous companions have become tools of an immense
and growing computing population. We should not overlook the new systems
environments which permit program and text editing and networking among groups
of users. In this context, complete arrangements of system design tools have
provided the basis for new businesses. Some of the most difficult problems
which programmers must face are those of adapting parallel processors to smooth
use of existing software, or of developing ways to reduce communication and
coherency overhead in such machines.

Turning to look at system demands, these have changed, principally due to the
increased dependence on uninterrupted computation, and on the sometimes
contradictory requirements of greater ease of use and greater security. But
perhaps most important, the cost of hardware relative to software, and the time
to produce it relative to software, are both down rather dramatically.

New software naturally has extended to new applications. Perhaps among the most
spectacular are those permitting associative recall and prototype learning done
on experimental machines simulating neural nets in organisms.

Perhaps the most insistent demand on systems, both large and small, has been
the call for increased availability. This has set new and more stringent
criteria for operating power systems, semiconductor device reliability and
also supporting software.

Along with the needs of the user, demands internal to system development and
manufacturing have intensified. With the laudable goal of shortening and making

more predicatable the system production cycle, the question is frequently
asked: How can design tools help? Will they in fact, help? Here the emerging
difficulties are closely related to the new complexity of chips and of entire
subsystems--multiplied by the factors coming from multiple designer
involvement. How does one relate preliminary analysis, software and local data
bases, to production design tools on a much larger data base suitable for
release to manufacturing? How does one smoothly record, check and incorporate
design changes?

As manufacturing becomes more automated, how does one relate tooling
development to a sufficiently stable laboratory-generated version of a new
machine? How early in the manufacturing processing cycle and how thoroughly
does it pay to test components, compared to the additional difficulty and
relevance of sub-system and system testing? How does one measure the degree of
relevance of system functional testing?

One must also look at the opportunities afforded by advances in technology. On
the level most visible in journals of electronics, one can ask about choices
between silicon and gallium arsenide, and between low temperature versus room
temperature operation. Both speed and power are significant. As cycle times
decrease, and threshold voltages decrease, though more slowly, noise
sensitivity increases. Wiring demand increases, as we know from Donath's work,
faster than proportionately to the number of devices interconnected. Multilevel
metal on chips, increased wiring plane count on packages both must result.

In this type of study, it is important to those emphasizing the development of
sharper design tools, that one consider what I may term the "packaging pay off
hierarchy". If one chooses, for example, reduction in cycle time as a
significant measure of payoff for technology improvement, one can ask where in
the hierarchy is the largest percentage reduction of propagation time or of
loading delay. From such analysis, one can quickly see that, in general, there
is, even in VLSI, more chance of a percentage return on investment in reducing
cable or broad wire length, than there is in reducing chip wire length. The
reasons for this are at least threefold: First, chip design tools have received
a great deal of concentrated attention, and so have the chip wiring and device
technologies. Second, one can hope to optimize over all package levels only by
iterative use of tools which take all package levels into account. It is
important that appropriate interactive but automated tools for this iteration
are complex to conceive and to build. We do not have such tools. A third factor
is that the manufacturing and change process cycle times increase rather
sharply up the hierarchy from chip to chip carrier to board or frame. This
makes rapid iteration of design up and down the hierarchy even less practical.

In this connection, management in industry and sometimes research supervisors
in universities have to ask: Do we want what we are devising sooner or better
performing? Those who claim both may be in danger of being looked at as playing
the role of sales people more than of engineering folks.

Finally some questions about trends. We can see that emphasis on and use of
design tools really dominates design. Given this situation, how are these tools
best developed and transformed into sturdy structures suitable for engineering
design by colleagues in industry or by the next generation of graduate
students?

Another question: How can analysis and software best penetrate the upper
regions of decision-making; (that is at the level where system alternatives in
architecture or packaging are chosen)?

And last, but not least, how do engineers spend or share their time, as users
or tool developers?

VLSI '87, C.H. Séquin (editor)
Elsevier Science Publishers B.V. (North-Holland)
© IFIP, 1988

THE ROLE OF HDLS IN THE DIGITAL DESIGN PROCESS

T.L. THORP and N.E. PEELING

Royal Signals and Radar Establishment,
Malvern, WR14 3PS, United Kingdom.

The traditional use of HDLs is to describe the structure of
networks of components and to give black-box models of
components. A newer use is as a notation to aid the process
of design which is the transformation of behaviour to
structure. The paper considers core behavioural and
structural constructs used in HDLs in the context of these
two uses.

1. INTRODUCTION

This paper is concerned with the use of Hardware Description
Languages (HDLs) in the process of designing digital electronics. It
is only concerned with the part of the design cycle dealing with
behaviour and structure; it will not be concerned with the
specification of requirements or of physical design. Particular
attention is paid to the traditional use of HDLs in black-box
modelling and also to their newer role in design, where they are
sometimes known as Hardware Design and Description Languages (HDDLs).
Whether design is done by man or by machine, it is crucial that a
language has the semantics to contain the appropriate information
from which the design transformation process starts. In addition a
good, readable syntax is vital if humans are to make good use of it.

Black-box modelling of components is particularly needed when the
interactions between a collection of components have to be checked by
simulation. In this case the interconnection structure is known
already, so that a relatively simple language to define the structure
is all that is needed. The main problem is to provide a modelling
language to describe a component's behaviour, that is the
relationships in time between signals on the component's pins.

The process of design is usually described as bottom-up, top-down or
meet-in-the-middle, which is a combination of the previous two. In
bottom-up design, the specification of a new structure is created by
combining the specifications of pre-existing structures. In top-down
design a specification which contains a mixture of behaviour and
structure is progressively transformed to one which contains more
structure: almost invariably any pre-existing structure is unchanged
– if some structure is found to be inappropriate, the design is
iterated back to an earlier behaviour and a new route to structure
explored; thus the process is essentially one of transforming
behaviour into structure. In practice, the behaviour transformation
process is guided, either by a human designer or by an algorithm in a
program, towards structures which are thought to be 'good', such as
those previously created by the bottom-up design process: This
meet-in-the-middle process is the way designers actually work, though
there is no consensus on the complexity of structures to be
incorporated from the bottom-up design process.

The descriptions (specifications) of behaviour and of structure,
which HDLs make possible, are used by designers to record the status
of their designs and to transmit information between designers,

between designers and CAD tools and between CAD tools. The quality of
the HDLs used for these purposes will have economic consequences. If
a language is difficult to understand or does not have the
appropriate expressive qualities, specifications will be
misunderstood leading to the building of the 'wrong' component. The
expressive power of the language will also have a bearing on the
ability of a designer to explore the design space rapidly, to find
the best implementation, to design with speed and accuracy and to
handle large designs of high complexity.

Important though the design of a language is, an excellent language
in a poor environment, may be of little use to a company with a heavy
design load (e.g. where there are a large number of designs and/or
difficult designs). In this situation the information contained in
the design language must be made available to, and be able to drive,
other tools through appropriate interfaces. Further, a company must
be able to 'tune' the language system to incorporate a company design
philosophy and indeed be able, if required, to 'coerce' designers to
conform to it. In this paper we are not principally concerned with
the support environment except in so far as the design of the
language spills over into the support environment, for example in the
ways library mechanisms work. In future, where the meaning allows it,
'language' means both the language and the environment in which the
language is embedded.

Throughout the paper, examples are given using VHDL[1-3] and
ELLA[4-6]/1/ - VHDL because a version is likely to become an IEEE
standard and because documentations of its various versions have been
widely circulated, and ELLA, not just because it is the language with
which the author is associated but, because it emphasises different
aspects of language design from VHDL. VHDL examples are generally
written in version 7.2 (now implemented) or where appropriate in
draft standard 1076. ELLA examples use a version which has been
implemented but not yet generally released.

2. Behaviour and Structure

It has already been said that the design process consists of
generating specifications from other specifications: structures from
behaviour in top-down design, structure from structure in bottom-up
design and a mixture in meet-in-the-middle design. The essential
requirements of a notation are that it:
(i) represents data (signals)
(ii) gives a method of describing structure
(iii) gives a method of describing behaviour
(iv) gives facilities to compose and decompose behaviour and
structure.
The first three of these are needed to describe specifications, the
fourth is particularly associated with the activity of transforming
specifications.

2.1 Representation of Data

Most modern HDLs such as ELLA, Helix[7], VHDL now agree that a rich
variety of data types and datastructuring facilities are required,
usually with strong type checking included in the compiler. This
acceptance is in common with decisions in designing programming
languages like Ada.

Signal data types like two and multivalued bits, integers (fixed and
user defined ranges) and reals, as well as user defined enumeration
types are needed. Sub-types are also a very elegant feature. In many
languages sub-types of numbers and enumeration types can be declared

(in VHDL, though not for reals; not at all in ELLA). For example, in
VHDL one can declare:

```
type INT_512 is -512 to 511;                          Example 2.1
type INT_64K is -65536 to 65535;
type TWO_BIT is (t,f);
type TWO_BITX is (t,f,x);
```

Thus the symbol 27 could be of type INT_512, INT_64K (and also of
built-in type INTEGER which is an integer of implementation dependent
range). A number symbol like 27 and similarly the symbols t, f are
thus 'overloaded'.

The reason why ELLA does not have subtypes is of interest as it
illuminates the interdependency of language design and other aspects
of the design system. Strictly as a language issue, sub-types are
clearly elegant and useful. However, there is a price to pay for
their inclusion. After an early trial it was decided to have no
overloading of types (i.e. sub-typing) as it was judged that the
consequent improved diagnostics outweiged the advantages of a more
elegant description capacity. The effect of this decison was also to
reduce the complexity and size of the compiler leading to improved
performance and robustness (c.f. the heavy overloading in Ada is
responsible for perhaps 30% of the compiler size and significant
reductions in compilation speed). VHDL has tended to favour the Ada
solution.

In some cases pointers are provided. On the whole those HDLs which
emphasise their connection with hardware do not provide them, while
those which also wish to have some of the attributes of a
conventional programming language, or need them for modelling, do
provide them. For example, VHDL1076 has them (access types), while
ELLA and VHDL7.2 do not.

In some cases (e.g. VHDL) there are a rich variety of types built
into the language, in others (e.g. ELLA) all types are user defined.
To the circuit designer, as ultimate user, it should not matter much
whether types are built-in or are part of a library.

Rows, arrays and structures are common for structuring data, but
unions or Pascal-like variant records are not always provided (e.g.
not in VHDL). That unions are not generally provided seems strange:
It is very common in hardware to have quite different sorts of
objects on a bus or in memory (e.g. data and instructions) and the
natural way of expressing this is by a union. An example in ELLA of
such a (tagged) union is:

```
TYPE instruction = NEW (add|sub|stop),                Example 2.2
     data = NEW d/(0..255),
     busvalue = NEW (inst&instruction|dt&data).
```

(Note ELLA integers are all tagged, in this case by the identifier
'd'; one value is d/253. The symbol '/' therefore does not mean
divide.)

The interpretation of busvalue is: busvalue can take two values inst
or dt; if it is of value inst, then another value of type instruction
is associated with it and can be accessed; if it is of value dt then
there is associated another value of type data; two possible values
are inst&add and dt&d/27.

Once an architecture has been decided, it is relatively easy to get a
design more or less right, but considerably more difficult to get all
the errors out. Facilities to define unknown, don't-care and other

exception values are very important, because they are a powerful
means of catching difficult faults. It is unfortunately a
particularly difficult area of language design to decide whether and
how to provide these exception values. In TWO_BITX from Example 2.1,
a value x was explicitly declared; this declaration does not define
what x means (e.g. don't know or don't care) rather its semantics are
defined by the set of operations done on it. In some languages every
type declared has a built-in catch-all value with pre-defined meaning
(e.g. NIL in LISP); VHDL does not have it and ELLA's is only
partially implemented. As a consequence, in the VHDL Example 2.1
INT_512 does not have an unknown value and one cannot be added in the
way the 'x' is for an enumerated type like TWO_BITX. In these
circumstances there is the danger that the user will extend the range
and define say 512 as the unknown value, but this is extremely
hazardous. ELLA can get round the problem through the use of its
union facility:

```
TYPE int_512 = NEW i/(-512..511),                          Example 2.3
     int_512x = NEW (x512|gd512&int_512).
```

The same issue reappears with rows and arrays. Consider,

```
TYPE row3_int_512x = [3]int_512x.                          Example 2.4
```

In this case an individual field or all fields could take on the
exception value, for example:

```
(x512,gd512&i/73,gd512&i/51)
```

but a designer might wish to distinguish between the value [3]x512
(equivalent to (x512,x512,x512)) and an exception value for the row
as a whole. If such a value is needed then a new type could be
declared:

```
TYPE int_512x_x = NEW(xxxx|gdrow&row3_int_512x)            Example 2.5
```

allowing values such as xxxx or gdrow&[3]x512 or
gdrow&(x512,x512,gd512&i/511)

While values such as these look a bit long-winded, they allow great
precision of expression. In our experience with users in industry,
this ability to define exception values is heavily used by engineers;
when searching for a fault, they find it particularly useful to
invent and slip in extra values, which are then often removed after
the fault has been cleared.

2.2. Representation of Structure

The two concepts of 'instantiation' and 'connection' seem to be
agreed to be the two fundamentals of structure and are the common
features in HDLs. They imply parallelism: two instances of an AND
gate are quite separate and do not affect each other. Further,
creating instances or joining them up in a different order, are
semantically equivalent as long as the same final structure is
created. Various syntactical ways have been used to describe
structure: schematic diagrams, net-list (textual) languages etc but
since they all express the same idea, that is have the same
semantics, they can in principle all be translated into each other's
format.

To illustrate how very different syntaxes can have the same
semantics, consider three structural descriptions of a full adder,
containing ANDs, OR and XORs, one in VHDL and two in ELLA:

First the VHDL (from [1]),

```
entity FULL_ADDER                                    Example 2.6
(X,Y:in BIT;
CIN: in BIT:='0';
COUT, SUM:out BIT) is
end FULL_ADDER;

architecture MY_STRUCTURE of FULL_ADDER is
MY_STRUCTURE_BLK:
block
component AND port (A,B: in BIT; C: out BIT);
component XOR port (A,B: in BIT; C: out BIT);
component OR port (A,B: in BIT; C: out BIT);

signal S1,S2,S3 : BIT;

begin
X1 : XOR port (X,Y,S1);
X2 : XOR port (S1,CIN,SUM);
A1 : AND port (CIN,S1,S2);
A2 : AND port (X,Y,S3);
OR1 : OR port (S2,S3,COUT);
end block;
end MY_STRUCTURE;
```

Second, the first ELLA version,

```
FN FULL_ADDER = (bool:x y cin) -> [2]bool:        Example 2.7
COM the two output fields correspond to carryout and sum MOC
BEGIN MAKE XOR:x1 x2,
           AND:a1 a2,
           OR:or1.
JOIN (x,y) -> x1, (x1,cin) -> x2,
     (x1,cin) -> a1, (x,y) -> a2,
     (a1,a2) -> or1.
OUTPUT (or1,x2)
END.
```

Third, another ELLA version,

```
FN FULL_ADDER = (bool:x y cin) -> [2]bool:        Example 2.8
BEGIN LET xor = XOR(x,y).
OUTPUT ( (xANDy) OR (cinANDxor),
          xorXORcin )
END.
```

Examples 2.6 and 2.7 use the familiar net-list style of programming.
(The main differences between them are associated with the way the
types and libraries work in the two systems. In VHDL the use of a
library component (like AND) is declared in the module, while in ELLA
this information is contained in the Support Environment.)

The meanings of the ELLA descriptions in Examples 2.7 and 2.8 are
exactly the same even though syntactically they are very different.
For example, the first of the two descriptions contains five
explicitly named components, while the second contains no named
components but only a single named wire. While Example 2.7 has the
net-list style of syntax, Example 2.8 has a functional form of syntax
commonly used, for example, in procedural languages. However in ELLA,
'invocations' of a FN (like AND) have the meaning, not of 'calls' of
a procedure, but of 'instantiations' of a component. It can be seen

that in both Examples 2.7 and 2.8 there are two instantiations of
AND, NOT and one of OR and also that the two networks correspond.
Note, in the OUTPUT statement of Example 2.8, that had XOR(x,y) been
used in the two places where xor was used, then there would have been
a total of three instances of XOR created and so a different network
would have been created.

In addition to the basic forms of structure description so far
described, languages must provide higher level features, in
particular the ability to parameterise structure. For example, an
N-bit adder is described below in two ways: the first, in VHDL, uses
structural replication, the second, in ELLA, structural recursion (in
net-list style). (Converse examples could be written; ELLA allows
structural replication and VHDL1076 structural recursion). First, the
VHDL example (from [1]):

```
entity MULTI_BIT_ADDER                                    Example 2.9
(A,B: in BIT_VECTOR;
CIN: in BIT;
SUM: out BIT_VECTOR;
COUT: out BIT) is
end MULTI_BIT_ADDER;
```

```
architecture REGULAR_STRUCTURE of MULTI_BIT_ADDER is
REGULAR_STRUCTURE_BLK:
block
signal C:BIT_VECTOR (A'RANGE);
component FULL_ADDER port (CI,I1,I2:in BIT;
                           CO,RES:out BIT);
begin
for I in A'RANGE generate
if I = 1 generate
FULL_ADDER port (A(I),B(I),CIN,C(I),SUM(I));
end generate;
if I>1 generate
FULL_ADDER port (A(I),B(I),C(I-1),C(I),SUM(I));
end generate;
end generate;
end block;
end REGULAR_STRUCTURE;
```

Second, the ELLA example:

```
MAC MULTI_BIT_ADDER{INT n} = ([n]bool:a b, bool: cin)    Example 2.10
                         -> (bool,[n]bool)#cout,sum#:
(FAULT IF n<1 THEN n "is an unreal length of adder" FI.
OUTPUT IF n=1 THEN FULL_ADDER(a[1],b[1],cin)
       ELSE (MAKE MULTI_BIT_ADDER{n-1}:mba,
             FULL_ADDER:fa.
         JOIN (a[n],b[n],mba[1]) -> fa,
              (a[1..n-1],b[1..n-1],cin) -> mba.
           OUTPUT (fa[1],fa[2]CONCmba[2])
           )
       FI
).
```

It should be noted that in Example 2.10, the parameter range (n)
appears explicitly in the description (such as the array size,
[n]bool) while in this particular VHDL example (2.9) the array size
is never explicitly declared ('unconstrained' arrays), but is worked
out by the system from the context in which MULTI_BIT_ADDER is used.
The programmer can get access to the range through the built-in
attribute 'RANGE.

Because the semantics of instantiation and connection are common to
all HDLs, it is possible in principle to translate from one language
to another. Indeed in simple cases like the Examples 2.7–2.8 it would
be easy. It would be a little more difficult to generate translators
betweeen VHDL and ELLA structural replication formats and a lot more
difficult from VHDL structural replication format to ELLA structural
recursion format which is what would be required to translate between
Examples 2.9 and 2.10.

2.3. Representation of Behaviour

We now turn to the behaviour description of a circuit, which is one
which relates inputs to outputs without implying any internal
structure. Unlike for structure, there appears to be no common
semantics.

2.3.1 Circuits without state

There is no fundamental disagreement on how to describe zero–delay
combinatorial components. All that is required is a way of giving a
mapping: one way would be to give a truth table, another a piece of
code from a sequential (imperative) programming language or even from
a declarative language.

For example the truth table to describe a 2–bit to decimal converter
could be described in ELLA by a (value delivering) CASE clause:

```
TYPE bl = NEW (h|l),                               Example 2.11
     int = NEWi/(0..3).

FN B2_TO_D = ([2]bl: ip) -> int:
CASE Ip OF
  (1,1):i/0,
  (1,h):i/1,
  (h,1):i/2,
  (h,h):i/3
ESAC.
```

or it could be described by a (value delivering) sequence clause:

```
INT n=2.                                           Example 2.12
TYPE int = NEW i/(0..(1SLn)-1).

FN BN_TO_D = ([n]bool: ip) -> int:
SEQ VAR answer := i/0;
    FOR j= 1..n DO
        answer := ABSip[j] + (i/2*answer);
OUTPUT answer
QES.
```

Here SEQ ...QES delivers an 'int' value, which is used to provide the
output of BN_TO_D. In SEQ an ephemeral variable 'answer' is declared
and initialised at the begining of each time step to i/0. The n+1
assignments in SEQ should be understood to execute sequentially, in
zero time.

2.3.2 Circuits with state

The real problem with describing behaviour is, however, that much
hardware has state and that in order to give a mapping, one would
have to give a mapping between input and output waveforms (i.e. time
evolutions); this can be done in temporal logic [8]. Current HDLs do
not have such waveforms as signals but only model instantaneous
values, such as those described by the TYPE declarations of section

2.1. The behaviour of the hardware is specified by describing how these values evolve through successive instances of time, usually using an imperative style of programming. These HDLs use different methods of handling time, none of them entirely satisfactory. Since the methods used can be quite different, in general it is not possible to translate between them. Similarly, because the semantics are different, the methods used to synthesise structure from them must also be different.

Given that there is no agreed behaviour semantics (model of time evolution) the qualities of the various methods of behaviour description must be measured against the two primary uses for the language – modelling and design. When used for modelling, the primary concerns are model accuracy at the chosen level of abstraction and simulator execution efficiency. Simulation execution efficiency really means speed but, for large simulations, efficient space allocation translates into speed when virtual memory, with its consequent paging overheads, has to be used. The most common current practice, for getting efficient simulation models, is to give the user direct access to the the simulation implementation; that is the user directly controls the event mechanism.

When behaviour descriptions are given for design, that is as a precursor to transforming the description to structure, the notation must help the designer in this creative process, as well as allowing the description to be animated by the simulator. In this case, it is not very helpful for the user to have to give his behaviour description in terms of the internal working of some simulator.

It was principally for this reason that the ELLA designers decided that users should see virtually nothing of the simulator. ELLA has delay as the primitive which gets time into the language, for example,

LET x= DELAY5 y   Example 2.13

If pure delay (i.e. a succesion of unit delays) were the only primitive, simulation efficiency would be very low, so other delays are given which filter the signals as they pass through and which can be made to give the effects of inertial, ambiguity etc delays. Inside the simulator, these delays are indeed implemented with an event mechanism, but the user knows nothing of this. The delay algorithms are carefully chosen so that the user does not need to understand the event algorithm to understand the filter characteristics of the delay. From this primitive and the constructor facilities of the language higher level timing functions can be made, such as RISESWITHIN{n} or LASTACTIVE (similar to the VHDL attribute of that name).

A further consequence of this type of primitive is that it makes ELLA 'backward' looking, that is the designer describes what is to happen now consequent on what signals are now and were in the past. This gives a very different feel to the language from forward looking languages; languages where the event mechanism is visible are forward looking because the designer predicts what will happen in the future consequent on signal values now. The ELLA designers thought that backward looking languages are a more natural mode of expression for designers and thus desirable in design languages.

The designers of VHDL, on the other hand, wanted the user to see the simulator through the language and to give him direct access to the event mechanism in the simulator. This is seen in register transfer statements like:

```
OUTPUT <= X after min NS;                           Example 2.14
OUTPUT <= INPUT after max NS;
```

In practice once the user is given this freedom and power, he has to
understand the quite complex simulator algorithm. First, if the
statements in Example 2.14 are treated as sequential (that is when
they are found in a 'process' body) the order of the statements
matters. Secondly, at times non-intuitive effects can be obtained.
This can occur with Example 2.14 for an input pulse of length p if:

(max-min)< p <min

Consider the case when max=6, min=4, p=3.

```
      h h h
1 1        1 1 1 1 1 1 1 1
```

then the output waveform is:

```
          x x
1 1 1 1 1 1 1    1 1 1 1
```

while if the statements are reversed, the output is:

```
          x x x x x x
1 1 1 1 1 1 1
```

Only a minimal understanding of the event setting mechanism is needed
to understand that reversing the statement gives a different answer
because setting a new event on the queue at time t deletes all
existing events after t. However a detailed understanding is needed
to know that pulses which obey the inequality are shortened, while
the rest are lengthed. It is even more difficult to understand the
effect in the more general case. For example in:

x <= a when <condition>   Example 2.15

<condition> can create events dynamically.

Such an effect can be seen in the following fragment of a process
statement:

```
z <= a after t1 NS;                                 Example 2.16
wait until <condition>;
z <= b after t2 NS;
```

If <condition> becomes true within a time t < t1-t2, then the first
assignment to z does not occur as its event is deleted from the
queue.

Even when the designers have given the users access to the event
mechanism, there are further choices to be made. For example, the
designers of VHDL7.2 give the user another direct control on the
event queue with the enable/disable construct, while VHDL1076 gives
him instead the higher level primitive 'wait' which gives VHDL1076
more the feel of a design language.

In VHDL more complicated effects can be obtained by making multiple
concurrent assignments to the same signal (creating several event
queues) and then using a resolution algorithm to determine the
combined effect. (The same mechanism is used for buses). A similar
effect can be obtained in ELLA by combining delays. Thus in both
cases very complicated effects can be created, but in VHDL this can
be, but does not have to be, effected by combining a relatively few

queues each incorporating a complicated algorithm, while in ELLA many
simple delays have to be combined. One would hope that the more
detailed and sophisticated the control of the queues, the faster
would be the simulation. However, arguments for simplicity similar to
those used for justifying reduced instruction sets for computers
could apply. For example, the ELLA event lists are all static in
implementation (i.e. their size and nature does not alter during
simulation) and therefore allow an extremely efficient, fully
compiled implementation in the simulator.

From the point of view of those wanting a modelling language, the
issues are:
(i) speed
What are the relative simulation efficiencies of the different
methods of controlling the event queue? Is direct control of the
event queues actually faster in simulation than indirect methods? Is
a faster simulator obtained by putting in more sophisticated
mechanisms to control the queue? Whatever the methods used to control
the queues, to what extent have the simulator implementers optimised
the simulator to obtain high speed and a small memory requirement?
How suitable is the simulation algorithm for implementation in a
hardware accelerator?
(ii) accuracy
Can a user understand the full effects of what he writes? If not, can
the model written under these circumstances ever be accurate?

From the point of view of those wanting a design language, the
central issues are:
(i) understandability – accuracy
The user must be able to understand the full implications of what he
writes, both for the structure he has created and the behaviour he
has specified.
(ii) understandability – transformation
Can a user write behaviour descriptions in a way which helps him
transform the behaviour into structure while efficiently exploring
all the options? This issue is considered in more detail in section 3
because it is transformation which is the basis of high level
synthesis.

If it is the case that extra speed is indeed obtained by very
detailed control of the event queues, then it is probable that there
is a trade off between speed and understandability and/or accuracy.
This clearly has implications on trade-offs between modelling and
design languages. More fundamentally, design and modelling languages
begin to merge because much structure has to be given to obtain
models of high timing accuracy, so that to obtain models of widely
different timing accuracy, languages need to combine behaviour and
structure to any degree required.

2.4 Separation of Behaviour and Structure

The mechanisms for packaging programs into managable parts and for
allowing the reuse of code are important parts of languages. In
programming languages, the procedure mechanism is used to do both
these functions. Similar mechanisms exist in HDLs: ELLA has the MACro
(with the FN as its un-parameterised form); VHDL has the 'design
entity' and 'subprogram'. Most HDLs use different mechanisms for
packaging behaviour and structure. For example, in VHDL subprograms
package behaviour only, while design entities can contain both
behaviour and structure. ELLA, however, uses the MACro (and FN) to
package behaviour, structure and any mixture of the two. The fact
that in some cases there is more than one mechanism, implies
restrictions on the way behaviour and structure can be combined. For
example, in VHDL there are restrictions on how subprograms may call

each other and also subprograms may not call design entities. These languge features can have repercussions on the ways design hierarchies can be composed.

One would expect to be able to compose behaviour from sub-behaviours and similarly for structure (components made from sub-components). Clearly also structure must be composable from behaviour: at the trivial level, an AND-gate or adder need to be able to be described by its behaviour. All modern HDLs provide users with these facilities. Less obviously, it is useful for behaviour to be able to contain structure. This facility is needed in meet-in-the-middle design to incorporate pre-existing structure into behaviour. If this cannot be done then either a behaviour description has to be totally converted into structure (i.e. more top-down design) or, instead of incorporating the structure of the pre-existing component, a behavioural representation of the pre-existing component must be substituted. This means that when composing bottom-up, an equivalent pure behaviour representation has to be grown in parallel with the structural description, which certainly means extra work to generate two representations. Further, in practice, it is nearly impossible exactly to match behaviour and structure models of any complexity. Because of the different ways of packaging behaviour and structure descriptions, VHDL suffers from this inability to describe arbitrary compositions and decompositions of behaviour and structure, while ELLA avoids it, by defining a specification interface (the MAC or FN declaration) which is used both for structure and for behaviour.

It will be seen in section 3.2 that functional languages have attractions for describing data-flow architectures. In ELLA this is done by making MAC and FN value delivering. This shows the close relationship between functions delivering results and components having wires. Also, other elements, such as CASE and SEQ statements, deliver values. To illustrate these points, consider:

```
FN AND4 = (bool:i1 i2 i3 i4) -> bool:            Example 2.17
SEQ VAR result:= AND(i1,i2);
        result:= AND(result, i3);
        result:= AND(result, i4);
OUTPUT result
QES.
```

Here, the three ANDs, which will normally have associated delay, are instantiated within a sequence (behaviour) statement, or alternatively the behaviour has been (partly) composed from structure. The AND gate instances and the SEQ clause all deliver values.

3. TRANSFORMATION

The design process is essentially one of the transformation of data and behaviour and of the incorporation of pre-existing designs.

3.1. Transformation of Data

Enumerated values can easily be mapped onto a bit representation (e.g. in Example 2.2 a possibility for 'instruction' is that add, sub, stop map to 00, 01, 10 respectively). There can still be a problem of which bit pattern to associate with which basic value – this is not unlike the state assignment problem. In some cases there are more values in the new type than required to represent the values in the old (e.g. value '11' is not used in the representation of 'instruction'), but this should be no problem, indeed one of the attractions of using the higher level types first, is that it makes

sure that no illegal values are used. A particular concern is the
representation of integers and reals. For example, there is ample
scope for rounding and other errors to occur in trying to transform a
real number into a number representation of lower precision. This can
be necessary, for example, in signal processing applications where a
high level representation could use a floating point real
representation but an implementation uses fixed point integer
arithmetic.

The structuring of values creates few problems. In many cases the
structure is for convenience only and all that is necessary that it
be 'flattened', while in other cases the structure contains valuable
information.

Unions also should create few problems. When they are used to
represent 'real' signals rather than exception values, they behave
very like enumeration values. For example, the two dissimilar types
'instruction' and 'data' of Example 2.2 could both map down onto an
array of bools. A problem with unions used to create exception values
is that as the design is refined new exception values are likely to
be needed. This is not difficult for a designer to do manually; it is
less obvious to what extent such exception values will be necessary
in automatic synthesis, which is presumed to be correct by
construction.

Bidirectional signals introduced as a high level representation of a
bus would normally be expected to be implemented as such. It would
only be in exceptional circumstances that a description could be
analysed to show that it could, for example, safely be replaced by a
multiplexer.

The biggest problem in transforming data is when the language allows
dynamic values, that is signals whose extent is not know at the
moment simulation starts, for example the range of an integer, the
width of a bit word, the creation of a list. (Note that MACros in
ELLA and unconstrained arrays in VHDL are not dynamic). In many
cases, as design progresses, these data-objects will later become
statically defined (e.g. range of integers, depth of stack) but it is
generally very difficult to show that such a transformation is valid
– see for example the problem of range checking in programming
languages like Ada. If these dynamic signals are actually intended to
be implemented then almost inevitably the implementation will have to
be done by using memory, as this is usually the only resource which
is assumed to be of infinite extent. However in place of true dynamic
values often a (large) static maximum value is assumed e.g. the
maximum possible range of user defined integers is implementation
dependent and restricted to what the machine provides.

Finally, conventional HDLs do not support any idea of the meaning of
signal values distributed in time i.e. a meaning to waveforms. Thus
an array of bits has a value and meaning at each instance in time,
but there is no simple way of expressing the fact that the collection
of eight successive bit values in time means a byte of data. This
problem arises from a fundamentally defective model of time; at
present, conventions have to be used to mitigate the problem, but in
the long term the best solution would appear to be to use quite new
language concepts, such as those in temporal logic[8]. With little
suport from the language, the transformation of a high level
description such as INTEGER in VHDL to a bit serial representation is
an enormous change, requiring the creation of a whole new clocking
scheme, creating sequencers etc. Although it is feasible to do this
automatically, the resulting hardware might not be considered to be
of acceptable quality for practical use.

3.2. Transformation of Behaviour

Transformation of behaviour centres on the core semantic constructs of the language. Case, sequence, variable assignment (time independent constructs) and delay, register assignment (time dependent constructs) are some of the common core behavioural primitives of HDLs. Synthesising hardware from behaviour requires decisions on how much parallelism (ie hardware) is acceptable or needed in the implementation. In general the more the parallelism the faster the implementation and the greater the amount of hardware. In practice it is necessary both to transform descriptions which have too much parallelism to ones with less, and vice versa.

The 'classic' behaviour compilation is from a source algorithmic sequential language, containing no time (i.e. case, sequence, variable assignment) to hardware including time [9]. The simplest approach is to transform all variables into registers which communicate by a bus to an operational unit (ALU) and to construct a sequencer to control register access and operational unit function. This process gives a machine which is a near relative of a Von Neumann processor. Optimisations can then be performed to eliminate unnecesary registers. The next stage is to study the data dependency graph for potential parallelisms and hence create a multiple bus and operational unit structure, with appropriate control. It is relatively easy to do all this precisely because programming languages have at their heart a model of computation predicated on an abstract Von Neumann machine. Hence, there is a close relationship between sequential and assignment constructs in programming languages and Von Neumann-like architectures which exhibit minimal parallelism and minimal hardware. There is correspondingly a close relationship between functional language constructs and maximally parallel, data-flow architectures. It is no accident that in front-end signal processing, where maximally pipelined, maximally parallel architectures are common, functional languages are often used (SILAGE in CATHEDRAL2 [10], ufp[11]). It would appear that to support behaviour compilation in its trade-offs between more or less parallelism, it is useful to have a clear understanding of the relationship between sequential and functional constructs in source languages, and be able to transform between them. ELLA examples are used for illustration since VHDL, which is a statement orientated (imperative) language, has virtually no support for a functional notation.

Consider, first, case clauses and the particularly simple Example 2.11 of B2_TO_D. The ELLA case clause is used to define a mapping and is an entirely parallel construct, that is the tests for (l,l) etc are deemed to be done in parallel in zero time. An obvious fully parallel implementation would be to use a PLA. The CASE statement can be transformed to a form, using the ELLA SEQuence clause, where each of the tests is done sequentially but still in zero time (in ELLA, program sequence steps are separated by semi-colons):

```
FN B2_TO_D = ([2]bool:ip) -> int:                    Example 3.1
SEQ VAR op:=i/0;
    CASE ip OF (l,l): op:=i/0 ESAC;
    CASE ip OF (l,h): op:=i/1 ESAC;
    CASE ip OF (h,l): op:=i/2 ESAC;
    CASE ip OF (h,h): op:=i/3 ESAC;
    OUTPUT op
QES.
```

(Note the case clause used here is not value delivering, but of the form usually met in programming languages.)

Next consider Example 2.12. The maximum parallelism is obtained if

FOR j=1..n DO answer:= (answer * i/2) + ABSip[j]

is transformed to parallel statements of the form:

```
FN BN_TO_D = ([n]bool:ip) -> int:                    Example 3.2
(LET answer0 = i/0,
     answer1 = ABSip[1] + (i/2*answer0),
     ....
     ....
     answern = ABSip[n] + (i/2*answern_1).
 OUTPUT answern
).
```

It can be seen that the body can be rewritten in functional form:
answern = ABSip[n] + i/2*(ABSip[n-1] + i/2*(ABSip[n-2] + ...)))),
see [6] for further details.

A natural way of writing BN_TO_D functionally is to use recursion:

```
MAC BN_TO_D{INT n} = ([n]bool:ip) -> int:            Example 3.3
IF n=1 THEN ABSip[1]
ELSE ABSip[n] + i/2*BN_TO_D{n-1}ip[1..n-1]
FI.
```

This can be seen to be identical to the transformed version (Example 3.2) but is in a pure functional notation with no naming of nets. The descriptions imply n each of *, +, ABS. This shows an example of converting sequential to functional constructs. It is essentially the same transformation that is used in transforming sequential languages via the data-dependency graph to a data-flow graph for programming data-flow machines [12].

These examples show transformations in both directions between parallel and serial representations - both occuring in zero time. A natural implementation of a functional description is as a dataflow architecture in which each function corresponds to a piece of hardware. Also increased speed can be obtained at the expense of higher latency by pipelining, through a further transformation to include latches in appropriate places.

Next consider the classic approach which produces minimally parallel hardware. A natural implementation of an algorithmic sequential construct is by transforming it to hardware where program sequence is converted to the corresponding time sequence. For example, in Example 2.12, the FOR loop could be transformed to allow it to execute in n time steps corresponding to the n program steps. The effect of doing this would be that there need only be one piece of hardware for each of the operations *, + and ABS. Assuming bit serial input, this could be:

```
FN B2_TO_D = (bool:seq ip) -> int:                   Example 3.4
SEQ VAR answer::=i/0;
CASE seq OF
    t: answer := ABSip + (i/2*answer),
    f:
ESAC;
OUTPUT answer
QES.
```

(The variable 'answer' is made 'persistent' by the use of the double colon in its declaration; that is its value is preserved in moving from one time step to the next. In this case it is initialised to i/0

at time zero.) The input 'seq' would be fed from a sequencer
generated from the precedence graph. By increasing the time to 3n
steps, the three separate pieces of hardware (*, +, ABS) could be
replaced by one programmable arithmetic unit.

We see that sequential expression naturally tends to produce minimal
hardware while functional expression tends to produce maximal
hardware. In ELLA, since it is possible to transform between
sequential and functional expressions, it should be possible to
adjust the amount of hardware synthesised. In general programming
languages, this transformation breaks down because of features whose
functional representations are not statically known e.g. a REPEAT
UNTIL loop (which ELLA has not included).

We now turn to the transformation of semantic constructs which
include time, such as register transfer and delay. In many
applications the writer of a behaviour description will have already
done some (human) synthesis: for example, a register transfer
statement was used because a register in the hardware was intended;
similarly, a register transfer or delay statement could be used to
model delays expected from a component. In this section, however, the
concern has been the use of behaviour statements as a stage in the
design process from which subsequent transformations are to be made.
For this use the most difficult problem is the transformation of
statements which were used for modelling, in particular those which
imply a knowledge of the event setting algorithm. If the event
setting is simple – for example, if transport delay, which implies no
overwriting of events, is used – then automatic translation
strategies would appear feasible. On the other hand if a description
implies complex manipulations of the event queue and if it is not
identifiable as a model of a known hardware component, then it is
unlikely that practically useful hardware could be created.

4. CONCLUSIONS

Significant advances have been made in the design of HDLs both for
modelling and as a notation for design. Modelling languages have
developed to give precise control over the simulator which animates
the description. Design languages are being developed which are more
concerned with the possibilities of transforming descriptions –
particularly of high level data to low level types and of behaviour
to structure. The most serious problem with current HDLs is a
defective model of time which makes difficult the expression of
time-serial data and the transformation of time-dependent behaviour
constructs. It is not yet clear to what extent efficient simulation
and good design notation can be combined in one language, but in our
judgement design languages offer a much better basis for the input to
a synthesis system than languages which are heavily biassed towards
modelling.

ACKNOWLEDGEMENTS

The authors are grateful for the advice of their colleagues C.
Newton, J. Morison and E. Whiting. The work is partially supported by
funding from the Alvey Directorate.

FOOTNOTES AND REFERENCES

/1/ ELLA is a registered Trade Mark of the Secretary of State for
Defence.

[1] VHDL User's manual, Vol 1 - Tutorial. Prepared for US Airforce by
Intermetrics Inc. August 85.
[2] IEEE Design and Test April 1986 (special issue on VHDL).
[3] VHDL Language Reference Manual, IEEE draft standard 1076B,
prepared for VHDL Analysis and Standardisation Group by CAD Languages
System Inc. April 1987.
[4] Morison, J.D.M., Peeling, N.E., Thorp, T.L., CHDLs and their
Applications. Koomen and Moto-aka (eds) p303 Elsevier, IFIP
1985.
[5] Morison, J.D.M., Peeling, N.E.P., Thorp, T.L., Whiting, E.V.,
EASE: A design support environment for the HDDL ELLA. To be published,
Design Automation Conference, Miami 1987.
[6] Morison, J.D.M., Peeling, N.E.P., Whiting, E.V., Sequential
program extensions to ELLA with automatic transformation to structure.
To be published, ICCD, New York 1987.
[7] Coelho, D.R., Van Cleemput, W.M., 3rd. Int. Conf. on semi-custom
ICs. London. Nov. 1983
[8] Moszkowski, B., Proc. 6th Int. Symp. on CHDLs and their
applications, Pittsburgh, Vehara and Barbacci (eds), North Holland
1983.
[9] Composano, R., Proc. ACM/IEEE Design Automation Conference 475-481
June 1985
[10] Hilfinger, P., Proc. IEEE CICC Conf. May 1985, pp 213-216
[11] Sheeran, M., MFP An algebraic VLSI design Language PhD thesis
Oxford University 1983
[12] Aho, A.V., Ullman J.D., Principles of Compiler Design,
Addison-Wesley 1977.

VLSI '87, C.H. Séquin (editor)
Elsevier Science Publishers B.V. (North-Holland)
© IFIP, 1988

An RTL Logic Design Aid

For Parallel Control VLSI Processor

Yukihiro NAKAMURA and Kiyoshi OGURI

NTT Electrical Communication Laboratories
1-2356 Take Yokosuka Kanagawa
JAPAN

1. Introduction

Logic design aids, like logic simulators or design editors for circuit diagrams, have already been implemented [1],[2]. Hardware description languages, which can describe the whole hardware structure in terms of the connective structure description at the gate or circuit levels, have been implemented as well [3].

Now, description at a higher level is needed. Several studies on Register Transfer Level (RTL) languages or functional simulators have been conducted[4]. However, a few of RTL languages aim at automating the hardware synthesis process [5],[6],[7]. An issue of great interest is whether an RTL CAD system is practical for designing a highly complex, parallel control, large scale VLSI processor. To the question of description capability, quality of expanded results, and how designers can adjust designs when using an RTL CAD system, no one has given an answer yet.

In designing digital equipment with parallel control parts using advanced control or pipelined control techniques, designers need to deal with macro-level conciderations, make mid-design evaluations and perform optimizations based on those evaluations. For these tasks, the author has developed an RTL description language called SFL (Structured Function description Language)[8],[9] which can be used to describe parallel control at the register-transfer level, a behavior simulator (SFLSIM), and a hardware synthesizer (SFLEXP) into a single system.

2. Behavioral Description Language

2.1 Characteristics of SFL

Table 1 shows a comparison of several typical RTL languages based on the following points [10]-[15]:

(1) Whether the combinatorial circuits are necessarily defined as hardware components (RTL facilities), i.e., can operators (e.g., +, −, *, /) be used or not;

(2) Whether the hardware is designed to put components into operation, i.e. whether time frames and description classes to explicitly indicate the controllable domains are employed;

(3) Whether descriptions of static relations between hardware components can be combined with behavioral description, i.e., whether connective description between hardware components is allowed.

Table 1. Comparison of RTL languages

(NOTE) ○ : YES
      × : NO
      — : NOT APPLICABLE

			Behavioral description language					Reference		
			CDL	DDL	FDL	SFL	SDL	HHDL	ISPS	VHDL
Definition of passive object (Def. of RTL facilities)			○	○	○	○	○	×	○	○
Necessity of combinatorial circuit definition as passive object (Operator usage of +, -, *, / prohibited)			×	×	×	○	○	—	×	×
Designed to put components into operation			○	○	○	○	×	—	○	○
Behavioral Description	Expression of Behavioral Procedures	Order relation only	○				—	—	○	
		State (machine cycle) transition		○		○	—	—		○
		Time and clock reference			○	○	—	—		○
	Hierarchy for behavioral description (Existence of active objects)		×	○	○	○	—	—	○	○
	Relation between active objects	Static expression — only by signaling terminals	—		○		—	—		
		Static expression — by passive object	—	○		○	—	—	○	○
		Dynamic expression	—	×	×	○	—	—	○	○
Description of static relation between passive objects (Connective description, between passive objects)			○	○	○	×	○	—	×	○

Nearly all RTL languages require the definition of registers, memories, and terminals as hardware components, but few of them require the definition of combinatorial circuits as hardware components. As shown in Table 1, only SFL explicitly defines combinatorial circuits as hardware components. This SFL characteristic makes it possible to trace the utilization rate of components and to generate an efficient structure. In a practical design process, the number and sorts of combinatorial circuits as well as those of registers are very important in that they have to be used effectively in order to optimize the hardware design. Therefore, it is considered absolutely necessary for a designer to be able to explicitly define the number and sorts of combinatorial circuits.

As stated above, SFL generalizes the concept of "behavior" not only by transfer between registers as in conventional languages, but also as a **procedure using hardware components** like combinatorial circuits, registers and so on (referred to as "passive objects").

In addition to this, SFL has made it possible to handle an entity corresponding to a passive object procedure as a hardware component (referred to as "active object"). This provides a recursive representation of the behavior. Therefore, SFL does not provide any description format for static relations between hardware components. In SFL, an active object is called a "stage." An entity similar to SFL's active object is called an "automaton" in DDL [11], a "node" in FDL [12], and a "process" in ISPS [14].

To express a design in SFL, the design is divided into active and passive object portions. Passive objects are I/O terminals, storage facilities, and I/O functional relations. Active objects are defined by the use of passive objects. In other words, the passive objects are external terminals, internal terminals, or functional units (e.g.,register, ALU) and the active objects are controllers.

In general, a hardware device can be functionally partitioned into several behavioral units (control parts or controllers), like instruction fetch or execution parts of CPU. Hardware design is usually carried out by designing each behavioral unit separately. In SFL, an active object, behavioral unit, control part or controller is the same concept and is designed as a stage.

2.2 SFL Behavior Model

Figure 1 shows a typical SFL behavior model of a highly complex, parallel control processor. SFL makes it possible to describe the following control parts:

(1) Main independent control part and dedicated subordinate control parts (stage S3 in Fig.1);

(2) Parallel operated subordinate control parts (main part waits for termination acknowledgement — stages S1 and S2);

(3) Leave behind control part (main part does not wait for task to finish — stage S4 and S6);

(4) Independent control part for transferring pipeline control (stages S8, S9 and S10);

(5) Independent control part for controlling priority (arbitration mechanism — stage S7);

(6) Temporary control parts for immediate operations (messenger M1, M2 and M3).

In SFL, besides the above–mentioned "stage," there is another type of active object, the "messenger," mentioned later.

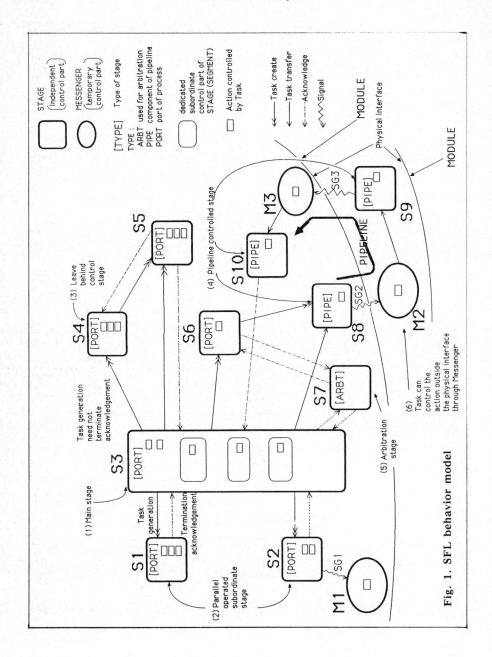

Fig. 1. SFL behavior model

A stage is activated by receiving a "hardware task" (which is a newly developed concept for synchoronizing stages and indicating their roles). A task is defined to be a process or a request that requires the functions of the corresponding stage. By introducing this new concept, SFL can provide the ability to explicitly describe the existence of a task within the corresponding stage and a task transition from one stage to another. Stage's behavior is defined in state transition format. In each state, the following actions are performed according to the received task type:

(1) use of passive objects;

(2) state transition;

(3) creation of a new hardware task for another stage (these two stages are both active);

(4) transfer of the hardware task to another stage (only last stage is active);

(5) termination of the hardware task;

(6) signal activation for the messenger.

All actions in one state of each stage are performed simultaneously. A stage is active until it terminates or transfers its own task. Some parts of a state transition (which are called "segments") can be shared like subroutines in software (as shown in stage S3).

A messenger is activated by a "signal" (which is a special concept for the temporary (immediate) control and introduction of structural hierarchy in behavior description) and performs the following actions while the signal is active:

(1) use of passive objects;

(2) creation of a new hardware task for another stage.

Three types of signals are applicable. One is for control inside the module which is a unit of structural hierarchy (SG1 in Fig.1). One is for inside to outside the module (SG2), and the other is for outside to inside the module (SG3). By these means, the control across the module (physical) interface is explicitly described in behavioral notation. Through these features, complex control logic can be expressed clearly in RTL behavioral description by SFL.

For example, Figure 2 shows a part of SFL description of the memory access controllers in a PROLOG machine mentioned later. The conditions and actions are as follows:

```
if (condition_1) {
        action_a;
        action_b;
}
if (condition_2) action_c;
if (condition_3) action_d;
```

are called a rule set. And all checks of conditions and actions of a rule set are performed simultaneously. Rule sets are separated by the following notations which define the state names of the stage.

```
<state name>
```

A state transition, a task transition and a task creation, respectively, are described in action part as follows:

```
=> <state name>;
=> stage name [task name];
=>=> stage name [task name];
```

Figure 2 indicates that arbitration mechanisms for four memory banks and a pipeline controlled bus can be clearly described in SFL.

```
stage:FETCH_A_REQUESTER(port)[F_A] {
<FETCH>
    switch( REG_A ) {
        case 1 : signal FETCH_A_REQ_BANK1 to MEM_CNT1;
        case 2 : signal FETCH_A_REQ_BANK2 to MEM_CNT2;
        case 3 : signal FETCH_A_REQ_BANK3 to MEM_CNT3;
        case 4 : signal FETCH_A_REQ_BANK4 to MEM_CNT4;
    }
    if (FETCH_A_OK from any) {
        ADRS_TERMINAL:=REG_ADRS;
        =>><MEM_PIPE1.[FETCH_A];
        =><WAIT>;
<WAIT>
    if (MEM_PIPE4.[FETCH_A]) REG_DATA<=DATA_TERMINAL;
}
stage:FETCH_B_REQUESTER(port)[F_B] {
<FETCH>
    switch( REG_B ) {
        case 1 : signal FETCH_B_REQ_BANK1 to MEM_CNT1;
        case 2 : signal FETCH_B_REQ_BANK2 to MEM_CNT2;
        case 3 : signal FETCH_B_REQ_BANK3 to MEM_CNT3;
        case 4 : signal FETCH_B_REQ_BANK4 to MEM_CNT4;
    }
    if (FETCH_A_OK from any) {
        ADRS_TERMINAL:=REG_ADRS;
        =>><MEM_PIPE1.[FETCH_B];
        =><WAIT>;
<WAIT>
    if (MEM_PIPE4.[FETCH_B]) REG_DATA<=DATA_TERMINAL;
}
stage:STORE_A_REQUESTER(port)[S_A] {
<STORE>
    switch( REG_A ) {
        case 1 : signal STORE_A_REQ_BANK1 to MEM_CNT1;
        case 2 : signal STORE_A_REQ_BANK2 to MEM_CNT2;
        case 3 : signal STORE_A_REQ_BANK3 to MEM_CNT3;
        case 4 : signal STORE_A_REQ_BANK4 to MEM_CNT4;
    }
    if (STORE_A_OK from any) {
        ADRS_TERMINAL:=REG_ADRS;
        DATA_TERMINAL:=REG_DATA;
        =>><MEM_PIPE1.[STORE];
    }
}

%macro:%MEM_CNT(
stage:MEM_CNT%1(arbt)[I] {
    <P>
        if (FETCH_A_REQ_BANK%1 from FETCH_A_REQUESTER !!
            FETCH_B_REQ_BANK%1 from FETCH_B_REQUESTER )
            signal BANK%1_FETCH_REQ to INT_CNT;
        if (STORE_A_REQ_BANK%1 from STORE_A_REQUESTER)
            signal BANK%1_STORE_REQ to INT_CNT;
        if (BANK%1_FETCH_OK from INT_CNT) {
            signal READ%1_START_SIGNAL to external;
            =><S1>;
            if (FETCH_A_REQ_BANK%1 from FETCH_A_REQUESTER)
                signal FETCH_A_OK to FETCH_A_REQUESTER;
            elseif (FETCH_B_REQ_BANK%1 from FETCH_B_REQUESTER)
                signal FETCH_B_OK to FETCH_B_REQUESTER;
        elseif (BANK%1_STORE_OK from INT_CNT) {
            signal WRITE%1_SIGNAL to external;
            =><S1>;
            if (STORE_A_REQ_BANK%1 from STORE_A_REQUESTER)
                signal STORE_A_OK to STORE_A_REQUESTER;
    <S1>            =><S2>;
    <S2>            =><S3>;
    <S3>            =><S4>;
    <S4>
        if (MEM_PIPE3.[STORE])   =><P>;
        else    =><S4>;
}
%MEM_CNT(1)
%MEM_CNT(2)

        signal READ%1_SIGNAL to external;
        if (FETCH_A_REQ_BANK%1 from FETCH_A_REQUESTER !!
            FETCH_B_REQ_BANK%1 from FETCH_B_REQUESTER)
            signal BANK%1_FETCH_REQ to INT_CNT;
        if (BANK%1_FETCH_OK from INT_CNT) {
            signal READ%1_START_SIGNAL to external;
            =><S1>;
            if (FETCH_A_REQ_BANK%1 from FETCH_A_REQUESTER)
                signal FETCH_A_OK to FETCH_A_REQUESTER;
            elseif (FETCH_B_REQ_BANK%1 from FETCH_B_REQUESTER)
                signal FETCH_B_OK to FETCH_B_REQUESTER;

%MEM_CNT(3)
%MEM_CNT(4)

stage:INT_CNT(arbt)[I] {
%macro:%PRIORITY(
    if (BANK%1_FETCH_REQ from MEM_CNT%1) {
        signal BANK%1_FETCH_OK to MEM_CNT%1;
        =><MEM%2>; }
    elseif (BANK%2_FETCH_REQ from MEM_CNT%2) {
        signal BANK%2_FETCH_OK to MEM_CNT%2;
        =><MEM%3>; }
    elseif (BANK%3_FETCH_REQ from MEM_CNT%3) {
        signal BANK%3_FETCH_OK to MEM_CNT%3;
        =><MEM%4>; }
    elseif (BANK%4_FETCH_REQ from MEM_CNT%4)
        signal BANK%4_FETCH_OK to MEM_CNT%4;
    elseif (FETCH_COMPLETION_REQ from MEM_PIPE4) ;
    elseif (BANK%1_STORE_REQ from MEM_CNT%1) {
        signal BANK%1_STORE_OK to MEM_CNT%1;
        =><MEM%2>; }
    elseif (BANK%2_STORE_REQ from MEM_CNT%2) {
        signal BANK%2_STORE_OK to MEM_CNT%2;
        =><MEM%3>; }
    elseif (BANK%3_STORE_REQ from MEM_CNT%3) {
        signal BANK%3_STORE_OK to MEM_CNT%3;
        =><MEM%4>; }
    elseif (BANK%4_STORE_REQ from MEM_CNT%4)
        signal BANK%4_STORE_OK to MEM_CNT%4;
)
<MEM1>
    %PRIORITY(1,2,3,4)
<MEM2>
    %PRIORITY(2,3,4,1)
<MEM3>
    %PRIORITY(3,4,1,2)
<MEM4>
    %PRIORITY(4,1,2,3)
}
stage:MEM_PIPE1(pipe)[STORE,FETCH_A,FETCH_B] {
    switch(tasktype) {
        case [STORE]    : [STORE][end];
        case [FETCH_A]  : [FETCH_A]=>MEM_PIPE4.[FETCH_A];
        case [FETCH_B]  : [FETCH_B]=>MEM_PIPE4.[FETCH_B]
        .....

stage:MEM_PIPE2(pipe)[STORE,FETCH_A,FECTH_B] {
```

Fig. 2. SFL description of memory access control

3. Behavior Simulator (SFLSIM)

SFLSIM is a system which integrates an editor, parser, simulator, and evaluator. The editor and parser parse the SFL text on demand, and point out any erroneous phrase with the cursor. The simulator directly interprets the design translated from SFL. Therefore, since it does not require an expansion process, SFLSIM can start simulation in a very short time. SFL's synchronous model and SFLSIM's message driven mechanism make interpretive simulation possible. The simulator traces changes in value/status and the activity of active objects, and detects contradicting behavior.

SFLSIM can trace task transfer or creation sequence. Since a hardware task is strongly bound to some part of the hardware (i.e., the stage), it is not concerned with time flow. For example, a time chart representing the pipeline processes consisting of three stages is shown in Fig.3. Task transfer sequences (task1–task2–task4 and task1–task3–task4) are different processes to realize different functions. In both cases, the task1s and task4s must be distinguished by SFLSIM. Then SFLSIM memorizes the time in the history storage when the task is transferred or created. SFLSIM also memorizes the task from which a particular task is transferred or created. In this way the task transfer flow or task creation flow becomes traceable. This is especially useful when a designer wishes to trace all changes resulting from a particular task.

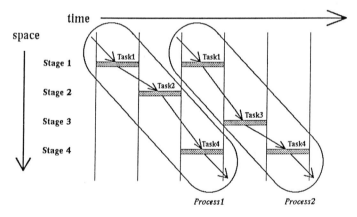

Fig. 3. Task activation flow and Process

Many commands for setting simulation status and inquiring about current status or history are available. Since these commands allow the variables to be used in their arguments, many types of inquiries are applicable. For example, an inquiry is possible which says " Display all active objects which have read a certain register (this register is the variable) that was written by a particular active object." The CAD environment also offers statistical information, such as the utilization rate of memory and ALU or the degree of parallel processing of independent parts or multi–memory banks. This information can be displayed graphically, in addition to the value trace data and time charts which are conventionally displayed.

Modification of hardware design during an SFLSIM session is also possible. This is a great advantage over conventional systems. Modification is available for every passive object and state of stages. Modification may result in some inconsistencies. SFLSIM points these out when it encounters them.

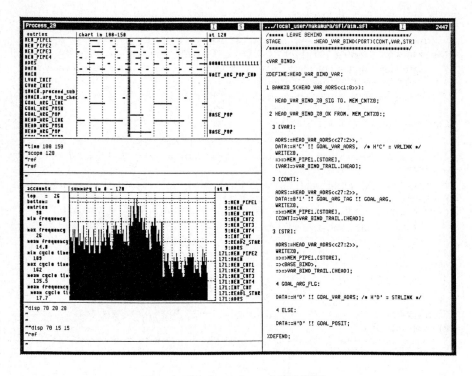

Fig. 4. Window view of SFLSIM

A window view example of the multi-window feature presented by SFLSIM when simulating a PROLOG machine executing a prolog program is shown in Fig.4. This program takes its subsets from three elements. One shell shows the SFL source codes for a stage (HEAD_VAR_BIND), one shows a time-chart indicating passive object values and active object status, and the other shows the degree of parallel activity in the inference cycle. The details of the PROLOG machine designed by SFL are described in Chapter 5.

4. Hardware Synthesizer (SFLEXP)

SFLEXP synthesizes control circuits and connects paths between active and passive objects from behavior description automatically. Since it does not synthesize the internal circuits of passive objects, these should be designed using conventional methods. However, this does not require much design effort, because most passive objects are already available in the component library. There are also ample design examples of passive objects, which can easily be modified by humans for a paticular target. This means fewer passive objects need to be newly designed. Moreover, even if a designer must design all the gate structures of these passive objects, the design effort required will not be significant compared to the total design effort. On the other hand, the control circuits for a paticular target are very difficult to design due to the semantic gap which exists between the behavior and connection. This is the reason for adopting the approach described in this paper.

In this synthesizing process, SFLEXP performs optimization processes by using the following pattern match algorithm methods with the net–list data: (1) gate step adjustment based on the clock cycle; (2) fan–out adjustment based on the cell library; and (3) polarity adjustment based on the polarity of passive object terminals.

Gate step adjustment means expanding logic circuits comprising critical paths. Two examples are described as follows (see Fig.5):

(i) If a control circuit which is constructed with 2–input AND gates and has some steps, it may be reconstructed with AND gates which have the maximum fan–in terminals allowed in the cell library;

(ii) If there are series of inverters in the net–list, they are removed.

Consequently, these reconstructed circuits have fewer steps and the critical paths are canceled.

Fan–out adjustment entails copying cells which exceed the fan–out limit and re–allocating the fan–out when the cell is synthesized. When the cell is defined by the designer, fan–out adjustment entails inserting buffer gates (see Fig.6).

Polarity adjustment involves selection from among many types of gates, selectors, and registers. This process starts the matching of polarity of output terminals on the synthesized gates with the polarity of input terminals on the passive objects, which has already been specified. This process also stops matching of the polarity of input terminals on the synthesized gates with the polarity of output terminals on the passive objects. Polarity is propagated between terminals on the synthesized gates. In this process, the polarity of the synthesized objects' terminals which have already been decided is not redefined. Finally, redundant inverters are removed (see Fig.7).

The optimization function is implemented as an expert system using KBMS (Knowledge–Base Management System)[16] developed in NTT.

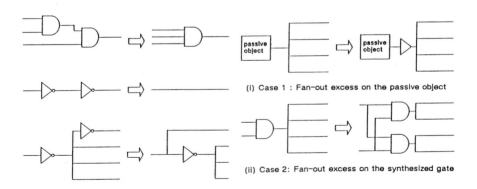

(I) Case 1 : Fan-out excess on the passive object

(II) Case 2: Fan-out excess on the synthesized gate

Fig. 5. Gate step adjustment example   **Fig. 6. Fan–out adjustment example**

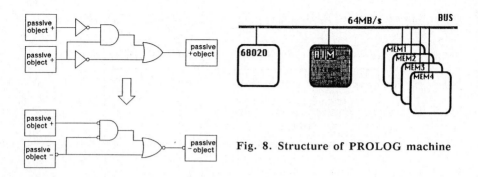

Fig. 8. Structure of PROLOG machine

Fig. 7. Polarity adjustment example

5. Design Outline of PROLOG Machine

5.1 Design Object

This SFL based hardware design environment was used to design a PROLOG machine. The general configuration of this PROLOG machine is shown in Fig.8. It includes a one–LSI chip inferential engine, an Advanced Inference Machine (AIM), an I/O co–processor, 4–way interleaved multi–bank storages (access time : 250ns) and a pipeline controlled bus (cycle time : 62.5ns).

AIM performs unification, backtracking, and cut–operation. The I/O co–processor is a Motorola 68020, and it processes built–in I/O predicates which can not be accelerated by specialized hardware.

The inference algorithm in AIM was taken from PROLOG interpreters on general purpose computers and was adjusted for hardware use. In order to show the effectiveness of this CAD environment, the details of highly complex, parallel processor, AIM, are described in the following.

To accelerate a process with hardware, it is necessary to divide the process into several sub–processes and control them in parallel. AIM's inference process was divided into 33 sub–processes, and 33 stages corresponding to these sub–processes were designed.

All stages in AIM are shown in Table 2.

For example, the details of the unification process in AIM are described in the following.

(1) Variable initialization: When the sequencer finds a candidate clause, it invokes this sub–process which automatically allocates and initializes the variables appearing in the clause. Both local and global variables are initialized simultaneously.

(2) Argument fetching: This sub–process is invoked preceding the main sequencer's examination of whether the goal and candidate head can be matched. Here too, argument fetching of goal and head are performed simultaneously.

(3) Variable binding and bind trailing: If either the goal or head arguments is found to be an unbound variable by tag decode operation, the sequencer invokes this sub–process which automatically performs binding and trailing functions.

Table 2. Stages in AIM

PROCESS	STAGE NAME	NUMBER of STEPS in SEL	NUMBER of TASKS	NUMBER of STATES
CONTROL of OTHER STAGES	MAIN_UNIFY	764	2	34
VARIABLE INITIALIZATION	VAR_NUM_FETCH , LVAR_INIT , GVAR_INIT	105	3	8
ARGUMENT COMPARISON	GOAL_ARG_FETCH/SKIP/POP, HEAD_ARG_FETCH/SKIP/POP, GOAL_ARG_PUSH, HEAD_ARG_PUSH	626	4	30
BINDING	GOAL_VAR_BIND, HEAD_VAR_BIND, VAR_BIND_TRAIL	245	8	5
RETURN DATA PUSHING	RETN_PUSH	94	1	4
BRANCH DATA PUSHING	BRCH_PUSH	179	1	8
BRANCHING	BRCH_POP1,BRCH_POP2, BRCH_POP3,BRCH_POP6	272	4	16
RESTORING	RETN_POP1,RETN_POP2, RETN_POP3,RETN_POP6	128	4	8
UNBINDING	UNBIND, UNBIND_EXEC	80	2	3
MEMORY ACCESS	INT_CNT, MEM_CNT,MEM_CNT, MEM_CNT,MEM_CNT, MEM_PIPE1,MEM_PIPE2, MEM_PIPE3,MEM_PIPE4	1,181	61	28
PREPARATION for NEXT DATA	NEXT_HEAD	40	1	4
TOTAL		3,718	91	144

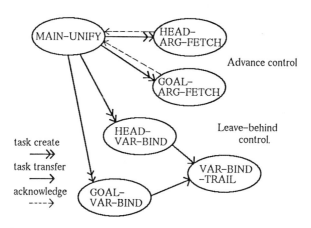

Fig. 9. Stages for unification processing

The AIM's stages for unification processing (as shown in Fig.9) is described as follows:

MAIN_UNIFY creates tasks on HEAD_ARG_FETCH and GOAL_ARG_FETCH to execute goal and head argument fetch simultaneously and, then, waits for the arrival of completion acknowledgements. Next, it decodes these arguments and creates new tasks to fetch the next set of arguments (advance control). If one of the arguments is a variable, MAIN_UNIFY creates a task on HEAD_VAR_BIND or GOAL_VAR_BIND to bind the variable to the other argument, and at the same time, it decodes the next set of arguments without waiting for that binding to be completed (leave-behind control). HEAD_VAR_BIND or GOAL_VAR_BIND transfers the task to VAR_BIND_TRAIL to trail this binding.

5.2 Simulation and Performance Estimation

Figure 10 shows a part of the simulation results of AIM in the evaluation process. From these results, high simultaneity was found to be attained. Nearly all memory accesses are efficiently used.

SFLSIM showed that AIM takes 105 machine cycles per one inference trial. To carry out the primary goal, this program generated 30 sub-goals (including 8 failures), and the machine cycle was set at 62.5ns. An AIM thus designed realized a performance of 111KLIPS.

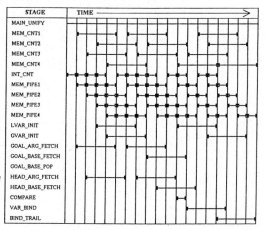

Fig. 10. Simulation result of stage operations

6. Summary of Evaluation

Several configurations could be easily evaluated for cost-performance using the CAD environment. The design was carried out as shown in Table 3, and examples of evaluation data are shown in Table 4.

(1st) The original design shown in Table 2 was evaluated. The total number of SFL statements is 3,867.

(2nd) Next, the design was re-configured to reduce and integrate inefficient active objects (stages), i.e., RETN_PUSH, RETN_POP1,2,3,4, BRCH_POP1,2,3,4.

(3rd) Finally, the number of passive objects and the passive objects themselves were optimized based on their usage frequency.

In the optimization process, the designer rewrites the SFL source and evaluates it using the CAD system cyclically.

This optimization effort took 3.8 person-months and the total design effort was only 7.8 person-months including 1 man-month for designing the passive objects, which is several times faster than can be accomplished using conventional CAD tools.

The information provided by SFLSiM was particularly useful in debugging and adjusting the design. Furthermore, simulation speed is 70 times faster than the well-known TEGAS-5E on IBM 3081K. The reason for speeding up the simulation execution time are as follows:

(1) Since the behavioral description can be made by using RTL macro statements, the number of facilities that the simulator has to evaluate decreased;

(2) It is sufficient to evaluate just the facilities which satisfy behavioral conditions only at the stages activated by tasks.

Table 3. Results of optimization

Optimization phases	Number of active objects	Number of gates	Performance (KLIPS)	Memory use frequency
1st	**33**	**23,119**	**111**	**0.41**
2nd	**23**	**20,045**	**121**	**0.52**
3rd	**23**	**18,213**	**130**	**0.60**

Table 4. Example of evaluation

OBJECT	EVALUATION ITEMS	RESULT of EVALUATION
BEHAVIORAL SIMULATOR SFLSIM	PROCESSING TIME	**38.7 sec** (23 Kgate, 300 clock) (70 times faster than TEGAS)
	FILE SPACE	**5.5 MB** (23 Kgate, 300 clock) (on IBM3081)
	SIMULATION/ ANALYZING OUTPUT	Resister Value, Terminal Value, Stage Activity, State Activity Conflicting Condition at Each Time, Time Chart, Average of Activity
EXPANDER SFLEXP	PROCESSING TIME	**108.2 sec** (23 Kgate) (on IBM3081)
	EXPANSION QUALITY (1st optimization phase)	13.8% 68.3% 9.2% Total : 23,119 gates (1st optimization phase) FUNCTIONAL CIRCUIT REGISTER SELECTOR CONTROL CIRCUIT (8.7%)
	CONFIDENCE	Results of behavioral simulation to SFL descriptions coincide with the results of TEGAS simulation for their expansion result.
RESULT of DESIGN	DESIGN EFFORT	SPECIFICATION DESIGN 2.0 BEHAVIORAL DESIGN by SFL (4.0) (1.0) Total : 7.8 Man-month BEHAVIORAL SIMULATION by the SFLSIM LOGICAL SIMULATION of COMBINATORIAL CIRCUITS by TEGAS (0.3) COMBINATORIAL CIRCUITS by COMMERCIAL TOOLS (0.5)
	QUALITY	GATE-NUMBER : **18,213 gates** (3rd optimization phase) MACHINE-CYCLE : **62.5 ns** SPEED : **100~150 KLIPS**

It was confirmed that the final design of this AIM realizes 100–150KLIPS performance for over 10 prolog programs at 62.5ns machine cycle. Its size ended up being 18,213 gates (using NTT 2μm CMOS cells). Automatically synthesized circuits accounted for 18.9% of AIM's gates. Quality, as expressed by the number of gates, of this automatically expanded part was found through sample checking to be 90% of that by human design. Overall, AIM requires only 2% more gates than when all the circuits are designed by hand.

The design output generated by this CAD environment has HSL [17] representation, which is NTT's connective description language. Now, AIM is under layout design process for VLSI.

7. Conclusion

This paper described an RTL description based CAD environment developed for the architecture, function, and logic design of VLSI processors under highly complex, parallel control. The paper also described the evaluation of the CAD system applied to a PROLOG machine design. This CAD system consists of an RTL behavioral description language (SFL), behavior simulator (SFLSIM), hardware expander (SFLEXP) and some evaluation tools.

The SFL describes the design in independent control parts (stages) and contains a "hardware task," which is a newly developed concept to make process synchronizing easier. The PROLOG machine used in the trial was realized by co-operation of 33 stages and was clearly described in 3,867 steps in SFL, which demonstrates that SFL has the ability to describe a considerably complex machine. SFL was very useful not only in design description, but also in design consideration.

SFLSIM is a conversational simulator which directly interprets the design described in SFL. Therefore, since SFLSIM does not require an expansion process, it can start simulation in a very short time. Furthermore, simulation speed is 70 times faster than the well-known TEGAS–5E. SFLSIM also provides some of the information used for debugging and tuning. It was found with the PROLOG machine that 4–way interleaved memory throughput and the parallel activity of 33 processes were very effective in providing accurate tuning.

By restricting synthesis to only control circuits and data paths between registers and functional units, it was possible to develop a practical hardware synthesizer (SFLEXP). Of the total number of gates in the PROLOG machine, only 18.9% were automatically synthesized. However, the design effort for the other circuits required only 12.8% of the person–months expended. This indicates how difficult behavior control design is. However, if this design were done with conventional circuit diagram methods, it would be even more time–consuming and difficult.

The PROLOG machine is a dedicated one–chip processor provided with several mainframe acceleration mechanisms, including advance control, leave–behind control, pipeline control, and interleaved multi–bank storages control. Work involved in this design took only 7.8 person–months using the CAD environment. This effort is one order of magnitude smaller than can be accomplished using conventional CAD tools. This proves that the SFL based CAD system is most effective in the architecture, function, and logic design of various special purpose VLSI processors or ASICs which have highly complex, parallel control structures.

Acknowledgment

The authors would like to thank Dr. I. Toda, Dr. A. Hashimoto, Mr. K. Yoshida and Mr. R. Nomura of NTT Communications and Information Processing Laboratories for their helpful suggestions and supports.

References

[1] M. Breuer, A. Friedman, and A. Iosupovicz, "A survey of the state of the art of design automation," IEEE Computer, Oct.1981, pp. 58–75.

[2] T. Sudo, T. Ohtsuki, and S. Goto, "CAD system for VLSI in Japan," Proc.IEEE, Vol.71, No.1, Jan.1983, pp. 129–143.

[3] W. M. vanCleemput, "A hierarchical language for the structural description of digital system," Proc.14th Design Automation Conf., 1977, pp. 378–385.

[4] M. R. Barbacci, "A comparison of register transfer languages for describing computers and digital systems," IEEE Trans. Computers, Vol.C–24, No.2, Feb.1975, pp. 137–150.

[5] L. Hafer, and A. Parker, "Automated synthesis of digital hardware," IEEE Trans. Computers, Vol.C–31, No.2, Feb.1982, pp. 93–109.

[6] A. Nagle, R. Cloutier, and A. Parker, "Synthesis of hardware for the control of digital systems," IEEE Trans. CAD of IC and Systems, Vol.CAD–1, No.4, Oct.1982.

[7] S. Shiva, "Automatic hardware synthesis," Proc.IEEE, Vol 71, No.1, Feb.1983, pp.76–87.

[8] Y. Nakamura, K. Oguri, H. Nakanishi, and R. Nomura, "An RTL Behavioral Description based Logic Design CAD System with Synthesis Capability," Proc. 7th International Conference on Comprter Hardware Description Languages and their Applications (CHDL 85), 1985, pp. 64–78.

[9] K. Oguri, Y. Nakamura, and R. Nomura, "Evaluation of Behavior Description Based CAD System Used in PROLOG Machine Logic Design," Proc. of the International Conference on Computer–Aided Design (ICCAD–86), 1986, pp.116–119.

[10] Y. Chu, "An ALGOL–like Computer Design Language," Comm. ACM, Vol.8, No.10, 1965, pp. 607–615.

[11] J. R. Duley and D. L. Dietmeyer, "A Digital System Design Language (DDL)," IEEE Trans. Computers, Vol.C–17, No.9, 1968, pp. 850–861.

[12] S. Kato and T. Sasaki, "FDL : A Structural Behavior Description Language," Proc. of the 6th International Conference on Computer Hardware Description Languages and their Applications, 1983, pp. 137–152.

[13] HELIX 1.3: HHDL Reference Manual, SILVAR–LISCO, Palo Alto and Belgium, 1983, 178p.

[14] M. R. Barbacci, "Instruction Set Processor Specifications (ISPS): The Notation and Its Applications, IEEE Trans. Computer, Vol.C–30, No.1, 1981, pp. 24–40.

[15] VHDL Language Reference Manual Version 7.2, IEEE, Aug. 1985.

[16] F.Hattori, N.Shimizu, H.Tsuchiya, K.Kuwahara and T.Wasano, "Knowledge Base Management System (KBMS)," Monograph of Technical Group on Knowledge Engineering and AI of Information Processing Society of Japan, 41–6, 1985.

[17] T. Hoshino, O. Karatsu and T. Nakashima, "HSL–FX: A Unified Language for VLSI Design," Proc. 7th International Conference on Comprter Hardware Description Languages and their Applications (CHDL 85), 1985, pp. 321–336.

VLSI '87, C.H. Séquin (editor)
Elsevier Science Publishers B.V. (North-Holland)
© IFIP, 1988

STRUCTURAL SYNTHESIS IN THE YORKTOWN SILICON COMPILER

Raul Camposano

IBM Thomas J. Watson Research Center
P.O. Box 218
Yorktown Heights, New York 10598

This paper deals with the synthesis of circuit structures from behavioral domain descriptions in the Yorktown Silicon Compiler (YSC). The approach differs in several ways from existing ones. Data path and control synthesis are integrated. Instead sequential and combinational aspects are separated. Combinational parts are designed using powerful logic synthesis tools. The synthesis of the structure is done in several steps. First the operations are assigned to control states so that each specified sequence of operations requires the minimum number of states. This initial design is consequently modified to optimize timing and the circuit area. The model used to represent both behavior and structure is based on directed graphs. The algorithms are formalized as graph transformations.

1. INTRODUCTION

The Yorktown Silicon Compiler (YSC) is being developed at the Thomas J. Watson Research Center in Yorktown Heights [1,2]. The origins of the YSC project date back to activities that started in the early 80's. The overall goal of this project is to study all aspects related to the automatic synthesis of digital systems.

The major goals of the YSC are:

● The **automatic** synthesis of a chip layout from a high-level behavioral description.

● The synthesis of designs that are **competitive** with custom manual designs in performance and silicon area.

● The design of **general** kinds of digital circuits, not constrained to a particular type of application. In particular, any digital circuit that can be described as one or more finite automata can be synthesized by the YSC.

The work described in this paper is the high-end of the YSC, i.e. the synthesis of circuit structures from behavioral descriptions. This activity started in 1986 using the already already existing compiler, which provided an excellent design environment including logic synthesis, layout design, optimization paths and verification techniques. The compile times are small enough to allow an intensive experimentation with different chips and the evaluation in real time.

Figure 1 shows the basic synthesis steps in the YSC. Starting from a behavioral specification of the circuit to design a structure is synthesized. This structure consists of registers, memories, combinational logic and their interconnection. Structural synthesis is discussed in this paper. The generated combinational logic is described separately and passed to logic synthesis [3,4]. Once the logic is minimized, the structure and the now minimized logic are passed to layout design [5] to generate the final chip image.

2. STRUCTURAL SYNTHESIS

Structural synthesis, often called "behavioral synthesis", is the synthesis of circuit structures from behavioral domain descriptions. Although structural synthesis is not yet a well understood problem, many efforts to develop design systems including structural synthesis have been and are being undertaken in academia and industry. Among others, DSL [6], MIMOLA [7], various approaches at Carnegie Mellon University [8,9,10], ADAM [11] and DAA [12], can be mentioned. Overviews can be found in [13,14].

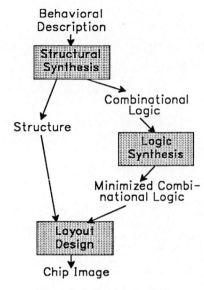

Figure 1. Synthesis in the YSC

In order to simplify structural synthesis and to be able to formalize the problems, we made several restrictions:

- Only synchronous systems described by finite automata are considered. This does not mean that the initial behavioral description is an automaton, but that the result of structural synthesis is one or more finite automata.

- Complex systems can be decomposed into several subsystems, each of them described by a finite automaton. A hierarchical behavioral description consisting of "modules" will lead to one finite automaton for each module. The communication among this automata is according to a fixed scheme. This paper does not deal with this mechanism, it is restricted to the synthesis of one finite automata.

- The behavioral specification we start with is given in an intermediate format rather than in a language. This format has an imperative semantics, i.e. it consists of partially ordered operations and variables. Imperative languages can be easily mapped onto this format by a compiler. All the comfort of a modern programming language and the syntactic sugar are left to the compiler. The language to describe the behavior we are using is V[15]. A compiler written by the developers of V produces YIF (Yorktown Intermediate Format, described in the next section).

The philosophy used to synthesize the structures differs from existing synthesis systems basically in two aspects. First, rather than separating the synthesis of control and the data path, both are synthesized together. What is separated instead are the sequential and the combinational aspects. Sequential aspects are taken care off at the beginning, determining the control states and the necessary registers. The combinational parts are then synthesized using extensively the powerful logic synthesis tools available in the YSC. Since the combinational logic usually takes only a small part of the total chip area, not too much effort should be spent at a high level to minimize this part of the design.

The second difference is that structural synthesis is restricted initially by a high level architectural decision: to minimize the number of control states needed for executing all operation sequences. The trade off, between the number of control states needed to perform a sequence of operations and the time period required to execute the operations within each control state (the cycle time), is always decided initially in favor of the minimum number of control states. Thus the number of clock cycles to complete all these operation sequences is minimized. This also leads to a small number of latches required for storing data used in different states. If static latches with scan path capabilities are used, latches are expensive compared to combinational logic.

Using these principles, the goal of structural synthesis is clearly defined. Initially, unknown parameters such as absolute speed or area, often estimated very poorly in structural synthesis systems, are not taken into account. The design obtained initially can be modified in subsequent steps using basically one transformation: control state splitting, i.e. assigning part of the operations to be executed during one control state to one or more new control states. Since each control state contains as many operations as possible in the initial design, control states can only be split, never merged.

In the rest of this section we will briefly introduce the format used to describe the behavior and show how a structure is synthesized from this description.

2.1. The Yorktown Intermediate Format (YIF)

YIF is the format used in the YSC to specify the behavior of a digital system at the algorithmic level. The main goal in designing YIF was to allow an easy compilation of programming languages with an imperative semantic into YIF while capturing all the information necessary to start a design. Related work can be found in [16,17].

YIF allows the definition of variables, operations and constraints. The basic control flow elements are sequence, conditional branching and iteration. The operators can be chosen according to the application and must be described at the logic level in an operator library. Also a mechanism for hierarchical and modular design is provided. Here only the subset of YIF relevant to this paper is described.

A YIF description $Y = (V, S, R_s, R_i, R_o)$ consists of

- A set of operations V. Operations represent atomic computations, e.g. **and, addition, shift-left**, etc. One element $v_f \in V$ called the first operation must be given.

- A set of variables S. They are equivalent to variables in a program. A variable s in YIF has a type$(s) \in$ {array, external, internal, register} . The type indicates whether a variable is an array, whether it represents a port to the outside (external), whether it is an internal variable or an architected register. During synthesis, the internal variables might be converted automatically into registers. Thus, the initially specified architected registers are a subset of the registers of the final design. (An initial specification might contain no architected registers at all).

- A precedence relation $R_s \subseteq V \times V$. It defines the control flow for the operations:

$$(v_1, v_2) \in R_s \text{ iff } v_1 \text{ before } v_2$$

"before" here means "immediate predecessor", as implied by an imperative semantics. The relation R_s is irreflexive.

- An input relation $R_i \subseteq S \times V$, indicating the variables used as inputs (are read) by each operation.

- An output relation $R_o \subseteq V \times S$, indicating the variables used as outputs (are written) by each operation.

The pair (V, R_s) can be seen as a digraph, the so called **precedence** graph. Node v_1 is said to be the (immediate) **predecessor** of node v_2 and, vice versa, v_2 is called the (immediate) **successor** of v_1. **Conditional branches**, i.e. the selection of one among many possible successor operations, are represented by a node with more than one successor, leading to a fork. **Iterations or loops** are represented by circuits in the graph. The operational semantics of YIF is defined as follows:

Operations are executed one at a time, starting with the first operation v_f. The next operation is a successor of the executed operation. If there is more than one successor, exactly one of them is chosen depending on the value in one of the variables. An operation v writes a new value to all variables s_o for which $(v, s_o) \in R_o$. It uses the values in the variables s_i such that $(s_i, v) \in R_i$. A variable retains its value until it is overwritten.

YIF also allows the specification of constraints such as the number of cycles one or more operations should take, and the specification of parallelism at the operation level. This features are not relevant for this paper.

2.2. Memory and port assignment

Variables in YIF in general will be mapped onto storage elements like registers or memories, onto nets (wires) or onto ports (pins). The type of a variable indicates how to implement it.

- Variables of type external are ports (pins) to the outside of the specified system. The ports specified in YIF are kept during the whole design.

- Variables of type internal will be implemented as registers only if necessary, otherwise as nets (wires). The system decides during synthesis how they are implemented.

- Variables initially of type register are the so called **architected registers**, i.e. registers already specified as those in the initial specification. A variable of type register is always implemented by a register.

- Variables of type array will be implemented by memories, registers or wires. The designer can either force them to be implemented by memories or let the decision of how to implement them to the system. In the latter case they are implemented according to the way they are referenced. Memories are modeled as registers, also multi port memories. The decision of which reference to a variable is assigned to which port of a multi-port memory is taken during synthesis.

Notice that architected registers need not to be specified, initially all variables can be of type internal. Synthesis determines which variables have to be registers and which can be nets.

2.3. Initial control state and register assignment

In this step an initial structure is obtained. This first design includes control and data path, all necessary registers (the memories were already assigned previously) and nets, and the combinational parts. Furthermore, this design minimizes the number of control steps for each possible sequence of operations in the behavioral specification.

The basic procedure for obtaining a structure from the behavior relies on the following ideas. Assume initially the design is supposed to contain just combinational logic. If this turns out to be correct, the circuit can be obtained just using logic synthesis. The same is true if there are registers present (and identified) but no sequential control is necessary. If more than one control state is necessary then it has to be decided, what operations have to be executed in what state (control state assignment). This is done by subsequently **splitting** an initial state that holds all operations. The operations are distributed among two new states. In each state splitting it is made sure, that as many operations as possible are scheduled in each of the new states. This assures that never two states will have to be merged again, as far as the number of states for performing the operation sequences is concerned. Operations can be assigned to more than one state. Each time a new state is introduced new registers might be necessary.

Given a YIF description $Y = (V, S, R_s, R_i, R_o, C_j)$ and the **type** of each variable type(s) $\in$ {external, internal, register} , the control state and register assignment algorithm constructs a set of states Z assigning to each state $z_i \in Z$ a set of operations ops(z_i) $\subseteq V$ to be executed during that state and determines which variables need to be implemented by registers. All operations scheduled to one control state are implemented by combinational logic and thus executed "in parallel". Operations scheduled into different control states are executed in sequence, thus they are alternative in time. Each operation is assumed to be implemented by a dedicated piece of hardware ("operator") in this step.

The algorithm works as follows:

1. **Control states due to loops.** For each loop (iteration, circuit in a graph) at least one control state must be introduced to allow the repetition of the operations in it. Loops are eliminated and the iteration is encoded into the control by providing appropriate state transitions. The algorithm proceeds as follows. It first finds the feedback edges $L \text{inc} R_s$ such that, in forming the transitive closure, A, of $(R_s - L)$ a partial order relation results. In our present approach, L is derived syntactically from operation tags. These tags are generated during compilation by considering the syntax of the iteration constructs of the high level language, e.g. WHILE and UNTIL iterations.

The operations of the resulting acyclic graph $(V, R_s - L)$ are now assigned to states. Let

$$V_L = \{v_f\} \cup \{v \in V \mid existl_{v'} [(v', v) \in L]\}$$

V_L contains all those operations that must form the starting point of a state. A state starting point is the first operation scheduled in that state, according to A. Operation v_f (the first operation of the whole YIF) clearly is such an operation. The other operations in V_L are the first operations in each loop; since loops according to the semantics of YIF must eventually be repeated, also these operations must be the starting point of a state.

A first automaton is built with as many states Z as $|V_L|$. The operations executed in each control state $z_i \in Z$ are

$$\text{ops}(z_i) = \{v_i \in V_L\} \cup \{v \in V \,|\, (v_i, v) \in A\}$$

Since our goal is to minimize the number of required states to execute all operation sequences, **all successors** in A of the first operations V_L are initially included in each state. Particularly, all successors from v_f, i.e. all operations, are scheduled in one state. Notice that one operation may be scheduled in many states.

2. **Control states due to module calls.** An operation can be either an atomic computation such as an addition or a reference to another YIF description. The latter is called a **module call**. If the called YIF description generates a combinational circuit, it can be treated as an atomic computation. If the resulting circuit is sequential, then it can not be treated as an atomic computation any more and an additional control state in the calling module must be introduced, splitting the original state. In the most general case, the number of control states (cycles) that a module call will need is unknown. For each of these module calls we introduce a new "waiting" control state. This module call waiting state does not perform any operation besides enabling the called module, until a **ready signal** is generated by the called module. Ready signals can be generated automatically by identifying control states that contain final operations in a module.

3. **Control states due to constraints.** Explicit timing constraints given in YIF, e.g. specifying that an operation should be performed in one cycle, might produce new control states. These new control states are added as specified.

4. **Control states due to data flow restrictions.** The first three steps yield a state assignment which is the starting point for data flow analysis. Data flow analysis detects

- which variables of type internal have to be converted into registers and
- which new control states are necessary due to data flow restrictions.

Data flow restrictions arise from the fact that during one cycle, a register can be written only once and, similarly, external variables (pins) may also hold only one value. A variable must be implemented by a register, if its value used (read) in a different state than it is generated (written). Since new registers might introduce new data flow restrictions, and new control states due to data flow restrictions might introduce new registers, an iterative algorithm of two steps is necessary:

a. Internal variables that are used as inputs (read) without having been used as outputs (written) before in the same state must hold a value that was written in another state. They must be converted into registers. These variables are defined by

$$S_{ir} = \{s \in S \,|\, \text{type}(s) = \text{internal} \,\wedge$$
$$exist l_{z \in Z,\, v \in V}[\, v \in \text{ops}(z) \wedge (s, v) \in R_i \wedge \forall_{v' \in \text{ops}(z)} [(v, v') \in A \vee (v', s) \notin R_o]\,]\,\}$$

They are used as inputs by the operation v in state z without being used as output by any operation v' before v in that state. Thus, the value of these variables must have been written in another state. To keep a value from one control state to another in hardware a storage element is necessary. Hence, the type of all variables $s \in S_{ir}$ is changed to $\text{type}(s) = \text{register}$. Unless architected, registers are only introduced where it is necessary.

b. Variables with $\text{type}(s) \in \{\text{register, external}\}$ create **data flow restrictions** if they are used as inputs and/or output more than a given number of times within one control state (cycle). A register can be written only once in a cycle, a one port memory can only be read or written once in a cycle, an external port might have only one value associated with it in each cycle. Control states in which this limitation is violated must be split into two or more states. For data flow constraints due to multiple use of a variable as output, these control states are obtained as follows. Given a state $z \in Z$ then if for some variable $s \in S$ with $\text{type}(s) \in \{\text{register, external}\}$ the set of operations that use this variable as an output

$$V_{zs} = \{v \in \text{ops}(z) \,|\, (v, s) \in R_o\}$$

has a subset $V_c \subseteq V_{zs}$ such that

$$\forall_{v_1 \neq v_2 \in V_c} [(v_1, v_2) \in A \vee (v_2, v_1) \in A] \wedge |V_c| > c_s$$

then z must be split. c_s is the maximum number of times the variable s can be written (used as output) in one state (during one cycle). By making $c_s > 1$ for memories, multiple port memories can be handled. The control state z must be split between both references (in this case output references) to the variable s. Input or mixed (input and output) data flow restrictions are treated in an analogous way.

Steps a. and b. are iterated until no changes occur.

After control state assignment the sequential control is explicit. A register holding the control state is introduced, and the state transitions are given by operations that load new values into this register. State assignment (i.e. encoding the states) may be done here if desired. The design at this stage is a finite state machine. All paths from a unique first operation to one last operation are performed in one cycle. This first design has the "extreme architecture" that minimizes the number of control states required for all operation sequences. The design is still represented in YIF. It is now an acyclic graph including the assignment and decoding of a new register holding the state.

Since the registers in the data path were also determined during control state assignment, also the data path is designed to some extent. Hence, control and data parts are synthesized together in a single step. The result is again represented in YIF.

In an imperative description, variables hold their values until they are overwritten, and therefore can be used many times. To generate a structure, each different use of a variable must be mapped in principle onto a different net or register. We call this **variable unfolding**. Variable unfolding introduces additional variables so that single assignment results, and changes the references accordingly. Variable unfolding occurs both for registers (and memories) and for internal variables implemented by nets.

Registers already meet the single assignment criterion due to the data flow restrictions imposed earlier. Nevertheless it must be identified, if an input or an output is being referenced: outputs are only loaded at the end of a cycle and are available only during at the next cycle. The unfolding consists of introducing new variables for the inputs whenever this is necessary. An example of register unfolding is given in figure 2. The operations listed are specified in that sequence and were all scheduled in the same state.

```
        REGISTER X
        INTERNAL A,B,C
                 . . .
                 A←X                                    . . .
1 cycle          X←B            becomes      A          ←X.output
                 C←X                          X.input←B
                 . . .                        C          ←X.input
                                                         . . .
```

Figure 2. Register unfolding of X

Internal variables which will be implemented by nets do not necessarily meet single assignment. For sequential assignment to these variables, new variables must be introduced. In doing this the necessity of introducing additional multiplexers might arise, as shown in figure 3.

```
        INTERNAL X,A,B,C,D
                 . . .
                 X←A                                . . .
                 IF C                               X←A
1 cycle            THEN B←X     becomes             IF C
                   ELSE X←B                           THEN B ←X
                 D←X                                  ELSE X'←B
                 . . .                              D←mux_C(X,X')
                                                    . . .
```

Figure 3. Internal variable unfolding of X

2.4. High level optimizations: control state splitting and folding

The basic structure synthesized so far was obtained without taking into account speed or size of circuits. Thus the architecture of the synthesized structure is still technology independent. This is very important since speed and size can only be *estimated* at this level.

To meet quality criteria optimizations have to introduced at this point (e.g. [18]). There are not any more technology independent and rely on estimations of speed and size of the real hardware. These optimizations are **control state splitting** and **folding**.

Splitting a control state means assigning part of its operations to one or more new control states. This is done for two reasons: First , if sequential operations within one control state are distributed among two or more states, the necessary time to execute all operations within one control state may be shortened (at the cost of a new control state). Second, if two operations that were executed in parallel within one control state are distributed among two control states, they are sequenced and may share hardware, thus trading increased execution time for less area.

To identify the states to be split, a goal has to be defined, e.g. a given maximal cycle time (specified as a timing constraint). State splitting already requires an estimation of the delays and areas not yet known at this stage. Successful state splitting can only be achieved with good relative estimates. In the YSC, area, power and delay are estimated using functions of arbitrary complexity stored in the module library, or by exercising logic synthesis using only fast algorithms.

Although we relieved structural synthesis from performing so called "high level optimizations" of combinational parts that can be done during logic synthesis, not all optimizations can be done by logic synthesis. Some optimizations arise from the sequential nature of the circuits. As an example, consider the circuits in figure 4.

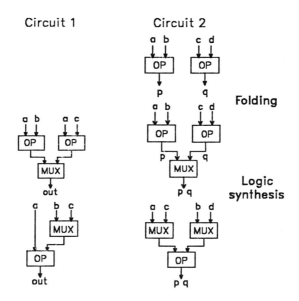

Figure 4. **Two examples of optimizations of combinational circuits**

The optimization of circuit 1 can be performed by logic synthesis; it will yield an optimal circuit (optimal according to the goals defined in logic synthesis) for any width of the operators, for some of the operators being constants, etc. The optimization in circuit 2 can not be performed by logic synthesis, because the operands are different for both operators. In fact the operations can only be implemented by one operator as indicated if they always occur in different control states, i.e. they are alternative in time. This optimization is done by structural synthesis in the YSC and is called **operation folding**.

Two operations v and v' can be folded, if

$$(v, v') \notin A \ \wedge \ (v', v) \notin A$$

i.e. they are alternative. Folding more than two operations corresponds to constructing the cliques of the complement of the symmetric closure of A.

A folding should result in some advantage. Our criteria are:

● The folding should result in an area gain. Areas are estimated considering the additional multiplexers required.

● The operations should be similar so that they can be folded. Similarity in the simplest sense means requiring the same function (e.g. an addition), only allowing different input and output widths. More refined similarity criteria can be table driven. The number of different operations is limited to the order of 10^2, so this approach is practicable. The circuit itself will be obtained by logic synthesis, so in principle any operations could be folded by multiplexing their output as shown in figure 4.

Also registers can be folded. They are generated according to the initial specification and during control state assignment and splitting. Besides the architected registers, registers were introduced if the value of a variable must be passed between two or more states. Clearly some of these variables might be "alternative", i.e. there is no situation in which they are both "alive". These variables can be mapped onto a single register. To detect which registers can be folded, techniques similar to "life-time" analysis in compiler construction are used. Folding of internal variables implemented by nets is basically the same problem generating buses instead of registers.

2.5. Control and network generation

At this point, the design is considered ready with respect to its sequential aspects. The YIF data format now satisfies the following properties:

● The predecessor-successor graph, which orders the operations (nodes in the YIF graph) is acyclic.

● The data flow graph defined by R_i and R_o, giving the connection between variables and operations, is also acyclic if the input and output sides of registers are considered separate.

● Indices selecting parts (bits) of variables are constants. Variable indices have been replaced by operations or memory calls.

● All operations can be implemented by combinational logic. If there were an operation requiring a sequential implementation it is a module call to another circuit also represented in YIF.

The goal at this stage is to produce

● the description of a network connecting module inputs, module outputs, registers, blocks of combinational logic, and calls to other modules and

● the logic specification of the combinational blocks.

For each operation specified in the YIF graph, a combinational function ("operator") must be chosen. A library of operators is supplied. Each operator is described by its **logic specification** and connection and control information. Also expressions to predict roughly the area, delay and power requirements are provided in the library for every feasible operation/operator combination. The expressions yield these estimates as a function of the width and the number of operands, and are used to make a default selection when several choices are feasible. By default one combinational function is instanciated for each operation, unless folding mapped more than one operation onto a single operator.

Remember that all combinational parts still have to be minimized during logic synthesis, so that for example the implementation of an increment by an ADD unit is *not* a waste of area or power. The library fixes only the logic behavior of the ADD unit. The actual hardware (gates) is only generated by logic synthesis reducing ADD with a constant input to a "real" incrementer. Thus, only a small amount of operators is necessary in the library.

Other tasks performed when mapping operations to operators are the adjustment of the widths of variables and constants, possibly (sign-) extending or truncating them. Multiplexers are inserted to write to nets which are the output of more than one operator, and to write to the inputs of operators whith more than one operation assigned to them due to folding. The multiplexers are stored in the YIF description in the same way as any other operator, and fetched from the same library.

Control signals are needed for the enable inputs of the registers, for the select input of multiplexers, and for the synchronization and communication with the "outside world" and other modules. A more complex control, e.g. for an ALU, is automatically generated: the control input of the ALU was assigned a constant for every operation that was folded on it. By multiplexing these constants, and the subsequent logic synthesis of this multiplexer with constant (data-) inputs, the proper control logic is obtained.

The control signals are generated inside each module as follows. Each node gets a control signal enabling it. The starting node gets a control signal from the outside or a constant "1" if no external enable is required. Control signals are propagated to the successors. At each fork, new control signals are created for the outgoing paths, "and-ing" the branch decision and the control signal of the fork node. At the joining of paths, the new control signal is created by "or-ing" the control signals corresponding to the incoming paths. The control signals created this way, are directly attached to the multiplexer inputs. The register enables might need a final "or-ing" of these signals if they are written by more than one operator. The different logic functions required for the creation of the control signals are obtained from the same library as the data path operations.

Basically, the above scheme generates a so called "one hot encoding". For example, the node which implements the branch on the value of the state register will produce one enable signal for every (used) state register value. However if the logic blocks which generate or use these enable signals, are passed as one unit to the logic synthesis, these enable signals remain internal to this unit, and might be removed while minimizing the logic. Thus the large number of enable signals are just part of the logic specification, and may not be present in the final realization.

As a last step combinational operators are grouped into larger units called groups that will be passed to logic synthesis. For the best minimization all the operators should be grouped into just one large group. However time and space complexity of logic synthesis limits the size. Also for layout design several smaller groups allow more flexibility. The grouping of operators is based on their connectivity having the maximum size of each group as a constraint. Again control and data path are not separated.

The resulting network is written in HND (Hierarchical Network Definition), a language suitable for machine and human reading. The logic specification of each group of logic functions, is written in YLL (Yorktown Logic Language) [19]. Also the logic specification in the library is written in YLL.

After all different modules of the chip hierarchy are generated they are linked to construct the hierarchy. The consistency of the interfaces is checked and the hierarchy is expanded, generating one output module for each different instanciation. The network information is written in a compact binary form, suitable for interfacing with the layout compilation step.

3. SOME EXAMPLES

We have done many designs using structural synthesis in the YSC, the largest one being the processor unit of an 801 processor [20,21]. Here we will report the results of two smaller examples to illustrate the concepts presented above and to give an idea of the performance of the system. To make the examples more clear, we will also give the results of logic synthesis, i.e. transistor count for combinational logic and the estimated delay using a 1 μ SCVS (Single Cascode Voltage Switch) technology.

The first example is the often used "Greatest Common Divisor" (GCD) algorithm. The self explaining V program is showed in figure 5. Besides the two 16 bit inputs to hold two non negative integers, also has a synchronous reset input *RST*. To know when the result is computed, a *READY* pin can be added automatically by the system.

The second example given in figure 6 is the also often used "Traffic Light Controller" (TLC). This version has a 4 bit counter to generate the "red" and "green" periods of the highway and the sideroad. "Yellow" is assumed to have the length of just one cycle.

The examples were synthesized on a IBM 3090 on a virtual machine of 2MB of memory (possibly less would have been enough). The results are given in figure 7. While GCD has a simpler sequential structure reflected in only 3 control states and a faster structural synthesis, its combinational part is more complicated than TLC's, mainly due to the 16 bit wide data path. TLC has only a 4 bit wide data path (the counter). In both examples the number of registers and the number of control cycles is minimal for the synthesis assumptions. The combinational part is probably smaller than a hand design due to the global logic minimization (no partition was required).

4. CONCLUSIONS AND OUTLOOK

Structural synthesis and the subsequent logic synthesis allow to generate automatically circuits without the intervention of a human designer. The practical limits of structural synthesis in our present system

```
MODULE GCD (XI:IN,YI:IN,RST:IN,OU:OUT);

EXTERNAL GCD;
 DCL XI   BIT(16),
     YI   BIT(16),
     RST  BIT(1),     /* Reset */
     OU   BIT(16);
INTERNAL GCD;
 DCL X    BIT(16),
     Y    BIT(16);

BODY GCD;
 DO INFINITE LOOP
  DO WHILE RST LOOP /* Wait */ ENDDO;
  X:=XI; Y:=YI;
  DO WHILE ¬(X=Y)
   LOOP
    IF X<Y THEN Y:=Y-X; ELSE X:=X-Y; ENDIF;
   ENDDO;
   OU:=X;
 ENDDO;
END GCD;
```

Figure 5. V program for the Greatest Common Divisor GCD

```
MODULE TLC (HIGHWAY:IN,SIDEROAD:IN,COLOR:OUT);

EXTERNAL TLC;
 DCL HIGHWAY  BIT(1),   /* Car on highway    */
     SIDEROAD BIT(1),   /* Car on sideroad   */
     COLOR    BIT(2),   /* Light on highway  */
     REDYEL   BINARY CONSTANT INIT(3),
     GREEN    BINARY CONSTANT INIT(2),
     RED      BINARY CONSTANT INIT(1),
     YELLOW   BINARY CONSTANT INIT(0);

BODY TLC;

 MODULE TIMER (LENGTH:IN);
 EXTERNAL TIMER;
  DCL LENGTH BIT(2);
 INTERNAL TIMER;
  DCL I      BIT(4);

 BODY TIMER;
  IF LENGTH=GREEN  THEN I:=15;ENDIF;
  IF LENGTH=RED    THEN I:=7 ;ENDIF;
  IF LENGTH=YELLOW THEN I:=1 ;ENDIF;
  DO UNTIL I=0 LOOP I:=I-1; ENDDO;
 END TIMER;

 DO INFINITE LOOP
  COLOR := GREEN;
  TIMER (GREEN);
  DO UNTIL SIDEROAD LOOP ENDDO;
  COLOR := YELLOW;
  TIMER (YELLOW);
  COLOR := RED;
  TIMER (RED);
  DO UNTIL HIGHWAY  LOOP ENDDO;
  COLOR := REDYEL;
  TIMER (YELLOW);
 ENDDO;

END TLC;
```

Figure 6. V program for a Traffic Light Controller TLC

are roughly 1000 operations for a 32 bit data path for the order of 1 CPU hour on an IBM 3090. Small designs like the examples shown take just a few CPU seconds. The results are comparable to hand design.

Design	GCD	TLC	
V lines	22	26	
V statements	16	27	
V compilation (CPU sec)	.87	1.2	
	GCD	TLC	TIMER
YIF lines before str. synthesis	94	84	118
YIF nodes before str. synthesis	13	12	17
Structural synthesis (CPU sec)	3.6	3.2	4.5
YIF nodes after synthesis	18	20	21
Control states	2	7	2
Total number of bits	113	4	14
Register bits	33	3	5
Combinational logic inputs	66	6	8
Combinational logic outputs	36	9	8
Logic synthesis (CPU sec)	1977	11	21
Levels	23	3	2
SCVS Trees	127	11	9
Transistors	965	69	66
Delay (ns)	51	3.3	3.0

Figure 7. Structural synthesis and logic synthesis results for two examples

The combinational logic can be grouped for logic synthesis, so that there should be no practical limit here. The quality of the design might decrease depending on how the logic is grouped because each group is optimized independently.

The above limits are for just **one** module, i.e. structuring a design "by hand" partitioning it already at the beginning into several modules (corresponding to one software routine in the behavioral description) is always possible and necessary. The structure given by the module partition is maintained throughout structural synthesis.

Although we can synthesize one finite automaton for each module and then connect them according to the specified hierarchy, more complex transformations like a general way of obtaining automatically a pipeline *with* all the appropriate control for interrupts, jumps, etc., are not possible. We indeed designed "by hand" in our system, describing the behavior of each stage and of the control explicitly.

Further work includes faster algorithms, the validation of large examples and higher level transformations like the synthesis of pipelines. The YSC provides an excellent framework for these applications.

REFERENCES

[1]   R.K. Brayton, N.L. Brenner, C.L. Chen, G. DeMicheli, C.T. McMullen and R.H.J.M. Otten, The YORKTOWN Silicon Compiler, ISCAS'85, June 1985

[2]   R.K. Brayton, R, Camposano, G. DeMicheli, R.H.J.M. Otten and J. van Eijndhoven The
       Yorktown Silicon Compiler System, to appear.

[3]   R.K. Brayton, C.T. McMullen, Synthesis and Optimization of Multistage Logic, ICCD'84, Port
       Chester, October 1984

[4]   R.K. Brayton, Algorithms for Multi-Level Synthesis and Optimization, Proceedings NATO ASI,
       L'Aquila, Italy, Martinus Nijhoff, 1986

[5]   R.H.J.M. Otten, Layout Compilation, Proceedings NATO ASI, L'Aquila, Italy, Martinus Ni-
       jhoff, 1986

[6]   R. Camposano, W. Rosenstiel, A Design Environment for the Synthesis of Integrated Circuits,
       Proc. 11th Symposium on Microprocessing and Microprogramming EUROMICRO'85, Brussels,
       1985

[7]   P. Marwedel, The MIMOLA Design System: Tools for the Design of Digital Processors, Proc.
       of the 21st Design Automation Conf., Albuquerque, New Mexico, June 1984

[8]   S.W. Director, A.C. Parker, D.P. Siewiorek, D.E. Thomas, A Design Methodology and Com-
       puter Aids for Digital VLSI Systems, IEEE Transactions on Circuits and Systems, Volume
       CAS-28, Number 7, July 1981

[9]   D.E. Thomas, C.Y. Hitchcock, T.J. Kowalski, J.V. Rajan and R. Walker, Automatic Data Path
       Synthesis, IEEE Computer, December 1983

[10]   C-J. Tseng, D.P. Siewiorek, Automated Synthesis of Data Paths in Digital Systems, IEEE
       Transactions on CAD, Vol. CAD-5, No.3, July 1986

[11]   J. Granacki, D.W. Knapp and A.C. Parker, The ADAM Advanced Design AutoMation System:
       Overview, Planner and Natural Language Interface, Proc. 22nd design Automation Conference,
       June 1985

[12]   T.J. Kowalski, D.J. Geiger, W.H. Wolf, W. Fichtner, The VLSI Design Automation Assistant:
       From Algorithms to Silicon, Design and Test of Computers 2(4), August 1985

[13]   R. Camposano, Synthesis Techniques for Digital Systems Design, Proc. 22nd design Automation
       Conference, June 1985

[14]   D.E. Thomas, Automatic Data Path Synthesis, in Advances in CAD for VLSI, Vol. 6, Design
       Methodologies, Edited by S. Goto, North Holland, 1986

[15]   V. Berstis, D. Brand, R. Nair, An Experiment in Silicon Compilation, Proc. of the ISCAS 85,
       IEEE, 1985

[16]   M. McFarland, The VT: A Database for Automated Digital Design, Technical Report, Carne-
       gie-Mellon University, 1978

[17]   R. Camposano, R. Weber, Semantik und interne Form von DSL, Interner Bericht Nr. 3.85, Fa-
       kultaet fuer Informatik, Universitaet Karlsruhe, 1985

[18]   W. Rosenstiel, Optimizations in High Level Synthesis, Microprocessing and Microprogramming
       (18), North Holland, 1986, pp.543-549

[19]   N.L. Brenner, The Yorktown Logic Language: an APL-like Design Language for VLSI Spec-
       ification, ICCD'84, Port Chester, October 1984

[20]   G. Radin, The 801 minicomputer, IBM Journal of Research and Development, Vol.27, Nr.3,
       May 1983, pp.237-246

[21]   R.K. Brayton, C.L. Chen, G. De Micheli, J. Katzenelson, C.T. McMullen, R.H.J.M. Otten and
       R.L. Rudell, A Microprocessor Design Using the Yorktown Silicon Compiler, Proc. ICCD'85,
       Port Chester, October 1985

VLSI '87, C.H. Séquin (editor)
Elsevier Science Publishers B.V. (North-Holland)
© IFIP, 1988

A Knowledge-Based CAD System for Synthesis of Multi-Processor
Digital Signal Processing Chips.

Jan Vanhoof, Jan Rabaey, Hugo De Man° (*)

IMEC v.z.w.
Interuniversity Micro Electronics Center
Kapeldreef 75
B-3030 Heverlee, Belgium
Phone : 16/281 211

Jack The Mapper, an expert tool for the synthesis of complex digital
signal processing (DSP) ASICs is presented. This CAD program is part
of Cathedral II, an integrated tool-box for the synthesis and
analysis of DSP chips. Jack The Mapper allows the system designer to
investigate and compare in an interactive way a number of silicon
implementations of a DSP algorithm.   The input is an applicative
behavioural   description   of a DSP algorithm, the output is a
customized data path and a controller specification in a register
transfer language.   Both the expert knowledge and the specifications
for the library modules have been acquired from manual top-down
designs of a number of industrial test-vehicles. The Cathedral-II
system is currently being used for the design of a number of complex
DSP systems.

1. INTRODUCTION.

The idea of silicon compilation was born from the observation that the ability
to produce complex application specific VLSI systems on a single chip will
soon be outrunning the ability to design them. In our opinion, a true silicon
compiler is a computer-aid which allows to produce a layout starting from a
behavioural description of a system. A first step towards a realization of
such a compiler is the choice of a suited design methodology. We have
selected the so called 'Meet-In-The-Middle' strategy [DeM85] (Fig.1) which
proposes a strict separation between silicon design and system design at the
level of LSI-modules, in an attempt to overcome the shortage of skilled
silicon designers.   In this way, a large number of system designers can use
their skills and experience to design complex VLSI systems without being
silicon experts.

Cathedral-II [DeM86] is a design environment which supports this
'Meet-In-The-Middle' design methodology. Its aim is to provide an interactive
aid in the synthesis process of ASICs which realize complex algorithms in the
intermediate frequency range belonging to the audio, speech and telecom
domain.   More specific, third generation DSP algorithms involving large blocks
of sampled data, subject to complex decision making algorithms are envisioned.
Some low-frequency back-end video applications are also within range.

A 'Meet-In-The-Middle' based synthesis system is naturally composed of three
basic environments (Fig.1).

(*)   Work sponsored by the EC under ESPRIT 97 contract.
 °   Professor K.U. Leuven.

- an LSI-module generation environment [Six86a][Six86b], which allows for the definition, characterization, verification and generation of the library modules in function of a set of parameters. The library consists of controller modules, data path structures, IO modules and regular arrays such as RAMs and ROMs.

- a synthesis environment for helping the system designer to translate a behavioural specification into an appropriate architecture. This step includes multiple tasks such as data path synthesis, controller scheduling, minimization of the interconnection cost and register minimization.

- a floorplanning environment to combine the selected modules and to verify the overall system performance.

This paper discusses the synthesis environment of the Cathedral-II system, and more particularly the expert synthesis tool called "Jack The Mapper". In section 2 the design methodology it supports is compared to that of other existing silicon compilers. Implementation details are given in section 3. Knowledge acquisition is an extremely important aspect of expert systems. Basic ideas are presented in section 4. Ideas on future work and conclusions can be found in section 5 and 6.

2. JACK THE MAPPER : THE SYNTHESIS METHODOLOGY.

In this paper we will concentrate on the following architectural synthesis problem :

> **Given a behavioural description of a synchronous DSP algorithm, generate both an area-efficient datapath specification and a controller specification within the timing constraints, only using modules which can be supplied by the available module generators.**

Before going into implementation details, some major aspects of the underlying synthesis methodology of Jack The Mapper will be explained. Jack differs from other systems in at least the following aspects :

2.1. Input language.

Some silicon compilers use a procedural (PASCAL or C like) input description [Mar86][Tri87]. In this case it is the task of the synthesis tool to find the maximum concurrency (if it is not indicated in the description by some kind of BEGINPAR ... ENDPAR construct). The control flow is indicated in the source code. If a fixed (customizable) microprocessor architecture is used, the top half of the compiler can basically use the same techniques as a traditional software compiler.

Other compilers use an input description on the register transfer level. In that case the control flow implementation is not indicated, but the maximum concurrency is fully specified. Since compilers usually try to maximize throughput, one can exploit this concurrency by mapping the flow graph on a data path on a one-to-one basis, at the cost of silicon area. More intelligent compilers try to multiplex as much hardware as possible by using a data path folding technique [Hit83]. However when a register transfer level input is used, the implementation efficiency depends heavily on the way the behaviour is described, because the lack of a translation step from high-level code into register transfers.

The input language of Jack consists of the following two seperated parts.

For describing the behaviour of the algorithm, the applicative language SILAGE [Hil85] is used (Fig.2). The main idea of SILAGE is to capture the signal flow graph of a signal processing algorithm (Fig.3). A SILAGE description contains no structural information and does not enforce any degree of concurrency. It does not contain information about the implementation of the control flow. This gives the compiler the full flexibility to select between the fastest and the cheapest implementation starting from the same behavioural input description. We consider this to be of prime importance, because of the excessive CPU-times needed to simulate the behaviour of complex DSP algorithms. In SILAGE, signals are represented by variables, which can be thought of as infinite arrays in time. The implicit time index is never written. The values of a variable at any moment in the past can be recovered by using a delay operator "@". So instead of writing a[t] and a[t-2] one writes a and a@2.

Relations between variables are expressed by explicit, time-discrete equations. The ordering of these equations is irrelevant. Each equation has to be considered true at any moment in time. Equations can be conditional. Loops can be used as a compact notational format (repetition) but they do not imply any control flow. Between the equations inside a loop, there might be precedence or not. A loop

> (i : 1 .. N) ::
> begin
> ....
> end;

is equivalent to the quantifier ∀ 1≤i≤n. Operations on variables are represented by function calls. A large number of functions suited for describing typical DSP operations is predefined. Word-lenghts of signals and finite word-length characteristics of operators can be fully specified (at this moment for fixed point operations only). Typing is almost completely implicit, but the designer can change the type of any variable by using a coercion.

The second part of the input description are compiler directives. Since SILAGE is applicative, the compiler must generate both a structure and the detailed timing of the micro-program. It will only be able to do so by using a very well defined target architecture. This allows both the compiler and the designer to make abstract decisions on a very high level and still perform a relevant cost evaluation, because bottom-up design information is continuously used when making high-level decisions. In the interactive concept of Cathedral-II the system designer is able to give structural hints to the compiler and this at as high a level as possible. This can be done by adding high-level directives, called "pragmas", to the behavioural description. So before giving a description of supported pragmas, the target architecture must be explained.

2.2. Target architecture.

In most present day synthesis tools the target of the compilation is rather ill defined. In order to generate a performant, area-efficient DSP chip, it is obviously not sufficient to consider only hardwired or even folded datapaths containing registers, busses, multiplexers and ALUs [Kow86][Tri87].

The key to efficient silicon compilation is the selection and precise definition of a specialized target architecture and its parameters [Cat87]. This should be combined with a highly specialized rule-base to translate high-level language constructs into efficient register transfers to be executed on that architecture. Only this way higher order constructs such as delay management, memory addressing and multiplication strategies can be translated efficiently, and dedicated optimization strategies can be applied. Architecture independent generation of structure cannot exploit the particular properties of a target library and is therefore bound to be sub-optimal in most cases. In order to cope with various levels of technological updates, a variety of mechanisms have been provided within Cathedral-II. Updates to rather closely related (e.g. scaled) technologies can be handled by the module generators. Updates to completely new libraries are handled by writing a completely new translation rule-base. This is only feasable if a powerful expert-system shell is available. Updates to new design methodologies inevitably require a completely different system and different optimization tools.

In Cathedral-II, a signal processing algorithm is translated into a set of concurrent processors. Each of those processors consists of a customized data path, which is an interconnection of modules, particularly suited for signal processing. Each processor has its own control structure. A global controller synchronizes the chip by generating the appropriate start pulses for the individual processor controllers. A restricted set of modules (execution units) and their parameters have been selected after an extensive study of the application area. The available execution units at this moment are :

- A general data path: an ALU-shifter unit.

- Dedicated accelerators : an array multiplier (with or without adding/subtracting accumulator), an iterative divider, a comparator unit for fast decision making algorithms, a normalizer unit for accelerating a limited set of floating-point operations.

- Memory : ROM, RAM, FIFO and an address calculation unit (ACU).

The modules are stored in a procedural way in module generators [Six86a][Six86b] with a well-defined set of parameters (word-length, number of overflow bits, optional presence of a shifter, ranges of programmable and fixed shifters, number of pipeline stages). Each of the execution units consists of two input register files (of at most 8 register fields) and some combinatorial logic to generate the desired function. The registers provide local storage of variables. RAM is used as background memory.

Scan-path registers and self-test structures for embedded RAMs are included in the modules. In the module generation environment a test view is included, which allows to generate all test vectors as a function of the parameters of the module.

A number of well-defined controller architectures have also been selected.

The maximum clock frequency depends on the library that is being used (10MHz for the current 3µm CMOS library). It is assumed that the module generators supply modules which can be clocked at this given frequency. The module generators will insert pipeline stages if the internal logic causes too much delay (e.g. because the word-length is too big) and they will select faster logic structures (e.g. a carry look-ahead instead of a carry-ripple adder) whenever appropriate. As a consequence, the synthesis tool only considers machine cycles and does not have to consider circuit delays of the execution unit logic. It has to know however the total number of machine cycles needed for an operation on a certain execution unit.

For this architecture, three types of pragmas are supported :

- pragmas for splitting up an algorithm into processors :
  pragma "pole, processor, 2" forces the function "pole" to be implemented on processor 2.

- hardware allocation pragmas :
  pragma "alloc(alu, 3)" allocates 3 ALUs in the datapath.

- pragmas for assigning an expression or a class of expressions to an
  execution unit instance :
  pragma "assign(pole(a,_).(_*y), alu, 2)" forces any multiplication using the
  local variable "y" in any function call "pole" with first argument "a" to be
  executed on ALU-instance 2.   Notice that the underscore '_' is used as a
  wild card.

2.3. The controller description language : ATOMICS.

During the synthesis the SILAGE code is translated into an equivalent
register-transfer level description.   Jack generates ATOMICS code [Goo86] to
describe the register transfer behaviour of the design.   ATOMICS differs
fundamentally from other existing RT-languages in the sense that the language
itself does not contain any keywords to indicate functions of operators.   The
user is allowed to define its own set of operations.   The transfer part and
the implementation part are seperated by a vertical bar "|".   A typical
register transfer looks like this :

IF c THEN s:reg1 <- a:reg2, b:reg3 | alu = add, bus2 = s, mux1 = bus2;

meaning that the variables "a" and "b", which are stored in the registers
"reg2" and "reg3", are added together on an execution unit called "alu", and
the result "s" is transferred via a bus "bus2" and a multiplexer "mux1" to a
register "reg1", if the boolean variable "c" has the value "true".

Because ATOMICS is applicative, the ordering of the statements is irrelevant.
Although a particular register file can be the target of more than one
register transfer, the name of the variable is used in combination with the
name of the register file to denote a register field.   In principle, a
register field can be the target of a register transfer only once.   The
ATOMICS scheduler [Goo86] is able to reorder the register transfers in such a
way that no resource conflicts occur, and the number of machine cycles to
execute the program is close to minimal.   The set of reordered register
transfers (Fig.5) is a procedural program which can be executed on the
generated data path (Fig.6).

2.4. Optimization criteria for a DSP silicon compiler.

Most existing compilers try to maximize the system throughput.   Since we deal
with DSP systems the data rate is usually fixed and known in advance.
Therefore the main task of a DSP silicon compiler is to minimize the area
within the timing constraints.   Often it is economical to generate a slow but
area-efficient structure to implement part of an algorithm, because the
arithmetic bottle-neck turns out to be the adjacent processor.   Eventually
other constraints may be imposed upon the compiler by the system designer,
such as restrictions on the type and the timing of I/O operations.
Nevertheless it should also be possible to use such a compiler for maximizing
the throughput of the chip within an area constraint by allowing the designer
to determine the hardware allocation.

2.5. Optimization mechanisms in Jack.

The above defined optimization criteria can be translated into a sequence of
optimization steps with decreasing importance :

  1. Minimize the number and size of execution units within the timing
     constraints
  2. Minimize the number of registers in the register files
  3. Minimize the interconnection cost (busses, multiplexers)

Busses have proven to be the least important cost as long as there are less
than 6 or 7.   This is a consequence of our layout strategy which applies

extensive abutment and over-the-cell routing using 5 uncommitted tracks.

The methodology, adapted in Jack, is to use a mixture of automated tools and user interaction to solve these complex minimization problems. In fact, it is our experience that a system designer often has a good idea of the computational bottle-necks of an algorithm, since this is the reason why he/she selected that particular algorithm. Therefore, the designer can fairly well estimate the required amount of parallelism and the type of accelerator functions. The most time-consuming and error prone part of the design job is not located in hardware allocation but in the detailed assignment of hardware, controller generation, register and bus minimization, and macro expansions. This is where the synthesis task has to come in and has to perform extremely good in order to be acceptable. E.g. a filter designer will not accept that a tap of a FIR filter takes two machine cycles if he knows that it can be performed in one cycle. Therefore, a synthesis system should allow user interference. This is however only possible if it can happen at high enough a level and if the user obtains enough feedback from the system to be able to pinpoint the problems and to interfere.

These considerations have led to the optimization strategy of Jack (Fig.4). Instead of trying to perform a global optimization, the design task is split up into the following sequence of subtasks :

- Hardware allocation.

    In a first step the designer estimates how much arithmetic power has to be put on a chip in order to be able to execute the algorithm within the timing constraints (e.g. 2 ALUs and 1 array multiplier). If no allocation is done by the designer, Jack tries to minimize the chip area by allocating the minimal hardware required to implement the algorithm.

- Automatic translation from high-level applicative code into primitive operations (register transfers) of the target architecture.

    This translation depends on the preceding hardware allocation step. A piece of high-level code which can both be executed on a general data path and on an accelerator will be compiled into different register transfers depending on the allocation of accelerators. Although this translation step selects the type of the hardware unit, it should not select the particular instance of the unit a particular operation will be executed on. This should be done in the next step.

- Hardware assignment and scheduling of register transfers.

    The set of register transfers generated in the previous step is ordered, and at the same time the particular execution unit instances on which the operations are executed are selected. The objective is to process the register transfer code in a close to minimum number of machine cycles through a full exploitation of the parallelism which was left open by the allocation step. The ordering has to take into account data precedence, pipeline delays of both data path operators and the controller, and resource conflicts [Goo87].

In order to generate a register transfer description and a detailed data path implementing the SILAGE description, a rule-based translation system is used. The rule-base stores the knowledge of architecture-design experts and knows a lot about efficiently translating SILAGE into architecture primitives. This turns out to be complicated for constructs such as multipication (parallel, serial-parallel, constant multipication), division, iteration, algorithmic delays, functions, matrices, etc. Translation rules showed to be very much dependent upon the target architecture.

The rule-base translates the SILAGE description into an initial solution with following properties :

- sufficient parallelism in terms of the allocated execution units.

- a separate register field for every variable (so that no register contention has to be taken into account).

- dedicated busses for each connection needed (so that no bus contention has to be considered). Multiplexers are put at the inputs of the register files.

The initial solution is then passed to a set of algorithmic minimization procedures. The cycle number is minimized by the controler scheduler ATOMICS [Goo87]. The datapath area is minimized by reducing as many storage and interconnection elements (registers and busses) as allowed by the timing constraints. The merging of busses may slightly increase the number of machine cycles but Jack estimates this increase accurately. Nevertheless, rescheduling and evaluation of the results is always necessary. Eventually this may cause backtracking (new design iterations) if the provided timing safety-margin is violated. The designer can enforce new design decisions by introducing pragmas.

Notice that the assignment of variables to register files is an automatic consequence of the operator assignment. The alternative is to perform the register assignment before the operator assignment, based on a lifetime analysis of the variables in the precedence graph [Tse86]. Our decision is based on practical, architectural grounds : in order to obtain area-efficient designs, registers are clustered in so called register files, situated at the two inputs of each execution unit. In this way, both input variables of an operator can be supplied at the same time. The problem of storage minimization thus reduces to the minimization of the number of fields in the register files which is achieved by means of a life time analysis following the scheduling of the register transfer statements. This strategy is flexible and allows for the duplication of variables in registers when this is required for a fast implementation. Note that the register count can also be lowered by storing long-living variables in a RAM, as can be indicated by a pragma.

3. Implementation.

3.1. Parser and preprocessor.

The SILAGE parser generates a syntax tree on which a limited set of local architecture-independent optimizations can be performed. Examples of these transformations can also be found in convential optimizing software compilers : reordering of operations and variables in order to minimize the number of operations and variable storage, elimination of common sub-expressions, etc. Trying to integrate these optimizations in the rule-base has proven to be highly impractical. The number of rules and the complexity of each rule grows too rapidly. Moreover, since these transformations are essentially architecture independent they should not be part of the rule-base.

3.2. The expert-system shell.

The expert-system shell of Jack is tuned towards synthesis problems : it offers data structures and manipulation routines for dataflow graphs and datapath structures, an inference engine, dedicated optimization procedures (scheduler, bus merger, register minimization), specialized graphics, an arithmetic tool box and a rule editor to specify translation rules.

All data structures in Jack are PROLOG lists. The list HLSet (Fig.7) contains the dataflow graph of the SILAGE description. It is gradually transformed into a list LLSet containing the register transfer description of the controller, and into a list AssList containing the structure of the data-path.

With each SILAGE equation in HLSet, a scope is indicated. This scope specifies the conditions under which the equation is valid. It also contains a stack indicating the nesting of the loops. The inference engine continuously optimizes the scopes of the register transfers in order not to introduce inefficiencies in the register-transfer code. E.g. transfers which are independent of a loop counter value are shifted out of the loop. Conditions are removed if this doesn't create any conflicts but increases efficiency (e.g. if both the 'then' and the 'else' part of a condition contain the same register transfer).

The engine also takes care of function expansions. There is no subroutine-calling mechanism provided : function calls are expanded by replacing the function call by the body of the function definition. During a function expansion the formal input and output parameters are unified with the actual ones. In order to generate unique variable names for the local variables, they are tagged with the name of the calling function.

E.g.

```
    a = my_function(b, c);

    func my_function(X, Y) =
    begin
       temp = X * Y;
       return = temp + X;
    end;
```

becomes after expansion:

```
    a = f(b,c).temp + b;
    f(b,c).temp = b * c;
```

The inference engine uses the information in the dataflow graph to decide which equation is to be mapped next. It also finds a rule which can be applied to this equation, taking into account relevant pragmas. The transformation process is demand-driven. The initial set of demands includes all the signals coming out of the data path : the data outputs and all the status flags needed for the evaluation of conditions or for controlling loops. The engine feeds a SILAGE equation with its scope to the selected rule, which performs following actions : fire procedures to generate additional information, store a number of register transfers in the LLSet, store structural information in AssList and put demands for the operands of the SILAGE equation in the DemandSet with their appropriate scope (Fig.7). This transformation process continues as long as the list DemandSet is not empty. The engine takes care not to compile any code more than once.

3.3. The rule base.

A description of the present status of the knowledge base is given below.

3.3.1. Logical operations on the data path.

The SILAGE primitives AND, OR and NOT can be directly implemented on on ALU. The EXOR function is not considered to be a SILAGE primitive, so no simulation model is incorporated in the SILAGE simulator MONKEY [Rob86]. The designer has to provide the model himself or take it from a function library. However, since EXOR is a primitive operation of the target architecture, the compiler will ignore the simulation model.

Logical operations on boolean variables are normally incorporated in the logic of the controller.

3.3.2. Addition and subtraction.

When the operands are not indices or addresses, additions and subtractions are always implemented on an ALU. A sign inversion is implemented as a subtraction from zero.

3.3.3. Multiplication.

A multiplication can be implemented on an array multiplier or on a multiplier-accumulator if the accumulator is initialized with a zero. It can also be expanded into a shift-add sequence on an ALU. In this case the ALU uses a special shift register to do the parallel-serial conversion of the multiplicator. Rules are provided for initialisation, the expansion of the iterative procedure, and for collecting the result. A multiplication with a power of two can also be implemented as a shift operation on a divider unit or on a normalizer unit. Finally there is a rule for converting a multiplication of a variable with a decimal constant into a minimal sequence of shift and add operations on an ALU. In this case the parallel-serial converter in the ALU is not needed.

3.3.4. Multiply-accumulation.

Rules have been designed for performing a multiply-accumulation (both for addition and subtraction) on an array multiplier. Initialisation of the accumulator is provided. If the multiplier-accumulator is pipelined, some extra rules have to be fired in order to generate additional pipeline register transfers. Another set of rules also allows for expansion of these operations on an ALU.

3.3.5. Division.

Dividing a variable by a power of two can be done by multiplying the variable with the reverse constant. All other divisions are either implemented on an iterative divider or in a shift-add way on an ALU. The divider is twice as fast as the ALU, and has its own control structure, so it only requires a start pulse. Two rules are provided for this divider: one for generating the start pulse, one for transfering the result after N clock cycles, where N is the number of outputs bits.

3.3.6. Shifting.

Left and right shifts are implemented on an ALU. Since the shifter is put at the output of the ALU, any regular ALU operation (addition, EXOR, sign inversion, ...) can be combined with a shift operation of the result in the same machine cycle. Shift operations over a variable shift field can only be implemented on a normalizer unit.

3.3.7. Accelerated non-primitive SILAGE functions.

The compiler is able to ignore the user-provided definition of the following functions, and to use special hardware to implement them. The maximum or the minimum of two numbers is normally computed in one cycle using a comparator. Absolute values and EXOR functions can be computed in one cycle on an ALU. An assignment pragma can be used to force the compiler to take the user-provided definition when implementing the function. This way the absolute value might be calculated on a comparator and the maximum and minimum function on an ALU. New user-defined functions (such as e.g. a Galois-addition) can easily be added by the user with the aid of the knowledge acquisition system (section 4).

3.3.8. Algorithmic delays.

Algorithmic delays can either be implemented by putting state variables in
register files or in RAM. RAM is used when the number of state variables is
too large to fit into a register file. A rule says this is the case when the
delays in the SILAGE description are not constants such as in a@2, but indexes
such as in a@i. This means a loop construct was used to enumerate them. If
no enumeration was used, the delays are known at compiler time (manifest) and
by default the compiler assumes the states fit into a register file. Rules
are provided to minimize the number of transfers and registers for realizing
delays in register files. If a RAM is used, an address computation unit is
needed to compute the rotating addresses. Such an address is computed by
decrementing a base address with the number of delays. The base address is
incremented each time a new input sample is taken, modulo N, where N is the
power of two which just includes the number of state variables.

3.3.9. Address computations.

Address computations are needed when dealing with indexed variables. Indexed
variables are always stored in RAM, except for two special cases. First, if
all the members of the array are manifest, such as the 128 coefficients of a
128-tap FIR filter, they may be stored in a ROM. Second, if the precedence
graph of the algorithm shows that each element of an array is computed by
using only one other array element, all the elements can share the same field
in a register file. Each array has an array header with index 0. The address
of the array header is called the base address of the array. The base address
of each array is stored as part of a micro-instruction in the micro-code ROM
of the controller. The RAM address of a particular array element can be
computed on an ACU (address calculation unit) by adding the index of the
element to the base address of the array. Whenever an indexed variable with a
non-manifest index is used in an equation, the equation must reside inside a
loop. Loops are implemented as iterations, where an ACU increments the loop
counter and checks the range of the loop. Since this loop counter is
available in one of the ACU register files, it can be thus used to calculate
addresses of array elements. On the other hand, if an array element with a
manifest index is used, the index is stored as a constant in one of the
register files of the ACU.

There are rules for incrementing and decrementing addresses on an ACU, and for
decrementing rotating base addresses. Rules are needed for computing
write-addresses when saving a variable in RAM, read-addresses when reading
from RAM, and both write and read-addresses when temporarily storing a
variable in RAM, which acts as a background memory in this case. Also a rule
is provided to transfer base addresses from the controller ROM to the address
register of a RAM or an input register of an ACU. All the rules concerning
read-operations from RAM, have an equivalent for ROM.

3.3.10. Constants.

Constant variables are most area-efficiently stored in a ROM. However it is
often convenient to store one or two constants in a field of a register file.
Rules are provided for this purpose.

3.3.11. Conditional equations.

Conditional equations are implemented by a set of register transfers which
compute the boolean condition variable, and a set of transfers implementing
the THEN and the ELSE part. Boolean condition variables may be any
AND-OR-NOT-EXOR-combination of boolean comparisons. The AND, OR, NOT and EXOR
functions are incorporated in the logic of the controller. Comparions (>, <,
>=, =<, ==, !=) are computed using a comparator or a general ALU according to
the following table :

a == b	"=="flag of comparator, or 2 times the sign bit of a 2's-complement subtraction on an ALU (there is no zero-flag)
a != b	NOT (a == b)
a > b	(a >= b) AND (a != b)
a < b	(b >= a) AND (b != a)
a >= b	">="flag of comparator, or sign bit of subtraction on ALU
a =< b	b >= a

The result of such an operation is not a variable on a data bus, but a condition variable (flag) in a condition register. The contents of these condition registers can be directly fed into the controller and the controller generates appropriate control signals for the data path some controller-pipeline delays later on. Conditions can be arbitrarily nested.

3.3.12. Loops.

As mentioned above, loops are implemented as iterations. Rules are provided for initializing a loop counter, incrementing a loop counter, checking the range of the loop, initializations for rotating-memory address calculation, and for initializing accumulators when iterative multiply-accumulation operations are used inside the loop. Loops can be arbitrarily nested.

4. Knowledge acquisition.

Rule editing tools provided in Jack are : a rule inspector to decompile the PROLOG code of a rule into a more readable format, a function to add or edit a rule and an adviser. The adviser makes an ordered list of all the rules which can be applied to a given SILAGE equation. From the point of view of a knowledge engineer, the scenario of adding new features to Jack is as follows :

- The knowledge engineer starts with investigating how the system reacts when a new type of SILAGE equation is presented to it by using the adviser. Jack will give warnings that it can find no match with any existing rule at all, or eventually it will report a match with one of the more general rules (which is most probably not the intention). Several matches may be possible, but they will be ordered.

- In order to insert a new rule to cope with the new kind of equation, the knowledge engineer can specify

  - prior to which of the previous shown matches (if any) he/she wants the new rule to match his equation in the future.

  - extra conditions, using predefined properties. E.g. the operators have to be indexed variables, may not be a power of two, etc.

  - the actions the rule has to perform : look for some missing data such as the word-length of one of the operands, perform some arithmetic operations, or update the datastructures.

The system will compile the rule into a PROLOG clause, save the source code separately for later use by the rule inspector, and generate the appropriate clauses at the right spot in the PROLOG rule-base. When the new rule is added to the rule-base Jack starts running a consistency check. By inserting a rule in front of some others, it may be possible that some equations are caught too early. Jack tries to find these equations. When the consistency check only finds the new equation everything is OK and one can use the adviser again to check whether the system performs as expected.

5. Future work.

The assignment of variables to particular register files and the assignment of operations to execution units is realized knowledge-based. The micro-code scheduler ATOMICS is being extended with analytical techniques to perform the hardware assignment in a more optimal way.

The automation of the allocation process in an optimal way has proven to be extremely hard for architectures as the one presented above : all options for which an accelerator execution unit exists can also be performed on a more general execution unit at the cost of extra machine cycles, while an arbitrary number of identical units can also be put in parallel. At IMEC, we are currently studying techniques to perform the operator allocation using ATMS techniques (assumption-based truth maintenance systems) [Gen86].

6. Conclusions.

Earlier experiences with PROLOG programming methodologies and design experience gained by performing complex manual top-down designs have been combined into a PROLOG CAD tool. This tool can help a system designer to perform the synthesis of DSP processor systems starting from a behavioural description.

The program Jack The Mapper contains a dedicated expert system shell : a rule editor, a number of transformation mechanisms, IO facilities and a library of predefined utilities. Jack also contains a knowledge base with about 100 rules, formally describing the features of the multi-processor target architecture used at IMEC.

Its run-time when mapping a design of industrial complexity lies in the order of a few minutes. Because of this short run-time and because of the integration of the tool in a tool-box of powerful simulation and analysis tools, module generators and floorplanners, a system designer can use this tool to explore a large design space succesfully.

Among the present applications are included : biquad and wave digital filters, a high-quality pitch extractor for vocoder realisations, an echo canceler for use in hands-free telephone and an adaptive interpolator for Compact Disk.

References.

[Cat87]   F. Catthoor et al. : "Architectural strategies for an application specific synchronous multi-processor environment", submitted to IEEE Transactions on Acoustics, Speech and Signal Processing.

[DeM85]   H. De Man : "Evolution of CAD-tools towards third generation custom VLSI-design", Digest European Conference on Solid-State Circuits, ESSCIRC, Toulouse, pp. 256-256c, September 1985.

[DeM86]   H. De Man et al. : "Cathedral-II : A silicon compiler for digital signal processing", IEEE Design and Test, December 1986, pp. 13-25.

[Gen86]   D. Genin et al. : "A knowledge based mapping tool", Internal report Tektronix, IMEC, Kapeldreef 75, B-3030 Heverlee, Belgium.

[Goo87]   G. Goossens et al. : "An efficient microcode compiler for custom multiprocessor DSP-systems", submitted to IEEE ICCAD '87, Santa Clara, November 1987.

[Hil85]   P. Hilfinger : "A high-level language and silicon compiler for digital signal processing", IEEE CICC conference, May 1985, Portland, pp. 213-216.

[Hit83]   C.Y. Hitchcock III, D.E. Thomas, "A Method of Automatic Data Path Synthesis", ACM IEEE 20th Design Automation Conference Proc. (Miami), 1983, pp. 484-489.

[Jai86]   R. Jain et al. : "Custom design of a VLSI PCM-FDM transmultiplexer from system specifications to circuit layout using a computer-aided design system", IEEE Transactions on Circuits and Systems, February 1986, Vol. CAS-33, No. 2, pp. 183-195.

[Jer86]   A. Jerraya et al. : "Principles of the SYCO compiler", Design Automation Conference, Las Vegas, July 1986, pp. 715-721.

[Kow85]   T.J. Kowalski et al. : "The VLSI design automation assistant : what's in a knowledge base ?", 22nd Design Automation Conference, pp. 252-258.

[Mar86]   P. Marwedel : "A new synthesis algorithm for the MIMOLA software system", 23rd Design Automation Conference, pp. 271-277.

[Rob86]   J.P. Robin : "Algorithmic description language and behavioural simulator", ESPRIT 97 report ESPRIT97/IMEC/9.86/C/1(4)/1-D, IMEC, Kapeldreef 75, B-3030 Heverlee, Belgium.

[Six86a] P. Six et al. : "An interactive environment for creating module generators", ESSCIRC, September 16-18, 1986, Delft, pp. 65-70.

[Six86b] P. Six et al. : An intelligent module generator environment", DAC '86, Las Vegas, pp. 730-735.

[Tri87]   H. Trickey : "Flamel : A high-level Hardware Compiler", IEEE Trans. on Computer-aided Design, Vol. CAD-6, No.2, 3/87, pp. 259-269.

[Tse86]   Chia-Jeng Tseng, D.P. Siewioreke : "Automated Synthesis of data paths in digital systems", IEEE Transactions on Computer-aided design, Vol. CAD-5, No. 3, July 1986, pp. 379-395.

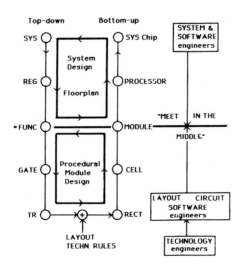

Fig. 1. The 'Meet-In-The-Middle' design methodology.

```
#define WORD num<20,0>

#define a11 0.625
#define a12 1
#define b11 0.5
#define b12 0.375
#define a21 7
#define a22 1
#define b21 0.3125
#define b22 0.78125
#define a31 0.5
#define b31 0.375

func main(In : WORD) Out : num =
begin
    Section1 = biquad(In, a11, a12, b11, b12 );
    Section2 = biquad(Section1, a21, a22, b21, b22 );
    Out = FirstOrder(Section2, a31, b31 );
end;

func biquad(input, a1, a2, b1, b2 : num) : num =
begin
    State = input + WORD(b1 * State@1) - WORD(b2 * State@2);
    return = State + WORD(a1 * State@1) + WORD(a2 * State@2);
end;

func FirstOrder(input, a, b : num) : num =
begin
    State = input + WORD(b * State@1);
    return = State + WORD(a * State@1);
end;
```

**Fig. 2. SILAGE description of a 5th order
         PCM filter.**

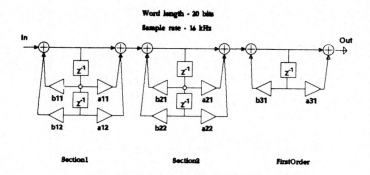

**Fig. 3. Signal flow graph of the PCM filter
         described in Fig. 2.**

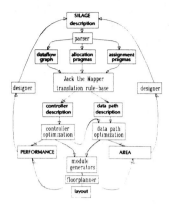

Fig. 4. The Cathedral II design cycle.

```
          .
          .
          .

Potential    1 :
----------------
'*60':reg_1_alu_1 <- '*65':reg_2_ram_1, '*60':reg_3_ram_1 |
  bus_2_alu_lbus_1_rom_ctrlbus_1_ram_lbus_1_alu_1 = '*60',
  ram = READ <0>;

Potential    2 :
----------------
'*68':reg_2_alu_1 <- '*62'@1:reg_2_alu_1, '*47':reg_1_alu_1 |
  alu = ADD&UPSH[1],
  bus_2_alu_lbus_1_rom_ctrlbus_1_ram_lbus_1_alu_1 = '*68' <0>;

          .
          .
          .


Potential   35 :
----------------
'*37':reg_2_alu_1 <- '*40':reg_2_alu_1, '*39':reg_1_alu_1 |
  alu = ADD,
  bus_2_alu_lbus_1_rom_ctrlbus_1_ram_lbus_1_alu_1 = '*37' <0>;
'*35':reg_3_ram_1 <- '*36':reg_2_ram_1, '*35':reg_1_ram_1 |
  ram = WRITE <0>;
```

```
<   0> /* Startup */
       UPD CREG[0]=sregStart, CREG[1]=CREG[0];
       JMP IF CREG[1] -> 2 || !CREG[1] -> IF CREG[0] -> 1 || !CREG[0] -> 0 FI FI

<   1> /* Potential 0 */
       CTL reg_2_ram_1:W[0,0], rom:const['&in',0]; UPD; JMP 3;

<   2> /* Potential 1 */
       CTL reg_1_alu_1:W[5,5], reg_2_ram_1:R[0,0], ram:read; UPD; JMP 4;

<   3> /* Potential 2 */
       CTL reg_2_alu_1:W[4,7], reg_2_alu_1:R[4,7], reg_1_alu_1:R[-1,5], alu:add&
       UPD;
       JMP 5;
          .
          .
          .
```

Fig. 5. Register transfer description generated by Jack and scheduled by ATOMICS.

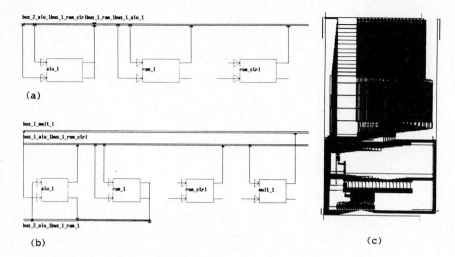

(a)

(b)   (c)

Fig. 6. Architecture generated by Jack
        (a) with one ALU (36 cycles).
        (b) with one ALU and one multiplier (15 cycles).
        (c) floorplan of solution (a). The controller
            PLA is drawn as a black box.

```
rule111([CREG,EXU,COND] = [(alu,I),(OP1 == OP2)],
    Scope, HLSet, LLSet, DemandSet, AssList,
    'Equality tested on ALU.'):-

  selectSEXU([(alu,I),(OP1 == OP2)]),

  ([(creg,s),(alu,I),( OP1-OP2)==0]
      = ( [(reg,1),(alu,I),OP1] - [(reg,2),(alu,I),OP2]), Scope) ---> LLSet,
  ([(creg,s),(alu,I),(-OP1+OP2)==0]
      = (-[(reg,1),(alu,I),OP1] + [(reg,2),(alu,I),OP2]), Scope) ---> LLSet,
  ((OP1 == OP2) = (not (OP1-OP2)==0 and not (-OP1+OP2)==0)) --> LLSet,

  ([(reg,1), (alu,I), OP1] = [_,OP1], Scope) ---> DemandSet,
  ([(reg,2), (alu,I), OP2] = [_,OP2], Scope) ---> DemandSet,

  [(creg,s),(alu,I),(-OP1+OP2)==0] --> AssList,
  [(creg,s),(alu,I),( OP1-OP2)==0] --> AssList.
```

Fig.7. PROLOG code of a rule for checking the equality of two
       variables OP1 and OP2 on an ALU. Since the ALU allows
       reversed subtraction, the sign bits of the 2's-complement
       subtraction OP1-OP2 and the reversed subtraction -OP1+OP2
       can be transferred to the condition register (creg,s)
       of the selected ALU-instance I. The controller action
       (negating the two sign bits and ANDing them) is also
       stored in LLSet. Demands for computing OP1 and OP2 and
       storing them in the register files of the ALU are put
       in DemandSet.

Session 3

SPECIFICATION AND VERIFICATION

VLSI '87, C.H. Séquin (editor)
Elsevier Science Publishers B.V. (North-Holland)
© IFIP, 1988

ALGORITHMS AND SPECIFICATIONS

Graham Birtwistle,
Computer Science Department,
University of Calgary,
2500 University Drive,
Calgary, Alberta, Canada T2N 1N4.

ABSTRACT

Hardware verification is a technique whereby VLSI designs may be formally proven to meet their specifications. Progress has been quite rapid over the last few years with a growing body of methodological experience and completed proofs of LSI designs. Further, verification techniques have been used to show the correctness of a VLSI design style. This paper looks at some current work in the field and discusses the long term possibilities for deriving layout from specifications and for CAD system support for specification driven design.

Key words. Hardware verification. Behavioural specifications. High level intermediate languages. Composition rules. Transformation algorithms. Hierarchical design. VLSI CAD tools.

1. INTRODUCTION.

Hardware verification is a technique by which a chip design may be proven to meet a specification of its intended behaviour. Currently chip designs are validated by extensive simulation at several levels, but the process is so time consuming that it cannot be done exhaustively for large designs. This inevitably results in some production chips being flawed. Many systems can tolerate minor flaws, but there are systems even now which cannot. The most obvious examples to quote lie in safety critical applications such as flight control, medical life-support chips (pacemakers), industrial plant control where failure may mean loss of life. The problems are of such magnitude in certain defence applications that the UK Ministry of Defence feels it cannot rely on commercial chips and has embarked on a program of producing formally verified chips to its own specification. Hospital, civil aviation, and transport boards in the UK will also use these chips. A second, less dramatic, area is afforded by industry where certain chips are used by the million. The flawed design of a telecommunications chip or of an automobile chip could force a massive and very expensive recall program. Again, simply because of location, it would be tremendously expensive to replace sensor chips installed on arctic pipelines or chips operating in remote regions of space. Yet a third potential application area is product redesign. Technology advances mean that chips have to be reworked into a new technology every two or three years, or even less. If a design has a verified hierarchy (specification tree), redesign will usually mean taking and changing the lower tree nodes. There can be no change to the overall chip specification when the behaviours of the replacement designs conform to the specification of their plug-in slot in the new tree. In this case, the new versions of the same part can be inserted into existing systems with a guarantee that they will not introduce bugs.

In this paper we argue that a formal specification language (suitably decorated) ought to serve as the central notation in future CAD systems. In section two we highlight selected recent work in hardware verification proofs and models. In section three we give a simple example of design verification in HOL (higher order logic) to give the flavour of specification and verification (and how tedious unautomated theorem proving can be). In section four, we show that many design views can be derived from a specification tree by transformation. We look at ideas for taking specification trees and using them as input to floorplanners, simulators at various levels, and for generating layout from specifications. (The specification hierarchy developed in section three is used to illustrate the techniques.) This opens up the possiblity of deriving (nearly) everything from specifications. Our viewpoint is that suitably annotated HOL can be used as a hardware description language at the sub-system and architectural levels as well as at the library cell level. If this turns out to be valid, it would ease many severe VLSI CAD problems notably version consistency and data-base management.

2. SOME RECENT VERIFICATION WORK.

Over the last few years we have seen the development of hardware verification in many areas. Below is a sampler of some of the work that is going on in three selected areas: transistor level models, proofs of sub-systems and architectures at the register transfer level [1, 2, 4-11, 17, 18], and proofs of design styles [9].

[14, 15, 27] present work at the transistor level. [15] details the specification and proof of a (supposedly) edge-triggered D-type flip flop and formalises waveforms very carefully (after all, timing is where many errors are made). The resulting specifications of a nand gate and the D-type are cumbersome - occupying 6 and 19 lines respectively. Hanna and Daeche show that this D-type is not really edge triggered at all, and that its ability to retain data is critically dependent upon the rapidity of the trailing edge of the strobe waveform. [27] discusses several transistor models and points out the flaws in each. Winskel presents a compositional model for the behaviour of MOS circuits when the input is steady, and shows how this leads to a formal logic. The model is based upon Mossim, but is compositional, and is now being extended to provide a full and accurate treatment for circuits with changing inputs. It is hoped that work in low-level models will provide us with rules for when we can use the more succinct register transfer level representations of circuits in VLSI proof work, eg. permit us to use the Dtype model below (instead of Hanna and Daeche's 19 liner)

$$\text{Dtype d ck q} = !t.\ o(t+1) = (ck\ t => d\ t\ |\ o\ t)$$

provided that we clock it at less than, say, 10 MgHtz. For a further example see Herbert and Gordon [14]. NB HOL uses ! to represent *for all*, ? to represent *there exists*, and *if a then b else c* is written $a => b\ |\ c$.

Work at the system level attempts to put verified LSI designs into silicon. Researchers at Cambridge have designed, verified, and fabricated a network interface chip [14]. Work at Calgary has produced the correctness proof of an existing large practical design implemented in off-the-shelf LSI [4], and an 8-bit processor, proven correct in [11, 18] was fabricated in December 1985. [17] describes the verification of a processor using the Boyer-Moore automated theorem prover. Perhaps the highest-profile achievement was accomplished by the Royal Signals and Radar Establishment (UK) who completed the (hand) verification of the VIPER processor and had it fabricated in gate array technology in 1986 [7, 8, 9]. Avra Cohn of Cambridge has since mechanised the VIPER proof following the structure of the RSRE proof closely [6]. The mechanical verification was a formidable task, but revealed several flaws in the original hand proof. Three were of a serious nature - a phase error in the fetch cycle, and there were two incomplete checks for illegal instructions due to unforseen conditions. Avra's work would seem to vindicate completely formal methods even when they are used solely for design verification work.

In [9], Inder Dhingra has formalised some rules of thumb for popular CMOS design styles, and used them to analyse the rules of the NORA design style. In this design style, there are two clock lines, inverses of each other, and two sorts of gate, the n-type and the p-type. The design rules govern how gates may be connected, what clock lines they are driven by, and if the output is to be guaranteed. In order to make the design style synchronous, a CMOS latch is used as a dynamic register. This further complicates the rules but gives rise to a design style that generates smaller and faster circuits than standard CMOS. Dhingra proves that the NORA design style can fail for large circuits, and then develops a refinement of NORA, called CLIC, using a two phase non-overlapping clocking scheme that is guaranteed. He also gives a formal motivation for CLIC using a simple transistor model with charge storage capability.

3. SPECIFICATION AND VERIFICATION IN HOL.

The specifications given in this section are in higher order logic, HOL [12, 13], a system developed by Gordon at Cambridge and used for many of the largest designs that have been verified or are in progress [3, 6, 18]. A specification is a relation that holds at any time between the outputs of a device and its inputs. As a simple example consider the correctness statement and proof of a combinational unit which compares words for equals, less, and greater. The parts hierarchy is shown in figure 1.

egl_unit

egl_slice

| and | nand | or | nor | inv |

| pwr | ptran | ntran | gnd |

Figure 1. Parts hierarchy for the comparator.

At the bottom end of the parts hierarchy we specify four basic CMOS building blocks using a bi-directional model. Other models may be found in [10, 27]. *pwr* whose output line b is always high, *ptran* whose source and drain are equal in value when the gate goes low. Definitions of *ntran* and *gnd* follow similar lines.

let pwr_spec = new_definition ('pwr_spec', "! b. pwr_spec b = (b=T)");;

let ptran_spec = new_definition ('ptran_spec', "! g a b. ptran_spec g a b = (~ g ==> (a=b))");;

let ntran_spec = new_definition ('ntran_spec', "! g a b. ntran_spec g a b = (g ==> (a=b))");;

let gnd_spec = new_definition ('gnd_spec', "! b. gnd_spec b = (b=F)");;

We may now specify an inverter and implement it from these parts and prove the equivalence of the implementation and the specification by:

let inv_spec = new_definition ('inv_spec', "! i o. inv_spec i o = (o = ~ i)");;

let inv_imp = new_definition
  ('inv_imp',
   "! i o. inv_imp i o = ?p1 p2.(pwr_spec p1)/\(ptran_spec i p1 o)/\ (ntran_spec i o p2)/\(gnd_spec p2)");;

let inv_imp_simp = EXPAND [pwr_spec; ptran_spec; ntran_spec; gnd_spec] inv_imp;;

let inv_correct = prove_thm
  ('inv_correct', "! i o. inv_imp i o = inv_spec i o",
   REPEAT GEN_TAC
   THEN REWRITE_TAC [inv_imp_simp; inv_spec]
   THEN BOOL_CASES_TAC "i" THEN REWRITE_TAC []
  );;

The subsidiary definition *inv_imp_simp* uses the built-in HOL rule EXPAND to remove hidden lines p1 and p2 from the implementation. The proof strips away the forall operator (REPEAT GEN_TAC), rewrites the stripped goal in atomic parts using REWRITE_TAC, and then does a straighforward by-case analysis. In a similar vein it is tedious but not difficult to specify, implement, and prove correct, nand2, and2, or2, and nor2 gates from the basic blocks and the inverter.

The comparator we are after is defined as a strip with lines esf, lsf, gsf (equal-so-far, less-so-far, greater_so_far) running into and out of each stage. Also input to each stage are the two bits a_k, b_k being compared at this stage. The specification, implementation, and proof of equivalence are:

let eglbox_spec = new_definition
  ('eglbox_spec',
   "! a b esf gsf lsf e g l. eglbox_spec a b esf gsf lsf e g l =
    (e = (esf /\ (a=b))) /\ (g = (esf /\ (a/\~ b)) \/ gsf) /\ (l = (esf /\ (~ a/\b)) \/ lsf)");;

```
let eglbox_imp = new_definition
  ('eglbox_imp',
   "! a b esf gsf lsf e g l. eglbox_imp a b esf gsf lsf e g l =
      ? p1 p2 p3 p4 p5 p6.
        (nand_imp a b p1)  /\ (and_imp p1 a p2)  /\ (and_imp p1 b p3) /\
        (nor_imp p2 p3 p4)  /\ (and_imp p4 esf e) /\
        (and_imp p3 esf p6) /\ (or_imp p6 lsf l)  /\
        (and_imp p2 esf p5) /\ (or_imp p5 gsf g)");;


let eglbox_imp_simp = EXPAND [nand_correct; nand_spec; and_correct;
               and_spec; nor_correct; nor_spec; or_correct; or_spec] eglbox_imp;;


let eglbox_correct = prove_thm
  ('eglbox_correct',
   "! a b esf gsf lsf e g l. eglbox_imp a b esf gsf lsf e g l =  eglbox_spec a b esf gsf lsf e g l",
   REPEAT GEN_TAC
   THEN BOOL_CASES_TAC "a"
   THEN BOOL_CASES_TAC "b"
   THEN REWRITE_TAC [eglbox_spec; eglbox_imp_simp; DE_MORGAN_THM]
   THEN EQ_TAC
   THEN STRIP_TAC
   THEN ASM_REWRITE_TAC []
   );;
```

The proof uses brute force running through the variety of input cases on a and b rewriting making use of selected previous definitions, and splitting into implications by EQ_TAC using the equivalence imp = spec and imp ⊃ spec ∧ spec ⊃ imp. We now have to make three auxiliary definitions for the =, <, and > operations on words, each which uses primitive recursion. Typically we have

```
let equal = new_prim_rec_definition
  ('equal',
   "(equal 0 (a:num->bool) (b:num->bool) = (a 0 = b 0)) /\
    (equal (SUC n) a b = (a (SUC n) = b (SUC n)) /\ (equal n a b))");;
```

before proceeding to the main result which specifies an n-bit comparator, defines an implementation using primitive recursion, and verifies their equivalence using induction. Notice that in these definitions, certain quantities are explicitly typed. Most of the time, the HOL system will deduce the correct type automatically, but sometimes it cannot and types have to be supplied. As a result, all quantities in HOL specifications and proofs obtain a type. In general, this prevents the Russell paradox; in hardware verification work, it supplies the number of bits on interconnecting wires.

```
let egl_spec = new_definition
  ('egl_spec',
   "!(n:num) (a:num->bool) (b:num->bool) (e:bool) (g:bool) (l:bool).
    egl_spec n a b e g l = (e = (equal n a b)) /\ (g = (greater n a b)) /\ (l = (less n a b))");;

let egl_imp = new_prim_rec_definition
  ('egl_imp',
   "(egl_imp 0 (a:num->bool) (b:num->bool) (e:bool) (g:bool) (l:bool)
      = eglbox_imp (a 0) (b 0) T F F e g l) /\
    (egl_imp (SUC n) a b e g l
      = ? (e1:bool) (g1:bool) (l1:bool). (egl_imp n a b e1 g1 l1) /\
         (eglbox_imp (a (SUC n)) (b (SUC n)) e1 g1 l1 e g l))");;
```

```
let egl_correct = prove_thm
  ('egl_correct',
  "!n a b e g l. egl_imp n a b e g l = egl_spec n a b e g l",
  INDUCT_TAC
  THEN REPEAT GEN_TAC
  THEN ASM_REWRITE_TAC [egl_imp; egl_spec; eglbox_correct; eglbox_spec; equal; greater; less]
  THEN EQ_TAC THEN STRIP_TAC
  THENL
    [ ALL_TAC;
      EXISTS_TAC "equal n a b" THEN EXISTS_TAC "greater n a b" THEN EXISTS_TAC "less n a b"
    ]
  THEN ASM_REWRITE_TAC []
  THEN REPEAT STRIP_TAC
  THEN EQ_TAC THEN STRIP_TAC THEN ASM_REWRITE_TAC []
  );;
```

Thus we now have a fully verified implementation of an n-bit comparator expressed in terms of n-slices, then each slice in terms of nand, nor, and, or, and inv gates, and finally each of the latter is given in terms of 4 basic CMOS building blocks. In the next section, we give support to our thesis that the specification tree should serve as the central representation for VLSI CAD systems by hinting how many views can be derived from annotated specifications

4. TRANSFORMATIONS FROM HOL.

Executing specifications. Some design capture languages that have been used for verification may be executed directly [22]. Other design capture languages, eg Lattice Logic's MODEL, are programs which can check syntax and semantics and hence things like connectivity. Simulations at various levels and gate-array layout are generated automatically from MODEL descriptions. But MODEL offer no help with proof. HOL specifications cannot yet be executed but work is going on in this direction at Cambridge. For a restricted (but very general) class of definitions including primitive recursive and operations upon lists, HOL definitions can be transformed into effective programs in a functional programming and then executed. The approach opens up usage of HOL as a program specification system too, but even for hardware verification, it would be a most useful aid in checking out specifications and proof attempts.

Floorplanning and placement Several researchers at Edinburgh University [23] have been working on first cuts at floorplanning and placement from wiring patterns. Their technique, derived from Heller's original work, first builds a graph using as nodes the chip elements to be floorplanned and placed. Nodes are joined together if the chip elements they represent are wired together. The interconnections are weighted according to the number of wires between the underlying chip elements. Then the graph is clustered so that heavily joined nodes come together as one supernode. Finally, mathematical techniques have been developed for examining the graphs and measuring their regularity and aplanarity and recognising those which fall into patterns that are easy to plan and place, eg. lines, arrays, stars, channels, datapaths, etc. If the graph configuration does not fall into a recognised pattern, it must be simplified, each part solved separately, and the parts glued together.

HOL specifications are typed and expressly name all ports so that node connections and their weights can be derived directly from HOL specifications. For example, from the definition of eglbox_imp, we can deduce that each box will have 9 nodes, that there are 8 external bit lines (a, b, esf, gsf, lsf flowing in, and e, g, l flowing out), and there are 6 internal 'node connecting wires' q1-q6, all bit lines. The algorithm tells to cluster the 4 tightly bound nodes, and then use the channel. The resulting floorplan is quite effective. In general, many more attributes may be considered in addition to pure wiring - area, wire lengths, critical path timing information, and additional constraints stating upon which walls input and output ports must lie. Constraint checkers and simulated annealing may then be used.

Timing and critical paths. We anticipate all library leaf cells will have been SPICEd. We then use a composition algorithm such as that of Lin and Mead [20; or 16, 24] to compose the electrical properties of the specification tree. In Lin's thesis, the electrical properties of any two port RC network are given in terms of 5 base parameters: series resistance R, total capacitance C, internal delay due to input D, total stored charge Q, and the internal delay due to stored charge D^*. These quantities are not independent, may be reduced to three in terms of which eventual equations are solved. Lin shows that all tree nets may be built from 5 primitive blocks and gives the composition algorithm for each primitive.

In our example, we decompose egl_imp into n eglbox_imp boxes then into a general network of nand, and, nor, or gates, and finally into ptran and ntran primitives simply be expanding the specification tree. All that remains is to express tree nodes in terms of Lin's 5 primitive node types - leaf, serial, parallel, side-port, and bi-directional. This can be done by typing the library leaf cells (this will have been done already) and traversing the specification tree filling in the Lin types of all intermediate nodes from their own specification. Lin's algorithm then traverses the graph, working from leafs backwards to the root. Cycles in the graph are detected and solved as separate clusters. In similar vein, the transistor level netlist or a higher level gate list (throw away leaf cells) can be used as input to other timing analysers in order to spot critical paths.

Constraints. To produce a design from the specification tree we start from the leaf level where information is complete and work our way back up the tree node by node. At each stage, we satisfy all internal constraints and replace them by synthesized border constraints or report an error. We then combine any inherited constraints with the synthesized border constraints. The process is repeated until we reach the root of the hierarchy. Now we find a solution to the constraint graph at the top level of the hierarchy, and recursively inherit down values for the border points of the component cells until we have dealt with the leaf cells. A topological sort is used to determine the order in which values are assigned to nodes in the constraint graph. To eliminate the interior constraints of a cell, we consider each border point α in turn from the bottom of the cell. We perform a depth first search on the constraint graph from α, but stop when we reach another border point β. Thus we reach each and every node accessible from the border point. By visiting the nodes in topological order we can derive for each border node β, such items as the length of the longest path from α to it. By repeating this operation for all border points, we derive the set of constraints involving only border points.

Layout from specifications? The program segments below specify an n-bit comparator in MODEL (Lattice Logic's design capture language) and HOL (transformed automatically from its previous recursive to iterative form). MODEL descriptions can be fabricated on many gate array lines. Expressing a MODEL description in HOL would enable the design to be verified by proof rather than 'validated' by simulation, thus assuring complete coverage, pinpointing errors, and limiting the scope of design alterations. The strong structural similarity between HOL specifications and the MODEL hardware language makes it easy to write a translator from HOL to MODEL.

Thus gate array chips can be made from specifications right now.

MODEL:
```
    PART EGL (n) [a(0:n), b(0:n)] -> e, l, g
      SIGNAL esf(0:n+1), lsf(0:n+1), gsf(0:n+1)
      INTEGER k
      esf(0) = T, gsf(0) = F, lsf(0) = F
      FOR k = 0:n CYCLE
        EGLBOX[a(k), b(k), esf(k), gsf(k), lsf(k)] -> esf(k+1), gsf(k+1), lsf(k+1)
      REPEAT
      e = esf(n+1), g = gsf(n+1), l = lsf(n+1)
    END
```

HOL:
```
    EGL n (a:num->bool) (b:num->bool) e g l =
    ? (esf:num->bool) (gsf:num->bool) (lsf:num->bool) .
    (esf 0 = T) ∧ (gsf 0 = F) ∧(lsf 0 = F) ∧
    FOR (0,n) (EQLBOX (a k) (b k) (esf k) (gsf k) (lsf k) (esf (SUC k)) (gsf (SUC k)) (lsf (SUC k)) ∧
    (e = esf(SUC n)) ∧ (g = gsf(SUC n)) ∧ (l = lsf(SUC n))
    )
```

In the HOL definition we have defined a looping construct FOR and used it to match the MODEL definition closely. Transformations from primitive recursive definitions to iterative ones are quite common and are easy to automate.

Generating custom from HOL specifications is a very hard problem. It is equivalent in difficulty to that of generating custom layout from gate level or switch level specifications. Much work is going on in this hard area - see [19, 21, 25, 26] for very different approaches - but all the results can be interfaced to HOL.

SUMMARY

Currently specification and proof is a separate exercise from layout. We would like to bend specifications into layout by correctness preserving transformations. In one approach, outlined herein, we elaborate a design hierarchically as a tree of nodes and formally specify the behaviour of each node. If we compose the behaviours of a node's children, we can check at once to see whether or not their composition agrees with their parent's specification. If they agree, we have a correct refinement of the design; if not, we know at the earliest possible stage that we are wrong. By deductive argument, we can show the correctness or otherwise of a complete design.

Proceeding in this way a design iteration is driven by the specifier - but he is but one member of a design team and needs feedback from the others. The trick is to keep other views, such as layout, isomorphic to the specification. Indeed they are to be obtained from it by transformation. This enables us to pick off concerns (floorplanning, placement, routing, timing) one at a time and study them separately using current standard tools (MOSSIM, TV, SPICE ...). A negative report is returned if they do not fit the constraints for this view. After all views have been evaluated, the specifier uses his new knowledge to change the specification tree and the next iteration begins. If no 'complaints' are received, ie all constraints have been passed, the chip is laid out from its specification (annotated with electrical properties, areas etc). The latter step is possible today only for gate arrays, but future advances can be interfaced to specification languages like HOL.

ACKNOWLEDGEMENTS.

This work is supported by an Operating Grant from NSERC, and also (1986-1989) by a Strategic Grant from NSERC in which LSI Canada and the Alberta Microelectronics Center are partners. It is a pleasure to record the verified help and encouragement of colleagues in the VLSI team at Calgary, Cambridge University European Silicon Structures, and Lattice Logic (all UK), and Schlumberger Alto Alto Research.

REFERENCES.

[1] H.Barrow. *Proving the correctness of digital hardware designs.* VLSI design, July 1984.

[2] C.Berthet and E.Cerny. *Verification of asynchronous circuits:* behaviours, constraints and specifications. Proceedings of the 1987 Calgary Verification Workshop. Ed. G.Birtwistle and P.A.Subrahmanyam, Kluwer 1987.

[3] G.Birtwistle, et al. *EDICT - an environment for designing ICs.* Research Report 84/155/13, University of Calgary, 1984.

[4] G.Birtwistle, J.Joyce, B.Liblong, T.Melham, and R.Schediwy. *Specification and VLSI design.* Proc. Edinburgh Workshop on Formal Methods in VLSI Design. Ed. G.Milne and P.Subrahmanyan. North Holland 1986.

[5] D.Dill, and E.Clarke. *Automatic verification of asynchronous circuits using temporal logic.* Chapel Hill Conference on VLSI, 1985

[6] A.Cohn. *A proof of correctness of the VIPER microprocessor: the first level.* Proceedings of the 1987 Calgary Verification Workshop. Ed. G.Birtwistle and P.A.Subrahmanyam, Kluwer 1987.

[7] W.J.Cullyer. *Hardware integrity.* The Aeronautical Journal of the Royal Aeronautical Society, August/September, 263-268, 1985.

[8] W.J.Cullyer. *Implementing safety-critical systems: the VIPER microprocessor.* Proceedings of the 1987 Calgary Verification Workshop. Ed. G.Birtwistle and P.A.Subrahmanyam, Kluwer 1987.

[9] *Designing a 32-bit processor that's 'fail-safe'.* Electronics Weekly, January 27, 53-55, 1986

[10] M.Gordon. *A model of register transfer systems with applications to microcode and VLSI correctness.* University of Edinburgh Research Report CSR-82-81, 1981.

[11] M.Gordon. *Proving a computer correct with the LCF-LSM hardware verification system.* University of Cambridge Technical Report 42, 1983.

[12] M.Gordon. *HOL a machine oriented version of higher order logic.* University of Cambridge Technical Report 68, 1985.

[13] M.Gordon. *HOL: a proof generating system for higher order logic.* Proceedings of the 1987 Calgary Verification Workshop. Ed. G.Birtwistle and P.A.Subrahmanyam, Kluwer 1987.

[14] M.Gordon and J.Herbert. *Hardware verification by formal proof.* University of Cambridge Technical Report 74, 1985.

[15] F.K.Hanna, and N.Daeche. *Specification and verification using higher order logic: a case study.* Proc. Edinburgh Workshop on Formal Methods in VLSI Design. Ed. G.Milne and P.Subrahmanyan. North Holland 1986.

[16] M.A.Horowitz. *Timing models for MOS circuits.* PhD Thesis, Stanford University 1984.

[17] W.A.Hunt. *FM8501: a verified microprocessor.* University of Texas at Austin Technical Report 47, 1985.

[18] J.Joyce. *Formal verification and implementation of a microprocessor.* Proceedings of the 1987 Calgary Verification Workshop. Ed. G.Birtwistle and P.A.Subrahmanyam, Kluwer 1987.

[19] P.W.Kollaritsch and N.H.Weste. *TOPOLOGIZER: an expert system translator of transistor connectivity to symbolic cell layout.* IEEE Journal of Solid-State Circuits, vol SC-20 (3), 799-804, 1985.

[20] T-Z.Lin *A hierarchical simulation timing model for digital integrated circuits and systems.* PhD Thesis, CalTech 1984.

[21] E.S.K.Liu. *Two dimensional IC layout compaction.* PhD Thesis, University of Calgary, 1986.

[22] B.Moszkowski. *Reasoning about digital circuits.* PhD Thesis, Stanford University, 1983.

[23] I.Nixon. *IF an idiomatic floorplanner.* Computer Science Research Report, CSR-170-84. Edinburgh University 1984.

[24] P.Penfield, and J.Rubinstein. *Signal delay in RC tree networks.* 18th Design Automation Conf., 613-617, 1981.

[25] R.Schediwy. *A CMOS cell architecture and library.* MSc Thesis, University of Calgary, 1986.

[26] S.Trimberger. *Automated performance optimisation of custom integrated circuits.* PhD Thesis, CalTech 1981.

[27] G.Winskel. *MOS models and logic.* Proceedings of the 1987 Calgary Verification Workshop. Ed. G.Birtwistle and P.A.Subrahmanyam, Kluwer 1987.

VLSI '87, C.H. Séquin (editor)
Elsevier Science Publishers B.V. (North-Holland)
© IFIP, 1988

Temporal Logic Based Fast Verification System Using Cover Expressions

Hiroshi Nakamura   Masahiro Fujita*   Shinji Kono
Hidehiko Tanaka

Department of Electrical Engineering, The University of Tokyo
7-3-1 Hongou, Bunkyo-ku, Tokyo 113, Japan

* FUJITSU LABORATORIES LTD.
1015 Kamikodanaka, Nakahara-ku, Kawasaki 211, Japan

We have developed a verification and synthesis method for hardware logic designs specified by temporal logic using Prolog, but this system was not satisfactory from the view point of speed and memory. Hence, we have implemented another verification system using the C language, where the combinational circuit part is handled in sum-of-product form (cover expressions).

While the time required for the verification in both systems are nearly equal in the cases of small designs, the larger the scale of design is, the more it takes to verify in the Prolog-version system (increases almost exponentially). The C-version system can handle much larger designs in comparison, and it has successfully verified a DMA controller about 1000 times faster than the Prolog-version system.

1 Introduction

In the past several years there has been an increasing interest in verifying, as distinct from simply testing, the proposed logic designs [2,6].

We have developed a verification and synthesis method for hardware logic designs specified by temporal logic with Prolog [4], but this system was unsatisfactory due to its deficiency in speed and memory. Hence, we have implemented another verification system using the C language. This system verifies the synchronous circuits of the synchronization part in the digital systems. In this system, the combinational circuit part is handled in sum-of-product form. Since the undefined values of the variables are directly expressed in this form, the stage of backtracking is reduced and the number of times required to trace the combinational circuit is also reduced.

In this system, we used **Tokio**[9] as a specification description language, which is based on temporal logic, and which enables us to describe a specification in any levels[7].

In this paper, we present the method of verification of hardware logic circuits using temporal logic. We will show the efficiency of this system implemented with the C language, and will compare the results with those implemented with Prolog.

1.1 contents

In the following sections, we discuss the following topics:

Section 2 The structure of the system.

2   The Structure of the Verification System

The structure of the verification system is as shown in Figure 1. This system verifies the synchronous circuits of the synchronization part in the digital systems. The synchronization part is generally small enough to be treated in sum-of-product form. The parts of translating **Tokio** into Linear Time Temporal Logic (**LTTL**; see section 3) and **LTTL** into state diagrams are implemented with Prolog [4]. In this paper, we will not discuss the method of translating **Tokio** into **LTTL**. The basic idea of the verification in this system (see section 3) is generally the same as that in the Prolog-version system. HSL is a hardware description language which only describes the networks among the gates.

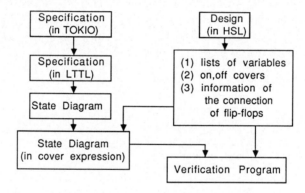

Figure 1: Structure of the Verification System

3   Temporal Logic and State Diagram

In this section, we first briefly introduce temporal logic, then describe the method of translating it into state diagrams, and finally explain the verification method using state diagrams.

3.1   Specifications in Temporal Logic

There are several kinds of temporal logic; here we use Linear Time Temporal Logic (**LTTL**)[11], which is an extension of the traditional logic with four temporal operators added, that is, ○ (next), □ (always), ◇ (sometimes), and U (until). **LTTL** is defined not on continuous states but on discrete states. The first three operators are unary and the last is a binary operator. The meaning of each temporal operator is as follows.

- P (without temporal operators): P is true at the current state.

- oP: P is true at the next state.

- □P: P is true in all future states.

- ◇P: P is true in some future state.

- P U Q: P is true for all states until the first state where Q is true.

LTTL can express a wide variety of properties of sequences, which make it easy to describe the specifications of the hardware. For instance,

> Every state (clock) where signal P is active is immediately followed by a state in which signal Q is active.

is described as

$$\Box(P \rightarrow o\, Q).$$

(From now on, "$A \rightarrow B$" means that "if A holds true then B must be true" .)

3.2 Translation into State Diagrams

Next, we describe the technique to translate **LTTL** formulas into state diagrams. The basic idea of this technique is that **LTTL** formula can be decomposed into sets containing formulas which are either atomic (that is, without temporal operators) or that have o as their main operator. The atomic sets are transition conditions and the rest excluding the outermost o operator are conditions in the next state (details are described in [10]). The decompositions are repeated until every condition in the next states produced during the decompositions are the same as those conditions already treated.

The decomposition rules are as follows.

- $\Box F = F \wedge o\Box F$

- $\Diamond F = F \vee (\sim F \wedge o\Diamond F\{F\})$

- $F1\ U\ F2 = F2 \vee (F1 \wedge \sim F2 \wedge o(F1\ U\ F2))$

(From now on, "$\sim$" represents negative.)
For example, let P, Q and R are atomic and we want to translate

(A) $\Box P$

(B) $\sim ((P \wedge o\Box Q) \rightarrow o\Box R)$

into state diagrams using above rules. It goes as follows;

(A) $\Box P = P \wedge o\underline{\Box P}$

□P

Figure 2: State Diagram (1)

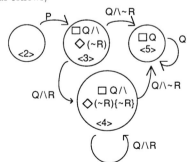

Figure 3: State Diagram (2)

Since the condition in the next state '$\Box P$' (underlined) is the same as the condition at the current state, the decomposition is completed and the corresponding state diagram is obtained as shown in Figure 2.

The translation of (B) goes;

(B) $\sim ((P \wedge o\Box Q) \to o\Box R)$

$= (P \wedge o\Box Q \wedge \sim (o\Box R))$

$= (P \wedge o\Box Q \wedge o\Diamond(\sim R))$

$= (P \wedge o(\Box Q \wedge \Diamond(\sim R)))$

$(\Box Q \wedge \Diamond(\sim R))$ is the next condition and decomposed as follows.

$(\Box Q \wedge \Diamond(\sim R))$

$= Q \wedge o\Box Q \wedge (\sim R \vee (R \wedge o\Diamond(\sim R)\{\sim R\}))$

$= (Q \wedge \sim R \wedge o\Box Q) \vee (Q \wedge R \wedge o(\Box Q \wedge \Diamond(\sim R)\{\sim R\}))$

Therefore, the corresponding state diagram is as shown in Figure 3.

Satisfiability   A **LTTL** formula is satisfiable iff it has at least one infinite sequence of state transitions when it is translated into a state diagram. The logic formula (A) is satisfiable because it has an infinite sequence of state transitions $< 1 >, < 1 >, \cdots$. Similarly, the logic formula (B) is satisfiable because it has an infinite sequence of state transitions $< 5 >, < 5 >, \cdots$. Obviously, an infinite sequence is nothing but a loop. Here, the sequence $< 4 >, < 4 >, \cdots$ is not infinite because it does not satisfy the eventuality $\{\sim R\}$. The eventuality $\{P\}$ means that P must eventually be true in all sequences of future states which follow the state $\{P\}$. Since '$\sim R$' is never true in the sequence $< 4 >, < 4 >, \cdots$, this sequence cannot be infinite.

It is easy to check the satisfiability of products of some logic formulas by tracing each state diagram concurrently. For example, we check the satisfiability of the formula

$\Box(Q \wedge R) \wedge \sim ((P \wedge o\Box Q) \to o\Box R)$.

To do so, we only have to trace the state diagrams shown in Figure 3 and Figure 4 concurrently. The result is as shown in Figure 5. Since there exists no loop (even the sequence $< 4,6 >, < 4,6 >, \cdots$ does not satisfy the eventuality), this formula is unsatisfiable.

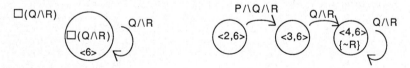

Figure 4: State Diagram (3)   Figure 5: State Diagram (4)

3.3   Verification Based on Temporal Logic

Here, we verify that the hardware designs satisfy the specifications. Let D be the temporal logic expression for the hardware design and S be that for the specification. We must investigate whether the following formula;

D $\to$ S

is valid. To do so, we show that the negation of the formula, that is,

D ∧ ∼ S

is unsatisfiable. In order to check this, we only need to do the following operations;

- Make state diagrams for ∼ S and D.
- Check whether there is any loop for both state diagrams ∼ S and D.

If there exists an infinite sequence, the design does not satisfy the specification (contradiction), and if it does not exist, the design is correct with respect to the specification S.

3.4 Implementation on Prolog

Here, we describe the method of obtaining the state diagram for the design on the Prolog-version system. This is where the difference between the Prolog-version system and C-version system is most obvious.

Since states for the design are nothing but the conditions of the flip-flops, in order to acquire the state diagram for the design, it is only necessary to trace all the gates and decide the next condition of the flip-flops provided that the current condition of them is given.

At first, the description concerning networks between gates is translated into Prolog. For example, AND-gate like in Figure 6 is described as

and2($[I1, I2, O1]$).

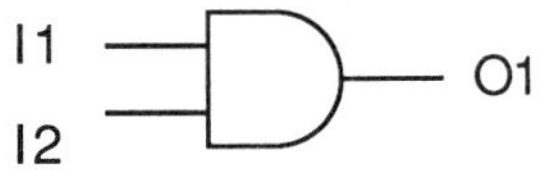

Figure 6: AND gate

There also exists a data base for the functional gates such as

and2([1,1,1]).
and2([A,0,0]).

$\vdots$

and so on. Therefore, if the values of $I1$ and $I2$ are both 1, the value of $O1$ is unified to 1 by unification. The next condition of the flip-flops is only acquired when this operation is executed throughout all the gates.

Here, we must consider the case that the current input values are not fixed such as external inputs. For example, let us consider that $I1 = 1$, and the value of $I2$ is not fixed in Figure 6. In this case, the value of $O1$ is unified to 1 at first because the value of $I2$ is unified to 1 using a data base, and tracing the gates is continued. Even if there does not exist a loop in this case, since there still remains the possibility of contradiction, the verification backtracks and the value of $O1$ is unified to 0 (the value of $I2$ is unified to 0), and the verification continues.

Therefore, in this system, all the gates should be traced every time in obtaining the next condition of the flip-flops and there also exist many backtrackings, which lead to the degradation in the efficiency of the verification. To raise the efficiency of the verification, the number of backtrackings and tracing gates should be reduced. Thus, we suggest two approaches for the efficiency;

1. Use triple-valued logic and handle undefined value.

2. Trace the combinational part of the design only once.

In the next section, we show the more efficient verification system in which these two approaches are implemented.

4   Logic Design Verification using Cover Expressions

The synchronous circuits are divided into the combinational part and flip-flop part as in Figure 7.

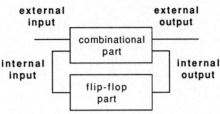

Figure 7: Structure of Synchronous Circuits

Here, we show the verification method by handling the combinational part as cover expressions [3].

At first, we briefly explain the cube and cover.

4.1   Cube and Cover

Let p be the product term associated with a sum-of-product expression of a logic function with n inputs $(x_1, ...x_n)$ and m outputs $(f_1, ..f_m)$. Then p is specified by a row vector $c = [c_1, .., c_n, c_{n+1}, .., c_{n+m}]$, where

$$c_i = \begin{cases} 10 & \text{if } x_i \text{ appears complemented in } p, \\ 01 & \text{if } x_i \text{ appears not complemented in } p, \\ 11 & \text{if } x_i \text{ does not appear in } p, \\ 0 & \text{if } p \text{ is not present in the representation of } f_{i-n}, \\ 1 & \text{if } p \text{ is present in the representation of } f_{i-n}. \end{cases}$$

For example, let us consider a logic function with 4 inputs and 2 outputs. For $f_1 = x_1 x_2 \overline{x_4}$, we have $c = [01\ 01\ 11\ 10\ 1\ 0]$.

The input part of c is the subvector of c containing the first n entries of c. The output part of c is the subvector of c containing the last m entries of c. A variable corresponding to 11 in the input part is referred to as an input don't care, and 00 never appears in the input part.

A set of cubes is said to be a cover C associated with a sum-of-product expression. For

$$f_1 = x_1 x_2 + \overline{x_2} x_3 + x_1 x_3;$$
$$f_2 = \overline{x_2} x_3 + \overline{x_3}\overline{x_4};$$

we have $C = \begin{bmatrix} 01 & 01 & 11 & 11 & 1 & 0 \\ 11 & 10 & 01 & 11 & 1 & 1 \\ 01 & 11 & 01 & 11 & 1 & 0 \\ 11 & 11 & 10 & 10 & 0 & 1 \end{bmatrix}$.

Intersection   Suppose that the intersection (logical and) of two cubes c and d, written as $c \cdot d$, is a cube e. Then, the entries e_i of the cube e are obtained from bit-and operation between the cube c and d.

$$f_1 = x_1 x_2 \quad [01\ 01\ 11\ 1]$$

Example. $\quad f_1 = x_2 x_3 \quad [11\ 01\ 01\ 1]$

$$\Downarrow \qquad\qquad \Downarrow$$

$$f_1 = x_1 x_2 x_3 \quad [01\ 01\ 01\ 1]$$

On-cover and Off-cover For a certain output variable f_i, the set of all cubes where f_i is 1 is called on-cover for the output variable f_i; similarly the set of all cubes which f_i is 0 is called off-cover for the output variable f_i.

4.2 Verification Method using Cover Expressions

The verification flowchart using cover expressions is shown in Figure 8. (From now on, the state diagram corresponding to the Negation of the Specification is called **NS**.) We explain Figure 8 by verifying an example. The example is the control part of a receiver by handshaking [5]. The design is shown in Figure 9 and the specification to be verified is

$$\Box(\text{Call} \rightarrow \Diamond\,\text{Hear})$$

with the condition that flip-flops are reset at the initial state.

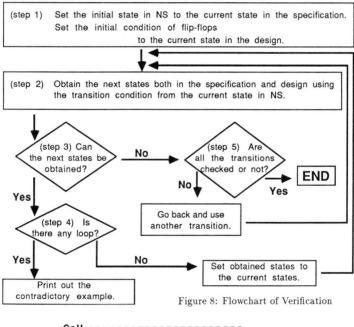

Figure 8: Flowchart of Verification

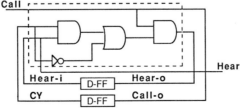

Figure 9: The Control Part of Receiver by Handshaking

(**preparation**) We describe each cube in the form of [Call, CY, Hear-i, Call-o, Hear-o, Hear] (input variables are Call, CY, and Hear-i; output variables are Call-o, Hear-o, and Hear). Then on-cover and off-cover of the combinational part of this circuit are as follows.

$$
\text{Con} = (\text{on-cover})
\begin{bmatrix}
01 & 11 & 11 & 1 & 0 & 0 \\
01 & 10 & 11 & 0 & 1 & 0 \\
01 & 01 & 01 & 0 & 1 & 0 \\
11 & 11 & 01 & 0 & 0 & 1
\end{bmatrix},
$$

$$
\text{Coff} = (\text{off-cover})
\begin{bmatrix}
10 & 11 & 11 & 1 & 0 & 0 \\
10 & 11 & 11 & 0 & 1 & 0 \\
11 & 01 & 01 & 0 & 1 & 0 \\
11 & 11 & 10 & 0 & 0 & 1
\end{bmatrix}.
$$

For example, the second and third rows of Con show that Hear-o is on in two cases, that is, either Call is on and CY is off or Call, CY, and Hear-i are all off.

The connections between flip-flops and the combinational part are described as oHear-i = Hear-o and oCY = Call-o.

The negation of the specification "$\sim \Box(\text{Call} \rightarrow \Diamond\text{Hear})$" is translated into a state diagram such as in Figure 10. This state diagram is nothing but **NS**.

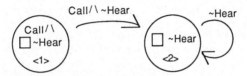

Figure 10: State Diagram for NS

(**step 1**) The initial state of NS is $< 1 >$ in Figure 10. The condition in which the flip-flops are reset is described in the cube form as

Ccond = [11 10 10 1 1 1].

(**step 2**) The transition condition from the state $< 1 >$ in NS is "Call $\wedge \sim$ Hear". The cube for the condition Call is

[01 11 11 1 1 1].

Then the cube for the condition "$\sim$ Hear" is

[11 11 10 1 1 1],

which is taken from the fourth row of Coff, because we only have to derive from the off-cover for the output variable Hear.

Therefore, we obtain the cover for "Call $\wedge \sim$ Hear" as

Ct = [01 11 10 1 1 1].

The next state in NS is $< 2 >$ and that in design are calculated from

Cnext-on = Ccond·Con·Ct

and

Cnext-off = Ccond·Coff·Ct.

(**step 3**) The next state in the design is obtained from Cnext-on and Cnext-off in the following way. If there is a certain output variable that has the value 1 only in the cover Cnext-on, that variable should be 1 at the next state. Similarly, if there exists a certain output variable that has the value 1 only in the cover Cnext-off, that variable should be 0 at the next state.

Here, since

Cnext-on = [01 10 10 1 1 0]

Cnext-off = [01 10 10 0 0 1],

Call-o and Hear-o are 0 and Hear is 1 at the next state. Considering the connections between flip-flops and the combinational part, the next state in the design is as follows.

Cnext = [11 01 01 1 1 1].

If there are some variables that have the value 1 both in Cnext-on and Cnext-off, the values for those variables at the next state can not be decided.

If there exists a variable that has the value 1 neither in Cnext-on nor Cnext-off, the next state in the design can not be obtained. In this case, verification flow goes to the (step 5) as shown in Figure 10.

(**step 4**) Check whether there is any transition loop both in NS and in the design. If there exists a loop and the loop satisfies eventuality, that is a contradictory example.

In this case, since there does not exist any loop, set $< 2 >$ to the current state in NS and set Cnext to the current state in the design (in other words, set Cnext to *new* Ccond), and go to the (step 2).

(**step 2**) The condition of the state transition in NS is
Ct = [11 11 10 1 1 1].
In this case, since Ct·Ccond = **nil**, both Cnext-on and Cnext-off are **nil**. and the next state in the design can not be obtained. Then go to the (step 5).

(**step 5**) Since there remains no state transitions in NS, verification has been finished.

5　Evaluation of Verification System

Here, we use two examples; one is a receiver by handshaking[5] and the other is a DMA controller for a mini computer[1]. As mentioned earlier, we have developed two verification systems; the Prolog-version[4] and the C-language version implemented this time. We verify these two examples using both systems, and discuss the results. We used VAX11/730 (0.2 ~ 0.3 MIPS) and UNIX C-Prolog, which was developed by Edinburgh University [8].

(1) Receiver

The design is shown in Figure 11.

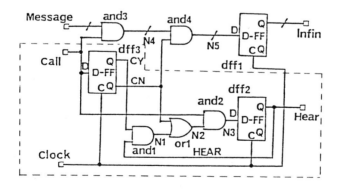

Figure 11: Receiver by Handshaking

We verify the specification

$\Box($ Reset $\rightarrow \Box($ Call $\rightarrow \Diamond$ Hear$))$.

The results are shown in Table 1.

CPU time [sec]		Prolog version		C language version		
		verification part memorizing states		HSL → cover	state diagram → cover	verification part without memorizing states
		without	with			
not filtered	bit width of data path — 1bit	9.88	4.28	2.3 (2.1)	0.7	0.6
	2bits	204.80	28.25	⋮	⋮	⋮
	3bits	5645.80	253.3	(not measured)	(not measured)	⋮
	4bits	⋮	⋮	5.2 (3.3)	1.4	1.4
	8bits	(Keep on increasing)		10.2 (4.7)	2.9	3.1
	16bits	⋮	⋮	26.8 (8.4)	9.1	10.2
filtered		0.87	0.93	*	0.4	0.4

* In C version, the design is filtered in making covers, and so the time depends on the bit width of data path. The time for each width is shown above in (parentheses).

$\left(\begin{array}{c} \text{VAX11/730} \\ \text{0.2~0.3 MIPS} \end{array} \right)$

Table 1: CPU time for Verifying Receiver

Filtering Design Description One technique for restraining the increase of verification time is *filtering design description* which is to extract the necessary part for the verification. For example, as for this specification, there is only one output variable Hear and therefore, we only need to verify the filtered part about Hear (it is surrounded by the broken lines in Figure 11). This technique is implemented on both systems.

Memorization of states In the verification flowchart as in Figure 8, when we get a state that has appeared before, we need not check this state again provided that every state that has appeared is remembered. This is called *memorization of states.*

The basic operation for obtaining the next state is the bit-calculation in this C-version system whereas it is unification in the Prolog-version system. Hence, it takes much more time to obtain the next state in the Prolog-version system than in the C-version. This means that the memorization of states is not so efficient in this system as in the Prolog-version, therefore we do not implement this method on this system.

(2) DMA controller

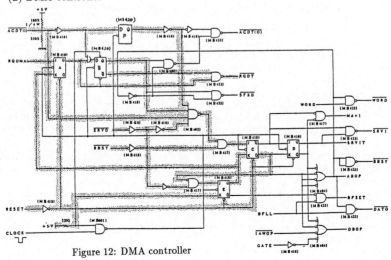

Figure 12: DMA controller

The design is shown in Figure 12. We verify these two specifications.

(1) $\Box((\text{Reset} \wedge \circ \Box \sim \text{Reset} \wedge \Box \sim \text{Acdt}) \rightarrow \circ\Box(\text{Rqdma} \rightarrow \circ \text{Rqdt}))$

(2) $\Box((\text{Reset} \wedge \circ \Box \sim \text{Reset} \wedge \circ \Box \sim \text{Rqdma}) \rightarrow \circ\Box(\text{Acdt} \rightarrow \circ \sim \text{Rqdt}))$

Filtered part is dotted in Figure 12, and the results are shown in Table 2.

CPU time [sec]		Prolog version		C language version		
		verification part memorizing states		HSL → cover	state diagram	verification part without memorizing states
		without	with		→ cover	
not filtered	(1)	> 60,000	> 60,000	22.5	4.5	7.9
	(2)	> 60,000	> 60,000	22.5	4.5	7.8
filtered	(1)	> 60,000	2672.05	18.6	2.1	2.8
	(2)	> 60,000	1923.35	18.6	2.1	2.7

("> 60,000" means over 60,000 seconds)   (VAX11/730 0.2~0.3 MIPS)

Table 2: CPU time for Verifying DMA Controller

Evaluation What differs most between the two systems is the way the combinational part is handled. In the Prolog-version system, all gates are traced every time in obtaining the next state in the design, whereas those are traced once in making covers Con and Coff in the C-version system. Moreover, because the undefined values cannot be handled in Prolog, there exists in the Prolog-version system a lot of needless backtrackings which do not exist in the C-version system.

Therefore, while the time required for the verification in both systems are nearly equal in the cases of small the designs, the larger designs are, the longer it takes to verify in the Prolog-version system (increases almost exponentially). The C-version system can handle much larger designs in comparison, and it verified DMA controller about 1000 times faster than the Prolog-version system. Also, it takes little time to make covers.

6 Verification Method using Terminal Variables

In case the designs become larger and the number of input variables increases, it is not easy to translate the combinational part of the designs into cover expressions. The number of cubes is 2^{n-1} in the worst case where n be the number of input variables. The more complicated the logic of the combinational part becomes, the more it becomes the worst case. Although that part of the synchronization part is not usually so large and complicated as that of the function part, covers may explode.

In this section, we present a verification method using terminal variables which prevents covers from exploding. Introducing terminal variables makes it easy to translate the design into cover expressions, since the logic for output variables becomes simple. This method, however, is not implemented yet.

In using terminal variables, the structure of the synchronous circuits is as shown in Figure 13. Terminal variables should be derived from the original designs on condition that the terminal inputs and outputs have one-to-one correspondence.

The flowchart of the verification is very similar to what is mentioned in section 3. Different points happen where on-cover and off-cover of the combinational part are used. That is,

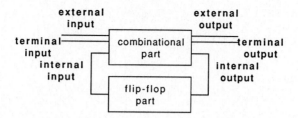

Figure 13: Structure of Synchronous Circuits using Terminal Variables

(1) translating a transition condition of the specification into cover expressions

(2) calculating the next state in the design.

(preparation) First, we get on-cover and off-cover of the combinational part of the circuit. The form of each cube is

[I,FI,TI,O,FO,TO].

Here, each column means as follows.

I : external input variables

FI : internal input variables

TI : terminal input variables

O : external output variables

FO : internal output variables

TO : terminal output variables

Input part consists of I, FI, and TI, and output part consists of O, FO, and TO.

(1) To obtain the cover Ct, which is the transition condition of NS. Ct has the form

[I,FI,TI,O,FO,TO],

and values of all the output variables are 1. Here, we remove terminal variables from the input part of Ct.

removal of terminal variables   In case that a terminal input variable TI_i is 01 (10), the input part of Ct is replaced by that part of the intersection between Ct and some rows of on-cover (off-cover) which corresponds to TO_i — TI_i and TO_i correspond to each other one by one —, and then the value of TI_i is changed into 11. This operation should be repeated until all the values of TI are changed into 11.

If a certain input variable, that is I, FI, and TI, is changed into 00 during this operation, that means "the cube is **nil**" and this cube should be deleted. If the cover Ct becomes **nil** during this operation, this means that this transition condition cannot be satisfied and another transition should be found.

(2) We remove the terminal variables in the same way from the input part of Cnext-on and Cnext-off, which are obtained as described in section 3.

The rest of the verification flowchart are the same as mentioned earlier.

7 Conclusions

We have presented the verification method using cover expressions. The verification system where this method is implemented can verify larger designs and it has verified a DMA controller about 1000 times faster than the Prolog-version system. This is due to handling the combinational part in cover expressions.

We have also presented the verification method using terminal variables. We intend to implement this method and to show the efficiency of this method in the case of much larger designs.

References

[1] *User Device Design Manual for PANAFACOM U-series.*

[2] H.G. Barrow. Verify: a program for proving correctness of digital hardware designs. *Artif,Intel.*, 24:437–492, 1984.

[3] R.K. Brayton, G.D. Hachtel, C.T. McMullen, and A.L. Sangiovannni-Vincentelli. Logic Minimization Algorithms for VLSI Synthesis. Kluwer Academic Publishers.

[4] M. Fujita. Logic Design Assistance with Temporal Logic. In *CHDL '85*, pages 129–138, IFIP, 1985.

[5] M. Fujita. Verification with Prolog and Temporal Logic. In *CHDL '83*, IFIP, 1983.

[6] M.J.C. Gordon. *Why higher-order logic is a good formalism for specifying and verifying hardware.* Technical Report 77, Cambridge University, 1985.

[7] M. Fujita and S. Kono and H. Tanaka. Aid to hierarchical and structured logic design using temporal logic and Prolog. In *Prodeedings.Pt.E*, pages 283–294, IEE, 1986.

[8] F. Pereira. C-prolog users manual version 1.5. 1984.

[9] S. Kono and T. Aoyagi and M. Fujita and H. Tanaka. Implementation of temporal logic programming language Tokio. In *Logic Programming Conference '85*, pages 138–147, ICOT, 1985.

[10] P. Wolper. *Synthesis of Communicating Processes from Temporal Logic Specifications.* Technical Report STAN-CS-82-925, Stanford University, 1982.

[11] Z. Manna and A. Pnueli. *Verification of Concurrent Programs Part1. The Temporal Framework.* Technical Report STAN-CS-81-836, Stanford University, 1981.

VLSI '87, C.H. Séquin (editor)
Elsevier Science Publishers B.V. (North-Holland)
© IFIP, 1988

THE DESCRIPTION AND VERIFICATION OF INPUT CONSTRAINTS AND INPUT-OUTPUT SPECIFICATIONS OF LOGIC SYSTEMS USING A NEW EXTENDED REGULAR EXPRESSION

Shinji KIMURA[†] and Shuzo YAJIMA[††]

[†]Dept. of Electronics Engineering, Faculty of Engineering, Kobe University,
Nada-ku , Kobe-city 657, Japan
[††]Dept. of Information Science, Faculty of Engineering, Kyoto University,
Sakyou-ku, Kyoto-city 606, Japan

The input constraint of a logic system is the assertion to be satisfied by the input to the system, and the correct behavior of the system is guaranteed for the input satisfying the input constraint. The input-output specification of a logic system specifies the correct behavior of the system. In this paper, a new description method of these assertions is proposed and the verification of these assertions are discussed. These assertions are described as sequence sets using a newly proposed concatenation. The verification method of these assertions are based on the decision algorithm of the inclusion of regular sets. The computation time needed to verify these assertions is proportional to the polynomial of the description size.

1. INTRODUCTION

The recent development of the VLSI technology makes it possible to construct large scale logic systems. Then the design of the logic system becomes more and more complex, and it is hard to design a correct system without the support of the computer. There are many studies on the design verification methods to decide the correctness of a given logic system and to find design errors systematically[1]-[12]. These methods are useful for small systems, but the computational complexity of these methods are inhibitive for large scale systems. In this paper, a new efficient verification method is proposed. This method can be applied to the timing verification and the functional verification in the same time. These verifications are normally done independently, but for the detection of design errors in asynchronous systems and communication hardwares these verification must be done in the same time.

In the design verification process, the description of the specification which specifies the correct behavior of the logic system is very important. If the specification is incorrect, the verification is nonsense. The description method shown in this paper is very simple. It corresponds to the timing chart widely used in the description of logic systems. Timing chart can be represented with the set of sequences assuming that time is discrete.

For the specification description, a new extended regular expression is proposed in this paper. The extended regular expression is the regular expression adding a newly proposed concatenation and a closure using the concatenation. These new operations correspond to the timing property of the logic system. The extended regular expression includes all regular expressions, thus the number of states of the deterministic finite automaton (DFA) accepting the sequence set described with the extended regular expression may be the exponent of the length of the description.

This situation makes it time-consuming to decide the set inclusion, set intersection, etc. Thus the restricted form of the extended regular expression is proposed. The number of states of the DFA accepting the sequence set written by the restricted form can be less than or equal to the double of the length of the expression. The restricted form is properly included by the regular sets, but many practical specifications of the logic system can be represented by the restricted form.

The specification is divided into two types. One is for specifying the input given to the system, such as the data input of a clocked D-flip flop must not be changed before and after the clock is up. This is called the input constraint of the system. The correct operation of the system is guaranteed only for the input sequences satisfying the input constraint. Thus if a logic system is constructed from the elements having the input constraint, the satisfaction of the input constraint of each element must be checked. This verification is called the structural verification in this paper.

The other is for specifying the relation between the input sequence and the output sequence. The verification of this specification checks the correct behavior of the logic system, and is called the functional verification.

The verification method proposed in this paper is based on the set inclusion problem. In the verification, the specification is given by the set of sequences, and the sequence set generated by the designed system is extracted. If the specified sequence set includes the extracted sequence set, the design is correct with respect to the specification. If the specifications are written with the restricted extended regular expression, the inclusion problem can be decided with the time complexity proportional to the polynomial of the length of the description.

Chapter 2 of this paper describes some basic definitions. The new extended regular expression is proposed in chapter 3, and the description of the specification of a logic system using the newly proposed extended regular expression is discussed in chapter 4. Chapter 5 discusses the verification of the input constraint of a logic system, and an example of the verification is shown. Chapter 6 discusses the verification of the input-output specification of a logic system, and an example of the verification is shown. Chapter 7 describes the conclusion.

2. PRELIMIMARIES

The definitions of the alphabet, the sequence, the regular expression, and the finite automaton are the same in the reference [13]. As the new concatenation is proposed in the following, the normal concatenation is defined for clarity. The concatenation of sequences x and y is a sequence 'xy' which is made by arranging x and then y. The concatenation is defined for any pair of sequences. The notation E^n is defined for $n = 0$ (E^0) as ε (null string) and for $n = i$ (greater than 0, E^i) as EE^{i-1}.

A logic system is defined by a tuple (Interface, Body). The 'Interface' is a 3-tuple (I, O, ICS), where I denotes a set of input terminals, O denotes a set of output terminals. ICS is a set of sequences satisfying the input constraint of the system. A terminal of a logic system is a tuple (N, Σ), where N denotes a name and Σ denotes an alphabet, the element of which denotes a value appearing at the terminal. Let I be $\{(I_i, \Sigma_i) \mid i = 1, ..., m\}$ and O be $\{(O_j, \Gamma_j) \mid j = 1, ..., n\}$, then the ICS is the subset of $(\Sigma_1 \times ... \times \Sigma_m)^*$, where $\times$ denotes the direct product.

The 'Body' of a logic system is specified by IOS and implemented by (S, C). IOS denotes the input-output specification and is the subset of $((\Sigma_1 \times ... \times \Sigma_m) \times (\Gamma_1 \times ... \times \Gamma_m))^*$. On the other hand, (S, C) corresponds the structural description of the logic system. S is a set of logic systems and C is the connection of these logic systems in S. Logic systems in S are defined recursively by the above definitions.

3. A NEW EXTENDED REGULAR EXPRESSION

In this chapter, a new concatenation and a new closure are proposed and the extension of regular expression with these operations are discussed. The restricted extended regular expression, which is accepted by a deterministic finite automaton with states less than or equal to the length of the expression, is also discussed.

3.1. A NEW CONCATENATION AND A NEW CLOSURE (# (SHARP) CONCATENATION AND # CLOSURE)

A new concatenation for sequences is proposed in the following manner. This new concatenation is called # (sharp) concatenation in this paper. In the definition, the first symbol of a sequence x is denoted as first(x), and the last symbol of x is denoted by last(x). For null string (ε), first(ε) and last(ε) are defined as ε.

[Definition 1] (# (sharp) concatenation)
For sequences x and y, the # (sharp) concatenation x#y is defined as

$$x\#y = \begin{cases} x'a^ny', & \text{if } x = x'a^n,\ y = a^ny',\ \text{last}(x') \neq a \text{ and first}(y') \neq a, \\ \varnothing, & \text{otherwise.} \end{cases}$$

$\varnothing$ denotes that the # concatenation cannot be done. For sequence sets X and Y (X, Y $\subseteq \Sigma^*$), X#Y is defined as $\{x\#y \mid x \text{ is in } X,\ y \text{ is in } Y,\ \text{and } x\#y \neq \varnothing\}$. □

For example, $01\#10 = 010$, $011\#110 = 0110$, $01\#01 = \varnothing$, $(011\#110)\#01 = 01101$, $(100+011)\#$ $(1100+001) = 1001 + 01100$, $1^*\#(10+001+110) = (10+110)$.

The # (sharp) closure is defined in the same manner as in the Kleene-closure (*) using the # concatenation.

[Definition 2] (# (sharp) closure)
The # closure $X^\#$ of a sequence set X is defined as follows.
(1) $\{\varepsilon\} \cup X \subseteq X^\#$.
(2) If x and y are in $X^\#$, x#y is in $X^\#$.
(3) All sequences in $X^\#$ are defined by applying the above rules. □

For example, $(0+1)^\# = \varepsilon + 0 + 1$, $(0^*1^* + 1^*0^*)^\# = (0+1)^*$, $(0011 + 1100)^\# = \varepsilon + 00(1100)^*(11 + 1100) + 11(0011)^*(00 + 0011)$.

For the # concatenation and the # closure, the following properties can be proved easily.
(Properties)
(1) The # concatenation satisfies the associativity.
(2) If X and Y are regular sets, X#Y is also a regular set.
(3) If X is a regular set, $X^\#$ is a regular set. □

The extended regular expression with the # concatenation and the # closure is defined. It is clear from the above properties that the sequence set expressed by the # expression is the regular set.

[Definition 3] (# (sharp) expression)
The # expression on an alphabet Σ is defined as follows.
(1) The regular expression is the # expression.
(2) X and Y are the # expressions, (XY), (X*), (X + Y), (X#Y), $(X^\#)$ are the # expressions.
(3) All # expressions are defined by applying the above rules. □

In the following, the sequence set expressed by the # expression and the # expression itself are regarded as the same. The priority *, $^\#$ > (concatenation) > # > + are assumed between the operations and the parentheses are omitted as long as possible.

3.2. RESTRICTED EXTENDED REGULAR EXPRESSION (FIRST # FORM)

The number of states of the deterministic finite automaton (DFA) accepting the regular set expressed by the regular expression is proportional to the exponent of the length of the expression in the worst case. Thus the restricted form of the extended regular expression called the first # form is proposed to solve the set inclusion problem efficiently. The number of states of the DFA, which accepts the sequence set represented with the first # form, is less than or equal to the double of the length of the expression.

At first, the 0-th form of the regular expression is defined.
[Definition 4] (The 0-th form of the regular expression)
The 0-th form of the regular expression on an alphabet Σ is defined in the following manner.
(1) A symbol 'a' in the alphabet Σ is the 0-th form.
(2) If $a_1, a_2, ..., a_n$ are symbols in Σ, $(a_1 + a_2 + ... + a_n)^*$ is the 0-th form.
(3) Let E_1 and E_2 be the 0-th form expressions. For any sequences x and xay $(x, y \in \Sigma^*, a \in \Sigma)$ in E_1, if a sequence az $(z \in \Sigma^*)$ is not in E_2, then $(E_1 E_2)$ is the 0-th form.
(4) Let E_1 and E_2 be the 0-th form expressions, a sequence set $x(a_1 + a_2 + ... + a_m)y$ be in E_1 and $x(b_1 + b_2 + ... + b_n)z$ be in E_2 $(x, y, z \in \Sigma^*; a_1, ..., a_m, b_1, ..., b_n \in \Sigma)$. If $(a_1 + ... + a_m) \supseteq (b_1 + ... + b_n)$, $(b_1 + ... + b_n) \supseteq (a_1 + ... + a_m)$ or $(a_1 + ... + a_m) \cap (b_1 + ... + b_n) = \varnothing$, then $(E_1 + E_2)$ is the 0-th form.
(5) All 0-th forms are constructed by applying the above rules. □

For example, aab, a*, $(a+b)(a+c)$, $aab+aac$ and $(a+b)(c+d)^*$ are the 0-th form, but $(aa)^*$, $(ab)^*$ and $(a+b)^*(a+c)^*$ are not the 0-th form. The length $|E|$ of the 0-th form E is defined as the number of symbols in the expression excepting the parentheses. For example, $|aa|$ is 2, $|(a+b)(a+c)|$ is 6, $|a^*|$ is 2.

In this paper, the following abbreviations are used.
(1) $(a_1+a_2+...+a_n)^{p,\ p}$ denotes the 0-th form $(a_1+a_2+...+a_n)^p$, and for q $(>p)$ $(a_1+a_2+...+a_n)^{p,\ q}$
   denotes the 0-th form $(a_1+a_2+...+a_n)^p+(a_1+a_2+...+a_n)^{p+1,\ q}$.
(2) $(a_1+a_2+...+a_n)^{p,\ *}$ denotes the 0-th form $(a_1+a_2+...+a_n)^p(a_1+a_2+...+a_n)^*$.

[Property 1]
The sequence set represented by the 0-th form E is accepted by the deterministic finite automaton with $|E|+1$ states or less. □

This property does not be satisfied for the non-restricted regular expression. For example, let R_1 be $(aa)^*$, R_2 be $R_1+(aaa)^*$, R_3 be $R_2+(aaaaa)^*$, ..., R_n be $R_{n-1}+(a^{n\text{-th prime}})^*$, then the length of the R_n is the sum of the primes from the first to the n-th. On the other hand, the number of states of the DFA accepting R_n becomes the product of the primes from the first to the n-th. The proof of this property is shown in the appendix.

The first # form of the extended regular expression is defined using the 0-th form.
[Definition 5] (The first # form)
Let E be the 0-th form satisfying the following conditions, $E^\#$ is the first # form.
(1) Let $A=\{a_1, a_2, ..., a_m\}$ and $B=\{b_1, b_2, ..., b_n\}$ be subsets of an alphabet. For any sequences xA^p and B^qy included in E, one of the following conditions is satisfied.
   (i) $m=n=1$.
   (ii) $A\cap B=\varnothing$.
   (iii) $p=$ * and and $A\supseteq B$ or $B\supseteq A$, or $q=$ * and and $A\supseteq B$ or $B\supseteq A$.
(2) If sequences xa^p, xa^pb^q and a^pb^qy are in E, a sequence b^qy is also in E, where 'a' and 'b' are symbols $(a\ne b)$, x and y are sequences satisfying $\text{last}(x)\ne a$ and $\text{first}(y)\ne b$.   □

For example, $(a)^\#$, $(a^*)^\#$, $(ab+ba)^\#$, $(ac+acd+cde+de)^\#$, $(a^2(b+c)^*+(b+c)^3a^2)^\#$ are the first # form, but $((a+b)^*+(a+c)^*)^\#$, $(a^2(b+c)^3+(b+c)^3a^2)^\#$ are not the first # form. The length of the first # form is defined in the same manner as in the 0-th form. Thus $|E^\#|$ is $|E|+1$.

[Property 2]
Let $E^\#$ be the first # form. The deterministic finite automaton accepting $E^\#$ can be constructed with $2|E^\#|$ states or less.   □

The proof of this property is shown in appendix.

4. THE DESCRIPTION OF INPUT CONSTRAINTS AND INPUT-OUTPUT SPECIFICATIONS USING THE EXTENDED REGULAR EXPRESSION

This chapter discusses the description of the input constraint and the input-output specification of a logic system using the restricted extended regular expression. The input constraint is the specification to the input sequences of a logic system, and the system's correct behavior is guaranteed for the input satisfying the input constraint. The input-output specidfication specifies the relation between the input sequence and the output sequence, and this denotes the system's correct behavior. These specifications are normally shown by timing charts. For example, timing charts in Fig. 1 shows the set-up time and hold time of a clocked JK flip flop. Timing charts can be represented as a set of sequences in the assumption that time is discrete.

The specifications represented by timing charts are divided into two types. One is the changelessness of the signal, and the other is the change of the signal. The changelessness can be represented by a^p, a^*, $(a_1+a_2+...+a_m)^p$ or $(a_1+a_2+...+a_m)^*$. The change can be represented by $(a_1+a_2+...+a_m)$ $(b_1+...+b_n)$ where $\{a_1, ..., a_m\}\cap\{b_1, ..., b_n\}$ is empty. These are the 0-th forms.

There are sequence sets which cannot be described with 0-th form such as $(a+b)^p(b+c)^q$. The sequence sets, however, has no clear changes and the sequence sets satisfying the input constraint or the input-output specification are ones which have clear changes.

The sequence corresponding to timing charts can be repeated as many times as needed. On the repetition, the specification of the signal change must be satisfied. If the # concatenation is used on the repetition, there happens no new signal change and the intervals between signal changes are not changed. Thus the specification is satisfied.

If E is a sequence set corresponding to the timing charts, a sequence in E#E, E#E#E, etc. are also satisfying the specification. Thus $E^\#$ represents the sequence set satisfying the timing specification represented by the timing chart.

An example of the specification description is shown in the following.
[Example]
Fig. 1 shows the specification and the implementation of a clocked JK flip flop. The implementation is shown in Fig. 1 (a), the input constraints called set-up time and hold time is shown in Fig. 1 (b), and the input-output specification is shown in Fig. 1 (c).

The timing chart shown in Fig. 1 (b) can be written as in Fig. 2 with the alphabet {[clock, J, K]^t | clock, J and K denotes the value of each terminal, and ^{t} denotes the transposition}. Fig. 2 (a) shows the case in which the clock input changes from 1 to 0. The set-up time before the clock changes from 1 to 0 is more than 6, this corresponds the super script "6, *" in Fig. 2 (a). The hold time after the clock changes from 1 to 0 is more than 1, this corresponds to the super script "+" in the figure 2 (a). Fig. 2 (b) shows the case in which the clock input changes from 0 to 1 or the case in which the clock does not change. The sequence set satisfying the specification is $\{(\text{Fig.2(a)}) + (\text{Fig.2(b)})\}^\#$.

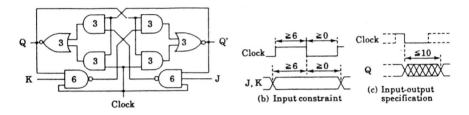

(a) A block diagram

(b) Input constraint

(c) Input-output specification

Fig. 1   The structural description of JK flip-flop.

$$\begin{bmatrix} \text{Clock} \\ J \\ K \end{bmatrix} = \left(\begin{bmatrix} 1 \\ 0 \\ 0 \end{bmatrix}^{6,*} + \begin{bmatrix} 1 \\ 0 \\ 1 \end{bmatrix}^{6,*} + \begin{bmatrix} 1 \\ 1 \\ 0 \end{bmatrix}^{6,*} + \begin{bmatrix} 1 \\ 1 \\ 1 \end{bmatrix}^{6,*} \right) \left(\begin{bmatrix} 0 \\ 0 \\ 0 \end{bmatrix} + \begin{bmatrix} 0 \\ 0 \\ 1 \end{bmatrix} + \begin{bmatrix} 0 \\ 1 \\ 0 \end{bmatrix} + \begin{bmatrix} 0 \\ 1 \\ 1 \end{bmatrix} \right)^+$$

(a) A sequence set satisfying the input constraint
(Clock value changing from 1 to 0)

$$\begin{bmatrix} \text{Clock} \\ J \\ K \end{bmatrix} = \left(\begin{bmatrix} 0 \\ 0 \\ 0 \end{bmatrix} + \begin{bmatrix} 0 \\ 0 \\ 1 \end{bmatrix} + \begin{bmatrix} 0 \\ 1 \\ 0 \end{bmatrix} + \begin{bmatrix} 0 \\ 1 \\ 1 \end{bmatrix} \right)^+ \left(\begin{bmatrix} 1 \\ 0 \\ 0 \end{bmatrix} + \begin{bmatrix} 1 \\ 0 \\ 1 \end{bmatrix} + \begin{bmatrix} 1 \\ 1 \\ 0 \end{bmatrix} + \begin{bmatrix} 1 \\ 1 \\ 1 \end{bmatrix} \right)^+$$

(b) A sequence set satisfying the input constraint
(Clock value changing from 0 to 1)

$$\begin{bmatrix} \text{Clock} \\ J \\ K \end{bmatrix} = \left(\begin{bmatrix} 0 \\ 0 \\ 0 \end{bmatrix} + \begin{bmatrix} 0 \\ 0 \\ 1 \end{bmatrix} + \begin{bmatrix} 0 \\ 1 \\ 0 \end{bmatrix} + \begin{bmatrix} 0 \\ 1 \\ 1 \end{bmatrix} \right)^* + \left(\begin{bmatrix} 1 \\ 0 \\ 0 \end{bmatrix} + \begin{bmatrix} 1 \\ 0 \\ 1 \end{bmatrix} + \begin{bmatrix} 1 \\ 1 \\ 0 \end{bmatrix} + \begin{bmatrix} 1 \\ 1 \\ 1 \end{bmatrix} \right)^*$$

(c) A sequence set satisfying the input constraint
(Clock value not changing)

Fig. 2 Sequence set satisfying the input constraint of JK flip flop.

The timing chart shown in Fig. 1 (c) is written as in Fig. 3 with the alphabet {[clock, Q]ᵗ| clock, Q denotes the value at each terminal, and ᵗ denotes the transposition}. Fig. 3 (a) shows the case in which the clock changes from 1 to 0. The value at the terminal Q can be unknown after the clock changes from 1 to 0. Fig. 3 (b) shows the case in which the clock changes from 0 to 1 or doesn't change. That is not shown explicitly in the timing chart, but the case is needed to the specification. These are all cases for the change of the clock. The sequence set satisfying the specification is {(Fig.3(a)) + (Fig.3(b))}*. □

$$\begin{bmatrix} Clock \\ Q \end{bmatrix} = \begin{bmatrix} 0 \\ 0 \end{bmatrix}^* \begin{bmatrix} 1 \\ 0 \end{bmatrix}^* + \begin{bmatrix} 0 \\ 1 \end{bmatrix}^* \begin{bmatrix} 1 \\ 1 \end{bmatrix}^*$$

(a) A sequence set satisfying the input-output specification
(Clock value changing from 0 to 1 or not changing)

$$\begin{bmatrix} Clock \\ Q \end{bmatrix} = \left(\begin{bmatrix} 1 \\ 0 \end{bmatrix}^+ + \begin{bmatrix} 1 \\ 1 \end{bmatrix}^+ \right) \left(\left(\begin{bmatrix} 0 \\ 0 \end{bmatrix} + \begin{bmatrix} 0 \\ 1 \end{bmatrix} \right)^{1,\,10} + \left(\begin{bmatrix} 0 \\ 0 \end{bmatrix} + \begin{bmatrix} 0 \\ 1 \end{bmatrix} \right)^{10} \left(\begin{bmatrix} 0 \\ 0 \end{bmatrix}^* + \begin{bmatrix} 0 \\ 1 \end{bmatrix}^* \right) \right) +$$

$$\left(\begin{bmatrix} 1 \\ 0 \end{bmatrix}^+ + \begin{bmatrix} 1 \\ 1 \end{bmatrix}^+ \right) \left(\cup_{i=1,9} \left(\begin{bmatrix} 0 \\ 0 \end{bmatrix} + \begin{bmatrix} 0 \\ 1 \end{bmatrix} \right)^i \left(\left(\begin{bmatrix} 1 \\ 0 \end{bmatrix} + \begin{bmatrix} 1 \\ 1 \end{bmatrix} \right)^{1,\,10-i} + \left(\begin{bmatrix} 1 \\ 0 \end{bmatrix} + \begin{bmatrix} 1 \\ 1 \end{bmatrix} \right)^{10-i} \left(\begin{bmatrix} 1 \\ 0 \end{bmatrix}^+ + \begin{bmatrix} 1 \\ 1 \end{bmatrix}^+ \right) \right) \right) \right)$$

(b) A sequence set satisfying the input-output specification
(Clock value changing 1 to 0)

Fig. 3 Sequence set satisfying the input-output specification of JK flip flop.

5. VERIFICATION OF INPUT CONSTRAINT

In this chapter, the verification of the input constrain of a logic system is considered. The input constraint is the assertion to the input sequences of the logic system, and the system's correct behavior is guaranteed for the input satisfying the input constraint. Thus if a logic system is constructed from logic elements which have the input constraints, the input constraint of each subsystem must be verified. Thus the verification of the input constraint is called the structural verification.

[Algorithm 1] (Structural Verification)
Let M be a logic system, ((I, O, ICS), (S, C)) be the structural description of M, and (I_m, O_m, ICS_m) be the interface of a sub-system 'm' in S.
(1) Construct a DFA A_I accepting the permissible input ICS of M.
(2) Select a sub-system 'm' which is not checked in S, and check it. If all sub-systems are checked, this algorithm terminates.
(3) Construct a DFA A_m accepting ICS_m of 'm'.
(4) Construct a DFA A which convert the primary input of M to the input of 'm'.
(5) Construct a DFA A_m' accepting a sequence set given to the input of 'm'. A_m' can be constructed using the modified method to construct the DFA accepting the intersection of $L(A_I)$ and $L(A)$, where $L(A_I)$ and $L(A)$ are the sequence sets accepted by A_I and A, respectively.
(6) Determine whether $L(A_m)$ includes $L(A_m')$. This can be done to decide whether $(\Sigma^* - L(A_m)) \cap L(A_m')$ is empty or not. If so, the input constraints of 'm' have been verified. Otherwise the correct behavior of 'm' cannot be guaranteed, thus it is reported that the input of 'm' is erroneous.
(7) Go to step (2).   □

The computation time of this algorithm is shown. The step (1) is proportional to the length of ICS assuming that ICS is described with the first # form. The step(2) to step (6) is repeated as the number of sub-systems, which is less than or equal to |M|. The step (3) is less than or equal to |M|. The step (4) and (5) can be done with the time proportional to $|A_M| \times |A| \le |M|^2$, and $|A_m'| \le |M|^2$. The step (6) can be done with the computation time less than or equal to $|A_m| \times |A_m'|$, because A_m is the DFA. (The automaton accepts $\Sigma^* - L(A_m)$ can be constructed by changing the final states of A_m.) Thus from the step (2) to the step (5) can be done with the computation time proportional to $|M|^3$. The total computation time is less than or equal to $|M|^4$.

In the following, an example of the structural verification is shown. Fig. 4 shows an example system using the JK flip flop shown in Fig. 1. The integer in Fig. 4 (a) shows the delay time of each logic gate. The pure delay is assumed for the logic gates. Fig. 4 (b) shows the input constraint of the system. The following shows the sequence set with the decimal symbol which denotes clock $\times 2^2 + s_0 \times 2 + s_1$.

$$\{(4+5+6+7)*(0+1+2+3)* +$$
$$\cup_{i=0,4}(4^{i,}*0^{10-i,}* + 5^{i,}*1^{10-i,}* + 6^{i,}*2^{10-i,}* + 7^{i,}*3^{10-i,}*)(4+5+6+7)^+\}^{\#}$$

In the expression, $\cup_{i=0,4}$ E(i) denotes that $E(0)+E(1)+..+E(4)$. Fig. 5 shows the DFA 'A$_i$' accepting the above sequence set. The number of states is 57.

Then the finite automaton that convert the primary input of the system to the input of the JK flip flop is shown. From Fig. 4 (a), the clock input 'f' of the JK flip flop is $\neg(\text{clock}^3 + (\neg s_0 \neg s_1)^6)^3$, where the super script correspond to the delay from each terminal to the terminal 'f'. On the conversion of the sequence set, only the difference of the delay time, which is 3 in this case, has the meaning. The input alphabet of the DFA is $\{0, 1, ..., 7\}$ where each number denotes clock $\times 4 + s_0 \times 2 + s_1$, but the $\{1, 2, 3\}$ and $\{5, 6, 7\}$ need not be distinguished. Thus the alphabet $\{0, \alpha, 1, \beta\}$ is used, where α denotes $\{1, 2, 3\}$ and β denotes $\{5, 6, 7\}$. The state set is $\{q_{abc} | a, b, \text{and } c \text{ is in } \{0, \alpha, 1, \beta\}\}$. The state q_{abc} denotes that the input symbol given 3 steps before is 'a', the input symbol given 2 steps before is 'b' and the input symbol given 1 steps before is 'c'. Thus the state transition function δ of the DFA is defined as $\delta(q_{abc}, d) = q_{bcd}$. The output of the DFA is defined as

$$\gamma(q_{abc}, d) = \quad 1, \text{ if } a \in \{\alpha, \beta\} \text{ and } d \in \{0, \alpha\},$$
$$0, \text{ otherwise.}$$

The number of states of the DFA is 4^3. We call this DFA as 'A'.

The input sequence given to the clock of the JK flip flop is accepted by the DFA constructed from A_I and A. The input constraint of the clock of the JK flip flop $(1^{6,}*0^+ + 0*1*)^{\#}$ can be accepted by the DFA with 8 state. Thus the computation time of this verification is proportional to $57 \times 4^3 \times 8$.

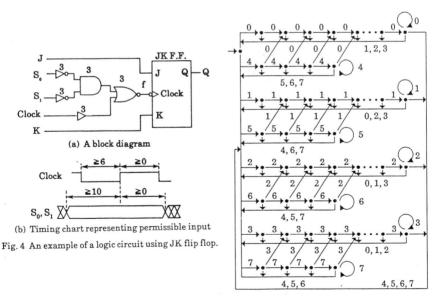

J

S_0 ▷ $\overset{3}{}$

S_1 ▷ $\overset{3}{}$

Clock ▷ $\overset{3}{}$ f

K

JK F.F.

J Q ─ Q

▷ Clock

K

(a) A block diagram

Clock ⊢ ≥6 ⊣ ⊢ ≥0 ⊣

S_0, S_1 ⊢ ≥10 ⊣ ⊢ ≥0 ⊣

(b) Timing chart representing permissible input

Fig. 4 An example of a logic circuit using JK flip flop.

Fig. 5 A DFA accepting the sequence set shown in Fig. 4(b).

6. VERIFICATION OF INPUT-OUTPUT SPECIFICATION

In this chapter, the verification of the input-output specification of a logic system is considered. The verification is called the functional verification, because this verification corresponds directly to the functional correctness of the logic system. The algorithm shown in this chapter resembles to the one shown in chapter 5.

[Algorithm 2] (Functional Verification)
Let M be a logic system, ((I, O, ICS), IOS) be the specification of M and (S, C) be the implementation of M.
(1) Construct a DFA A_I accepting ICS.
(2) Construct a DFA A_{IO} accepting IOS.
(3) Construct a FA A which convert the primary input of M to the primary output of M by (S, C).
(4) Construct a FA A' accepting a sequence set appeared at the output of M when $L(A_I)$ is given. A' can be constructed from A and A_I.
(5) Check whether $L(A')$ is included in $L(A_{IO})$ or not. If included, the verification is done. If not, there may be design errors. ☐

The computation time is proportional to $|M|^3$, this can be checked by the estimation same as in the estimation of the algorithm 1.

In the following, the functional verification of a JK flip flop in Fig. 1 is shown. Fig. 6 shows the DFA accepting the ICS of the JK flip flop. The number of states of the DFA is 26. From the implementation of the JK flip flop shown in Fig. 1 (a), Q is $(\neg Q' + \neg clock \cdot (Q' \cdot J \cdot clock)^6)^6$ and Q' is $(\neg Q' + \neg clock \cdot (Q \cdot K \cdot clock)^6)^6$. The FA converting the primary input of the JK flip flop to the primary output is the FA storing the input symbols during 6 steps. Thus the state set is $\{q_{abcdef} \mid a, b, c, d, e, \text{ and } f$ are in $\{clock \times 2^4 + J \times 2^3 + K \times 2^2 + Q \times 2 + Q'\}\}$. The number of states is $(2^5)^6 = 2^{30}$. As there are symbols that need not be distinguished such as in the example of chapter 5, the number of states becomes 10^6 or so.

The IOS of the JK flip flop is shown in Fig. 1 (c). This is accepted by the DFA in Fig. 7 which has the 24 states. The functional verification can be done by the decision that $L(A_{IO})$ includes $L(A_I \cap A_M)$. The computation time is proportional to $26 \times 10^6 \times 24$.

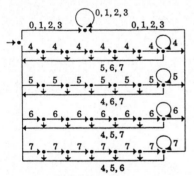

Fig. 6   A DFA accepting $((0+1+2+3)^*$
$(4+5+6+7)^* + (4^{6,*} + 5^{6,*} + 6^{6,*} + 7^{6,*})$
$(0+1+2+3)^+)^*$.

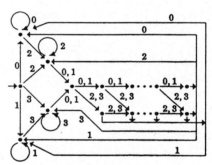

Fig. 7   A DFA accepting the sequence set shown in Fig. 1(c).

7. CONCLUSION

This paper proposes a new extended regular expression with a new concatenation and a new closure, and shows the verification method of the specification represented with the extended regular expression. The description method is very suitable for the timing specification shown by timing charts.

The verification problem reduces to the sequence set inclusion problem, and it is solved using a finite automaton accepting the sequence set. That has been considered very time consuming, as the number of states of the DFA accepting the regular expression may be the exponent of the length of the expression. This paper proposes a restriction for the extended regular expression, such that the number of states of the DFA accepting the restricted expression is less than or equal to the double of the length of the expression. The restriction is practical for the description of the specification of the logic systems.

ACKNOWLEDGEMENTS

The authors thank to Dr. Yasuura of Kyoto University for helpful suggestions to writing this paper, and thank to Professor Haneda of Kobe University for his support to writing this paper. The discussions with the colleagues of the Yajima Lab. at Kyoto University are very helpful.

REFERENCES

[1] H. E. Krohn : "System Verification of Large Scale Scientific Computers", Proc. 14th DA Conf., pp. 431-438, 1977.

[2] M. A. Wold : "System Verification and Performance Analysis", Proc. 15th DA Conf., pp. 264-270, 1978.

[3] T. M. McWilliams : "Verification of Timing Constraints on Large Digital Systems", Proc. 17th DA Conf., pp. 139-147, 1980.

[4] H. Eveking : "The Application of CONLAN ASSERTIONS to the Correct Description of Hardware", Proc. 5th Int. Symp. on CHDL, pp. 37-50, 1981.

[5] T. Sakai, Y. Tsuchida, et. al., "An Interactive Simulation System for Structured Logic Design - ISS'" Proc. 20-th DA Conf., pp. 747-754, 1982.

[6] G. V. Bochmann : "Hardware Specification with Temporal Logic: an Example", IEEE Trans. Comput., vol. C-31, no. 3, pp. 223-231, 1982.

[7] F. Maruyama and M. Fujita, "Hardware Verification," IEEE Computer, 1985.

[8] P. Amblard, P. Caspi, and N. Halbwachs : "Describing and Reasoning about Circuits Behavior by means of Time Function," Proc. 7th Int. Symp. on CHDL , pp. 39-48, 1985.

[9] G. J. Milne : "Simulation and Verification: Related Techniques for Hardware Analysis," Proc. 7th Int. Symp. on CHDL , pp. 404-417, 1985.

[10] F. K. Hanna and N. Daeche : "Specification and Verification using Higher-Order Logic," Proc. 7th Int. Symp. on CHDL , pp. 418-433, 1985.

[11] J. Herbert : "The Application of Formal Specification and Verification to a Hardware Design," Proc. 7th Int. Symp. on CHDL , pp. 434-451, 1985.

[12] K. J. Supout and S. J. Friedman : "A New Method for Verifying Sequential Circuits," Proc. 23rd DA Conf., pp. 200-207, 1986.

[13] J. E. Hopcroft and J. D. Ullman, Introduction to Automata Theory, Languages and Computation, Addison-Wesley, 1979.

APPENDIX

This appendix describes the proof of the properties of the extended regular expression shown in chapter 3.

[Property 1]
The sequence set represented by the 0-th form E is accepted by the deterministic finite automaton with $|E| + 1$ states or less. □

(Proof)
The construction of the deterministic finite automaton (DFA) with $|E| + 1$ states or less accepting the 0-th form E is shown. In the proof, the stronger condition is also proved that if the DFA accepting E has a transition to the initial state, the number of states of the DFA is less than or equal to $|E|$.

The DFA accepting a symbol a can be constructed with 2 states, and the DFA accepting $(a_1 + ... + a_n)^*$ can be constructed with 1 state. These satisfy the stronger condition.

Let M_1 be the DFA accepting the 0-th form E_1, and M_2 be the DFA accepting the 0-th form E_2. The DFA M accepting $(E_1 E_2)$ can be constructed by a direct sum of M_1 and M_2, and then adding state transitions from the final states of M_1 to the states of M_2 that can be reached from the initial state of M_2 with one symbol. If the initial state of M_2 is the final state of M_2, the final states of M_1 and those of

M_2 are final states of M. Otherwise, the final states of M_2 are the final states of M. There is no non-deterministic state transition by the condition of the 0-th form. The length of (E_1E_2) is $|E_1|+|E_2|$. If there is no transition to the initial state of M_2, the initial state of M_2 is not needed in M, thus the number of states in M is less than or equal to $(|E_1|+1)+(|E_2|+1)-1=|E_1|+|E_2|+1$. If there exist transitions to the initial state of M_2, the number of states of M_2 is less than or equal to $|E_2|$, thus the number of states of M is $(|E_1|+1)+|E_2|$. The stronger condition is satisfied if there exist transitions to the initial state of M_1.

The DFA M' accepting (E_1+E_2) can be constructed by a direct product of $M_1=(Q_1, \Sigma, \delta_1, q_{01}, F_1)$ and $M_2=(Q_2, \Sigma, \delta_2, q_{02}, F_2)$. In the usual case, the number of states of the DFA made by the direct product becomes the product of the numbers of states of each DFA. In this case, however, the number of states is the sum of those of each states. Let (q_1, q_2) be a state of M, W_1 be $\{x\in\Sigma^*|\ \delta_1(q_{01}, x)=q_1\}$, and W_2 be $\{y\in\Sigma^*|\ \delta_2(q_{02}, y)=q_2\}$. From the condition of the 0-th form, $W_1\supseteq W_2$ or $W_2\supseteq W_1$ is satisfied. Thus if $W_2\supseteq W_1$, (q_1, q_2) can be represented by q_1, and if $W_2\supseteq W_1$, (q_1, q_2) can be represented by q_2. Thus the number of states of M' is $(|E_1|+1)+(|E_2|+1)=(|E_1|+|E_2|+1)+1=|(E_1+E_2)|+1$. The stronger condition can be checked easily.   □

[Property 2]
Let $E^\#$ be the first # form. The deterministic finite automaton accepting $E^\#$ can be constructed with $2|E^\#|$ states or less.   □

(Proof)
For the 0-th form E, the DFA accepting E with $|E|+1$ states can be constructed from the property 1. Let the DFA accepting E be $M_X=(Q, \Sigma, \delta, q_0, F)$ and the DFA accepting $E^\#$ be M.

The idea of the construction of M is as follows. Let the state set of M be $Q\times Q$, and a state (q_1, q_2) of M be reached with a sequence $x=x'a^n$ $(\text{last}(x')\neq a)$. The first state q_1 is used for a transition with x $(q_1=\delta(q_0, x))$, and the second state q_2 is used for a transition with a^n $(q_2=\delta(q_0, a^n))$. The check of the overlapping part is done using the second state q_2. If q_1 is a final state of M_X, there may be a state transition with a symbol b $(\neq a)$ from a state q_2 from the definition of the # concatenation.

M is $(Q\times Q, \Sigma, \delta', (q_0, q_0), \{(q_0, q_0)\}\cup(F\times Q))$, where δ' is defined as follows. For a symbol 'a', if $\delta(q, a)$ is a sink state and there exists a state q' such that $q=\delta(q', a)$, it is called in-only for a state q . If there is no state q' such that $q=\delta(q', a)$ and $\delta(q, a)$ is a sink state it is called incompatible . If $\delta(q, a)$ isn't a sink state and there is no state q' such that $q=\delta(q', a)$ it is called out-only for a state q. Otherwise it is called in-out. A sink state is written as q_s.

$\delta'((q_1, q_0), a) = \begin{cases} (\delta(q_1, a), q_0), & \text{if } a \text{ is in-out for } q_1, \\ (\delta(q_1, a), \delta(q_0, a)), & \text{if } a \text{ is out-only for } q_1. \end{cases}$

$\delta'((q_1, q_2), a) = \begin{cases} (\delta(q_1, a), \delta(q_2, a)), & \text{if } a \text{ is in-out for } q_1 \text{ and } q_2, \\ (\delta(q_1, a), q_0), & \text{if } a \text{ is in-out for } q_1 \text{ and isn't in-out for } q_2, \\ (\delta(q_1, a), \delta(q_0, a)), & \text{if } a \text{ is out-only for } q_1. \\ (\delta(q_2, a), \delta(q_0, a)), & \text{if } a \text{ is incompatible for } q_1, a \text{ is out-only for } q_2, \text{ and } q_1 \text{ is a final state.} \\ (q_s, q_s), & \text{otherwise.} \end{cases}$

$\delta'((q_s, q_s), a) = (q_s, q_s).$

The states of M are the direct product of the states in M_X, but the state (q_1, q_2) can be represented by q_1 or q_2 in the same manner as in the proof of property 1. The state q_1 may be the representative of a state (q_1, q_2) and a state (q_1, q_0). Thus the number of states of M is less than or equal to $2|M|=2|E|$.

The sequence in $\{\varepsilon\}\cup E$ is clearly accepted by M. Let sequences $x=x'a^n$ and $y=a^ny'$ be accepted by M, the state transition sequence for x be $q_x(q_{11}, q_{12})(q_{21}, q_{22}) ...(q_{n1}, q_{n2})$, where q_x is a state transition sequence for x', and the state transition sequence for y be $(q_0, q_0)(q_{21}, q_0) ...(s_{n1}, q_0)s_{y'}$, where $s_{y'}$ is a state transition sequence for y'. Then the sequence $q_x(q_{11}, s_{21})(q_{21}, s_{31}) ...(q_{n1}, s_{n2})s_{y'}$ is also the state transition sequence of M, and accepted by M. Thus the sequences in $E^\#$ are all accepted by M.

Let $(q_0, q_0)(q_{11}, q_{12})(q_{21}, q_{22})...,(q_{n1}, q_{n2})$ be the state transition sequence of a sequence $x=a_1a_2...a_n$ accepted by M. If $(0\leq i\leq n-1)$ $q_{i+1, 1}$ is $\delta(q_{i1}, a_i)$ for any i, x is in E and thus x is in $E^\#$. If there exists i $(1\leq i\leq n)$ such that $q_{i, 1}$ isn't $\delta(q_{i-1, 1}, a_i)$, there exists j $(j\leq i-1)$ such that x is $a_1a_2...a_{i-1}\#a_ja_{j+1}...a_n$ from the definition of M. If $a_1a_2...a_{i-1}$ and $a_ja_{j+1}...a_n$ are accepted by M_E, x is in $E^\#$. If not, the above discussion for a sequence x can be done for sequences $a_1a_2...a_{i-1}$ and $a_ja_{j+1}...a_n$. Thus x is in $E^\#$.   □

VLSI '87, C.H. Séquin (editor)
Elsevier Science Publishers B.V. (North-Holland)
© IFIP, 1988

Efficient, Stable Algebraic Operations on Logic Expressions

Patrick C. McGeer

Computer Science Division,
The University of California at Berkeley,
Berkeley, CA,
94720.

Robert K. Brayton

IBM TJ Watson Research Center,
Yorktown Heights, NY,
10598.

The set of multivariate boolean functions over the variables $x_1, \ldots, x_m$ is considered as the set of multilinear polynomials with coefficients in [0,1] over the literals $\{x_1, \overline{x}_1, \ldots, x_m, \overline{x}_m\}$. We denote this set of polynomials as $\mathbf{B}[\overline{x}]$, and call the set of polynomial operations over them *algebraic* operations. It is shown that the multiplication of two members of $\mathbf{B}[\overline{x}]$ is contained in $\mathbf{B}[\overline{x}]$ iff their supports are disjoint. It is shown that every algebraic operation may be made stable with optimum time complexity. In particular, this permits the development of linear-time algorithms to perform algebraic or "weak" division, a problem previously thought to be of $\theta(n \log n)$ time complexity.

1. Introduction

Multi-level boolean minimization is an important problem in the synthesis of VLSI circuits. A major component of boolean minimization is that of obtaining optimal *factored forms* of boolean functions; that is, of converting a standard sum-of-products form of a logic function into a form with fewer, but potentially more complex terms. This involves repeated use of multiplication and division procedures.

Boolean procedures, however, are extremely difficult. Hence it is desirable to exploit fast, heuristic algorithms. Algebraic algorithms have been suggested by Brayton [Bra86a], since one can devise fast algorithms for algebraic manipulation, and the results have been shown experimentally to approach those found by boolean procedures [Bra82] [Bra86a].

In this paper, we pursue the question of the optimum efficiency for algebraic operations to be used as part of fast heuristics in a logic synthesis system. In particular, we study the basic algebraic operations of division, multiplication, equality test, addition and algebraic subtraction.

In current systems for multi-level synthesis, the speed of division and equality test for algebraic expressions are limited by the requirement that the terms of the expressions under manipulation be sorted [Bra82]. If we can guarantee that the input expressions to division or equality test are already sorted and that the results remain sorted, then we might hope to achieve optimum linear-time algorithms for these operations. We call operations that preserve sorted order *stable*.

This research has been sponsored by the Defense Advanced Research Projects Agency (DoD) ARPA Order No. 4871. Monitored by Space and Naval Warfare Systems Command under Contract No. 00039-84-C-0089.

2. Definitions

For a logic expression f, its *support*, denoted $sup(f)$, is defined as the set of literals $\{l_i \mid l_i \text{ appears in } f\}$.

We say that a logic expression f is a *cube* iff f is written as a product of literals. If $f = f_1 + \ldots + f_n$, f_i is a cube for all i, we say that the size of f, denoted $|f|$, is n.

We say that a logic expression f is *cube-free* iff there is no cube c s.t. $f = qc$.

We say that logic expressions $f = f_1 + \ldots + f_n$ and $g = g_1 + \ldots + g_m$ are *algebraically equal*, written $f = g$, iff for each cube f_i there exists g_j s.t. $f_i \equiv g_j$, and for each g_j there exists f_i s.t. $f_i \equiv g_j$.

3. Logic Expression Representation and Orderings

A logic expression $f = f_1 + \cdots + f_n$ is represented as a list of its cubes f_i. The cubes are represented as sets of literals. Hence for c_1, c_2 cubes $c_1 c_2 = c_1 \bigcup c_2$; $\dfrac{c_1}{c_2} = c_1 - c_2$ (as sets). The empty set of literals, ϕ, is the representation of the cube **1**. The set of sets over $\bar{x}$ is denoted as $\mathbf{C}(\bar{x})$.

3.1. Representation of Cubes.

In the multi-level synthesis system MIS[Bra86b], cubes are represented as subsets of some set of literals, Ψ. If the sets are represented in the manner of Pascal's bit-vectors [Jen78], the set operations are often single machine instructions. Strictly speaking, such set operations are linear in $|\Psi|$. This is dependent upon representation, so for the remainder of this paper we express complexity in terms of set operations; the reader concerned with exact machine complexity should multiply the complexity figures given here by $|\Psi|$.

3.2. Valuations and the Natural Valuation

The representation of cubes in MIS, together with the Pascal representation of sets allows us to associate a unique integer $v(c)$ with a cube c using the obvious interpretation of c's bit-vector representation. We call $v(c)$ the *natural valuation* on $\mathbf{C}(\bar{x})$.

We do not wish to restrict the algorithms given here to a bit-vector representation of cubes, and hence we generalize this notion to that of a *valuation* as follows:

We say that a 1-1 mapping $v : \mathbf{C}(\bar{x}) \to \mathbf{Z}$ is a *valuation* on $\mathbf{C}(\bar{x})$ if

$v(\phi) = 0$

$v(x) > 0 \quad x \neq \phi$

$v(c_1 c_2) \leq v(c_1) + v(c_2)$

$v(c_1 c_2) > v(c_1) \quad c_2 \neq \phi$

We say that v is a *normal valuation* if $v(c_1 c_2) = v(c_1) + v(c_2)$.

For the remainder of this paper, if $v(c_1) > v(c_2)$ we shall often write $c_1 > c_2$ when the meaning is clear from context.

3.3. Ordering of Logic Expressions and Stable Operations

We say that a logic expression $f = f_1 + \ldots + f_n$ is *ordered* with respect to a valuation function v iff $v(f_i) > v(f_j)$ for $i < j$. Note that there are no duplicate cubes in an ordered logic expression. This permits us to define more precisely stability: we say that an $n{:}m$ operation $\Gamma : \Gamma(u_1, \ldots, u_n) = > (v_1, \ldots, v_m)$ is *stable* if u_i ordered for all i implies v_j ordered for all j.

Theorem 2.1: Let f, g be ordered logic expressions. Then $f = g$ iff $f \equiv g$.

Proof: Let f, g ordered. Then if $f_1 < g_1$, $f_i < g_1$ for all i and hence $f \neq g$. Similarly if $f_1 > g_1$ $f \neq g$. Hence if $f = g$ then $f_1 = g_1$. It is trivial to extend this argument to show that if $f = g$, f, g ordered then $|f| = |g|$ and $f_i = g_i$ for all i. The converse is trivial. Hence the theorem. ∎

With this in hand, we describe the basic objective of this paper. As we mentioned above, current systems support linear-time algorithms for multiplication. Addition, subtraction, equality, and division all seem to be $O(n \log n)$, since the best known algorithms order the input functions before operations are begun, and the time for sorting is the critical path of the operation.

Now, we can clearly start with an initial set of sorted logic expressions. Therefore, if we can devise stable algorithms for the basic algebraic operations of division, multiplication, addition, and subtraction we may be able to achieve linear time algorithms. Further, since the outputs of these operations are themselves sorted, manipulations can continue in linear time.

4. Addition, Subtraction, and Equality

Algebraic equality is simply a comparison of the elements of two sorted lists to determine if they are identical; addition is simply a merging of two sorted lists into a single list. $h = f - g$ is defined for all logic expressions f, g; c is a cube of h iff c is a cube of f and c is not a cube of g. h may be formed, ordered, by taking the difference of two sorted lists.

It is easy to see that equality is $O(\mid f \mid)$; addition and subtraction are $\theta(\mid f \mid + \mid g \mid)$.

5. Stable, Linear Algebraic Multiplication

The multiplication operation over $\mathbf{B}[\overline{x}]$ is defined as it is over the polynomial domain $\mathbf{Z}_2[\overline{x}]$. We wish to define a linear multiplication algorithm on $\mathbf{B}[\overline{x}]$ such that, if $f = gh$ for g, h in $\mathbf{B}[\overline{x}]$, ordered, then f is in $\mathbf{B}[\overline{x}]$ and ordered.

Theorem 5.1: Let $f = gh$, f, g, h in $\mathbf{B}[\overline{x}]$. Then $sup(g) \bigcap sup(h) = \phi$.

Proof: Suppose not. Let $x \in sup(g) \bigcap sup(h)$. Then there is some cube g_i of g and h_j of h such that $x \in g_i \bigcap h_j$. Then $x^2 \in g_i h_j$. Hence f not in $\mathbf{B}[\overline{x}]$ ∎.

This theorem justifies the restriction found in [Bra86a]; $f = gh$ is defined iff $sup(g) \bigcap sup(h) = \phi$. Following this tradition, we assume this restriction.

This theorem is the key distinction between algebraic and boolean operations. It is easy [Bra86a] to see that if multiplication of logic expressions of non-disjoint supports is permitted, then the division operation over logic expressions is either ill-defined, or intractable, or both. What we have shown here, formally, is that without this restriction we cannot apply polynomial algorithms to the problem of obtaining factored forms.

Note, by the way, that if this restriction is assumed then the natural valuation becomes a normal valuation.

Theorem 5.2: Let $f = gh$, g, h ordered. Then for each cube f_i of f, there is no cube f_j, $i \neq j$, $f_i = f_j$.

Proof: Let $f_i = g_k h_l$, $f_j = g_p h_q$. If $f_i = f_j$ then $g_k h_l = g_p h_q$. Since $c_1 c_2 = c_1 \bigcup c_2$ and since $g_r \bigcap h_s = \phi \ \forall \ r, s$, we must have $g_k = g_p$ and $h_l = h_q$. Since h, g ordered, $k = p$ and $l = q$, hence $i = j$ ∎.

Theorem 5.3 (The Counting Theorem): Let $f = gh$, g, h ordered. Then $\mid f \mid = \mid g \mid \mid h \mid$.

Proof: Clearly $\mid f \mid \leq \mid g \mid \mid h \mid$. If $\mid f \mid < \mid g \mid \mid h \mid$, then there are k, l, q, p $k \neq p$, $l \neq q$ such that $g_k h_l = g_p h_q$, contradicting theorem 5.2. Hence $\mid f \mid = \mid g \mid \mid h \mid$ ∎.

Corollary 5.3: The set of cubes of f is simply the pairwise union of the set of cubes of g and the set of cubes of h.

5.1. The Stable Multiplication Problem.

An obvious algorithm for multiplication is produceed by Corollary 5.3; simply form the pairwise union of the cubes of g with the cubes of h. The stable multiplication problem is the problem of forming the unions in such a way that the product is ordered if the factors are ordered. An upper bound is given by $O(\mid g \mid \mid h \mid \log \mid g \mid \mid h \mid)$, and a lower bound by $O(\mid g \mid \mid h \mid)$.

Under the natural valuation v, this problem is a specialization of Berlekamp's problem[Har75]. Given sorted lists of integers X, Y, $\mid X \mid = n$, $\mid Y \mid = m$, and a matrix B, $B_{ij} = X_i + Y_j$. Can B be sorted any faster than $nm\log nm$? The question is open: there is an information-theoretic lower bound of nm, but no algorithm has yet been found faster than the naive upper bound given by a standard sorting algorithm.

It is easy to see that the stable multiplication problem is a special case of Berlekamp's problem; take $X_i = v(g_i)$, $Y_j = v(h_j)$; by theorem 5.1, g_i and h_j are disjoint for all i,j, and hence X_i and Y_j are bit-disjoint; that is, their binary representations have a bitwise *and* of 0. Of course, this means that $v(g_i h_j) = X_i + Y_j = $ the bitwise *or* of X_i and Y_j $\forall\, i,j$.

Figure 1: Computation of fg -- Matrix Method

101010
100010
001010
000010

010100
010001
010000
000001

f = uwy + uy + wy + y   g = vx + vz + v + z

	f1	f2	f3	f4
g1	111110	110110	011110	010110
g2	111011	110011	011011	010011
g3	111010	110010	011010	010010
g4	101011	100011	001011	000011

fg = uvwxy + uvwyz + uvwy + uvxy + uvyz + uvy + uwyz + uyz
    + vwxy + vwy + vxy + vxz + vy + wyz + yz

An example is shown in figure 1. In this example, the literals are ordered alphabetically: $u > v > w > x > y > z$.

A study of the matrix in figure 1 is instructive, and provides the essential clue to the remainder of this paper. Each element of the first two columns of the matrix is greater than any element of the remaining columns of the matrix. Hence, to produce the result in ordered form, we can take a vertical slice through the matrix, forming the product cubes in the first two columns and prepending these to the product cubes in the last two columns. Now, focussing on the first two columns, notice that any element of the first three rows is greater than any element of the last row. In fact, we shall see below that we can always take either a vertical or horizontal slice through *any* multicolumn, multirow multiplication matrix, and thus split the problem into two parts. Since the resulting two matrices are themselves multiplication matrices, we can apply this procedure recursively to form the ordered product.

Although this observation gives some hope that this specialization of Berlekamp's problem may be solved efficiently, it is easy to show that searching for the appropriate horizontal or vertical slice at each recursive step of the algorithm must yield an $O(n^2 m^2)$ complexity.[1] Hence it is critical that all the slices for a problem be determined statically, before the multiplication is begun. We attack this problem using a new data structure, the *slicing tree* of a logic expression.

---

[1] the recurrence relation for the worst case of such an algorithm is $T(n,m) = n + m + T(n-1,m)$, or $T(n,m) = n + m + T(n,m-1)$; using symmetry of the variables, solving $T(n) = n + T(n-1)$ yields the solution.

5.2. The Slicing Tree of a Logic Expression

If we refer to the matrix of figure 1 again, we observe that the high-order bit is set to 1 in columns 1 and 2, and 0 in columns 3 and 4. Similarly, for the first two columns, the second-highest order bit is 1 in rows 1-3 and 0 in row 4. Of course, in any non-constant sorted list of integers, we have some highest-order bit that changes, which we'll call the *change bit*. Now, consider Berlekamp's problem as given above. Both X and Y have change bits, $change_X$ and $change_Y$. Since X and Y are bit-disjoint, $change_X \neq change_Y$. If we consider the outer-product sum B, B has a change bit, $change_B$. Now, clearly if a bit changes from 1 to 0 in B, it must also change somewhere in X or Y. Hence $change_B = max(change_X, change_Y)$. Further, every integer in B with $change_B$ set to 1 is greater than any integer in B with $change_B$ set to 0.

These considerations lead to the realization that the change bits of the lists of integers correspond to the positions of the slices that we saw in the matrix of figure 1. Further, we can certainly determine the positions and values of the change bits of X and Y statically, and organize them in a tree. We now formalize, generalize and prove these notions, which lead directly to a stable, linear, multiplication algorithm.

Of course, change bits are associated with a particular representation, which we've used to motivate these ideas. For the remainder of this section, we return to the notions of literals, sets of literals, and valuations.

We define $on(f) = \{x \in f_i \ \forall \ i\}$. The *most significant literal* of f, $msl(f)$, is the highest-value literal of $sup(f) - on(f)$.[2]

Figure 2: Difference Array and Slicing Tree of f

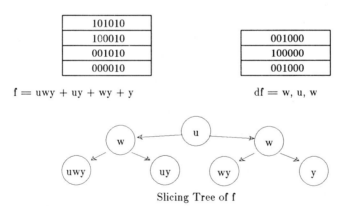

Slicing Tree of f

We define the *slicing tree* of f, S_f recursively. If f is a cube, then f is a slicing tree of height 0. If f is an ordered, non-cube logic expression, then let $x = msl(f)$, and let i be such that $x \in f_i$, $x \notin f_{i+1}$. Then x is the root of f's slicing tree. The left subtree is the slicing tree of $f_1 + \dots + f_i$, and the right subtree the slicing tree of $f_{i+1} + \dots + f_n$.

Let $f = f_1 + f_2 + \dots + f_n$ be a ordered logic expression. We define the *difference array* of f, df_i for $1 \leq i \leq n-1$ as the highest-valued literal of $f_{i+1} - f_i$. The difference array of a logic expression is of use in constructing its slicing tree.

The difference array and slicing tree of the expression f of figure 1 is shown in figure 2.

---

[2] Note that in our previous discussion, $msl(f)$ is the change bit of f's representation as a list of integers

We have devised a $\theta(n)$ algorithm for the construction of slicing trees. The algorithm is conceptually simple, but has a difficult proof of correctness and a non-trivial derivation for its bound. We leave its discussion to Appendix A. For the moment, we state the principal result of the appendix:

Theorem A.3: $S_f = buildSliceTree(f)$ can be formed in time $\theta(\,|\,f\,|\,)$.

Proof: See Appendix A.∎

5.3. Performing the Multiplication

Here we formally state and prove the observations we made above that underlie the multiplication algorithm.

Lemma 5.1: The leaves of the slicing tree of f are its cubes, and they are in order.

Proof: Induction on the height of the slicing tree, $h(S_f)$. If $h(S_f)=1$, the result follows by definition. Assume true for $h(S_f)<r$. If $h(S_f)=r$, let x be the root. Then the leaves of the left subtree of x are $f_1, \ldots, f_i$ and the leaves of the right subtree of x are $f_{i+1}, \ldots, f_n$. Since both subtrees are slicing trees of height $<r$, the leaves of both subtrees are in order. Since an inorder presentation of the leaves has the leaves of the left subtree followed by those of the right, the result follows. ∎

Condition 5.1: We say that a be a valuation v on $\mathbf{C(\overline{x})}$. satisfies Condition 5.1 if $v(x)>v(y)$, $v(x)>v(z)$ implies $v(x)>v(yz)$, for $x,y,z \in \mathbf{C(\overline{x})}$.

Condition 5.1 is a restriction on the type of a valuation that is required for the multiplication algorithm given below to operate correctly. It is easy to see that the natural valuation v satisfies condition 5.1. Let x be a single literal. Then $v(x)=2^k$, some k, and
$$max(v(\prod_{v(y)<v(x)} y))= \sum_{v(y)<v(x)} v(y)=2^k-1.$$

Lemma 5.2: $x=msl(f)$. Then $x \in f_i, x \notin f_j$ implies $f_i > f_j$.

Proof: $v(f_i) \geq v(on(f))+v(x)$ and $v(f_j)<v(on(f))+v(x)$, hence $v(f_i)>v(f_j)$

Lemma 5.3: Let $h=fg$. Then $msl(h)=max(msl(f),msl(g))$.

Proof: Let $z=msl(h)$. We have z is the highest-valued literal of $sup(h)-on(h)$. Now, $on(h)=on(f)\bigcup on(g)$, $sup(h)=sup(f)\bigcup sup(g)$. By the definition of set difference, z is the max of
$$(sup(f)\bigcap \overline{on(f)}\bigcap \overline{on(g)})\bigcup(sup(g)\bigcap \overline{on(f)}\bigcap \overline{on(g)})$$

Noting that $sup(f)\bigcap \overline{on(g)}=sup(f)$ and $sup(g)\bigcap \overline{on(f)}=sup(g)$ and applying the definition of set difference we have z is the max of $(sup(f)-on(f))\bigcup(sup(g)-on(g))$. Since these sets are disjoint, z is in precisely one of those sets, and hence is the greater of $msl(f)$ or $msl(g)$ ∎.

These lemmas suggest the following recursive algorithm for stable algebraic multiplication.

```
multiply_algebraic(f, g)
{
  sliceF <- buildSliceTree(f);
  sliceG <- buildSliceTree(g);
  return(multiplySliceTrees(sliceF, sliceG));
}
multiplySliceTrees(sliceF, sliceG)
{
  if(sliceF is a leaf) {
    prod <- nil;
    foreach leaf c of sliceG prod <- prod, c.val ⋃ sliceF.val;
    return prod;
  }
  if(sliceG is a leaf) {
```

```
        prod <- nil;
        foreach leaf c of sliceF prod <- prod, c.val ⋃ sliceG.val;
        return prod;
    }
    if (sliceF.val > sliceG.val) {
        leftproduct <- multiplySliceTrees(sliceF.leftson, sliceG);
        rightproduct <- multiplySliceTrees(sliceF.rightson, sliceG);
    } else {
        leftproduct <- multiplySliceTrees(sliceG.leftson, sliceF);
        rightproduct <- multiplySliceTrees(sliceG.rightson, sliceF);
    }
    prod <- leftproduct,rightproduct;
    return prod;
}³
```

Theorem 5.4: *multiplySliceTrees(S_f, S_g)* for f,g ordered, returns the ordered product of f, g.

Proof: By induction on $t = h(S_f) + h(S_g)$. If $t=0$, S_f and S_g consist of the cubes f_1, g_1, and $h = f_1 g_1$. Now, assume true for all $t < T$. For $t = T$, we have two cases:

Case A: One of S_f, S_g is a leaf. WLOG assume it is S_f. Hence $g = g_1 + ... + g_m$, $h = h_1 + ... + h_m$, $h_i = g_i f_1$. Further, since v is a normal valuation, $h_i > h_j$ if and only if $g_i > g_j$. Hence the cubes of h are in order if the leaves of S_g are in order, as they are by lemma 5.1.

Case B: WLOG assume $S_f.val > S_g.val$. By lemma 5.3 $S_f.val = msl(h) = z = df_i$. By lemma 5.2, every cube of h containing z is greater than any cube of h not containing z. The cubes of h containing z are $f_k g_j$ for $k \leq i$, which are the cubes of *leftproduct*. Hence the cubes of h are the cubes of *leftproduct* followed by those of *rightproduct*, and hence *multiplySliceTrees* returns an ordered product if the cubes of *leftproduct* are ordered and the cubes of *rightproduct* are ordered. The formation of the cubes of *leftproduct* and *rightproduct* are *multiplySliceTree* problems with $t = T-1$, and hence by the inductive assumption ordered. ▮

Theorem 5.5: *multiply_algebraic(f, g)*, $|f| = n$, $|g| = m$, is in $\theta(mn)$.

Proof: The cost of *multiply_algebraic* is the cost of *buildSliceTree(f) + buildSliceTree(g)* + the cost of *multiplySliceTrees(S_f,S_g)*. The cost of the last is the cost of forming the products (in $\theta(mn)$) + the cost of the recursion. Each recursive call entails a traversal of one edge in either S_f or S_g, and it is easy to verify that each edge is traversed at most once. There are $2n-2$ edges in S_f, and $2m-2$ in S_g. Hence the cost of the recursion is in $\theta(m+n)$. The cost of the calls to *buildSliceTree* are in $\theta(m)$ and $\theta(n)$, respectively, by theorem A.3. Hence the cost of *multiply_algebraic(f, g)* is in $\theta(mn)$ ▮.

---

³ A. Wang suggested [Wan86] that *multiplySliceTrees* can easily be modified to return not simply the logic expression $h = fg$, but rather its slicing tree, thus saving the computation of the slicing tree of h if it is required in future. In effect, Wang suggests that slicing trees may be a more feasible representation of logic expressions than the conventional sum-of-products list of sets. This suggestion has merit; however, in practice, we see that many algorithms (cf the division algorithms below) use the list catenation operation, an $O(1)$ operation; insertion into a slice tree, on the other hand, is potentially $O(n)$. Merging sorted lists, as in addition, also does not fit well with the notion of slicing trees. Hence these algorithms would require that we first dispatch the slicing tree structure, and then reconstruct it, an operation hardly less expensive than constructing the slicing tree at the beginning of the multiplication algorithm, where, in any case, it does not affect the complexity.

6. Division

6.1. Definition of the Division Operation

Let f,g be two arbitrary boolean functions. We define $(q,r)=alg\_divide(f,g)$ iff:
(a) the product gq is defined;
(b) the product gq and r partition the cubes of f ($f=gq+r$); and
(c) there is no cube $c\neq0$ s.t. gc is a set of cubes of r.

We establish that the above definition of the division operation yields a unique quotient and remainder.

Theorem 6.1: Consider the sets

$$\frac{f}{g_i}=Q_i=\{q_{ij}\mid q_{ij}g_i=f_j,\ q_{ij}\bigcap sup(g)=\phi\}$$

Then the set of cubes of the quotient of $\frac{f}{g}$, $q=\bigcap_i Q_i$.

Proof: It is easy to see that $q\subseteq\overset{|g|}{\underset{i}{\bigcap}}Q_i$ since if $q_k\in q$ there exists $f_{k(1)},\ldots,f_{k(m)}$, $f_{k(i)}=q_kg_i\ \forall\ i$, and hence $q_k\in Q_i\ \forall\ i$. Conversely, if $q_k\in\bigcap_i Q_i$, $\exists\ f_{k(1)},\ldots,f_{k(m)}$, $f_{k(i)}=q_kg_i$. Now, the $f_{k(i)}$'s are distinct since the g_i's are. If $f_{k(i)}=f_{h(j)}$, we have $g_iq_k=g_jq_h$, and by corollary 5.3 $h=k$, $i=j$. Hence gq_k is a subset of the cubes of f, hence $q_k\in q$, hence $\bigcap_i Q_i\subseteq q$, hence $q=\bigcap_i Q_i$. ∎

Corollary 6.1: $(q,r)=alg\_divide(f,g)$ is unique.

6.2. Division by a Cube

The simplest case of division occurs when $|g|=1$, i.e., g is a cube. Then $q=\sum_{f_i\supseteq g}(f_i-g)$, $r=\sum_{f_i\not\supseteq g}f_i$. This is captured in the following algorithm:

```
divide_by_cube(f, g) {
  q <- nil;
  r <- nil;
  foreach cube f_i of f {
    if( f_i ⊇ g) q <- q, (f_i-g);
    else r <- r, f_i;
  }
  return(q, r);
}
```

The cubes of r are ordered if the cubes of f are ordered, since the cubes of f are examined in order and appended to the end of the appropriate list. Under a normal valuation, if $v(c_1)>v(c_2)$, $c_1\supseteq c_3$, $c_2\supseteq c_3$, then $v(c_1-c_3)>v(c_2-c_3)$. Hence the cubes of q are ordered if the cubes of f are ordered.

Each cube of f is examined exactly once, hence this is a $\theta(|f|)operation$.

6.3. Exact Division

Theorem 6.2: Let $f=gh$, ordered logic expressions f, g. Then h is the quotient produced by $divide\_by\_cube(f,g_1)$.

Proof: Since by definition $Q_i=divide\_by\_cube(f,g_i)$, if $f=gh$ then all the Q_i are equal by corollary 5.3. Hence theorem 6.1 gives $h=\bigcap_i Q_i=Q_1$. ∎

This suggests a fast algorithm to test for and perform exact division:

```
exactly_divides(f, g) {
  (cofactor, r) <- divide_by_cube(f, g₁);
  if( |cofactor| * |g| != |f| ) return (FALSE, nil);
  if( sup(cofactor)∩sup(g) != φ ) return (FALSE, nil);
  f1 <- multiply_algebraic(cofactor, g);
  if(algebraic_equality(f1, f)) return (TRUE, cofactor);
  else return (FALSE, nil);
}
```

If f is ordered, so is $cofactor$. By the counting theorem, if $f = cofactor\ g$ then $|f| = |cofactor|\ |g|$. Hence $multiply\_algebraic(cofactor, g)$ is in $\theta(|f|)$, and we know that $divide\_by\_cube$ and $algebraic\_equality$ are in $\theta(|f|)$. Hence $exactly\_divides(f, g)$ is in $\theta(|f|)$.

6.4. General Algebraic Division

General algebraic division follows the same strategy as exact division. A trial quotient and remainder q, r are found by dividing f by g_1. Then each cube q_j of q is tested: q_j is a cube of the final quotient iff $(g_2 + ... g_m)q_j$ is a subset of the cubes of r.

The naive algorithm for algebraic division suggested by this fact has poor complexity. The upper bound on $|q|$ is $|f|$. Hence the complexity of the naive algorithm is in $O(|g|\ |f|)$. To get a $\theta(|f| + |g|)$ bound the individual cubes of gq must be formed in order, and compared immediately against the cubes of r. Suppose for the moment that the cubes of gq may be formed in order, and the top *remaining* cube of r is being compared against the just-formed cube of gq. Here r_1, $(gq)_1$ refer to these cubes. There are three cases:

(a) $r_1 > (gq)_1$. Then $r_1 > (gq)_i\ \forall\ i$. Hence r_1 is in the final remainder, and may be deleted from r;

(b) $r_1 < (gq)_1$. This cube of the product gq matches no remaining cube of r. Let $(gq)_1 = g_i q_j$. Then $q_j g$ is not a subset of the cubes of r, hence q_j is not a cube of the quotient, and is deleted from the candidate quotient.

(c) $r_1 = (gq)_1$. This cube of the product matches this cube of r, and no other cube of the product can match this cube of r. We pop r. If $(gq)_1 = g_{|g|} q_j$, then $q_j g$ is a subset of the cubes of r, and q_j is added to the quotient.

We encode these cases in the following routine. We have slightly optimized case (a) so that *every* cube of $r > (gq)_1$ is deleted. Each call to this routine results in the deletion of at least one cube of r or a cube of q, and if this routine empties either r or q, then this routine terminates the algebraic division routine. Since $|q| \leq |f|$, $|r| \leq |f|$, this routine can be called at most $2|f| - 1$ times. The return value of this routine is the next undeleted cube of q, and a flag indicating whether this cube of gq found a match in the cube of r, or not. The resulting quotient is maintained in the global variable $Quotient$.

```
disposeOfTerm( g_cube, q_cube ) {
  prod <- g_cube.val ∪ q_cube.val;
  while(r₁ > prod) {          /* case (a) */
    pop(r);
    if(r = nil) TERMINATE;
  }
  if(r₁ = prod){              /* case (c) */
    if( g_cube.index = |g| ) Quotient <- Quotient, q_cube.val;
    pop(r);
    if(r = nil) TERMINATE;
    return(TRUE, q_cube.next);
  } else {                    /* case (b) */
```

```
    q_cube <- delete(q_cube);
    if( q_cube = nil ) TERMINATE;
    return(FALSE,q_cube);
  }
}
```

The *TERMINATE* call terminates the calling algorithm, with the result left in *Quotient*. Of course, *Quotient* could be passed in as an argument, modified and returned; similarly, the *TERMINATE* non-local return could be implemented as a flag, and a set of return statements in the calling procedure. For the moment we prefer the current formulation, as it simplifies the code of the calling routine.

With *disposeOfTerm* in hand, we proceed to generating the cubes of *gq* in order. The *multiplySliceTrees* algorithm generates product cubes in order, so we take it as a starting point. Simply calling *disposeOfTerm* from *multiplySliceTrees* does not suffice; the deletions of cubes from *q* during the course of the multiplication dynamically changes *q*'s slicing tree, and the algorithm must keep track of the changes. Conceptually, part of *q*'s slicing tree, *SliceQ*, is burned out through deletions of leaves, and we do not wish to form products from a burned-out tree.

We do this through two modifications to the slicing tree and two to the *multiplySliceTrees* algorithm. The leaves of *SliceQ* are now maintained as a doubly-linked list, so that deletion of a cube is $O(1)$; further, the deletion routine always returns the next undeleted cube (which is, of course, also the leftmost undeleted leaf to the right of the just-deleted leaf). Each non-leaf node v of *SliceQ* now maintains the index of its initial rightmost leaf; this is used to determine whether or not a particular node is to the right of v's subtree.

The algorithm below, *divideUsingSliceTrees* is a modification of *multiplySliceTrees* that exploits the property that the first product cube formed in the subtree headed by v will always contain v's *leftmost* leaf, and that the first product cube formed *after* the product formed by v's subtree will contain the leftmost leaf to the *right* of v. We modify *multiplySliceTrees* to pass in the leftmost leaf of v (and hence form the first product easily) and to return the leftmost leaf to the right of v (since this is the leftmost leaf of a left sibling or uncle of v). The algorithm follows:

```
divideUsingSliceTrees(SliceG, SliceQ, LeftQ) {
  if(SliceG is a leaf) {
    matched <- false;

    /* Form products until you run out of leaves of SliceQ or find a match in r.
    SliceQ.rightnum is the rightmost leaf of SliceQ; LeftQ is the leftmost
    undeleted leaf of SliceQ. When disposeOfTerm returns matched = FALSE,
    we know we have deleted the leftmost leaf of SliceQ, hence LeftQ must change */

    while((!matched) && (LeftQ.index <= SliceQ.rightnum)) {
      (matched, nextLeftQ) <- disposeOfTerm(SliceG, LeftQ);
      if(!matched) LeftQ <- nextLeftQ;
    }

    /* if(!matched) we've run out of leaves. Hence LeftQ and RightQ are
    identical (no undeleleted leaves in this subtree) */

    if(!matched) return(LeftQ, LeftQ);

    /* Once we have identified LeftQ, we may form the products normally;
    when we run out of leaves, Q = RightQ */

    Q <- nextLeftQ;
```

```
  while(Q.index <= SliceQ.rightnum) (matched, Q) <- disposeOfTerm(SliceG, Q);
  return(LeftQ, Q);
}


/* if SliceQ is a leaf, form the products as in multiplySliceTrees until
we fail to find a match for any term of the product. If we fail,
then LeftQ = RightQ = nextQ. Otherwise, LeftQ = SliceQ, RightQ = nextQ */


if(SliceQ is a leaf) {
  foreach leaf g of SliceG {
    (matched, nextQ) <- disposeOfTerm(g, SliceQ);
    if(!matched) return(nextQ, nextQ);
  }
  return(SliceQ, nextQ);
}


/* Recursive case. As before, only passing in and out the appropriate
pointers to leaves. */


if(SliceG.val > SliceQ.val) {
  (NewLeft, NewRight) <- divideUsingSliceTrees(SliceG.leftson, SliceQ, LeftQ);
  (NewLeft, NewRight) <- divideUsingSliceTrees(SliceG.rightson, SliceQ, NewLeft);
  return(NewLeft, NewRight);
} else {
  (NewLeft, NewRight) <- divideUsingSliceTrees(SliceG, SliceQ.leftson, LeftQ);
  (NxtLeft, NewRight) <- divideUsingSliceTrees(SliceG, SliceQ.rightson, NewRight);
  return(NewLeft, NewRight);
  }
}
```

One can see by analogy with *multiplySliceTrees* that *divideUsingSliceTrees* forms the products of gq in order. It is further easy to see that *divideUsingSliceTrees* always returns the leftmost node of *SliceQ*, and the leftmost node to the right of *SliceQ*. We observe that at most $2 \mid q \mid + 2 \mid g \mid + 4$ comparisons are made, by the same argument that established this bound for *multiplySliceTrees*. Further, since $\mid q \mid \leq \mid f \mid$, we may bound the comparisons at $2 \mid f \mid + 2 \mid g \mid + 4$.

All that remains is to write the division algorithm:

```
alg_divide(F, g) {
  (cand_q, r) <- divide_by_cube(F, g_1);
  foreach cube c of cand_q if (c ∩ sup(g) != φ) delete(c);
  restG <- g_2+...+g_m;
  sliceQ <- buildSliceTree(cand_q);
  sliceG <- buildSliceTree(restG);
  Quotient <- nil;
  divideUsingSliceTrees(sliceG, sliceQ, cand_q_1);
  prod <- multiply_algebraic(g, Quotient);
  Remainder <- algebraic_difference( F, prod );
  return(Quotient, Remainder);
}
```

By the discussion above, it is clear that *divideUsingSliceTrees* with *disposeOfTerm* generates the quotient q. Hence the remainder is $f - gq$. For complexity, we note that at most $2 \mid f \mid$ products are formed during the execution of $divideUsingSliceTrees$, and that at most $2 \mid f \mid + 2 \mid g \mid$ comparisons are made. Hence the cost of $divideUsingSliceTrees$ is in $\theta(\mid f \mid + \mid g \mid)$. $algebraic\_difference$, $divide\_by\_cube$, and the first call to $buildSliceTree$ are all in $\theta(\mid f \mid)$, and the second call to $buildSliceTree$ is in $\theta(\mid g \mid)$. Hence alg_divide is in $\theta(\mid f \mid + \mid g \mid)$.[4]

7. Summary

In this paper, we have demonstrated stable, linear procedures for the principal algebraic operations on logic expressions. A summary of the results, with a comparison to the performance results of unstable algorithms, is shown in the table below. Optimum performance is also given; these lower bounds are trivially obtained by considering the size of the result or by observing that the result is dependent upon every cube of one or both arguments.

Stable vs Unstable Complexity			
Operation	Stable Complexity	Unstable Complexity	Lower Bound
$f+g$	$\theta(\mid f \mid + \mid g \mid)$	$\theta(\mid f \mid \log \mid f \mid + \mid g \mid \log \mid g \mid)$[5]	$\Omega(\mid f \mid + \mid g \mid)$[5]
$\dfrac{f}{g}$	$\theta(\mid f \mid + \mid g \mid)$	$\theta(\mid f \mid \log \mid f \mid + \mid g \mid \log \mid g \mid)$	$\Omega(\mid f \mid + \mid g \mid)$
fg	$\theta(\mid f \mid \mid g \mid)$	$\theta(\mid f \mid \mid g \mid)$	$\Omega(\mid f \mid \mid g \mid)$
$\dfrac{f}{g}$ (exact)	$\theta(\mid f \mid)$	$\theta(\mid f \mid \log \mid f \mid)$	$\Omega(\mid f \mid)$
$f = g$	$\theta(\mid f \mid + \mid g \mid)$	$\theta(\mid f \mid \log \mid f \mid + \mid g \mid \log \mid g \mid)$	$\Omega(\mid f \mid + \mid g \mid)$
$f - g$	$\theta(\mid f \mid)$	$\theta(\mid f \mid \log \mid f \mid + \mid g \mid \log \mid g \mid)$	$\Omega(\mid f \mid)$

8. Acknowledgements

Thanks to Joe Sharp, Bill Bush, Gino Cheng, and Al Despain for support; to Carl Ponder and Antony Ng for many illuminating conversations; to Albert Wang, Rick Rudell and Alberto Sangiovanni-Vincentelli, who kindly read early drafts of this manuscript and provided many insightful and helpful suggestions; and to the other members of the Berkeley Design team and the Aquarius Project for providing the environment which stimulated this research.

9. References

[Bar86] K. A. Bartlett, R. K. Brayton, G. D. Hachtel, R. Jacobi, R. Rudell, and A. L. Sangiovanni-Vincentelli, "Algorithms for Multi-Level Logic Minimization Using Implicit Don't-Cares", *ICCD 86*, November, 1986.

[Bra82] R. K. Brayton and C. T. McMullen, "The Decomposition and Factorization of Boolean Functions", *ISCAS Proceedings*, April, 1982.

---

[4] It has been suggested that $divideUsingSliceTrees$ may produce the remainder as well as the quotient, since case (a) of $disposeOfTerm$ identifies cubes in the candidate remainder that are in the final remainder. This would save the final multiplication and subtraction steps in alg_divide. However, it is possible for a cube r_i of the candidate remainder to be matched (case (c) of $disposeOfTerm$) by a product cube involving a cube of the candidate quotient which is subsequently deleted. r_i is therefore a cube of the final remainder which is not detected by $disposeOfTerm$

[5] The best possible bound for addition is to simply stick the cubes together. This solution is $O(1)$, but it permits the resulting expression to have duplicate cubes which must be eliminated before most other operations may be performed. The counting theorem and its corollary do not apply if this is used. Most current systems use the counting theorem to do quick tests to avoid unnecessary division and an $O(1)$ escape from equality test. These cannot be used if $O(1)$ addition is used. Hence we argue that an appropriate bound for the unstable algorithm is $\theta(\mid f \mid \log \mid f \mid + \mid g \mid \log \mid g \mid)$, and the lower bound is $\Omega(\mid f \mid + \mid g \mid)$.

[Bra84a] R. K. Brayton, G. D. Hachtel, C. T. McMullen, and A. L. Sangiovanni-Vincentelli, *Logic Minimization Algorithms for VLSI Synthesis*, Kluwer Academic Publishers, Boston, September, 1984.

[Bra84b] R. K. Brayton and C. T. McMullen, "Synthesis and Optimization of Multistage Logic", *ICCD 84*, October, 1984.

[Bra86a] R. K. Brayton, "Algorithms for Multi-Level Logic Synthesis and Organization", *NATO Advanced Study Institute on Logic Synthesis and Silicon Compilation for VLSI Design*, L'Aquila, Italy, July 1986.

[Bra86b] R. K. Brayton, A. Cagnola, E. Detjens, S. Krishna, A. Ma, P. McGeer, L-F Pei, N. Phillips, R. Rudell, R. Segal, A. Wang, N. Weiner, R. Yung, T. Villa, A. R. Newton, A. Sangiovanni-Vincentelli, and C. H. Sequin, "Multiple-Level Logic Optimization System", *ICCAD 86*, November, 1986.

[Bre84] N. Brenner, "The Yorktown Logic Language: An APL-like Design Language for VLSI Specification" *ICCD 84*, October, 1984.

[Har75] L. H. Harper, T. H. Payne, J. E. Savage, and E. Strauss, "Sorting X + Y", *Communications of the ACM*, 18, 6, June, 1975.

[Jen78] K. Jensen and N. Wirth, *Pascal: User Manual and Report*, 2d ed, Springer-Verlag, New York.

[Wan86] A. Wang, *Personal Communication*.

10. Appendix A: A $\theta(n)$ algorithm to Build Slicing Trees

Recall from section 5 that the difference array of f, df, df_i is the highest-valued literal of $f_{i+1}-f_i$. Here we show that the internal nodes of S_f, the slicing tree of f, are the elements of df. First we need a technical lemma.

Lemma A.1: Let df be the difference array of f, f ordered. Let $df_i=df_j$ for $j>i$. Then $\exists\ k\ |\ i<k<j,\ df_k>df_i$

Proof: Let $x=df_i=df_j$. Hence $x\in f_i$, $x\notin f_{i+1}$, $x\in f_j$. Let k' be the least $k\ |\ i<k<j,\ x\notin f_k$. Now either $f_{k'}<f_{k'+1}$, contradicting assumption that f ordered, or $\exists\ y>x,\ y\in f_{k'}-f_{k'+1}$. Hence $df_{k'}\geq y>x$, QED ∎.

Lemma A.2: Let $f=f_1+...+f_n$ be an ordered logic expression with difference array df, and $x=msl(f)$. Then x is the maximum element of the difference array df.

Proof: Let $x=msl(f)$. Now, for some $1\leq i<n$, $x\in f_i$, $x\notin f_{i+1}$, hence $x=df_i$. If $y=df_j \geq x$, then $y\in f_j$, $y\notin f_{j+1}$ implies $y=msl(f)\Longrightarrow y=x, i=j$, QED. ∎

For any node v in an acyclic digraph, where $outdegree(v)\leq 2$, we denote the set of nodes reachable through the right son of v as $R(v)$ and through the left son as $L(v)$. $C(v)=R(v)\bigcup L(v)$ is the set of descendants of v. We define the index function, $I(v)=i$ for v a node in this graph if $v=df_i$ or $v=f_i$. If $indegree(v)\leq 1$ and $indegree(x)=1\ \forall\ x\in C(v)$, then v is called a *tree node*.

Theorem A.1: Let $G=(V,E)$ be any full binary tree such that $V=\{f_1,\ldots,f_n,df_1,\ldots,df_{n-1}\}$. G is the slicing tree on $f=f_1+...+f_n <=>$
(a) The f_i are the leaves of G.
(b) $df_j>df_k\ \forall\ df_k$ descended from df_j
(c) For each df_k in V, if $u\in L(df_k)$, then $I(u)\leq k$. If $u\in R(df_k)$, then $I(u)>k$

Proof: $(=>)$. Let G be the slicing tree on f. Proof by induction on $h(G)$, the height of G. If $h(G)=1$, (a)-(c) follow from the definition of the slicing tree. Assume for $h(G)<r$. If $h(G)=r$, then (a) - (c) hold for both subtrees by the inductive assumption. Let $x=msl(f)$, x is the root of S_f, and, by lemma A.2, x is the maximum of df, df_i. Hence df_i is the root of G. By definition, $df_i>df_j$ for $j\neq i$, hence (b) holds. The leaves of G are the leaves of the subtrees, and hence (a) holds. The left subtree of G consists of the nodes $\{f_1,\ldots,f_i,df_1,\ldots,df_{i-1}\}$, the right subtree

consists of the nodes $\{f_{i+1}, \ldots, f_n, df_{i+1}, \ldots, df_n\}$ and hence (c) holds.
($<=$) Induction on $h(G)$. If $h(G)=1$, the only tree satisfying (a) - (c) is the slicing tree on f_1+f_2. Now assume true for $h(G)<r$. If $h(G)=r$, by (b) the root of the tree must be the maximum of the difference array, df_i. By (c), the nodes of the left subtree must be $\{f_1, \ldots, f_i, df_1, \ldots, df_{i-1}\}$, and of the right subtree $\{f_{i+1}, \ldots, f_n, df_{i+1}, \ldots, df_{n-1}\}$. These are precisely the nodes of the left and right subtrees of f, and they are of height at most $r-1$. By the inductive assumption they are therefore the left and right subtrees of the slicing tree of f, respectively, and by lemma A.2 df_i is the root. Hence G is the slicing tree on f ∎.

Theorem A.1 gives a set of conditions which permit us to determine if a given binary tree is the slicing tree on f.

10.1.1. Building The Slicing Tree

We begin the construction of the slicing tree for $f=f_1+ \cdots + f_n$ by constructing the digraph on the nodes f_i and df_i pictured in figure 3. For each node of the tree we have fields *indegree, leftson, rightson, leftparent* and *rightparent*. For any node u, $u.leftparent = v$ iff $v.rightson = u$. The *rightparent* and *leftparent* fields are not graph edges.

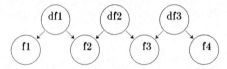

Initial Slicing Graph

The graph of figure 3 is the initial graph used by the *buildSliceTree* algorithm. This algorithm essentially runs a tournament. If w,x share $v=w.rightson=x.leftson$, they are compared. If $w>x$, x becomes w's *rightson*, and the parentage of v is resolved. If the parentage of x becomes contentious with w's claim (in other words, x is already some other node's *leftson*), x is placed on the stack of nodes whose parentage must be resolved in this fashion. When this stack is empty, the algorithm terminates.

```
buildSliceTree(f) {
 (fGraph, twoParents) <- makeInitialGraph(f);

 /* twoParents is the list of nodes that have two parents (indegree = 2) */

 while(twoParents != nil) {
  u <- pop(twoParents);
  v <- u.leftparent;
  w <- u.rightparent;
  if (v.val > w.val) {
   v.rightson <- w;
   w.leftparent <- v;
   u.leftparent <- nil;
   if (++w.indegree = 2) push(w,twoParents);
  } else {
   w.leftson <- v;
   v.rightparent <- w;
   u.rightparent <- nil;
   if (++v.indegree = 2) push(v,twoParents);
  }
  u.indegree = 1;
 }
```

foreach node u in fGraph if (u.indegree = 0) return u; /* u is the root */
}

We now show that this algorithm builds the slicing tree, and does so in time $\theta(n)$. All the remaining results in this subsection operate on the graph $G = (V,E)$, the graph under construction by this algorithm.

Lemma A.3: At any time t $indegree(v) \leq 2$ $\forall$ $v \in V$, and there is at most one non-leaf $v \in V$ s.t. $indegree(v) = 2$.

Proof: Clearly if $v = f_i$ (v is a leaf) then $indegree(v)$ is initially 2 and is never increased, since $outdegree(v) = 0$. At any time t, one node's $indegree$ is increased by one and another's is decreased by one. If v is not a leaf, then its $indegree$ is 0 initially and may be increased. But $indegree(v)$ is increased to 2 at $t = T$, it is reduced to 1 at $t = T+1$ since $twoParents$ is a stack ∎.

Lemma A.4: Let u be a non-leaf descendant of non-leaf v. Then $u < v$.

Proof: Induction on n, the number of edges from u to v. If $n = 1$, then $u < v$ directly from the algorithm. Suppose true for all $n < N$. If $n = N$, let w be the son of v and ancestor of u. By the inductive assumption $w > u$ and $v > w$ ∎.

Corollary A.4: G is acyclic.

We now turn to an extremely important result, which establishes immediately that the algorithm *buildSliceTree* builds the slicing tree on f. This result is also vital to deriving the bound on the algorithm. Lemma A.5 below, the Interval Lemma, states that all the nodes in $L(df_i)$ have indices in the interval $[i-j,i]$ for some $j \geq 0$, and that no node with index in the interval $[i-j,i]$ lies outside $L(df_i)$. Similarly, all nodes in $R(df_i)$ have indices in the interval $[i+1,i+k]$, $k > 0$, and no node with index in the interval $[i+1,i+k]$ lies outside $R(df_i)$. In other words, the subtrees of df_i form an unbroken interval of nodes adjacent to df_i.

Lemma A.5 (The Interval Lemma): Let $I(v) = i$. At time t, let the minimum index of $L(v) = i - j$, and the maximum index of $R(v) = i + k$. Then $j \geq 0, k > 0$, and

$$L(v) = \{f_{i-j}, f_{i+1-j}, \ldots, f_i, df_{i-j}, \ldots, df_{i-1}\}$$

$$R(v) = \{f_{i+1}, \ldots, f_{i+k}, df_{i+1}, \ldots, df_{i+k-1}\}$$

Proof: Induction on t. At $t = 0$, true by inspection. Now, assume true for $t = 0, \ldots, N-1$. Assume that at $t = N$, we are considering the situation where $w.rightson = v.leftson = y$. Now, by the inductive hypothesis, if $w = df_l$, $v = df_i$, we have the situation pictured in Figure 4. A contains all nodes with indices $l - l_1, \ldots, l-1$, and f_l. B contains those with indices $l+1 (= i - i_1), \ldots, l+l_2 - 1 (= i-1)$, and $f_{l+l_2} = f_i$, and C those with indices $i+1, \ldots, i+i_2 - 1$, and f_{i+i_2}. The situation pictured in figure 5 is for the case $w > v$. In this case, $L(w)$ remains unchanged, and hence obeys the result. $R(w) = B \cup C$ and hence consists of all nodes with indices $l+1, \ldots, i+i_2 - 1$, and f_{i+i_2} and hence satisfies the result. The case for $w < v$ follows by symmetry ∎.

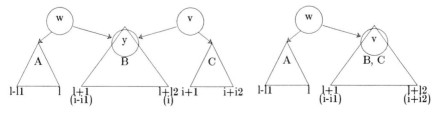

Figure 4: Situation at t = N-1   **Figure 5: Situation at t = N**

Corollary A.5: $R(df_k) \cap L(df_k) = \phi \ \forall \ k$

Theorem A.2: *buildSliceTree* builds the slicing tree on f.

Proof: By corollary A.4, *buildSliceTree* builds an acyclic digraph. By inspection, one can see that there are $2n-1$ nodes in the graph and $2n-2$ edges. The graph is connected since edges are only removed from nodes with *indegree*=2, and only one edge is removed from such a node. Further, *indegree* ≤ 1 for each node in the graph. Hence *indegree*=1 for all nodes except one, for which *indegree*=0. Hence *buildSliceTree* builds a tree. Since the *outdegree* of each node is preserved by the algorithm, the leaves of the tree are the cubes of f, satisfying theorem A.1(a). Theorem A.1(b) is satisfied by the Interval Lemma, and theorem A.1(c) by lemma A.4. Hence by theorem A.1 *buildSliceTree* builds the slicing tree on f ∎

Now that the correctness of *buildSliceTree* is established, we turn to its complexity. We observe that when all nodes have *indegree* ≤ 1, the algorithm terminates. Hence we wish to find the number of comparisons required to reduce the *indegree* of each node to 1. We begin by asking which nodes may have *indegree*=2 at any given time.

Consider any non-leaf node u of the graph. Denote the set of nodes on the path from u to its leftmost (rightmost) leaf as the *spine* of $L(u)$ $(R(u))$; and the remainder of the nodes of $L(u)$ $(R(u))$as the *interior* of $L(u)$ $(R(u))$.

Lemma A.6: Let u any non-leaf node in G. Then $\forall \ v$ in the interior of $L(u)$ $(R(u))$, $indegree(v)=1$.

Proof: We show this for $L(u)$. Suppose $indegree(v)=2$ for v in the interior of $L(u)$. $v=w.leftson=x.rightson$. Since v is in the interior of $L(u)$, by the Interval Lemma $x \epsilon L(u), w \epsilon L(u)$, and w is in the interior of $L(u)$. Hence x and w share some common ancestor, z, and $w \epsilon R(z)$, $x \epsilon L(z)$. Hence $v \epsilon R(z) \cap L(z)$, contradicting corollary A.5 ∎

Lemma A.7: Let $indegree(v)=2$. Then $\forall \ u \in C(v)$, $indegree(u)=1$.

Proof: Suppose not. Then $indegree(v)=2$, $u \in C(v)$, $indegree(u)=2$. Suppose $u \epsilon L(v)$. Now, $v=x.rightson$, some x. Hence $u \epsilon R(x)$. But u is in the interior of $R(x)$, contradicting lemma A.6. The case for $u \epsilon R(v)$ follows by symmetry. ∎

Theorem A.3: *buildSliceTree* is in $\theta(n)$.

Proof: Once a node v of the graph is a tree node, it remains a tree node and is not considered during the course of the algorithm. By lemma A.7, each comparison creates at least one tree node. There are $2n-1$ nodes in the graph, and the algorithm terminates when all the nodes are tree nodes. Hence the algorithm makes at most $2n-1$ comparisons ∎

Session 4
PLACEMENT AND ROUTING

VLSI '87, C.H. Séquin (editor)
Elsevier Science Publishers B.V. (North-Holland)
© IFIP, 1988

TOP DOWN HIERARCHICAL GLOBAL   ROUTING   FOR   CHANNELLESS   GATE   ARRAYS
BASED ON LINEAR ASSIGNMENT

Ulrich Ph. Lauther

Siemens AG
ZTI DES V, P.O. Box 830953
D–8000 Munich 83, FRG

We present a new hierarchical top down global routing algorithm for
channelless gate arrays that is based on linear assignment or network
flow optimization. The top down partitioning scheme, cost function,
cut—line position optimization and computational complexity are discussed. Experimental results are reported which show that the router
is fast and compares favorably with previously published results.

1. INTRODUCTION

Most systems for placement and routing on PCB's or VLSI—chips divide the total
design task into subtasks that are easier to handle: Placement, global routing
and detailed routing.

The main tasks of global or "loose" routing, which is carried out after at
least a preliminary placement has been defined, are to determine the rough topology of nets so as to achieve a uniform and low wiring density and to partition the overall routing problem into smaller, more or less independent and
maybe specialized subproblems that are better understood and easier to solve.
Sometimes global routing also performs adjustment of cell placement in order to
improve routability.

The exact definition of and methods for global routing depend crucially on
technology and design style used.

In this paper we consider the global routing problem for channelless gate arrays (sea of gates). Here we have a regular array of basic cells without any
wiring channels set aside for routing. Groups of one or more adjacent basic
cells are personalized by adding local wiring and are wired together to form
functional blocks (intracell wiring). After placement these functional blocks
are connected according to a netlist to implement the required overall functionality of the circuit under development (intercell wiring). Intercell wiring
is done in free tracks over personalized or unused base cells.

We assume that a regular grid of rectangular routing blocks is superimposed on
the gate array in such a way that one block corresponds to a constant number
and fixed configuration of basic cells of the gate array. We further assume
that detailed routing is done block by block connecting all nets that have terminals within the block or that pass through the block as proposed by Kessenich
and Jackoway for PCB's [10].

The question to be answered by global routing in this setting is: How   should nets be assigned to routing blocks so that the resulting local routing problems can be solved by the detailed routing phase.

For this purpose we assume that wire—capacities are specified for block boundaries, describing how many wires may cross each boundary. Boundary capacities depend on the type, number and distribution of cells that have been placed on the gate array, on characteristics of unused basic cells and on the density of wiring local to a block. We assume that these capacity values are available.

Of course, wirability for a given global routing result depends on the specific router used for detailed routing. For the purpose of this paper we assume that a configuration is routable if nets are assigned to blocks in such a way that no boundary capacities are exceeded.

Throughout the rest of the paper we will use the following terminology (cf. Fig. 1) :

Base—cell: Smallest "atom" from which functional cells are built. Contains a fixed number of transistors (typically 4 .. 7). The core of a sea of gates master is made up of a regular array of these base—cells.

Cell: Functional block that consists of one or more base cells plus intracell wiring. Usually the outline of a cell is rectangular, but this is not essential for our method of global routing.

Terminal: A point on a functional block where intercell connections must be made.

Net: A set of terminals to be connected.

Routing—block: A rectangular block of base cells to be processed as one unit in detailed routing. The task of global routing is to assign nets to routing blocks. Routing blocks form a regular two-dimensional array.

Partition: A set of routing blocks with rectangular outline and the set of terminals that belong to these blocks.

Cut—line: A horizontal or vertical line separating one partition into two sub-partitions.

Section: A cut—line is divided into sections which correspond to boundaries between adjacent routing blocks.

Capacity: With each section a capacity is associated that defines the maximal number of wires that may cross the section.

Pseudo—terminal: Pairs of terminals are generated by our algorithm where nets cross routing block boundaries; they describe the global topology of nets.

Overflow: A net that could not be assigned to routing blocks without violating capacity—constraints.

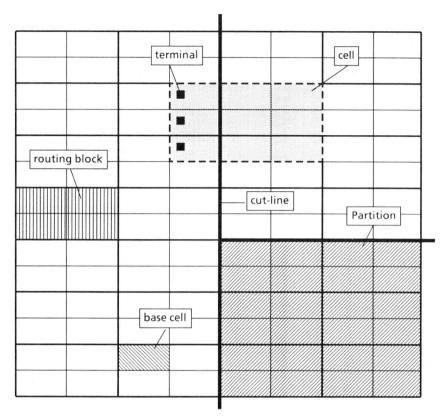

FIGURE 1
Basic structure of gate array with base–cells, cells, routing blocks and partitions.

2. PREVIOUS WORK

Some authors have discussed similar problems as the one described above:

Goto et al. [1] used a maze router to approximate Steiner trees for each net and a rip–up and reroute scheme to take care of nets which failed in the first attempt. Of course, the result of these sequential net by net methods depends heavily on the order in which nets are processed.

Li and Marek–Sadowska [2] developed an "outer–most loop algorithm", a set of heuristics that try to identify unique portions of the solution (look ahead) and to avoid congestion in the center of the chip. Backtracking is used when all else fails.

In another paper Marek–Sadowska [3] used an AI–based rip up and rerouting scheme to improve on results of a hierarchical bottom up router.

Kirkpatrick et al. [4] used simulated annealing to achieve a uniform density distribution; since nets may be (re-)assigned many times one achieves quasi-simultaneous processing of nets. This approach does not naturally solve the second subtask of global routing, namely to define smaller subproblems for detailed routing.

Burstein and Pelavin [5] report on two different hierarchical approaches that both reduce the problem to that of finding Steiner trees on a 2 by n grid.

The first approach reduces the problem further to a series of 2 by 2 problems. It classifies nets into types and net embeddings into patterns. All nets are processed simultaneously. Using linear programming one determines how many nets of each type should be embedded according to each pattern, but the question which net should use which pattern is not answered.

The second approach proceeds net by net and does assignment of patterns to nets. It uses dynamic programming to construct Steiner trees on the 2 by n grid.

A method very similar to that to be described in this paper has been developed independently and at the same time as this work was done by Marek-Sadowska of UCB [6]. The main difference is that she aims not at channelless gate arrays but at global routing of channel-structured macro cell designs.

3. BASIC CONCEPT

In our approach the basic goal is to combine positive aspects of previous methods: First, to be order independent we aim at simultaneous processing of nets. Second, we want to find an embedding (in terms of routing blocks) for each net. Third, for speedup and simplicity, we prefer a hierarchical, recursive approach.

The basic idea is to use divide and conquer: We divide the whole chip by a horizontal or vertical cut-line into two subchips (partitions) of approximately equal size. Now with each of these subchips we have a subproblem of smaller size.

In order to solve these two subproblems independently we first have to look at the interface between these two problems. This interface is made up of those nets that cross from one partition into the other, nets that have at least one terminal on each side of the cut-line. If we decide for each of these nets where to cross the cut-line and then introduce two pseudo-terminals at this position, one on each side of the cut-line, then each of the two partitions can be solved independently applying the same technique recursively.

The whole problem thus boils down to the question of how to assign nets to positions along the cut-line. Since we are dealing with global, not detailed routing we need only "rough" positions for crossing nets. For this purpose, the cut-line is divided into sections. Each section corresponds to the border between two adjacent routing blocks that define the coarse grid used for global routing. Now we identify the subset of nets that have to cross the cut-line and assign these nets to sections. Each assignment is recorded by generating a pseudo-pin in the two routing blocks adjacent to the section.

Postponing details of the method used for assignment we are now ready to give a high level description of our global routing algorithm:

```
Initial partition := (total chip, all terminals);

push initial partition on stack;

while stack not empty do begin

    pop partition from stack;

    select cut-line position and orientation;

    split partition along cut-line;

    identify nets crossing the cut-line;

    divide cut-line into sections;

    assign crossing nets to sections;

    for each assigned net generate a pseudo-pin in both routing
    blocks adjacent to the section the net was assigned to;

    for both subpartitions do begin

        if subpartition contains more than one routing block
        then push subpartition on stack

    end

end
```

4. ASSIGNMENT OF NETS TO CUT-LINE POSITIONS

Assignment of a net to a section of the cut-line should be done in such a way that the increase of wire length of that net becomes as small as possible. Using this criterion, many nets may compete for the same section. On the other hand, the number of nets to be assigned to one section is limited: This is the capacity of the block-boundary. To find a good assignment of nets to sections we have to consider both, increase of wire length and capacity of sections.

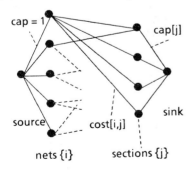

This problem can be stated as a generalized linear assignment problem or as a Hitchcock-type transport problem: We build a complete bipartite graph $G = (V,E)$ with two sets of nodes, one set $Vn = \{i\}$, $|Vn| = N$ representing nets, the other one $Vs = \{j\}$, $|Vs| = S$ representing sections of the cut-line. Edges (i,j) connect net-nodes with section-nodes. Edges (i,j) are labeled with weights $c[i,j]$ indicating the cost (to be discussed later) for assigning net i to section j. Assignment is subject to capacities $cap[j]$ associated with nodes from $\{j\}$.

FIGURE 2
The transport network corresponding to the assignment problem.

There are two approaches for solving this problem. One involves splitting each node j into cap[j] different nodes representing together one section; thus the problem is transformed into a classical linear assignment problem without capacities on nodes.

The other one (cf. Fig. 2) introduces additional source and sink nodes connected to nodes from Vn and Vs respectively. Capacity 1 is assigned to edges incident to the source node, capacity cap[j] to edges connecting a node j to the sink node and capacity 1 to the original edges (i,j). Cost zero is assigned to all the auxiliary edges. That way we have constructed a network problem the integer min-cost maximal flow solution of which gives us an optimal assignment of nets to sections.

Standard methods (least cost augmenting paths [7–9]) may be used to solve this problem.

5. COST FUNCTION

Experimental results have shown that choosing an appropriate cost function is crucial for the approach outlined above to achieve good results. Values of the cost function are stored in a N by S matrix and specify the cost for assigning crossing net i (i = 1 .. N) to one of the sections j (j = 1 .. S). (Note that the maximal number of nets crossing any cut-line determines the size of the problem; this number should be minimized by a good placement algorithm).

In our implementation the cost function contains two additive terms, one describing the increase of wire length left of the cut-line, the other one that right of the cut-line. The following discussion is concerned with only one of these terms.

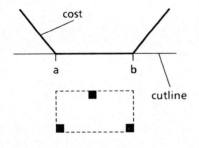

For each net to be processed we store and maintain the minimal rectangular box enclosing its true and pseudo terminals. Let the interval (a,b) be the projection of this box on the cutline. For all sections that are part of this interval we assign cost zero because the enclosing box will not increase more than it has to inevitably. For sections outside this range we assign cost values increasing linearly with the distance from the interval (a,b).

FIGURE 3
Parameters and shape of the cost function

The slope of this cost function outside (a,b) is not the same for all nets: The nearer the enclosing box lies to the cut-line the higher a slope is used. Therefore, nets that are already near to the cut-line "try harder" to stay within or near the interval (a,b) whereas more distant nets are forced to detour if not enough capacity is available for routing in the "ideal" range.

6. MULTIPLE CROSSINGS

For simplicity we have presented a primitive version of the algorithm that allows for only one crossing of a net over a cut—line. We get much better results if we allow multiple crossings. Multiple crossings fill otherwise unused capacities at higher levels of the hierarchy and provide connections that, without multiple crossings, would have to be made at lower levels.

Of course, only such additional crossings should be generated that do not result in an undue increase of wire length. To find such crossings for a net, we first calculate a minimal spanning tree (MST) on the complete graph induced by all the terminals of the net in the two partitions involved.

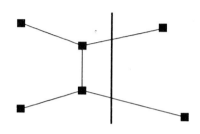

The MST edges can be separated into two subsets, those which cross the cut—line, and those which do not. Deleting the crossing edges would break the net into subnets that are totally contained in one of the two partitions. Now the assignment process described above is applied to these subnets, assigning not nets but crossing edges (connections between subnets) to sections of the cut—line.

FIGURE 4
MST crossing the cut—line twice

7. SELECTION OF CUT—LINES

Experimental results have shown that careful selection of cut—lines improves results considerably. We define criticality of a cut—line as the difference D — C between density D of the cut—line and total capacity C of the cut—line. Here the total capacity is the sum of capacities of cut—line sections, and density of a cut—line is the number of nets that have to cross over the cut.

Whenever we attempt to cut a partition, criticality is first calculated for all horizontal and vertical candidate positions. Then one with maximal criticality is selected.

For uniform distribution of terminals and capacities this method would result in producing an alternating sequence of horizontal and vertical cuts roughly bipartitioning chip and subchips; in general we get quite a different and more suitable pattern of cuts.

Calculation of capacities and densities at all potential cut positions can be done in one plane sweep per orientation over the partition. Adding up capacities is the most time consuming step in this process, taking o(m*n) steps for a partition of m rows by n columns of routing blocks.

8. COMPUTATIONAL COMPLEXITY

We will give only a rough estimate of computational complexity. For this purpose we assume a square chip of l rows by l columns of routing blocks, uniform capacities and a constant number k of nets crossing each block boundary in the final distribution of nets. We further assume a regular sequence of horizontal and vertical cuts bipartitioning the regions under consideration.

In the first partitioning step we have l sections and n = k*l nets to be assigned, resulting in an l by n cost matrix. Solving the assignment problem takes o(l*n) time on the average (experimental result). This results in c*k*l*l steps for solving the first subproblem (c constant). The next two subproblems have cut-line length l/2 requiring c*k*l*l/4 steps each. Thus we get a total of 1.5*c*k*l*l steps for the first level of hierarchy.

On the next level we have to solve 4 problems on l/2 by l/2 subchips which takes 4*(1.5*c*k*l*l/4) steps, the same number as for the previous level. Thus, the number of steps is the same for all levels of the hierarchy.

Since the number of steps is constant per level, the total expected time for the assignment process is of order o(k*l*l log l). The process of finding the best cut positions is o(l*l) as we have seen above which is dominated by the complexity of the assignment problem.

If we further assume that k is proportional to the number N of nets for fixed l, we can expect overall time complexity of o(N*l log l).

9. SHORTCOMINGS OF THE APPROACH

Exact solution of the global routing problem would involve calculation of Steiner trees which is known to be NP-hard in the general case. Therefore, we can not expect to get optimal results for our global routing heuristic. The main reasons that suboptimal solutions are generated are these two:

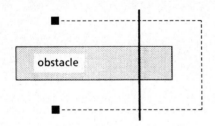

First, the hierarchical top down partitioning process imposes a very special topology on trees generated for the nets, which may not be optimal in some cases. For instance, a two-terminal net will never cross a cut-line twice or — in other words — U-shaped connections are not generated for these nets even though that might be useful for detouring crowded chip regions.

FIGURE 5
Typical situation where algorithm fails

Second, we may make final decisions on higher levels of the hierarchy that might turn out unfavorably at lower levels; there is no way (other than backtracking) to fix such problems at the lower level.

10. EXPERIMENTAL RESULTS

The algorithms described above have been implemented in PASCAL under UNIX on a VAX 11/780 and tested using both randomly generated test data and data from real chips.

The following table shows results for random net lists. To show how run—time depends on size of the grid and number of nets, these parameters have been varied. The number of terminals per net is randomly selected from a uniform distribution between 2 and 5 and terminal locations are uniformly distributed over the chip area.

	without	with	without	with
	cut—line optimization		cut—line optimization	
size	25 x 25		50 x 50	
nets	100 200	100 200	100 200	100 200
run—time [sec]	10 18	13 25	22 38	34 60

TABLE 1

The data of table 1 confirm our complexity considerations: Run—time approximately doubles if the linear dimension of the array is doubled (keeping the number of nets constant) and also increases as expected with the number of nets for constant grid size.

We also see that selecting a appropriate cut—line takes a considerable fraction of total run—time.

Table 2 shows results achieved with a practical example used as a bench mark in previous literature and compares the performance of various algorithms.

Number of nets   464

Number of terminals   1693

Algorithm	1	2	3	4	5	6
Overflows	0	19 0	0	15	46	0
Wire length	5366	????	4086	(4104)	(3713)	4101
run—time [sec]	1020	120 31	30	215	17	23

TABLE 2

Algorithms used are:

1.   Mesh routing with 1—step look ahead and backtracking [2].

2.   Bottom up hierarchical routing with rip—up and rerouting [3]. The table shows two entries, before and after the rip—up / reroute phase.

3.   Simple sequential maze router implemented by the author for comparison.

4.   Burstein's hierarchical algorithm based on linear programming.

5.   Top down hierarchical routing by linear assignment without cut—line optim-
      ization.

6.   Top down hierarchical routing by linear assignment with cut—line optimiza-
      tion.

Note, that wire length can be compared only if there are no or few overflows.

Obviously algorithm (6) does better on this example both in terms of wire
length and run—time than previously published algorithms. Comparison with (5)
shows that optimization of cut—line position and orientation is indispensable
to achieve satisfactory results.

The maze router also competes well in this case, but it slows down considerably
in larger examples and gives, in general, considerably lower completion rates.

Fig. 6 shows the global router in action. Some cut—lines have already been processed and the assignment of nets is indicated graphically.

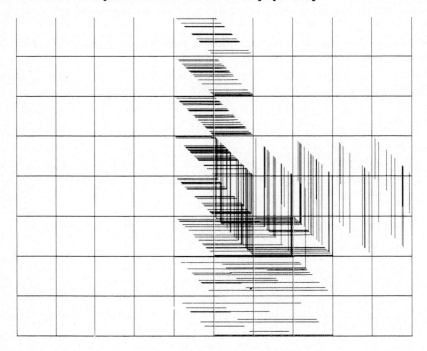

FIGURE 6
Global router in action. Snapshoot after a few cut—lines have been processed.
Nets assigned to positions sections along the cuts are shown as short pieces of
wiring.

11. CONCLUSIONS

A new hierarchical top down global routing algorithm based on linear assignment
(or network flow optimization) has been presented that processes at each level
of hierarchy all affected nets in parallel and calculates an embedding for nets
in terms of routing blocks.

The algorithm is easy to implement and compares favorably with previous results
for a practical example from published literature both in terms of run–time as
well as in terms of completion rate and wire length.

Since, after dividing a partition, the two subpartitions can be processed independently, the algorithm could also be implemented efficiently on parallel
processors.

ACKNOWLEDGEMENTS

The work reported here was done at the EECS department of the University of
California at Berkeley during a sabbatical leave from the Central Technology
Group of Siemens at Munich. My students Ren–Song Tsay and Young Hwan Kim imple-
mented a similar global router as a course project, experimenting with dif-
ferent cost functions. Caterina Willms–Peters implemented and evaluated
Burstein's algorithm and Doris Zepf did the drawings.

REFERENCES

[1] S.Goto, T. Matsuda, K.Taksmizawa, T.Fujita, H.Mizumura, H.Nakamura,
F.Kitajama, "LAMBDA, an Integrated Master–Slice LSI CAD System", Integration, The VLSI Journal, Vol. 1, No. 1, April 1983, pp. 53 – 69
[2] J.Li, M.Marek–Sadowska, "Global Routing for Gate Array", IEEE Trans. on
CAD, Vol. CAD–3, No. 4, Oct 1984, pp. 298 – 307
[3] M.Marek–Sadowska, "Global Router for Gate Array", Proc. ICCC 1984
[4] M.Vecchi, S.Kirkpatrick, " Global Wiring by Simulated Annealing", IEEE
Trans. CAD, Vol. CAD–2, no. 4, Oct. 1983, pp. 215– 222
[5] M.Burstein, R.Pelavin, "Hierarchical Wire Routing", IEEE Trans. CAD,
Vol. CAD–2, no. 4, Oct. 1983, pp.223–234
[6] M.Marek–Sadowska, "Route Planner for Custom Chip Design", IEEE International Conf. on Computer–Aided Design, Nov. 1986, Santa Clara, Digest of
Technical Papers, pp. 246 – 249
[7] R.E.Burkard, U.Derigs, "Assignment and Matching Problems: Solution
Methods with Fortran–Programs", Springer Verlag, 1980
[8] J.Edmonds, R.Karp, "Theoretical Improvements in Algorithmic Efficiency
for Network Flow Problems", Journal of the ACM, Vol. 19, No. 2, April
1972, pp. 248 – 264
[9] N.Tomizawa, "On Some Techniques Useful for Solution of Transportation
Network Problems", Networks, 1, pp. 173 –194, John Wiley & Sons, 1971.
[10] J. Kessenich, G. Jackoway, "Global Forced Hierarchical Router", Proc. of
the 23rd Design Automation Conf., Las Vegas 1986, pp. 798 – 802

VLSI '87, C.H. Séquin (editor)
Elsevier Science Publishers B.V. (North-Holland)
© IFIP, 1988

A Gridless Router : Software and Hardware Implementations

Kei Suzuki *   Tatsuo Ohtsuki *   Masao Sato **

* Department of Electronics and Communication Engineering
Waseda University, Tokyo Japan

** Department of Information Engineering, Faculty of Engineering
Takushoku University, Tokyo Japan

1.Introduction

Routing is one of the most important and probably one of the most successfully automated phases of VLSI design.   Among various algorithms, the Lee algorithm with its extensions is most general, and many existing auto-routers use it exclusively, or initially use some other algorithms to rapidly interconnect most of the nets, and then employ it in order to interconnect the remaining nets.   A disadvantage of the Lee algorithm is that it requires $O(L^2)$ time for finding a path of length L, which is becoming serious as the size of VLSI circuits continues to grow.   A possible solution to the size vs. processing time problem is to build special-purpose hardware which physically implements the Lee algorithm, and the recent VLSI technology has made it realistic.   For example, the authors have developed a hardware Lee router which finds a path of length L in O(L) time using N/2 processor elements for an N x N grid [1].   However, this kind of hardware routers based on parallel processing need more memory than software implementation.

The negative feature, i.e., $O(N^2)$ memory requirement, in the Lee algorithm has given rise to another class of routing methods which are referred to as **line search algorithms** [2],[3].   However, it turned out that the line search algorithms, unless the routing area is very simple, do not run as fast as the maze algorithms [2], or do not guarantee finding a path even if one exists [3].   Moreover, there is no rigorous analysis of computational complexity and data structures are only ambiguously described in the original papers [2],[3].

In this paper we present an improved line search algorithm which runs much faster and requires less memory than grid-based algorithms or classical line search algorithms, and of course it guarantees finding a solution whenever one exists.   The proposed algorithm can be viewed as a **gridless router** as it does not exploit a grid but directly consider polygonal regions as space for routing.   In Section 2, it is described how the improved line search algorithm leads to a minimum bend path.

Section 3 is devoted to data structures for software implementation of the proposed algorithm.   As the routing space can be viewed as a polygonal region in the plane, we analyze the algorithm based on computational geometry and extract from it a basic geometrical search problem.   Then it is shown that, if the routing space is represented by **priority search trees** [4], the geometrical search problem can be solved in $O(\log n)$ time with O(n) space, where n is the number of vertices of the polygonal region.   This implies that the improved line search algorithm runs in $O(n \log^2 n)$ time in the worst case with O(n) space.

In order to further accelerate the algorithm and to simplify complicated coding for data structure management, we propose an architecture for its hardware implementation. The essential part of the proposed architecture is Content Addressable Memory (CAM), which enables us to solve the basic geometrical search problem in constant time. This implies that the improved line search algorithm runs in O(n) time with O(n) units of CAM. In Section 4, the proposed architecture for hardware implementation of the algorithm is described, and its performance measured on a prototype machine we developed is compared with the results of the software implementation.

Finally, some concluding remarks are given in Section 5.

2. The Improved Line Search

In this section we shall describe the improved line search algorithm for point-to-point connections in single-layer routing space. We assume for simplicity that the routing space is a polygonal region bounded only by horizontal or vertical edges. Such a region is called a **rectilinear region**. Note that the polygon edges bounding the routing space is determined by obstructions and pre-assigned nets (see Fig. 1). The wiring paths to be found are also restricted to those rectilinearly oriented.

In the initial stage of routing, we virtually shrink the polygonal region for routing by taking wiring width/space rules into account. The concave vertices (270°) of the shrunk polygon are called **corner points** (marked with ● in Fig. 1). Then we generate horizontal and vertical lines incident with each corner point, where the endpoints of such lines are determined by the boundary of the shrunk polygon as obtained above. The line segments obtained in this way are called **escape lines** (denoted by thin solid lines in Fig. 1). The set of horizontal and vertical escape lines are stored into separate working storages WH and WV, respectively.

An efficient way of implementing the above initialization steps is to use balanced binary search trees for representing the polygonal regions. Then, by means of the plane sweep method, the operations of shrinking an n-vertex polygon and of generating escape lines can be done in O(n log n) time with O(n) space [5]. Note that an n-vertex polygon leads to O(n) corner points and escape lines. A key consideration here is not to find intersection points of escape lines in advance in order to get rid of using O(n²) memory space.

A (minimum bend) path connecting a pair of points S(source) and T(target) can be found as follows.

Step 1 (preprocessing): Generate an additional escape line incident with T (called a **target line**) and insert it into either WH or WV. Generate another line segment incident with S (called **source line** and regarded as the escape line of level 0 and put it into a queue (denoted by Q). In Fig. 1, the target line and source line are denoted by dotted lines.

Step 2: Delete an escape line (of level i) from Q and enumerate all escape lines that intersect it (regarded as those of level (i+1)) by searching WH or WV.

Step 3: If one of them is the target line, then backtrace to generate a path and go to Step 5.

Step 4: Otherwise, delete the enumerated escape lines from WH or WV and put them into Q with appropriate backtrace codes. Return to Step 2. If Q is empty, there is no path.

A Gridless Router   155

Step 5 (postprocessing): Update the set of escape lines (WH and WV) by
regarding   the   path   just   found   as   an   obstruction   for   subsequent
interconnections.

In the example of Fig. 1, three escape lines of level 1, seven escape
lines of level 2 and eight escape lines of level 3 are found in this order.
Now one of the escape lines of level 3 is the desired target line, thus the
backtrace leads to the path as shown in Fig. 2.   After the path is found,
some of old escape lines are either deleted or shrunk and then new corner
points corresponding to the bends of the path are placed to generate new
escape lines in Step 5.   The updated escape lines are shown in Fig. 2, and
new corner points are marked with O.

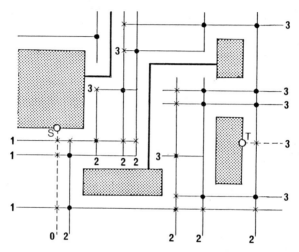

Fig. 1   Improved line search.

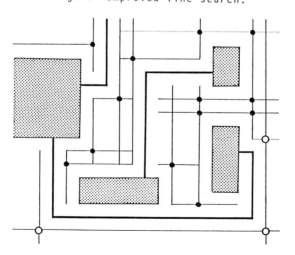

Fig. 2   Generated path and updated escape lines.

By analyzing the above algorithm, we see that the intersection is checked at most once per escape line.   Note that, if an escape line of level i has been confirmed to intersect another escape line of level (i-1) in Step 2, it is then deleted from WH or WV in Step 4 so as not to consider any more intersection with the other escape lines of level (i-1).   The intersection points actually considered in the above algorithm are marked with X in Fig. 1. Since there are only O(n) escape lines, a path can be generated in O(nt) time, .where t is the upper bound of the time to delete an escape line or to ·enumerate escape lines intersecting a query line segment from WH or WV.

This algorithm always leads to a minimum bend path [6], because escape lines of lower level are searched with higher priority.   Note that, if a path with b bends is to be found, the target line receives a level number b.

The improved line search algorithm can be extended to more general cases. For connecting a multi-terminal net, we first connect two of the terminals, and then repeat the procedure of finding a tree-to-point connection.   This procedure can be realized with an obvious modification of the above algorithm. For multi-layer interconnections, the essential modification is to store the escape lines in separate working storages classified by the available wiring layers, and a path can be found with the same order of time complexity.

3. Data Structures for Software Implementation

In the improved line search algorithm presented in the preceding section, the following geometric search problems play an essential role.

Problem A: **Rectilinear Line Segment Adjacency Search.**
For a set H of n horizontal line segments and the upward (downward) vertical half line incident with a query point P, find the lowermost (uppermost, resp.) line segment of H intersecting the half line (see Fig. 3).

Problem B: **Rectilinear Line Segment Intersection Search.**
For a set H of n horizontal line segments and a vertical line segment query V, enumerate all line segments of H intersecting V (see Fig. 4).

Although we will only discuss here the problems just defined above, the equivalent ones derived by interchanging x and y coordinates can be treated in the same way.   For our purpose, Problems A and B are **dynamic** ones in the sense that operations of the above searches and of updating H (inserting or deleting items) are invoked in a random sequence.

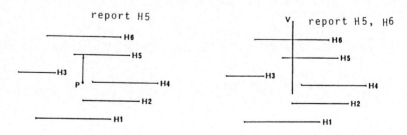

Fig. 3 Line segment
adjacency search.

Fig. 4 Line segment
intersection search.

There are several data structures [4],[7],[8],[9], applicable to the above dynamic search problems. Among those requiring only linear memory space, we claim that the priority search tree proposed by McCreight [4] is the best available. By means of this data structure, we can manage a set D of n points in the plane with O(n) units of memory and insert (delete) a point into (from, resp.) D in O(log n) time. Furthermore, for a query rectangular region $R=\{(x,y)| \; x \leq a, \; b_1 < y < b_2\}$, we can (a) find the lowermost (uppermost) point of R in O(log n) time and (b) enumerate all points of R in O(log n + k) time, where k is the number of enumerated points.

It is interesting to see here that the above search problems (a) and (b) are equivalent to Problems A and B with the set H of horizontal line segments displaced by that of rightward half lines. Note that the set D of points in the above paragraph is associated with the set of endpoints of the half lines.

The basic idea for dealing with the original line segments in Problems A and B is to divide the problem into O(log n) subproblems concerning half lines as follows. We bisect the plane by vertical slice line in such a way that the numbers of line segments to the right of and to the left of the bisector are balanced. Then we associate the root of a tree (**external tree**) with the line segments intersecting the bisector, and the right (left) subtree with those entirely lying to the right (left, resp.) of the bisector. The line segments cut by the bisector are represented by two priority search trees (**internal trees**), one representing the pieces of the cut segments to the right of the bisector, and the other representing those to the left. In each of these priority search trees, the line segments can be viewed as half lines. We recursively continue the bisection until every line segment is cut by a bisector. Note that the whole line segments are managed by a **two-level** tree; the external one is a binary search tree with respect to x-coordinates of the bisectors and the internal ones are priority search trees representing the fictitious half lines [10].

For a vertical segment query V, there are O(log n) priority search trees which we have to look into to report line segments intersecting it. Each such a tree corresponds to a recursive level of bisections. Any line segment in the other priority search tree has no intersection with the query segments. Thus, the solution of the problem can be obtained from the solutions of O(log n) subproblems of reporting half lines intersecting V. Therefore, we can report all horizontal line segments intersecting V in $O(\log^2 n + k)$ time. Furthermore, for a segment to be inserted into (or deleted from) H, the priority search tree to be inserted into (or deleted from) can be found in O(log n) time and it is updated in O(log n) time. An obvious modification of the above algorithm leads to an algorithm for Problem A, where $O(\log^2 n + k)$ search time is of course reduced to $O(\log^2 n)$. It is clear that the two-level tree requires only O(n) space as each line segment is stored in only two priority search trees.

Now we shall recall the improved line search algorithm described in Section 2. In step 2, Problem B is invoked with respect to escape lines stored in WH or WV. This step is repeated at most n (number of escape lines) times, and the total number of actually searched intersection points are of O(n). Problem B is also invoked in Step 5 to enumerate the escape lines intersecting the path just found, but it is invoked only (b+1) times, where b is the number of bends of the path. In order to generate source and target lines in Step 1 and to generate new escape lines in Step 5, Problem A has to be invoked with respect to the set of line segments defining obstructions. Again, it is invoked at most O(n) times. Consequently, the improved line search algorithm runs in $O(n \log^2 n)$ time in the worst case. To be more specific, "search" (running in $O(\log^2 n)$ time) and "updating" (running in O(log n) time) are repeated at most O(n) times.

An alternative way, which is theoretically interesting, of implementing
the proposed algorithm is to use the data structure called **segment tree**
[7],[8],[9], which is not applicable to the dynamic search problems.   Then
the algorithm runs in O(n log n) time, but instead O(n log n) memory space is
required.   As another interesting result, a minimum bend path algorithm with
O(n log n) time and O(n) space is available if the routing space is single-
layered [11].

The authors have implemented the improved line search algorithm in an
experimental program, written in FORTRAN run on IBM 3033 computer.   Since the
processing time for finding a particular path depends on the   number of
searched line segment, we consider here a worst case where the respective data
structures for n line segments are constructed once and then n searches
(Problem A or B) and n updating operations are invoked in a random sequence.
The average time for processing the above sequence of operations, depending on
data structures, is plotted in Fig. 5, where N, L, and P denote naive data
structure based on linked list, layered segment tree [7] and priority search
tree, respectively.   It is observed that priority search tree is much more
efficient than layered segment tree.   The reason is that the layered segment
tree requires more time for constructing and updating the data structure and
much more memory space than the priority search tree, although the former
achieves better search time than the latter [12].

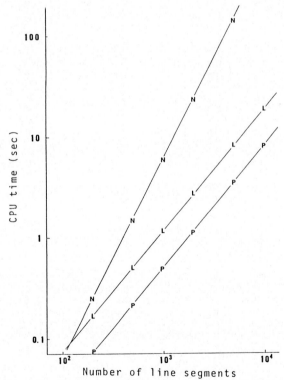

Fig. 5 Comparison of data structures.
        N: naive method based on linked lists
        L: layered segment tree
        P: priority search tree

4. CAM-Based Architecture for Hardware Implementation

In order to further speed up the improved line search algorithm, we propose in this section a new architecture for its hardware implementation based on **Content Addressable Memory** (CAM), or elsewhere called **Associative Memory**. The **equivalence search** in hardware, the basic function of early bit-parallel CAM, can be extended several more sophisticated searches on m-bit words by means of a sequence of $O(m)$ or $O(\log m)$ basic searches [13],[14],[15]. Then, provided that the number m of bits per word is fixed, hardware implementation of such searches achieves constant processing time independent of number of words. Among them the following searches play an essential role for our purpose.

Threshold Search : For a given search key word K, which is stored in Index Register, enumerate all the words greater than (or less than) K with respect to a partial content specified by Mask Register (see Fig. 6).

Extremum Search : Find the word with maximum (or minimum) value with respect to a partial content specified by Mask Register (see Fig. 7).

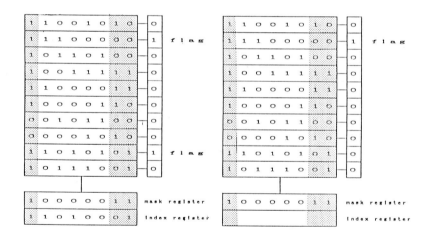

Fig. 6 Threshold search   Fig. 7 Extremum search
by means of CAM.   by means of CAM

The above functions of CAM can be applied to the geometric search problems posed in Section 3 by storing each horizontal line segment data in a CAM word as shown in Fig. 8. Then Problem A, for a query point $P=(X_0, Y_0)$, can be solved by means of the following sequence of basic operations.

Fig. 8 Representation of
line segment data.

   Step 1 :   Select the words such that XR $\geq$ X$_0$ (Threshold Search with respect to field XR).

   Step 2 :   From the words selected in Step 1, select those such that XL $\leq$ X$_0$ (Threshold Search with respect to field XL).

   Step 3 :   From the words selected in Step 2,   select those such that Y$<$ Y$_0$ (Threshold Search with respect to field Y).

   Step 4 :   Find the word with the minimum Y value among those selected in Step 3 (Extremum Search with respect to field Y).

   Problem B can also be solved in a similar way.   Now it is clear that the geometric search problems posed in Section 3 can be solved in constant time due to the word-parallel nature of CAM.   This implies that the hardware implementation based on CAM enables the improved line search algorithm run in O(n) time in the worst case.

   Outlined in Fig. 9 is the architecture of the proposed CAM-based layout engine, which is designed to be used as a slave processor controlled by a host computer.   This layout engine is intended to accelerate not only the improved line search algorithm but also variety of gridless routers [10],[16] and other geometrical problems involved in VLSI design,   such as design rule checking, layout compaction, artwork generation, etc.

   The layout engine includes four major parts: CAM,   microprogram controller, RAM and ALU.   For the CAM part, we are currently using the 4K bit (128 32-bit words) CAM chips developed by NTT [17],   which will be replaced by 20K bit (512 40-bit words) CAM chips [18].   Our machine is designed to embed a maximum of 64 such chips.   NTT's CAM circuits are operated by instructions synchronized by a clock pulse.   The 4K bit CAM has 30 instructions, and each instruction is carried out within a 140ns clock cycle.   The more details of

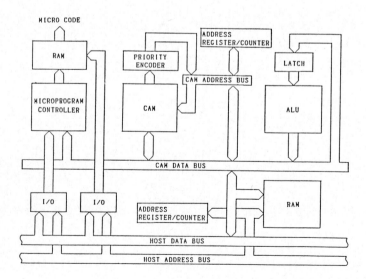

Fig. 9   Structure of layout engune using CAM chips.

the 4K bit CAM chip is given in Table 1.   Since the simple scheme, in which a
CPU directly gives instructions to CAM,   cannot follow this high speed clock,
the microprogram controller is used to drive microcodes.   RAM chips are used
for data swapping with the host computer and for working storages.   ALU is
used for other operations which are not suitable to CAM.

Table 1   Specification of 4Kbit CAM chips.

word structure	128w x 32b
operational modes	30 (search, write, read, etc)
cycle time	140 ns
power supply	5 Volts
power dissipation	250 mW (200 ns)
I/O interface	common I/O, TTL level
package	64 pin FP
process	3 µm CMOS, 2 layer Al.
transistors	71,300
chip size	10.3mm x 8.4mm

For the improved line search algorithm, two words (64 bits) of 4K bit CAM
chips are assigned.   Then the Line Segment Adjacency Search (Problem A in
Section 3) can be processed within 300 cycle time.   Fig. 10 demonstrates the
performance   improvement   the   CAM-based   hardware   confers   over   software
implementation.   The performance for small number of line segments was
measured on the first version of our prototype machine (4 CAM chips are
embedded)   and   that   for   large   problems   were   extrapolated   by   means   of
simulation.   It is observed from Fig. 10 that the more line segments there
are,   the   more   effective   the   CAM-based   approach   is.   Moreover we have
confirmed   that   the   signal   delay,   which   might   invalidate   the   constant
processing time assumption on word-parallel property of CAM,   is negligible in
a circuit with several tenth of such CAM chips.

5. Conclusion

A new gridless routing algorithm (the improved line search) has been
presented together with considerations on its implementations in both software
and hardware.   The algorithm,   in software, finds a path in $O(n \log^2 n)$ time
with $O(n)$ memory space, by means of an extensive use of priority search trees.
This is more efficient than existing grid-based algorithms and early line
search algorithms. It also has flexibility in accommodating complicated design
rules which are typically seen in recent VLSI chips.

The   hardware   implementation   based   on   CAM   further   accelerates   the
algorithm and achieves linear time and space complexity.   The proposed
architecture is applicable not only to the improved line search but also to
variety of layout problems.   This flexibility is due to the feature of CAM-
based approach that complicated coding for sophisticated data structures,
depending on subproblems,   is not involved.   A future direction the authors
expect is that higher density CAM chips with variable length words will come
out.

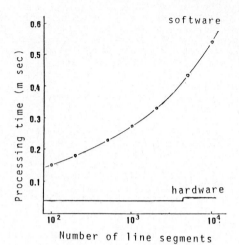

Fig. 10   Comparison of processing time:
software vs. hardware.

Acknowledgment

This research was partly supported by the National Science Foundation under Grant ECS-8201580.

References

[1] K. Suzuki et al., "A Hardware Maze Router with Application to Interactive Rip-Up and Reroute," IEEE Trans. Computer-Aided Design, vol.CAD-5, No.4, pp.466-476, 1986.
[2] K. Mikami and K. Tabuchi, "A Computer Program for Optimal Routing of Printed Circuit Connections," Proc. IFIPS, Vol.H47, pp.1475-1478, 1968.
[3] D. W. Hightower, "A Solution to Line-Routing Problem on the Continuous Plane," Proc. 6th Design Automation Workshop, pp.1-24, 1969.
[4] E. M. McCreight, "Priority Search Trees," SIAM J. Comput., Vol.14, No.2, pp.257-276, 1985.
[5] M. Sato et al., "An O(n log n) Algorithm for LSI Layout Resizing Problems," Proc. of ISCAS 85, pp.25-28, 1985.
[6] W. Lipski,Jr., "Finding a Manhattan Path and Related Problems," NETWORKS, Vol.13, pp.399-409, 1983.
[7] V. K. Vaishnavi and D. Wood, "Rectilinear Line Segment Intersection, Layerd Segment Trees, and Dynamization," Algorithms, Vol.3, pp.160-176, 1982.
[8] W. Lipski,Jr., "An O(n log n) Manhattan Path Algorithm," Information Processing Letters, Vol.19, No.2, pp.99-102, 1984.
[9] H. Imai and T. Asano, "Efficient Algorithms for Geometric Graph Search Problems," SIAM J. Comput., Vol.15, No.2, May 1986.
[10] T. Asano et al., "LAYOUT DESIGN AND VERIFICATION Chapter 9 Computational Geometry Algorithms," Advances in CAD for VLSI, Vol. 4, (North-Holland, Amsterdam, 1986).
[11] M. Sato et al., "A Fast Line-Search Method Based on A Tile Plane," to appear at ISCAS 87.

[12] M. Sato and T. Ohtsuki, "Dynamic Line Segment Intersection Search
     Algorithms Based on Computational Geometry and Their Applications,(in
     Japanese)" Bulletin of Centre for Informatics, Waseda Univ., Vol.2,
     AUTUMN, pp.1-12, 1985.
[13] E. H. Frei and J. Goldberg, "A method for resolving multiple responces in
     a parallel search file," IRE Trans. Electron. Comput., vol. EC-10,
     pp.718-722, Dec. 1961.
[14] A. D. Falkoff, "Algorithm for parallel-search memories," J. ACM, vol.9,
     pp.488-511, Oct. 1962.
[15] W. A. Davis and D. Lee, "Fast Search Algorithms for Associative
     Memories," IEEE Trans. Comput., Vol.c-35, No.5, pp.456-461, May. 1986.
[16] T. Ohtsuki and M. Sato, "Gridless Routers for Two-Layer Interconnection,"
     Proc. of ICCAD84, pp.76-78, 1984.
[17] T. Ogura et al., "A 4Kbit Associative Memory LSI," IEEE J.Solid-State
     Circuits, Vol.SC-20. pp.1277-1282, Dec. 1985.
[18] T. Ogura et al., "A 20Kb CMOS Associative Memory LSI for Artificial
     Intelligence Machines," Proc. of ICCD-86,
     pp.574-577, Oct. 1986.

VLSI '87, C.H. Séquin (editor)
Elsevier Science Publishers B.V. (North-Holland)
© IFIP, 1988

Mosaico: An Integrated Macro-Cell Layout System

J.Burns, A.Casotto, M.Igusa, F.Marron, F.Romeo,
A.Sangiovanni-Vincentelli, C.Sechen[†], H.Shin, G.Srinath[‡], H.Yaghutiel

Department of Electrical Engineering and Computer Sciences
University of California, Berkeley

ABSTRACT

In this paper a new, integrated, macro-cell layout system called Mosaico is presented. Mosaico implements a complete layout pipeline from high-level description to final layout. Well-tested tools like the channel routers Yacr and Chameleon are used together with recently-developed tools for power and ground routing, channel definition and ordering, and floorplanning and placement. The system handles macro-cells of any rectilinear shape and efficiently uses all the interconnect layers offered by the technology. Cells with floating pins and variable aspect ratios can be accommodated. Unlike other layout systems, no rectilinear slicing-structure placement is required; this is due to a new, generalized channel definition and ordering algorithm. Every tool in Mosaico runs from and generates symbolic-layout views of the design. A spacing program takes the results after detailed routing in symbolic form and performs a compaction while guaranteeing that the design rules are satisfied. The Oct data manager is used to store the design at each stage of the layout process. The amount of data stored at each stage is stated in a set of policies that are respected by all tools, making the system modular and extensible. Mosaico is tightly coupled with synthesis and verification tools in the Berkeley design environment.

1. INTRODUCTION

A critical component of an efficient IC synthesis system is a set of optimized placement and routing tools. Some of the early silicon compilers [1], [2] had a fixed floorplan, resulting in serious inefficiencies with respect to the area occupied by the design. Recently attention has focused on layout systems tightly coupled with logic synthesis [3]. This paper describes **Mosaico**, a complete set of placement and routing tools tightly coupled with logic synthesis, module generation, compaction, verification, and timing analysis.

One of the main requirements for a layout system in a general design environment such as the one being developed at Berkeley [4] is the ability to support a variety of layout styles. The ThunderBird system [5] has previously been developed to place and route standard-cell designs. The Mosaico system consists of a set of tools for the placement and routing of macro-cells, a design style that is rapidly gaining in importance. Other tools have been developed over the years to place and route macro-cells, both in industry, e.g., the systems described in [6], and in universities, e.g., the PI system [7] and the BBL system [8]. Mosaico differs from other systems in several ways, the most important difference being that no constraints are imposed on the layout style used to implement the macro-cells. Furthermore Mosaico is tightly coupled to Berkeley's logic synthesis system [4] through the use of module generators. That is, each macro-cell is optimized at the logic level with the characteristics of the target implementation style accounted for. The Mosaico floorplanner is then used to produce specifications for the aspect ratio and pin positions of the macro-cell. The combination of the optimized logic equations and the geometric information from the floorplanner comprise the input to the module generator; the generator output is then used in the placement phase of Mosaico.

In Mosaico the floorplanning and the placement (F&P) tasks are considered in a unified framework; in fact the same program is used for both tasks. The process starts as floorplanning with some or all of the

---

† C.Sechen is presently with the Electrical Engineering Department at Yale University.

‡ G.Srinath was a visiting Fellow from AMD during this work. He is presently with Daisy Systems Corporation.

cells not fully specified, and becomes placement as soon as all the macro-cells have fixed implementations. The tool used for F&P is based on simulated annealing. Simulated annealing has proven to be a robust optimization technique that consistently produces results with high area efficiency. In addition its flexibility makes it attractive for applications such as the macro-cell problem where there are many degrees of freedom.

The routing part of the system targets the fabrication technologies now emerging that provide multiple interconnect layers. To achieve design-rule independence the entire Mosaico system operates at the symbolic-layout level, rather than at the physical-layout level. A spacing step is carried out prior to mask generation to ensure that the layout is design-rule correct.

Mosaico has been configured in a highly modular manner to ease the introduction of new tools into the system. The modularity has been achieved by using a unified data representation for the design, regardless of the stage in the design cycle. No transformation between representation formats is required, and all data is stored using a common data manager.

The remainder of the paper is organized as follows. In Section 2 the overall structure of the system is presented. In the following sections, the tools that comprise the system are described in the order in which they appear in the design flow. Results obtained on a number of test cases are then presented, followed by some of the directions for future development of Mosaico.

2. MOSAICO OVERVIEW

An overview of the structure of Mosaico, the management of the design data, and the initialization of the system are given in this section.

2.1. Pipeline Structure

Mosaico consists of five basic steps that are nominally executed in sequence, that is, as a *pipeline*. The pipeline is represented in Figure 1 together with the sequence of symbolic views that are stored at each step in the Oct data manager [9]. Each step is described in detail in the following sections.

In an ideal situation each step in the pipeline would be executed once only. In reality iteration of some or all of the steps is often required. For example, if the routing area estimated in the placement phase is not

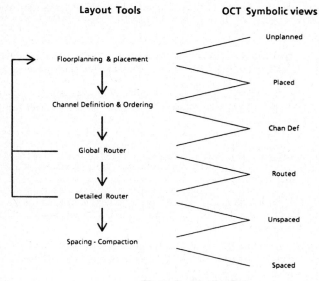

Figure 1. Mosaico System.

sufficient, at least one of the macro-cells must be moved. This in turn may require that the unrouted areas be re-processed by the channel definition procedure. A description of the feedback loops in the Mosaico system is included later in this paper.

2.2. Data Management

Figure 1 illustrates one of the most important feature of the Mosaico system, namely its modularity. Modularity is achieved by enforcing the rule that all the information produced at each stage of the pipeline must be stored via the data manager. Each of the tools in the pipeline reads its input data from a view in the data manager and produces as its output another view which contains the previous data updated with the information added by the tool. Of course, new views need not be created; the original view can be annotated in place by each tool if desired. This modularity provides the Mosaico system with a great deal of flexibility since every tool in the pipeline can be replaced with an equivalent one that requires the same input data and provides the same output data.

The key issue in achieving this flexibility is to control the structure of and the amount of data stored at each stage of the pipeline. The set of data has to be rich enough to provide each tool with the information it needs while being general enough to allow interfacing different tools based on different algorithms. This task is made easy by the characteristics of the design data manager Oct. Oct provides the user with a general way to store the data items and the dependency relations among them. The tools read and write Oct views using a library of procedures. As a result, the tools need not be concerned with the storage format used by Oct, nor are they affected by any changes to the internal structure of Oct.

The particular data items used, and the relations among them, are not part of Oct; rather, they are decided upon by the community of tool-makers. An example of such a decision is the manner used to describe the permutability of terminals. This set of decisions is referred to as the *policy* for the design. Since the policy is not part of Oct it can be changed easily; and since all concerned parties participate in the definition of the policy it provides them with an efficient protocol for storing and exchanging information at each stage of the pipeline.

Another important advantage of storing all intermediate results in the data manager is that the pipeline can be restarted at every level. Moreover all the intermediate results can be graphically displayed by Vem, a general-purpose graphics editor for Oct views [9]. Vem can be used to view the design at any point, from the floorplan stage down to the complete design after detailed routing and spacing. Finally, tools that complete more than one of the steps outlined in Figure 1 can easily be inserted in the pipeline, at the expense of losing the ease with which the intermediate steps of the layout procedure can be unbundled and re-executed.

2.3. Pipeline Initialization

The set of input data required for Mosaico is a set of instances of macro-cells interconnected by a net-list. The implementations of the macro-cells are generated separately, either by an automatic module generator or by manual design; when the Mosaico pipeline is started not all of the macro-cells need to be completely specified. Initially the input information is expressed in the Bdsyn language [3]. The Bdsyn description is used to automatically produce the corresponding Oct symbolic view, which is named *unplanned*.

3. FLOORPLANNING AND PLACEMENT

In the Mosaico environment, the activity of floorplanning and placement is handled in a unified framework; in fact there is no distinction between floorplanning and placement at the algorithmic level. At the floorplanning stage some of the parameters of the macro-cells (aspect ratio, pin positions) may be varied; at the placement level all the macro-cell parameters are fixed and the only remaining degrees of freedom are the positions and orientations of the cells. The F&P phase maintains a global view of the chip and directs the interactions with module generation and timing verification.

The F&P iterations are started by an initial floorplanning operation in which the most detailed description available for each cell is retrieved from the data manager. For some macro-cells the complete layout may be known. For others only a set of constraints, such as requirements on pin positions or aspect ratio, may exist. Other cells may be described at the logical or behavioral level. For such cells, called *soft cells*, an area estimation is performed, based on the complexity of the cell and on the features of the module generator that will be used to produce it. The terminals of a soft cell are free to move about the border of the cell unless constraints are present.

After each iteration the floorplanner produces as output the position and orientation of each cell and also the shape and pin positions for those cells that were not completely specified. This information is passed to the module generators, namely Gem [10], Wolfe [11], and Topogen [12]. The generators differ in the layout styles they implement. Gem produces macro-cells using a gate matrix approach featuring multiple row and column folding. Wolfe generates macro-cells by assembling standard cells using the TimberWolfSC package [13] combined with the channel routers Yacr [14] and Chameleon [15]. Topogen produces individual cells in the standard-cell style; these cells may be combined into larger cells using Wolfe.

The input to the module generators comes from two sources, one being the floorplanner which specifies geometric constraints as described above. The other data is the logic description produced by the logic optimization tool Mis [3]. If a module generator is unable to satisfy all the constraints imposed on a particular cell, the actual shape of the generated cell is fed back to F&P and a new iteration is started. An example of the interaction between F&P and the module generator Wolfe is shown in Figure 2. Figure 2A represents the target cell as specified by the floorplanner. Figure 2B shows the result produced.

The F&P module also interacts with the timing analyzer Hummingbird [16]. The purpose of the timing analyzer is to critique the floorplan. It performs two tasks; first it checks the arrival times of signals required for the correct functioning of the circuit, then it marks each net with information about the maximum and minimum delay through that net. If the requirements are not met, a new iteration of the floorplanner is necessary. The timing information is used to update the constraints imposed by F&P on the maximum or minimum length of the nets. Correction of violations of the timing requirements may require more than just a new placement. In fact, for some cells a transistor re-sizing may be necessary, or some may need to be re-synthesized with new delay targets. In both cases the intervention of the designer is required at present.

As the F&P task is repeatedly executed, more and more refined representations of the chip are generated. As the macro-cells gain their physical implementations, the information available to the F&P tool increases, and the floorplanning task becomes a placement task.

3.1. F&P Algorithm

The tool presently used for F&P is the TimberWolfMC package [17]. The package is based on the simulated annealing algorithm, which provides it with the flexibility that is needed in order to use one tool for both tasks.

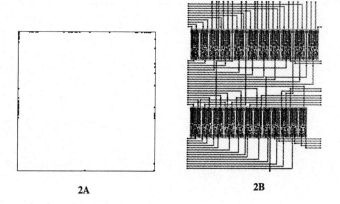

2A   2B

Figure 2.   Floorplanner and Module Generator Interaction.

A list of basic features includes:

- Cells representable by any set of Manhattan polygons are allowed
- Cells are allowed to have aspect ratios that vary over a range
- Cells can have multiple implementations (the most suitable will be selected)
- Cells may have variable pin positions
- Weights can be assigned to each net to bias the placement

During F&P the total estimated interconnect length is minimized, and a penalty function approach is used to drive the total amount of cell overlap toward zero at the end of the annealing procedure. The length of each net is estimated using the half-perimeter of the bounding box of the pins connected to the net; the calculation is based on the exact pin locations. A dynamic algorithm [17] is used to estimate the routing area necessary around each cell to complete the routing. The use of this estimation algorithm has resulted in the generation of placements which require very little modification during detailed routing.

After the placement is completed TimberWolfMC performs a placement refinement based on a more accurate estimate of the routing area required. The estimate is obtained through a coarse global-routing step. Based on the results of the global router and on the track spacing required by the technology, an estimate of the area required for each routing region is computed and the placement is consequently modified. The procedure is repeated until convergence is obtained.

4. CHANNEL DEFINITION AND ORDERING

The *channel definition* task is to partition the available routing area into smaller regions for the subsequent global and detailed-routing phases. Once the regions are determined they have to be *ordered* so that each region can be routed in a sequence such that its width can be adjusted independently of all previously-routed regions.

Otten [18] presented a channel definition algorithm which produces a feasible routing order on a restricted class of placements called *rectilinear slicing structures*. The advantage of the slicing method is that it induces a simple hierarchical decomposition of the routing problem into independent subproblems. The chip is divided by the first slice into two blocks; the slicing procedure is then recursively repeated on the subblocks. Each slice represents a single routing area and the order in which the slices are found is the reverse of the routing order. In the original work [18] the routing regions were restricted to channels; the removal of this restriction will be described below.

The ordering and independence properties described above are properties of the slicing structure *concept*, regardless of the actual shape of the slices. Typically, the term *slicing structure* refers to rectilinear configurations where each slice is a straight cut. However, if the channel definition algorithm is generalized to handle structures where the slices can have bends, no constraints need to be imposed on the placement. The lack of constraints is particularly important in Mosaico since the simulated-annealing-based F&P produces structures that are more general than the rectilinear slicing structure.

In Mosaico the slices are allowed to have bends. The configuration of a slice determines the type of its corresponding detailed routing problem. For example, in the simple case where the slice has no bends, the problem is an ordinary channel-routing problem with two fixed sides and two open sides. A single-bend slice produces an "L-shaped" channel.

It was proven in [19] that if only rectangular cells are present, an L-shaped slice is the most complex shape that can result from the slicing algorithm. However this result does not hold if the cells are general Manhattan shapes. In this case *k-bend* slices (*k=0,1,2,3,...*) are necessary to guarantee a feasible slicing of the placement for any combination of cells. In Figure 3 an example of a one-bend slice is presented.

The generalized slicing algorithm inherits all the properties of the ordinary slicing strategy and handles a larger class of problems. As in the simple case, no switch-box router is necessary since all the generalized channels have floating terminals on two open sides.

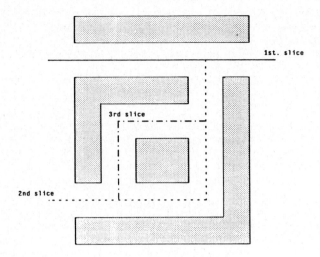

Figure 3.   Zero and One-Bend Slices.

4.1. Channel Definition Algorithm

A divide-and-conquer strategy similar to the one used to find a rectilinear slicing structure is employed. The differences compared to the standard algorithm are in the method used to determine the next slice. The algorithm consists of the following steps:

1. Use a scan-line approach to generate a floorplan graph [19].
2. Repeatedly subdivide the chip into sub-blocks up to the point in which each sub-block contains only one macro-cell. Each subdivision is determined by choosing the slice across the sub-block that minimizes a cost function.
3. The routing order is LIFO, i.e., the last slice found is the first to be routed.

The algorithm is implemented in a program called **Atlas**. The *cost* of a slice is determined by the number of bends in the slice, the number of orthogonal edges in the slice, and the number of external junctions [19] that are created by the slice. Note that the selection of a path with the smallest number of jogs and the maximum number of orthogonal edges to the path will eliminate as many potential jogs in future slices as possible. This is a greedy approach to finding the set of slices with the smallest total number of bends. Presently a more sophisticated algorithm is under development.

The hierarchy introduced by the slicing procedure corresponds to a binary tree that is added to the Oct design data. This routing order is used in the router server described below.

5. GLOBAL ROUTING

After the channel definition and ordering step described in the previous section, the data must be prepared for the global router. The channel graph, with the positions of the terminals on its edges, and a net list, are the inputs necessary for global routing. In the channel graph, nodes represent intersections between channels while edges represent channels or sections of them. Each edge in the graph is assigned a weight that represents the maximum number of tracks that can be accommodated in the channel. Once the channel graph is built, all the connected terminals of each macro-cell instance are projected to the closest edge in the graph. The weights on the edges are interpreted as *capacity constraints*. It is important to note that the input to the global router is completely symbolic and therefore totally independent of the layout style.

When the global router finishes, each net is represented by a sequence of subnets, each of which is assigned to one of the edges of the channel graph. When a net exits one channel to enter another one a *pseudo-terminal* is created.

Presently two different algorithms to perform the global route can be selected. The first algorithm is based on simulated annealing and it gives results that are marginally better at the expense of longer computation time. The second algorithm is faster and may be used interactively. The two algorithms are briefly described in the following.

5.1. Simulated-Annealing-Based Global Router

The simulated-annealing global routing algorithm has been developed as part of the TimberWolfMC package mentioned previously. The algorithm has the following features:

- No dependence on the routing order
- Multi-pin nets are handled in the same fashion as two-pin nets
- Electrically-equivalent pins are utilized to minimize the routing length

The algorithm has two basic stages; during the first stage it attempts to generate the M shortest routes for each net, a task which can readily be accomplished for two-pin nets [20]. For nets consisting of more than two pins, an algorithm has been developed which generalizes the approach in [20].

The second stage of the algorithm selects a single route from the M alternatives for each net. Let n_i represent a net, where $i \in \{1, \cdots, N\}$ and N is the number of nets. Furthermore, let n_i^k represent the k-th alternative route for net n_i, where $k \in \{1, \cdots, M\}$. A simulated annealing algorithm is then used to select alternative $n_i^{k_0}$ for each $i \in \{1, \cdots, N\}$ such that the total routing length is minimized subject to the channel-edge capacity constraints. This approach enables the global router to avoid the routing-order-dependence problem. Rip-up and re-route strategies are never needed to complete or improve the global routing.

5.2. N-Layer Global Router

Nlagr is a global router that can handle multiple layers of interconnect and over-the-cell routing. Over-the-cell routes are represented by fixed-capacity edges in the graph, while routing areas between cells are represented by edges whose capacities can be exceeded with a penalty. Nlagr has the following characteristics:

- The number of bends and the number of channels through which a net passes are minimized.
- User-specified critical nets are routed first. The routing order for all other nets is shortest-length (estimated) first. The estimate used is one-half the perimeter of the minimum enclosing rectangle of the net.
- Nets can be weighted to prefer or avoid specific layers.

Two different algorithms are incorporated in Nlagr. The first is an extended shortest-path algorithm that can route multi-terminal nets. At each iteration a path is determined from the existing partial path to the nearest unconnected pin on the same net. The search for the new connection is performed by expanding first the nodes of the channel graph that are close to the existing path. The expansion proceeds until an unconnected pin is reached. In the expansion procedure no particular direction is privileged since no unconnected pin has been selected as the target. For this reason the method is referred to as *undirected search*. The results produced by the method depend on the choice of the first pin and several heuristics are provided to select it.

In the second algorithm, called *directed search*, the pins of the net are connected in a specified order. First a least-cost path is found from the first pin to the second pin. Next the least-cost *incremental* path is found to the third pin (i.e., the first pin among those not yet connected) and so on as in [21]. The order in which unconnected pins are processed is determined by sorting them according to a cost which consists of two terms. The first term is the cost of the path connecting the expanded nodes in the channel graph to the already-existing path. This cost is the same as that used in the first algorithm. The second term is an estimate of the distance between the unconnected pin and the closest expanded node. The presence of the second cost term makes the search proceed rapidly in the direction of the target. This algorithm is strongly dependent on the pin ordering. Several schemes are provided for ordering the pins prior to routing.

According to experimental results undirected search seems to be better than directed search, although slower. The dependency of directed search on pin ordering can be used to provide interactive optimization. In this mode of operation the global router is typically run first in the undirected-search mode. The order in which the pins are connected is preserved and is used to back-annotate the net list. Next the optional interactive mode is entered; the user may then modify the pin order and run the router in directed-search mode.

6. DETAILED ROUTING

The router server **Spider** facilitates the detailed routing of the circuit based on the placement, the global router output, the channel order, and the design rules. Spider can handle k-bend routing regions with irregular edges, and wires with different widths, which is a crucial feature necessary in routing special nets like power and ground along with the standard signal nets. Spider chooses the best layer for floating pins whenever more than one layer is permitted.

The detailed routing is performed one channel at a time. The order is determined by Atlas as described in Section 4 of this paper. Spider retrieves the channel order from the data manager by traversing the binary tree that represents the hierarchy in depth-first order. Then it selects one of the symbolic routers available according to the nature of the channel being processed. Presently the library of routers that can be used by Spider consists of three symbolic routers: the two-layer channel router Yacr2 [14], the multi-layer channel router Chameleon [15], and the general-area router Mighty [22]. The selection of the router is based on a set of rules, such that the simplest router that can successfully route the area is selected. For example an L-shaped channel, routed by Mighty, is shown in Figure 4. To make it easy to extend the tool library by adding new symbolic routers, the selection rules are kept separate from the core of the program by storing them in a file that can be modified by the user.

Once the symbolic router is selected, Spider prepares the router's input data in the suitable format. Since all of the routers in the Mosaico library are grid-based, Spider starts by defining a grid. The symbolic grid in the "vertical" direction (the columns) can be built in two different ways. The first choice is to use a uniform grid, where the spacing between grids is determined by the wire widths, the contact widths, and the spacing rules. The second approach uses a non-uniform grid. In this case the vertical grid lines are placed to obtain the best possible alignment with the actual locations of the pins. This method is especially useful in dealing with wires that differ in width. Regardless of the type of grid selected, it is not always possible for every pin to be located exactly on a grid line. In this situation, an attempt is made to obtain a better alignment of the terminals on the two sides of the routing area by slightly varying the offset between the macro-cells on either side. After the alignment procedure each pin that is still not on a grid line will be connected to the nearest adjacent one by a jog. In the "horizontal" direction, the grid lines (rows) are initially spaced uniformly. If the general-area router is used, the situation is a little more involved since an estimate of the space necessary to complete the routing must be computed. The spacing

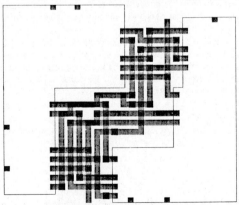

Figure 4.   L-Shaped Channel.

is definitively determined only after the routing is completed and the actual width of each wire has been computed.

After the selected router completes, a post-processing step is performed to attempt to reduce the number of jogs by shifting wires while maintaining the design rules. A simple optimization step is then performed to minimize the number of vias.

When the routing of a particular region is completed, a compactor is invoked to space the region and the adjacent macro-cells according to the design rules. The combination of the cells and the routing is then considered to be a new, large macro-cell for the following steps in the layout process. A word of caution is in order about the use of the compactor in this channel-by-channel manner. By compacting one channel it is possible to generate a misalignment in the next channel to be routed, possibly increasing its density and possibly increasing the area of the chip. To avoid this problem a more global view of the routing problem is necessary, which is accomplished by looking at the next area to be routed and passing constraints to the compactor to avoid increasing the density in the next channel.

7. POWER AND GROUND ROUTING

The routing of the power and ground nets is more involved than the routing of signal nets because of the following two considerations. First, voltage drops due to the finite conductance of interconnect and contacts have an adverse effect on the noise margins of the cells. Second, the maximum current densities tolerated by the interconnect layers cannot be exceeded. As a consequence, power and ground nets may have variable wire-segment widths.

In modern technologies the presence of two layers of metal makes it unnecessary to require planar routing techniques for power and ground connections. The policy used in Mosaico is to use the same set of tools to route both the standard signals and power and ground. However, power and ground connections require some additional processing. The complete details of the procedure will be described below.

It is assumed that there are power and ground rings around the periphery of the chip. The existence of these rings is important for insuring correct functionality of the chip. If the power pads were not connected through a ring, some of them might be at different potentials due to wiring inductance; this in turn might result in latch-up problems in a CMOS design. Furthermore, since no assumption is made on the amount of current that can flow through a macro-cell without damaging its internal power (ground) connection, it follows that each macro-cell must be connected directly to the rings.

The following steps describe the algorithm used to route power and ground.
1. Before the placement stage, the power (ground) net is decomposed into subnets. Each of these subnets contains two sets of equivalent pins, one being the power (ground) pins of a given macro-cell, and the other is the set of all the power (ground) pins on the ring. Then the original power (ground) net is discarded. The new nets are treated as signal nets, but with higher priority in the placement and global-routing stages in order to keep their lengths as short as possible.
2. After the global routing stage, the power (ground) nets are merged in such a manner that every channel contains at most two power (ground) nets. The upper limit of two occurs when two nets enter the channel from its opposite ends and both terminate inside the channel. An implication of this merging is that all the nets which stem from the same power (ground) pad are merged into a single net. This step is shown in Figure 5.
3. Once the nets are merged, the current requirements of the power (ground) nets are found at the boundaries of the channels.
4. After the symbolic detailed routing of each channel, the actual sizing of the nets in the channel is performed. The result of this step is shown in Figure 6.

8. LAYOUT SPACING

As noted above, all steps in the Mosaico pipeline are carried out at the symbolic-layout level. In addition, the module generators used in the system generate symbolic layouts. Symbolic layout spacing (or compaction) is thus an essential part of the system for several reasons. First, all designs must be spaced to

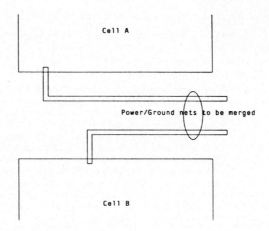

Figure 5. Merging of Power Nets.

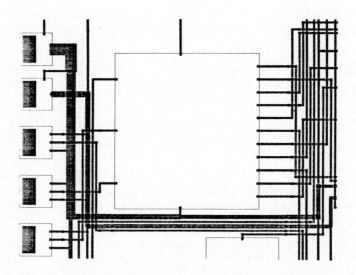

Figure 6. Sized Power Nets.

ensure that they are design-rule correct; this has the advantageous effect of eliminating design-rule checking, since the layouts are correct-by-construction. Second, the use of generalized symbolic layout provides a mechanism for producing technology-independent designs. The spacing techniques used in
Mosaico are capable of updating the symbolic layout primitives themselves (e.g., transistors, contacts), as
well as the spacings between them. Also, by the use of a variety of spacing techniques, various optimizations of the layout can be performed over a range of area/cpu-time tradeoffs. Presently two spacers are
available in Mosaico; each is described below.

8.1. One-Dimensional Spacing

Sparcs [23] is a constraint-based x-y spacer that has been designed to be as general as possible. Some of the features of Sparcs are:

- Support of upper-bound and user-defined constraints
- Adjustable positioning of non-critical-path circuit elements
- A hierarchy and technology-independent symbolic layout abstraction
- Terminal merging of arbitrary layout elements

Sparcs consists of two major modules: a constraint-graph builder and a constraint-graph solver. Sparcs uses successive one-dimensional spacings in alternating directions. The constraint graph for a particular direction is constructed from the relative placement of the symbolic layout elements and a table of spacing rules. The graph is analyzed to determine the locations of the layout elements in that dimension through a two-phase process, the first phase being a critical-path analysis. The elements that lie on the critical path determine the extent of the layout and are placed at their minimum legal positions. Considerations such as fabrication yield or delay optimization are used to locate the elements that are not on the critical path. Since both upper-bound and lower-bound constraints are allowed, overconstrained problems may arise. Such problems are identified in the solution process so that they may be corrected.

8.2. Two-Dimensional Spacing

Zorro is a two-dimensional spacing tool [24] which is based on the idea of 'zone refining' as used in the purification of crystal ingots. The approach followed in Zorro combines a generalized one-dimensional compaction procedure with sophisticated lateral movements of the elements to be compacted. Some of the features of Zorro are:

- Automatic jog generation
- Merging of contacts or wires

In close analogy to the zone-refining of crystals, individual circuit components or small clusters of components are peeled off row-by-row from a precompacted layout, moved across the open zone, and reassembled at the other end of the zone in a denser configuration. These lateral movements in effect 'shake' the individual components into a more densely-packed arrangement. In this process, both coordinates of the components are altered. In addition jogs may be introduced in the connecting wires between components; this provides additional flexibility in placing them, thereby reducing the layout area.

9. PIPELINE ITERATION

The two loops shown in Figure 1 are provided to account for situations in which the routing area available after placement is not sufficient to complete the routing. This situation can occur during global routing and during detailed routing. In both cases the extra routing area that is required can be provided by spacing apart the macro-cells delimiting the routing region. If the additional area can be provided without drastically changing the order and structure of the routing areas then the pipeline is started again from the point where the exception occurred. In this situation all of the work already completed is preserved.

If the addition of the extra area requires a change such that the organization of the routing area is no longer feasible then two possible solutions exist. In the first the channel definition procedure is re-executed to reorganize the areas not yet routed. The second is performed when the first solution fails; the pipeline is re-started at the placement stage using a more conservative estimate for the routing area requirements.

The number of times the feedback loops are excited is closely related to the accuracy of the routing area estimation performed at the placement stage. The routing area estimation algorithm used in TimberWolfMC together with the placement refinement stage are such that all the text cases available were routed by Mosaico in one pass of the pipeline.

10. INTERACTIVE CAPABILITIES

The Mosaico pipeline is operated by means of a script that executes either the entire pipeline or subsections of it. The script-based approach provides the user with a great deal of flexibility; the script can be modified both in the sequence of calls to the tools and in the parameters supplied to the tools, e.g., the parameters used in the simulated-annealing procedures.

In addition to the tools described in the previous sections, a set of interactive graphical aids is provided to help the user judge the quality of the layout and modify it at any stage of the pipeline. Presently three types of interactive tools are provided.

The first type consists of three tools that are aimed at judging the quality of the layout. One of these tools allows the user, for a selected macro-cell, to see a representation of its connections with the other cells, drawn from cell-center to cell-center. The second tool allows the user to see the optimal position of a selected macro-cell as computed by a force-directed algorithm. Both of these programs may be used at any point following the placement step. A third tool uses the information available after the global router completes. It allows the user to select a terminal and highlight the path of the net connected to that terminal as determined by the global router. This aid is used to judge the quality of the placement combined with the channel definition and global routing, prior to detailed routing.

The second set of tools allow the user to modify the macro-cells either by grouping some of them together to form a new macro-cell, or to decompose a macro-cell into more elementary macros. The grouping tool requires the user to select the set of macro-cells that must be merged. Mosaico is then run to determine the layout of the new, grouped macro-cell. The new macro-cell is then stored in the database and is used from then on as a single macro-cell. The dual of the grouping tool is provided to perform the decomposition procedure.

The third set of tools allow the user to gather statistical information about the length of nets, their electrical characterists (capacitance, resistance), etc., once the layout is completed.

All the tools are developed as Remote Procedure Calls [9]. They are completely independent of the algorithms used in Mosaico. The tools are closely linked to Vem [9] and are presented to the user as menu options. The time required to develop any such application is very short and the required knowledge of the data manager is limited to the amount of information stored in the view. The interactive tools together with the other Vem editing capabilities allow the user to modify existing views, quickly evaluate the effect of modifications on the quality of the layout, and determine whether or not to run the complete pipeline.

11. APPLICATIONS AND RESULTS

The Mosaico system is presently under test on a set of macro-cell examples provided by industry. The examples, whose characteristics are summarized in Table 1, consist of macro-cells with fixed aspect ratios and fixed pin-positions. Table 2 contains the area statistics after placement, routing, and spacing. The cpu time required to place and route the examples is reported in Table 3 while the results for the two largest cases are depicted in Figures 7 and 8.

Circuit	#Macro-Cells	#Pads	#Nets	#Pins	#Channels
ck1	8	5	29	58	17
ck2	12	39	262	691	54
ck3	23	17	129	458	43

Table 1.   Test Circuit Characteristics.

Circuit	Placed	Routed	Compacted	Area savings (%) after compaction
ck1	1592x1415	1678x1562	1533x1433	16
ck2	17305x15620	17033x14982	15670x14982	1
ck3	2902x3607	4245x4904	4036x4112	20

Table 2. Area, Various Stages of Pipeline (λ).

Circuit	Placement	Routing		Compaction
		Global	Detailed	
ck1	140	5	22	21
ck2	n.a	926	482	960
ck3	1203	74	140	480

Table 3. CPU Time (sec., VAX-8650).

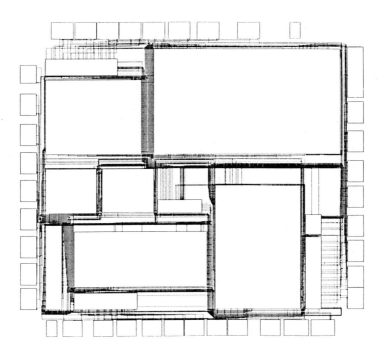

Figure 7. Layout of Example ck2.

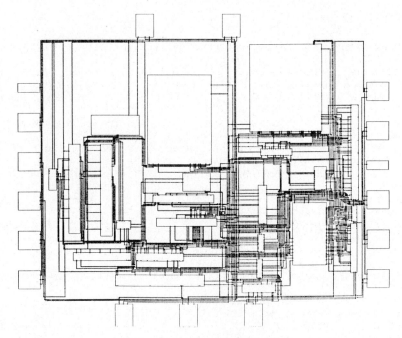

Figure 8.   Layout of Example ck3.

12. CONCLUSIONS

An integrated set of tools for macro-cell layout, called Mosaico, has been presented. Mosaico is designed to interact closely with the other tools in the Berkeley design system. A major point of interaction occurs in the floorplanning stage, where Mosaico exchanges information with module generators and timing analyzers. All the layout procedures are carried out at the symbolic-layout level, which provides the system with technology independence. Mosaico uses the data manager Oct to achieve an open system with a great deal of modularity and flexibility.

In Mosaico well-tested tools like the detailed routers Yacr and Mighty coexist with new tools that have been developed explicitly for the system, such as the channel definition and ordering procedure and the power and ground router.

Future development will occur on all stages in the pipeline. In particular an area router is presently under development. The area router will provide Mosaico with an alternative path in the pipeline that will replace the channel definition - global router - detailed router sequence with a single step. Mosaico will also be extended to deal with printed circuit boards and analog circuit layout. These cases are in fact rather different from digital integrated circuits. In printed circuit boards, placements of components on the two sides of the board and efficient use of all the layers of interconnect available must be considered. In analog circuit layout, the actual paths of interconnections between cells may affect the performance or even the functionality of the circuit.

Acknowledgements
The Mosaico project began in a course on integrated circuit synthesis at the University of California, Berkeley, in the Spring Semester of 1986. We acknowledge Professor A.Newton, Professor C.Sequin, and the other participants in that class for the valuable comments they provided throughout the development of Mosaico. We acknowledge the financial support of SRC under contract 82-11-008, DARPA under contract N00039-86-R-0365, and the California State Micro program.

13. REFERENCES

1. D. Johannsen, Bristle Blocks: A Silicon Compiler, *Proc. 16th Design Automation Conf.*, June, 1979, 310-313.
2. J. R. Southard, MacPitts: An Approach to Silicon Compilation, *Computers*, Dec., 1983.
3. R. Brayton, A. Cagnola, E. Detjens, S. Krishna, P. McGeer, L. Pei, N. Phillips, R. Rudell, R. Segal, T. Villa, A. Wang, R. Yung and A. Sangiovanni-Vincentelli, Multiple-Level Logic Optimization System, *Proc. ICCAD*, Nov., 1986, 356-359.
4. A. R. Newton, A. Sangiovanni-Vincentelli and C. H. Sequin, The Berkeley Synthesis Project, *ee290-cs292 Final Report*, University of California, Berkeley, CA, May, 1986.
5. D. Braun, C. Sechen and A. Sangiovanni-Vincentelli, ThunderBird: A Complete Standard-Cell Layout System, *Proc. CICC*, May, 1986.
6. T. Sudo, T. Ohtsuki and S. Goto, CAD Systems for VLSI in Japan, *Proceedings of the IEEE*, Jan., 1983.
7. R. Rivest and C. Fiduccia, The 'PI' (Placement and Interconnect) System, *Proc. 19th Design Automation Conf.*, June, 1982, 475-481.
8. N. P. Chen, C. P. Hsu, E. S. Kuh, C. C. Chen and M. Takahashi, BBL: A Building-Block Layout System for Custom Chip IC Design, *Proc. ICCAD*, Nov., 1983, 40-41.
9. D. Harrison, P. Moore, R. L. Spickelmier and R. Newton, Data Management and Graphics Editing in the Berkeley Design Environment, *Proc. ICCAD*, Nov., 1986.
10. S. Devadas, Synthesis of Logic Networks in Silicon, *Masters Report*, University of California, Berkeley, CA, 1986.
11. R. Rudell, Wolfe: A Standard-cell Based Module Generator, *ee290-cs292 Final Report*, University of California, Berkeley, CA, May, 1986.
12. G. Adams, S. Devadas, K. Eberhard, C. Kring, F. Obermeier, P. Tzeng, R. Newton, A. Sangiovanni-Vincentelli and C. Sequin, Module Generation Systems, *ee290-cs292 Final Report*, University of California, Berkeley, CA, May, 1986.
13. C. Sechen and A. Sangiovanni-Vincentelli, TimberWolf3. 2: A New Standard Cell Placement and Global Routing Package, *Proc. 23rd Design Automation Conf.*, June, 1986, 432-439.
14. J. Reed, A. Sangiovanni-Vincentelli and A. Santomauro, A New Symbolic Channel Router: YACR2, *IEEE Trans. on Computer-Aided Design*, July, 1985, 208.
15. D. Braun, J. Burns, S. Devadas, H. K. Ma, K. Mayaram, F. Romeo and A. Sangiovanni-Vincentelli, Chameleon: A New Multi-Layer Channel Router, *Proc. 23rd Design Automation Conf.*, June, 1986.
16. N. Weiner, Aspects of Pre-Layout Timing Prediction and Rectification, *ee290-cs292 Final Report*, University of California, Berkeley, CA, May, 1986.
17. C. Sechen, Placement and Global Routing of Integrated Circuits Using Simulated Annealing, *Ph.D. Thesis*, University of California, Berkeley, CA, 1986.
18. R. H. Otten, Automatic Floorplan Design, *Proc. 19th Design Automation Conf.*, June, 1982, 261-267.
19. W. M. Dai, T. Asano and E. S. Kuh, Routing Region Definition and Ordering Scheme for Building-Block Layout, *IEEE Trans. Computer-Aided Design*, July,, 1985, 189-197.
20. E. Lawler, *Combinatorial Optimization: Networks and Matroids*, Holt, Rinehart and Winston, 1976, 102-104.
21. G. T. Hamachi, An Obstacle-Avoiding Router for Custom VLSI, *Ph.D. Thesis*, University of California, Berkeley, CA, 1986.
22. H. Shin and A. Sangiovanni-Vincentelli, MIGHTY: A 'Rip-up and Reroute' Detailed Router, *Proc. ICCAD*, Nov., 1986, 2-5.
23. J. L. Burns and A. R. Newton, SPARCS: A New Constraint-Based IC Symbolic Layout Spacer, *Proc. CICC*, May, 1986, 534-539.
24. H. Shin, A. Sangiovanni-Vincentelli and C. Sequin, Two-dimensional Compaction by 'Zone Refining', *Proc. of 23rd Design Automation Conf.*, June, 1986, 115-122.

Session 5
PLACEMENT REFINEMENT

VLSI '87, C.H. Séquin (editor)
Elsevier Science Publishers B.V. (North-Holland)
© IFIP, 1988

USE OF TRIANGULATION FOR GLOBAL PLACEMENT

F. M. Johannes

Institute of Computer-Aided Design
Department of Electrical Engineering
Technical University of Munich
Munich, West Germany

An improved global placement method is proposed that not only considers the net–list of a circuit but also the sizes of its cells. The procedure consists of three major steps. First, a global placement is calculated from the net–list as usual. Then, by triangulation an adjunct network is determined weighting its nets with a function of the cell sizes. From this adjunct network one more global placement is generated that will preserve the spatial relationships of the initial global placement but will move the cells such that cell overlap is reduced. The algorithm treats all cells simultaneously. It is especially well suited for floorplanning problems in VLSI design. Its computational complexity is low. Average computing times increase nearly linear with the number of cells. The method is illustrated by a floorplanning example.

1. INTRODUCTION

Given the net–list of a circuit, the placement task is to determine locations for the circuit cells such that the subsequent wiring can be performed by spending a minimum amount of silicon area under the geometrical and electrical design rules. Since successful wiring depends strongly on the chosen locations, the placement algorithm is crucial for the quality of the final circuit layout. Rising quality demands and increasing circuit complexity require advanced design procedures to rely on the top-down approach. Therefore, early placement steps should emphasize the global connectivity of the circuit thereby neglecting (geometrical) details. Later placement steps may use the output of the previous step and solve the remaining problems locally.

One common strategy of this type is the min–cut placement method. For reference see [Laut79, PoDi86], e.g.. The placement region is hierarchically partitioned into subregions and the cells are assigned to them so that the number of nets crossing the cut-lines between the subregions is minimized. Eventually each subregion contains only one cell and the partitioning defines the neighboring cells in the plane. If not all cells are equally sized, postprocessing must eliminate the overlaps between cells using heuristics, e.g..

This paper deals with a second well-known concept which partitions the placement task into a global and a final placement subtask. From the net–list input and by neglecting most geometrical constraints the global placement procedure determines an intermediate result named global or relative placement, which defines the optimal spatial relationships for the cells in the plane with respect to a function of the total air–line wiring length. Figure 1 shows a typical global placement with the cell contours included. In the final placement phase all cell overlaps have to be eliminated under the objective that the area of the rectangle enclosing all cells and wiring areas is minimized. This problem has been dealt with by many authors [ChKu84, JuKJ86, e.g.] and is beyond the scope of this paper.

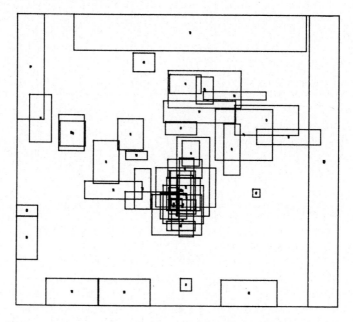

Figure 1. Global placement of the original network with cell contours

The possibility to profit from the global placement depends strongly on its quality. Especially in floorplanning for VLSI circuits the global placements often are as clustered as illustrated by figure 1, since the number of nets can be very high compared to the number of cells and since the cell areas are not considered sufficiently accurate during global placement. To obtain a better global placement with low additional effort a new strategy applying triangulation methods is proposed in chapter 4. The basic properties of global placement and triangulation algorithms are shortly reviewed in chapters 2 and 3. Results obtained with a floorplanning example are presented in chapter 5.

2. GLOBAL PLACEMENT

Many global placement methods have been published, e.g. [QuBr79, AnJK82, Otte82, ChKu84, Blan85, ShDu85, JuKJ86, FrKa86]. They all have in common that a function of the air–line interconnection lengths is minimized and that a linear or nonlinear equation system is formulated to simultaneously obtain coordinates for all cells as a solution. Although the coordinate values rather than their differences are often used as an initialization for the subsequent final placement process, they should only be interpreted as spatial relationships *between* cells. The elements of the system matrix of the equation system are determined from the net–list. Most algorithms allow the specification of net weights that are used advantageously in this paper.

As already mentioned, the cell areas are mostly neglected during global placement. Only few algorithms allow to specify the terminal positions of the cells. In [ShDu85] the cell areas are taken into account, which cause a high computational complexity. Most global placement algorithms consider from one to three constraints on the coordinates to distribute the cells on the plane as uniform as possible.

There are two basic methods for global placement. The coordinate vectors can be calculated by Eigenvector decomposition where it is difficult to consider preplaced cells. They can easily be taken into account if the equation system is solved by direct or iterative solution methods.

The computational complexities differ considerably. E.g., the asymptotic worst–case complexity of the global placement algorithm used in this paper [JuKJ86] is O(number of cell terminals).

3. TRIANGULATION OF A SET OF POINTS

For application to global placement the following definitions and properties of a triangulation are important. The reader is referred to the excellent text-books [Mehl85, PrSh85] for details.

Let P be a set of $|P|$ distinct *points* p in the plane. In our application they represent the cell locations in the global placement. A *triangulation* of set P is a partition of the plane if all its bounded regions form triangles $(p_1, p_2, p_3) \in P \times P \times P$. Equivalently, a triangulation of P is a planar graph $T=(P,E)$ with the maximum number of edges (straight–line segments) in E. A *Delaunay triangulation* is a triangulation such that the circumcircle of any triangle in the triangulation contains no point of P in its interior (*circle criterion*). Figure 2 shows a Delaunay triangulation of nine points, where big circles indicate points and solid or dashed lines denote edges. The edges forming the *convex hull* of P (rubber band enclosing all points, marked by dashed lines in figure 2) are members of the edge set E of the triangulation. The *minimum spanning tree* of the point set P is a subgraph of the (Delaunay) triangulation. A (Delaunay) triangulation contains at most $3 \cdot |P| - 6$ edges (Euler's formula for planar graphs). Thus, the average degree of a point $p \in P$ does not exceed

6. A (Delaunay) triangulation can be found in $O(|P| \cdot \log|P|)$ time, and this is asymptotically optimal.

The Delaunay triangulation can be determined directly by applying the circle criterion above [LeSc80]. It can also be derived from the *Voronoi diagram* of P. Every edge of the Voronoi diagram (dotted lines in figure 2) is a segment of the perpendicular bisector of a pair of points $(p_1, p_2) \in P \times P$. All points on a perpendicular bisector are equidistant from its two defining points. A Voronoi node is the intersection of three Voronoi edges, i.e. it is equidistant to three points. Therefore, every *nearest neighbor* $p_2 \in P$ of a point $p_1 \in P$ results in a Voronoi edge. All these edges form the Voronoi polygon enclosing p_1. Since the Delaunay triangulation is the straight-line dual of the Voronoi diagram, points that are nearest neighbors are connected by edges in the Delaunay triangulation.

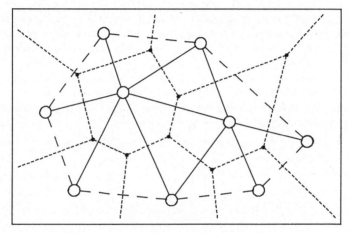

Figure 2. Delaunay triangulation and Voronoi diagram

The algorithms for constructing the Delaunay triangulation as well as the Voronoi diagram are tailored using the divide-and-conquer paradigm. A rough sketch of the Voronoi diagram procedure is as follows:

Step 1. Partition the point set P into two subsets P_1 and P_2
         of approximately equal sizes by median x-coordinate.
Step 2. Construct the Voronoi diagrams of sets P_1 and P_2 recursively.
Step 3. Merge both Voronoi diagrams of sets P_1 and P_2
         to obtain the Voronoi diagram of point set P.

On the bottom recursion level the Voronoi diagram of two or three points is determined analytically.

The concepts of Delaunay triangulation and Voronoi diagram have been introduced here in the Euclidian plane. They can easily be generalized to L_1 or L_∞ metrics with the same low time complexity such that the triangulation is even better adapted to the layout situation.

4. AN IMPROVED GLOBAL PLACEMENT STRATEGY

The global placement is commonly considered a convenient initial place-ment, since it provides a transformation of the cell connectivity (net-list) to op-timal cell coordinates in the plane for all cells simultaneously. To obtain a final overlap-free placement, a human designer will easily pick out the geomet-rically adjacent cells to be placed close to each other (if he can zoom into the clusters). He will move the cells to provide enough space for each cell while maintaining the spatial relationships and minimizing the chip area.

This process may be thought of as the continuous growth of cells from zero size to their real dimensions. A similar strategy has been published to perform placement and routing simultaneously [Souk79].

A realization of this idea yields the following five- step procedure:

Step 1.   Generate an initial global placement for the original network.
Step 2.   Determine all nearest neighbors by Delaunay triangulation.
Step 3.   Replace the original net-list by an adjunct network with
           the same cells (points) but interconnected by two-point nets
           corresponding to the edges of the Delaunay triangulation.
Step 4.   For all two-point nets calculate net weights
           decreasing with the sizes of the adjacent cells.
Step 5.   Generate an improved global placement of the adjunct network.

In steps 1 and 5 any existing global placement algorithm can be inserted provided that weighting of the nets is supported. During step 3 edges between preplaced cells (pads) can be eliminated, since they have no effect on the result-ing placement. The weights of all nets (i,j) interconnecting non-preplaced cells can be calculated, e.g., by

$$\frac{1}{A_i + A_j} \quad , \qquad \frac{1}{A_i} + \frac{1}{A_j} \quad \text{or} \qquad\qquad (1a,1b)$$

$$\text{constant} - A_i - A_j \qquad\qquad (2)$$

$$\text{where } A_i = a_i \quad , \qquad A_i = a_i / d_i \qquad\qquad (3a,3b)$$

$$\text{or} \quad A_i = \sqrt{a_i} \quad , \qquad A_i = \sqrt{a_i / d_i} \qquad\qquad (4a,4b)$$

and a_i is the cell area associated with point i

and d_i is the degree of point i in the adjunct network.

Nets connected to preplaced cells (pads) should be given a high positive weight to "pull" the respective cells to the pads. The algorithm used for global place-ment [JuKJ86] in this paper allows to specify an arbitrary subset of cells to be moved to the periphery. This can be used to "pull" all cells outward which are located at the rim of the adjunct network.

The obove procedure results in an improved global placement where the adjacencies of the cells are largely preserved with respect to the initial global placement. If the adjunct network and the graph model used in the global placement algorithm keep certain conditions, it has been proved [BeHo87] that the topological ordering of the cells is not changed.

The computing times of the proposed method are determined by the global placement algorithm applied, although the asymptotic computational complexity of the triangulation algorithm may be higher. Like the original global placement algorithms the proposed improvement method treats all cells of the circuit simultaneously in every step.

5. RESULTS

To verify the usefulness of the proposed method, the net-list of a VLSI chip known for its difficulty was taken at floorplanning level. It contains 39 macro-cells, 8 sets of pads and 839 nets. The pad sets were preplaced to allow a comparison of the results with the existing chip layout.

The applied global placement algorithm [JuKJ86] required 63 seconds computing time on a VAX11/750 under the ULTRIX operating system to generate the initial global placement shown in figure 1. Since the dense cluster of cells makes a processing during subsequent final placement extremely difficult, the triangulation method was applied. In figure 3 the initial placement is drawn again showing the adjunct network obtained by Delaunay triangulation in 2 seconds computing time.

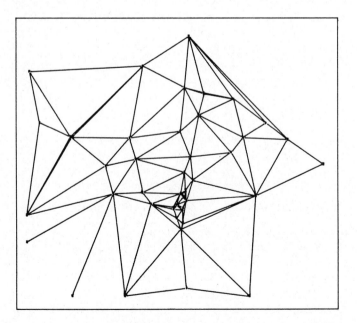

Figure 3. Original global placement with the adjunct network included

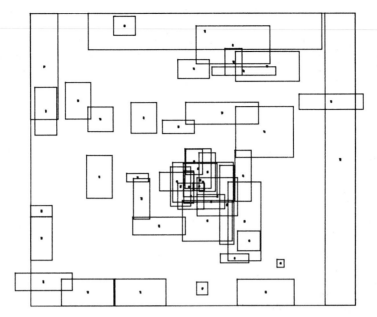

Figure 4. Improved global placement of the adjunct network with cells

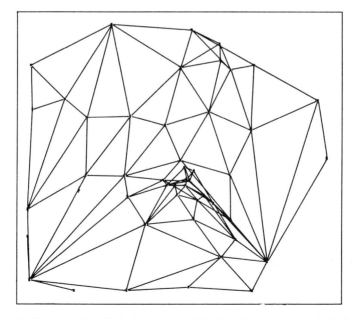

Figure 5. Improved global placement with the adjunct network included

Tests were made to compare the effect of different weighting functions. To measure the quality of the improved placement, the reduction of overlaps between cells was evaluated. It proved better to consider the cell areas (equations 3) rather than their square roots (equations 4). The weighting functions including the degree of a point (equations 3b and 4b) generally performed better. Although there was not much variation in the results, it seems that functions 1b and 2 yield comparable results and both are better than 1a. A global placement of the adjunct network from figure 2 is shown in figures 4 and 5 where the weights were determined by equations 1b and 3b. It was calculated in only 11 seconds computing time, since the adjunct network is planar and therefore has only 122 two-point nets (with an average node degree of about 5.2). Obviously the clustering has been considerably reduced. The amount of overlap-free cell area has been increased from 31% to 53% of the total area of the non-preplaced cells.

When comparing figure 5 with figure 3 it is evident that most spatial relationships are preserved as expected. The reason for the two minor exceptions in this example is probably the consideration of constraints in the global placement algorithm, which are used to spread the cells in the plane.

6. CONCLUSIONS

A method for global placement was presented that allows not only to consider the net-list but also the cell areas of a circuit. The procedure is based on existing placement algorithms. It solves the global placement problem simultaneously for all cells and it requires little additional computing time. Since the modeling is very flexible, it will be worthwhile investigating further improved strategies. The triangulation algorithm and the adjunct network as well as the net weight calculation will be integrated in one program, such that existing·limitations disappear. The possibility to choose net weights more freely and to preplace points (cells) lying on the periphery of the adjunct network close to the pads will further improve the results. If the x- and y-coordinate vectors are determined from separate equation systems in the global placement algorithm, it is also possible to model the aspect ratio of the cells by using different adjunct networks for both directions.

REFERENCES

AnJK82   Antreich, K.J., F.M. Johannes and F.H. Kirsch, »A New Approach for Solving the Placement Problem Using Force Models«, Proceedings ISCAS, 1982, pp. 481-486.

BeHo87   Becker, B. and G. Hotz, »On the Optimal Layout of Planar Graphs with Fixed Boundary«, SIAM Journal on Computing (to appear 1987).

Blan85   Blanks, J.P., »Use of a Quadratic Objective Function for the Place-
         ment Problem in VLSI Design«, PhD thesis, The University of
         Texas at Austin, 1985.

ChKu84   Cheng, C.-K. and E.S. Kuh, »Module Placement Based on Resis-
         tive Network Optimization«, IEEE Transactions CAD-3, 1984, pp.
         218-225.

FrKa86   Frankle J. and R.M. Karp, »Circuit Placements and Cost Bounds
         by Eigenvector Decomposition«, Proceedings ICCAD, 1986, pp.
         414-417.

JuKJ86   Just, K.M., J.M. Kleinhans and F.M. Johannes, »On the Relative
         Placement and the Transportation Problem for Standard-Cell Lay-
         out«, Proceedings DAC, 1986, pp. 308-313.

Laut79   Lauther, U., »A Min-Cut Placement Algorithm for General Cell
         Assemblies based on Graph Representation«, Proceedings DAC,
         1979, pp. 1-10.

LeSc80   Lee, D.T. and B.J. Schachter, »Two Algorithms for Constructing a
         Delaunay Triangulation«, International Journal of Computer and
         Information Sciences, 1980, pp. 219-242.

Mehl84   Mehlhorn, K., »Multi-Dimensional Searching and Computational
         Geometry«, Monographs on Theoretical Computer Science,
         Springer-Verlag, 1984.

Otte82   Otten, R.H.J.M., »Eigensolutions in Top-Down Layout Design«,
         IEEE Proceedings ISCAS, 1982, pp. 1017-1020.

PoDi86   Potin, D.P. and S.W. Director, »Mason: A Global Floorplanning
         Approach for VLSI Design«, IEEE Transactions CAD-5, 1986, pp.
         477-489.

PrKa86   Preas, B.T. and P.G. Karger, »Automatic Placement: A Review of
         Current Techniques«, Proceedings DAC, 1986, pp. 622-629.

PrSh85   Preparata, F.P. and M.I. Shamos, »Computational Geometry, An
         Introduction«, Texts and Monographs in Computer Science,
         Springer-Verlag, 1985.

QuBr79   Quinn, N.R. and M.A. Breuer, »A Force-Directed Component
         Placement Procedure for Printed Circuit Boards«, IEEE Transac-
         tions CAS-26, 1979, pp. 377-388.

ShDu85   Sha, Lu and R.W. Dutton, »An Analytical Algorithm for Place-
         ment of Arbitrarily Sized Rectangular Blocks«, Proceedings DAC,
         1985, pp. 602-607.

Souk79   Soukup, J., »Global Router«, Proceedings DAC, 1979, pp. 481-
         484.

VLSI '87, C.H. Séquin (editor)
Elsevier Science Publishers B.V. (North-Holland)
© IFIP, 1988

Global Spacing of Building-Block Layout

Wei-Ming Dai and Ernest. S. Kuh

Department of Electrical Engineering and Computer Sciences
and the Electronics Research Laboratory
University of California, Berkeley, CA 94720

ABSTRACT

In contrast to the constraint-graph approach, the *ridge spacing method*, which we use for global spacing, operates on the tile planes, and is composed of small steps which iteratively partition the layout into two pieces, and performs cutting or expanding only on the spaces which lie in between the two partitioned pieces. The main contribution of our work is precisely formulating the ridge spacing problem as the bottleneck path problem based on the concepts of tile planes and space tile adjacency graphs. While previous methods require $O(n^2)$ time to find a monotonic ridge (without optimization), we can find an optimal monotonic ridge in $O(n)$ time. Furthermore, we have generalized the spacing ridges to be non-monotonic, and developed $O(n\log n)$ time algorithms for finding an optimal one. The global spacing algorithms have been implemented in a new building-block layout system named BEAR. The experimental results are very promising.

1. Introduction

By *global spacing*, we mean global compaction and decompaction or placement modifications performed after global routing to obtain a better match of the placement and the topological routing to minimize the final layout area. Placement defines the capacity of the routing area around the blocks and global routing defines the density (net assignment) of the routing area. Regarding detailed routing, the desirability of a particular global routing on a given placement depends on the degree of the match of the capacity and the density. After placement and global routing, we can change the density by global rerouting or change the capacity by global spacing (global compaction or decompaction). In order to achieve high density of the final layout, we iterate these two operations to obtain a satisfactory match of the capacity and the density of the routing area before the detailed routing.

Global spacing is much more effective for optimizing the final layout compared with the local optimization of detailed routing. It is also efficient for achieving a better match between the placement and the routing since no detailed wiring yet presents. From our previous experience with the first generation of building-block layout system (BBL) developed at U.C. Berkeley, we found global spacing is a crucial step in a building-block layout system [4].

The most popular compaction method is constraint-graph approach [2] [3] [9]. This approach operates on a constraint graph derived from a placement, and performs compaction by finding the longest path in the graph. The major drawback of the approach is that all objects are pushed toward the boundary as much as possible or evenly distributed, for which some moves do not contribute to the reduction of the chip dimensions. Furthermore, they may make the wire lengths longer or prevent further compaction in the orthogonal direction. This drawback is particularly undesirable for global spacing. We would like to preserve the topology of the placement as much as possible since the job of global spacing is to match a reasonably good placement and a reasonably good global routing. If there is a bad mismatch, we should redo at least one of them or even both.

In contrast to the constraint-graph approach, the *ridge spacing method*, which will be discussed in this paper, operates on the tile planes [11] [6], and is composed of small steps which iteratively partition the layout into two pieces, and performs cutting or expanding only on the spaces which lie in between the two partitioned pieces.

2. A Brief Review of Ridge Spacing Method

The idea of "compression ridge" (called "monotonic compression ridge" in our paper) was first proposed by Akers et al. in 1970 [1]. It was only illustrated by hand drawing pictures (Fig. 1) together with a set of simple rules. It was not implemented until eight years later — the SLIP [8] and STICKS [13] systems demonstrated the success of the ridge spacing method. Manually driven ridge compaction was used in LTX2 system [5]. More recently, the ridge spacing method was applied to building block layout by successive deletion of vacant area from a finished layout [10]. To the best of our knowledge, not much work has been done for the ridge spacing method, mainly because that the computational complexity $O\left(n^2\right)$ (where n is the total number of vertices of the polygons representing the objects to be compacted) was too high to be practical in a VLSI design [3].

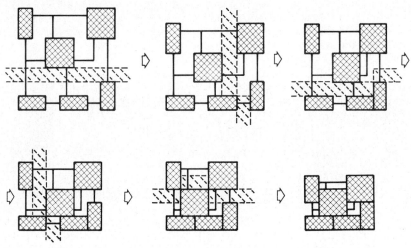

Fig. 1. Akers's compression ridge idea.

The main contribution of our work is precisely formulating the ridge spacing problem as the bottleneck path problem based on the concepts of tile planes and space tile
adjacency graphs. While previous methods require $O\left(n^2\right)$ time to find a monotonic
ridge (without optimization), we can find an optimal monotonic ridge in $O\left(n\right)$ time.
Furthermore, we have generalized the spacing ridges to be non-monotonic, and
developed $O\left(n\log n\right)$ time algorithms for finding an optimal one.

3. Tile Planes and Space Tile Adjacency Graphs

The entire area of a layout is covered with rectangles referred to as *tiles*. There are
two kinds of tiles: *solid tiles*, which represent building blocks, and *space tiles*, which
represent empty space for routing between the blocks.

Given the placement of rectilinear-shaped and arbitrary-sized building blocks, we
define two tile planes: the *horizontal tile plane*, where all space tiles are maximal horizontal strips, and the *vertical tile plane*, where all space tiles are maximal vertical strips
(Fig. 2(a) and (b)). The tile planes may be implemented using the corner stitching data
structure [11]. In a tile plane, each space tile has four edges. Two of them are called the
spans of the tile (completely covered by solid tiles or the layout boundary); the other
two, the *sides* of the tile. The size of the spans and the sides of a space tile are referred
to as the *widths* and the *lengths* respectively.

To represent the adjacency relations between space tiles in a horizontal tile plane,
we construct the *space tile adjacency graph*: $G = (V, E)$, where V represents space tiles
and there is an arc (v_i, v_j) in E if the space tile corresponding to v_i and the space tile
corresponding to v_j are adjacent. If the tile corresponding to v_i is on the top of the tile
corresponding to v_j, the arc (v_i, v_j) is called *forward arc*; otherwise, it is called *backward
arc* (Fig. 2(a)). The space tile adjacency graph in a vertical tile plane can be defined
similarly with *forward arcs* from left to right (Fig. 2(b)). The subgraphs induced by all
forward arcs, named *forward space tile adjacency graphs*, or induced by all backward
arcs, named *backward space tile adjacency graphs*, are acyclic. G is a directed graph with
two distinguished vertices, a *source s* and a *sink t* (Fig. 2(a) and (b)) which are the
source and sink of the corresponding forward space adjacency graph respectively. In the
rest of this paper, whenever we say adjacency graphs we mean space tile adjacency
graphs. Reversing the direction of the arcs in a forward adjacency graph results in the
corresponding backward adjacency graph and vice versa.

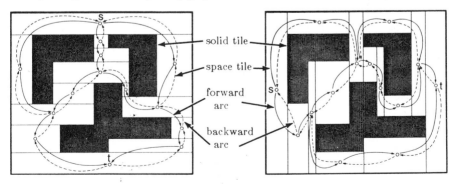

(a) Horizontal tile plane.   (b) Vertical tile plane.

Fig. 2. Tile planes and space tile adjacency graphs.

4. Optimal Spacing Ridges

Let us consider the forward adjacency graph derived from a horizontal tile plane. Corresponding to the vertices of a path p from s to t in the graph, the sequence of consecutive space tiles, referred to as *path's tiles*, divides the layout into two pieces (Fig. 3(a)). If we compress the length of every path's tile by Δ, the horizontal dimension of the bounding box of the layout will be decreased by Δ (Fig. 3 (a) and (b)) (by bounding box, we mean the smallest rectangle which encloses the blocks in a layout). For a given forward adjacency graph derived from a tile plane, a *monotonic compression ridge* is defined by a sequence of consecutive space tiles T corresponding to a path p from s to t in the graph and an integer Δ, the *ridge width*, i.e. the amount to be compressed. If instead, we expand the length of every path's tile by Δ, we have a *monotonic expansion ridge*.

When there is no horizontal (vertical) monotonic compression ridge, is it true that by moving any block or blocks in horizontal (vertical) direction we will not decrease the horizontal (vertical) dimension of the layout? Not necessarily. (See Fig. 3(c) and (d)). In an adjacency graph derived from a tile plane, a path p from s to t in the graph may contain forward and backward arcs, which means the compression ridge may not be monotonic (Fig. 3(c)). As before, the corresponding path's tiles divide the layout into two pieces. However, some of the path's tiles need to be compressed and others expanded in order to decrease the dimension of the bounding box of the layout. To be precise, any tile corresponding to a vertex into which a forward arc enters and from which a forward arc leaves need to be compressed. Similarly, any tile corresponding to a vertex into which a backward arc enters and from which a backward arc leaves need to be expanded. The rest is unchanged. Figure 3(c) and (d) illustrate these three cases. The *expansion ridges* are defined in a similar way. We call compression ridges or expansion ridges *spacing ridges*. Figure 3(e) and (f) shows an example of a vertical compression ridge spacing.

As a greedy strategy, for compaction, we want to find a *maximal compression ridge*, i.e. a compression ridge which will result in a maximal decrease in the dimension of the bounding box. For decompaction, we want to find a *minimal expansion ridge*, i.e. an expansion ridge which will result in a minimal increase in the dimension of the bounding box. We call maximal compression ridges or minimal expansion ridges *optimal spacing ridges*

In order to find optimal spacing ridges in a tile plane, we need the concept of residual capacities of arcs and paths in the corresponding adjacency graph.

5. Residual Capacities of Arcs and Paths

For each tile t in a tile plane, we denote the capacity of t by $cap\ (t)$, which is the length of t in this case, and the density of t by $den\ (t)$, which is some measure of global routing density of t [7]. The *compaction residual capacity* of t is given by $compRes\ (t) = cap\ (t) - den\ (t)$. We can compress a tile t up to $compRes\ (t)$. The *decompaction residual capacity* of t is given by $decompRes\ (t) = den\ (t) - cap\ (t)$. We need to expand t by the amount $decompRes\ (t)$.

Let $G = (V, E)$ be an adjacency graph derived from a tile plane. Let v_i denote the vertex in the adjacency graph which corresponds to a tile t_i in the tile plane. For each arc $(v_i,\ v_j)$, we define the *compaction residual capacity compRes* $(v_i,\ v_j)$ and the *decompaction residual capacity decompRes* $(v_i,\ v_j)$ as follows. We shall treat forward arcs and backward arcs differently.

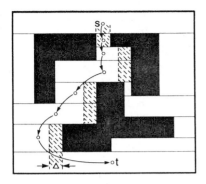

(a) Monotonic compression ridge.

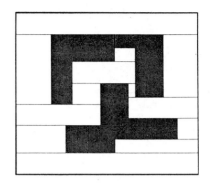

(b) After horizontal compaction.

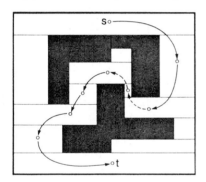

(c) Non-monotonic compression ridge.

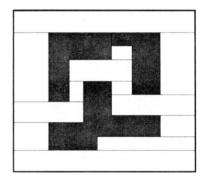

(d) After another horizontal compaction.

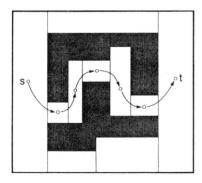

(e) Vertical compression ridge.

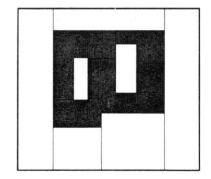

(f) After vertical compaction.

Fig. 3. Ridge spacing.

For compaction, the residual capacity of a forward arc (v_i, v_j), $compRes\ (v_i, v_j)$, is given by min $\{compRes\ (t_i),\ compRes\ (t_j)\}$, the maximal amount which can be compressed by both tiles. The capacity of a backward arc (v_j, v_i), $compRes\ (v_j, v_i)$, is set to ∞ since there is no limit for expanding t_j and t_i.

For decompaction, the residual capacity of a forward arc (v_i, v_j), $decompRes\ (v_i, v_j)$, is given by min $\{decompRes\ (t_i),\ decompRes\ (t_j)\}$ if $decompRes\ (v_i, v_j) > 0$ and is set to ∞ otherwise. This will guarantee that we have expanded every tile which need to be expanded when there is no decompaction ridge left. Notice that it is different from the compaction where we do not have to compress every tile which can be compressed. We define the residual capacity of a backward arc (v_j, v_i) as $decompRes\ (v_j, v_i) = \min\ \{compRes\ (t_j),\ compRes\ (t_i)\}$ because we would not compress t_j and t_i below the density. We delete all the backward arcs (v_j, v_i) which have $compRes\ (v_j, v_i) < 0$ to prevent compressing t_j and t_i.

The compaction residual capacity of a path p, denoted by $compRes\ (p)$ is the minimum value of $compRes\ (v_i, v_j)$ for (v_i, v_j) an arc of p. Substituting $compRes\ (v_i, v_j)$ by $decompRes\ (v_i, v_j)$ above, we have the definition for a decompaction residual capacity of p.

6. Finding Optimal Bottleneck Paths

In an adjacency graph, for a given vertex v, a *maximal bottleneck path* from s to v is a path that maximizes the compaction residual capacity of the path. Similarly, a *minimal bottleneck path* from s to v is a path that minimizes the decompaction residual capacity of the path. We call maximal bottleneck paths or minimal bottleneck paths *optimal bottleneck paths*. Therefore, finding a maximal compression ridge amounts to finding a maximal bottleneck path from s to t; likewise finding a minimal expansion ridge amounts to finding a minimal bottleneck path from s to t. We shall denote the residual capacity of a maximal bottleneck path p from s to v by $compRes\ (v)$, and for a minimal bottleneck path, $decompRes\ (v)$.

With the above definitions, we devise the following dynamic programming algorithms for finding maximal or minimal bottleneck paths. First, we state the recurrence relations of residual capacities.

For finding a maximal bottleneck path in G (Fig. 4):

$compRes\ (s) = \infty$;

$compRes\ (v_j) = \max\limits_{(v_i, v_j)\ \in\ E} \{\min\ \{compRes\ (v_i),\ compRes\ (v_i, v_j)\}\}$ for $v_j \neq s$;

in particular $compRes\ (t)$ is the compaction residual capacity of a maximal bottleneck path in G.

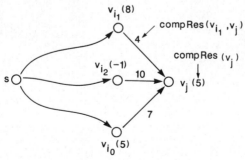

Fig. 4. Computation of $compRes\ (v_j)$.

For finding a minimal bottleneck path in G (Fig. 5):

$decompRes\ (s) = \infty;$

$decompRes\ (v_j) = \min\limits_{(v_i,\ v_j)\ \in\ E}\ \{\min\ \{decompRes\ (v_i),\ decompRes\ (v_i,\ v_j)\}\}$ for

$v_j \neq s;$

in particular $decompRes\ (t)$ is the decompaction residual capacity of a minimal bottleneck path in G.

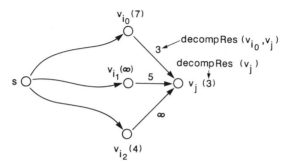

Fig. 5. Computation of $decompRes\ (v_j)$.

Let v_{i_0} be the predecessor of v_j when the maximal value of $compRes\ (v_j)$ or the minimal value of $compRes\ (v_j)$ is reached during the above computation. For each vertex v_j, if we record the v_{i_0} by keeping a pointer $back\ (v_j)$, we can trace back the maximal or minimal bottleneck path from t to s.

We initialize $compRes\ (v) = 0$ and $back\ (v) = $ **null** for all $v \neq s$. Then select an arc $(v_i,\ v_j)$, such that $compRes\ (v_j) < \min\ \{compRes\ (v_i),\ compRes\ (v_i,\ v_j)\}$. Replace $compRes\ (v_j)$ by $\min\ \{compRes\ (v_i),\ compRes\ (v_i,\ v_j)\}$ and $back\ (v_j)$ by v_i. Repeat the above step until $compRes\ (v_j) \geq \max\limits_{(v_i,\ v_j)\ \in\ E}\ \{\min\ \{compRes\ (v_i),\ compRes\ (v_i,\ v_j)\}\}$ for

$v_j \neq s$. We have found a maximal bottleneck path and its compaction residual capacity. Similar steps may be taken for finding a minimal bottleneck path.

The above algorithm may require an exponential time if we do not have an appropriate order of visiting vertices. Let us first consider the case of a forward adjacency graph G. Since G is acyclic, an appropriate visiting order is *topological* : we order the vertices reachable from s so that if $(v_i,\ v_j)$ is an arc, v_i appears before v_j in the order. Such topological order can be found in $O\ (|V|)$ time. We only need to visit each vertex once in order. So we have the following theorem:

Theorem 1: A maximal or a minimal bottleneck path in a forward space tile adjacency graph can be found in $O(|V|)$ time.

Corollary 1: Given a tile plane, a maximal monotonic compression ridge or a minimal monotonic expansion ridge can be found in $O(n)$ time, where n is the total number of vertices of the polygons representing the blocks.

Now let us consider the general case, namely in an adjacency graph G which may contain cycles. For each arc $(v_i,\ v_j)$, we define the *priority* of the arc as follows: $prio\ (v_i,\ v_j) = \min\ \{compRes\ (v_i),\ compRes\ (v_i,\ v_j)\}$ for compaction or $\min\ \{decompRes\ (v_i),\ decompRes\ (v_i,\ v_j)\}$ for decompaction. We begin by classifying the vertices into three classes: *visited* vertices, those connected together by paths have been visited; *fringe* vertices, those adjacent to visited vertices but not yet visited; and *unseen* vertices, those that have not been encountered at all yet (Fig. 6). We begin with one vertex, namely the source s on the fringe — all others unseen — and perform the following steps until the sink t is moved to the visited: select an arc (v_i, v_j) with the highest *prio* (v_i, v_j), where v_i is in the visited and v_j is in the fringe. Visit v_j, that is assign *compRes* (v_j) or *decompRes* (v_j) according to the above recurrence relations, then move v_j from the fringe to the visited, and put any unseen vertices adjacent to v_j on the fringe. For every arc (v_j, v_k), where v_k is not visited, assign *prio* (v_j, v_k). Such visiting order is referred to as *priority first*. In the priority first order, one visit per vertex suffices due to the following theorem. The proof will be omitted.

Theorem 2: If the visiting is priority first, once a vertex v is visited, *compRes* (v) or *decompRes* (v) is the residual capacity of an optimal bottleneck path from s to v.

All the arcs from visited vertices to fringe vertices are stored in a priority queue: the priority of an arc (v_i, v_j) is assigned and the arc is inserted to the queue when v_i is visited; the arc is deleted from the queue when v_j is visited. The destination vertex of the arc with the highest priority in the queue is the one to be visited next or moved from the fringe to the visited. Since $|E|$ is $O(|V|)$ in an adjacency graph, in other words, adjacency graphs are sparse, we implement the priority queue as a heap [12]. The worst case time complexity is indicated by the following theorem:

Theorem 3: A maximal or a minimal bottleneck path in a space tile adjacency graph can be found in $O(|V| \log |V|)$ time.

Corollary 2: Given a tile plane, a maximal compression ridge or a minimal expansion ridge can be found in $O(n \log n)$ time, where n is the total number of vertices of the polygons representing the blocks.

The optimal bottleneck path algorithms proposed above are similar to the shortest path algorithms. However, we improve the performance by storing arcs rather than vertices in the priority queue. In the conventional shortest path algorithms, the fringe vertices are stored in a priority queue so when the priority of the vertices changes, the queue need to be reorganized. In contrast, in our algorithm, after an arc is inserted into a priority queue, its priority will never be changed. There is one big difference between the optimal bottleneck path problem and the shortest path problem: unlike the negative cycles for the shortest path problem or the positive cycles for the longest path problem, negative cycles or positive cycles do not introduce any difficulties for solving the optimal bottleneck path problem.

7. Experimental Results

The preliminary results indicate our ridge spacing algorithms are very promising. Figure 7 shows a compaction example. The shaded area is one of the two partitions separated by the ridge. Even though we set densities of all tiles to zero, performing the extreme of global compaction — block packing, the topology of the placement does not change very much.

8. Remarks

In the implementation of the global spacing algorithms, we need not to construct the adjacency graphs explicitly since the adjacency of vertices can be obtained by neighboring search on the tile plane. Once a tile plane is being updated, the implicitly represented adjacency graph is also being updated. Our experience has demonstrated that the neighboring search of tiles and the update of tile planes can be performed

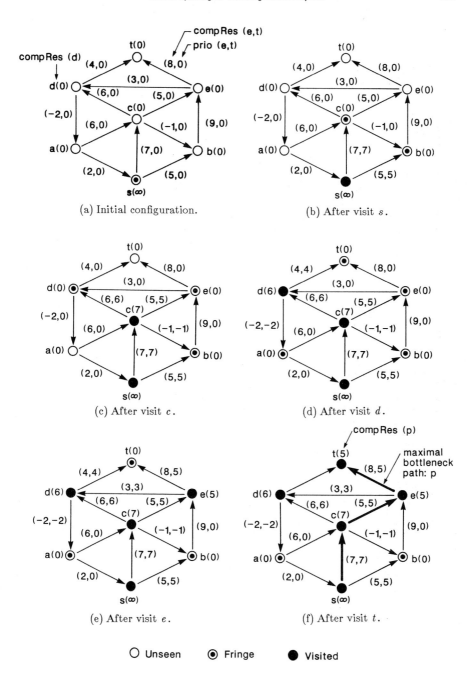

(a) Initial configuration.

(b) After visit s.

(c) After visit c.

(d) After visit d.

(e) After visit e.

(f) After visit t.

○ Unseen ◉ Fringe ● Visited

Fig. 6. Finding a maximal bottleneck path.

W.-M. Dai and E.S. Kuh

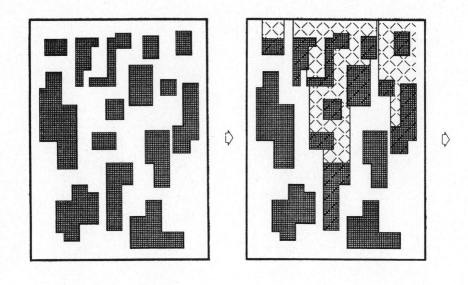

(a) Original placement.   (b) Vertical compaction.

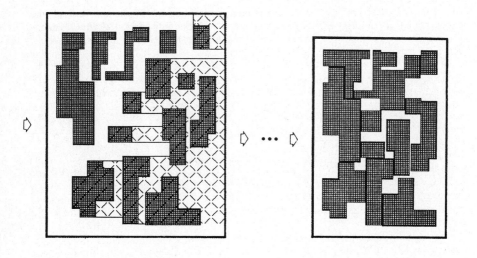

(c) Horizontal compaction.   (c) Final placement.

Fig. 7. An example of compaction.

efficiently using the corner stitching data structure.

A space tile is called *bottleneck* if both sides are covered by the sides of its adjacent space tiles (Fig. 8). If the width of a bottleneck tile is equal to zero, the tile is regarded as a *bottleneck line*. Either the set of bottleneck tiles (lines) on the horizontal tile plane or that on the vertical tile plane is sufficient for specifying global routing information [7]. For simplicity, we could assign the density of all non-bottleneck tiles to zero so only bottleneck tiles are considered in the global spacing.

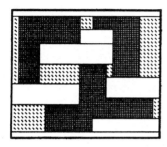

(a) Horizontal bottleneck tiles.

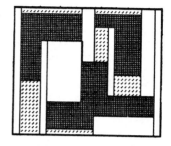

(b) Vertical bottleneck tiles.

Fig. 8. Bottleneck tiles.

Although the ridge spacing algorithms described above were motivated by the global spacing without detailed wires, they could be applied to the spacing with detailed wires as well. Given a building-block layout with blocks and Manhattan wire segments (Fig. 9(a)), we construct the horizontal tile plane containing the blocks and vertical wire segments and the vertical tile plane containing the blocks and horizontal wire segments (Fig. 9(b) and (c)). Any block together with the horizontal (vertical) segments attached to it is treated as one object in the vertical (horizontal) tile plane. While the capacity of a tile remains the same as above, i.e. its length, the density of a tile is determined by the minimal separation rules. Figure 9(c) illustrates a compression ridge in the vertical tile plane and 9(d) shows the result after compacting the ridge. Necessary jog points can be identified on wire segments efficiently by local search on the tile planes, thus jogs may be generated during the ridge spacing operations (Fig. 9(e) and (f)). Therefore, for spacing with detailed wires, the complexity of our ridge spacing algorithms remains the same.

To conclude, we would like to give another remark. Even though we space a ridge in one direction at each step, if we alternate between horizontal spacing and vertical spacing, the method has the inherent nature of two dimensional spacing. Optimal one dimensional compaction amounts to finding maximal flow in one of the space tile adjacency graphs. The unique feature of such one dimensional compaction is minimizing the block move.

The global spacing algorithms have been implemented in a new building-block layout system named BEAR (Building-block Environment Allocation and Routing system). It will have both automatic and interactive capabilities (for example, users can specify a spacing ridge on a tile plane interactively) including other features which BBL dose not have. BEAR is being developed using the C language for color and black-and-white displays that support the X window manager, which runs under 4.3 BSD UNIX. EDIF will be our primary input and output (also CIF).

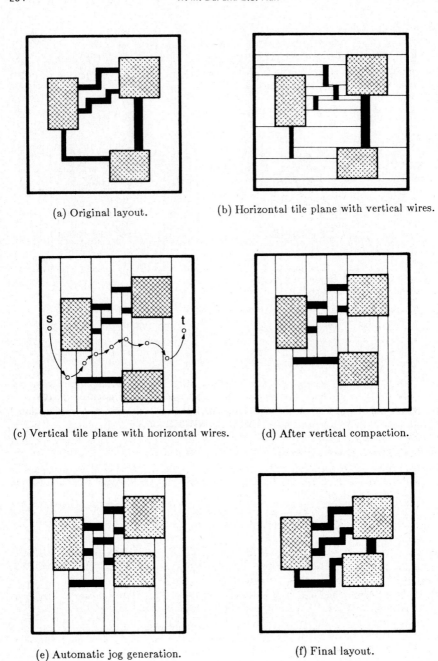

(a) Original layout.   (b) Horizontal tile plane with vertical wires.

(c) Vertical tile plane with horizontal wires.   (d) After vertical compaction.

(e) Automatic jog generation.   (f) Final layout.

Fig. 9. Compaction with detailed wires.

Acknowledgement

Dr. Masao Sato provided valuable comments and suggestions on the drafts of the paper. This research was supported by the Semiconductor Research Corporation under the Grant SRC-82-11-008 and National Science Foundation under the Grant ECS-85-06901.

References

[1] S. B. Akers, J. M. Geyer, and D. L. Roberts, "IC mask layout with a single conductor layer," in *Proc. 7th Design Automation Workshop*, pp. 7-16, 1970.

[2] Y. E. Chao, A. J. Korenjak, and D. E. Stockton, "FLOSS: an approach to automated layout for high-volume design," in *Proc. 14th Design Automation Conf.*, pp. 138-141, 1977.

[3] Y. E. Chao, "A subjective review of compaction," in *Proc. 22nd Design Automation Conf.*, pp. 396-404, 1977.

[4] N. P. Chen, C. P. Hsu, and E. S. Kuh, "The Berkeley building-block (BBL) layout system for VLSI design," in *Dig. Tech. Papers, IEEE Int. Conf. on Computer-Aided Design*, pp. 40-41, 1983.

[5] B. W. Colbry and J. Soukup, "Layout aspects of the VLSI microprocessor design," in *Proc. 1982 IEEE Int. Symp. on Circuits and Systems*, pp. 1214-1228, 1982.

[6] W. M. Dai, T. Asano, and E. S. Kuh, "Routing region definition and ordering scheme for building-block layout," *IEEE Trans. on Computer-Aided Design of ICs and Syst.*, Vol. CAD-4, No. 3, pp. 189-197, 1985.

[7] W. M. Dai, M. Sato, and E. S. Kuh, "A dynamic and efficient representation of building-block layout," to appear in *Proc. 24th Design Automation Conf.*, 1987.

[8] A. E. Dunlop, "SLIP: symbolic layout of integrated circuits with compaction," *Computer-Aided Design*, Vol. 10, No.6, pp. 387-391, 1978.

[9] M. Y. Hsueh and D. O. Pederson, "Computer-aided layout of LSI circuit building blocks," in *Proc. Int. Symp. on Circuits and Systems*, pp. 474-477, 1979.

[10] M. Ishikawa, T. Matsuda, T. Yoshimura, and S. Goto, "An automatic compaction method for building block LSIs," in *Proc. Int. Symp. on Circuits and Systems*, pp. 203-206, 1985.

[11] J. K. Ousterhout, "Corner stitching: a data-structuring technique for VLSI layout tools," *IEEE Trans. on Computer-Aided Design of ICs and Syst.*, Vol. CAD-3, No. 1, pp. 87-100, 1984.

[12] R. E. Tarjan, *Data structures and network algorithms*, CBMS Regional Conference Series in Applied Mathematics 44, Society for Industrial and Applied Mathematics, Philadelphia, 1983.

[13] J. D. Williams, "STICKS — graphics editor for high-level LSI design," in *Proc. National Computer Conference*, pp.289-295, 1978,

Session 6
HIGH-PERFORMANCE TECHNOLOGIES

VLSI '87, C.H. Séquin (editor)
Elsevier Science Publishers B.V. (North-Holland)
© IFIP, 1988

HIGH-PERFORMANCE BIPOLAR VLSI — THE ONLY WAY

George Wilson
Bipolar Integrated Technologies
Beaverton, OR, USA

INTRODUCTION

The next decade should see a continuation of the rapid improvement in VLSI system speeds. The major change will be a migration in technology for high speed applications from CMOS to bipolar.

Bipolar is now causing rapid advances in speeds of single-chip systems with complexities up to 20,000 gates. A logical questions would be "Why bipolar and why now?" That will be the topic of this discussion

Figure 1 offers a perspective of speed versus complexity of today's practical technologies.

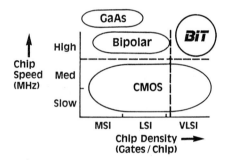

FIGURE 1.   HIGH PERFORMANCE VLSI

Two varieties of Bipolar are listed here:

1)   Conventional MSI/LSI bipolar - although very fast, it is limited in density due to relatively large transistors and complex processing techniques, both adversely effect yield. Additionally its high power adversely effect maximum die size.

2)   High density bipolar - using simplified processing and self-aligned transistors, can achieve CMOS yields and densities. System speeds are 3 to 5 times faster than CMOS, and power is 1/4th that of conventional bipolar.

Gallium arsenide is not a VLSI technology and is not expected to be. Both low yields and slower speed at VLSI density will be major obstacles.

CMOS will continue to dominate low and medium performance systems but will be unable to compete with high density bipolar in speed. The reasons for this will be discussed.

The primary requirements for a successful high performance VLSI technology are:

   a)   VLSI yields.
   b)   Device packing density limited by metal pitch.
   c)   Small loaded power delay product.

VLSI YIELDS

VLSI yields are an obvious necessity for any candidate technology. The process should yield 2 defects per cm2 or less to be economically viable.

PACKING DENSITY

Packing density of both CMOS and high density bipolar (HDB) are limited by metal pitch, and have similar densities. Further improvements in photolithography will produce like improvements in the density of both processes.

POWER DELAY PRODUCT

Power delay product is a key parameter of any candidate process. Although CMOS has low power at low to moderate clock speeds its loaded gate delays are inferior to HDB. HDB, on the other hand, dissipates significantly more power than CMOS but can readily achieve sub-nanosecond loaded gate delays.

Loaded gate delays are the key. If the unloaded delays are below 300ps per gate, most of the delay will be in the interconnect in a VLSI system. Technologies that strive to reduce unloaded delays below this point at the expense of density and yield will probably not be competitors.

Interconnect delay can be minimized by improving the density, thus reducing the load capacitance and by improving the transconductance of the transistor. Figure 2 gives a simplified view of the problem. Transconductance (gm) is the ratio of the output current to input voltage. The rise and fall speeds are proportional to gm and inversely proportional to C_l (mainly interconnect capacitance).

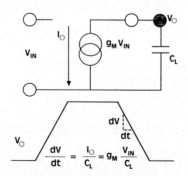

FIGURE 2.   TRANSISTOR TRANSCONDUCTANCE (gm)

If gm is determined by geometry and material properties of the transistor, an interesting phenomenon occurs in an MOS transistor as the gate length is reduced below about 2 microns and is shown in Figure 3.

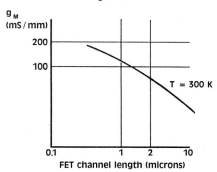

FIGURE 3. gm OF A SILICON FET TRANSISTOR VS GATE LENGTH

For gate lengths greater than two microns, the transconductance increases nearly linearly with reduction in gate lengths. Below two microns, a critical field is reached in the channel (under the gate) that causes a phenomenon known as scatter limited velocity where the carrier velocity cannot increase significantly. Consequently the gm of the device is limited to a maximum of about 200 ms/mm even at temperatures as low as 77°K. This is a fundamental limit of a silicon majority carrier device (FETs are majority carrier devices and bipolar transistors are minority carrier devices). The consequence of this phenomenon is a limit in the MOS transistors current drive capability and limits the speed in heavily interconnected systems.

Gallium arsenide FETs are very fast when lightly loaded, but also have a transconductance limitation. Figure 4 compares the maximum transconductance of MOS and GaAs FETs and a HDB transistor. The numbers have been normalized as a function of gate or emitter length.

— MOS   **200 MS / MM**

— GaAs   **400**

— BIPOLAR   **3800**

FIGURE 4.   MAXIMUM TRANSCONDUCTANCE

The full advantage of the gm ratios are not realizable in HDB gates, primarily because PNP transistors are not available. Practical systems do realize speed improvements to 3X or greater over CMOS, the only other VLSI technology.

Improvements in bipolar VLSI densities have continued over the last decade and many of the improvements have been "borrowed" from MOS advances. An illustration of bipolars evolution can be seen in Figure 5. By comparing size reduction in state of the art transistors over the last seven years. The areas have decreased from over 200 square microns to 14 with significant improvement in speed at low currents. The minimum size of these transistors is limited only by metal pitch, putting them on a par with MOS transistors in area but maintaining a much higher current drive capability.

FIGURE 5.   SIZE REDUCTION IN BIPOLAR TRANSISTORS IN THE PAST SEVEN YEARS.

The ability to integrate larger systems with HDB technology has increased dramatically over the same period. Figure 6 shows a production 20,000 gate floating point ALU system on a 9mm X 9 mm die. The maximum die size of these products is limited by power dissipation rather than yield. At 0.3mw per gate plus output driver, a die this complex will dissipate about 10 watts.

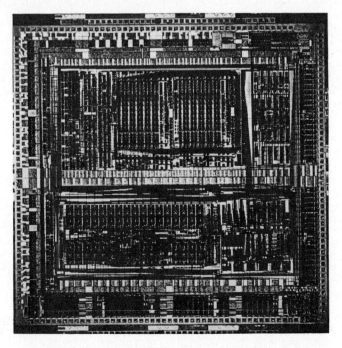

FIGURE 6.   20,000 GATE PRODUCTION HDB SYSTEM

There are no obvious competitors to bipolar speed in single chip VLSI systems and integration levels should improve following expected advances in photolithography. Figure 7 is the authors projection of bipolar system density improvements over the next several years.

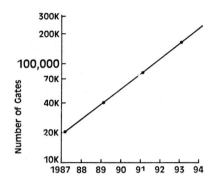

FIGURE 7. HDB FUTURE DENSITY INCREASE FOR A 9 X 9 mm CHIP AT 10 WATTS

In exchange for the higher power, the chip delivers 3 to 5 times higher speeds than comparable CMOS products. This technology will be used to manufacture a single chip RISC microprocessor capable of performance in excess of 50 VAX MIPS.

In summary, it now appears that although CMOS will remain the technology of choice in low and medium performance systems and GaAs will find a niche at much lower levels of integration, HDB will be the only choice for the highest performance single chip VLSI systems.

VLSI '87, C.H. Séquin (editor)
Elsevier Science Publishers B.V. (North-Holland)
IFIP, 1988

PROSPECTS FOR HIGH SPEED BIPOLAR LSI TECHNOLOGY
- DIGITAL LSI APPLICATIONS -

Shoji Horiguchi, Masayuki Ino and Masao Suzuki

NTT Atsugi Electrical Communications Laboratories
Atsugi-shi Kanagawa Pref.
Japan

This paper discusses the current status and future potential of high
speed bipolar LSI technology. Through comparative studies between Si
bipolar LSI and GaAs MESFET LSI, bipolar LSI technology will continue
playing a major role in ultra high speed digital LSI applications.

1. INTRODUCTION

High speed LSIs are the key components in the creation of higher
performance information processing systems such as mainframe computers, super
computers, real time image processing systems and optical fiber transmission
systems. Various high speed LSI technologies such as Si bipolar, GaAs FET,
HEMT and HBT have been developed using novel device structures, fabrication
technology and circuit designs.
State of the art high speed digital LSI technology is reviewed first.
Next, from the results of computer simulation techniques using scaled down
devices, the bipolar transistor because of its fast switching and high driving
capabilities will be the most promising for high speed LSI applications.

2. CURRENT STATUS OF HIGH SPEED LSIs

Ring oscillator delay time for various devices (1)(2) is shown in Fig.-1.
The shortest delay time of 5.8ps was achieved by HEMT (0.35um) at 77K. At room
temperature, GaAs MESFET (0.4um) has a delay time of 9.9ps. From this figure,
compound FETs seem superior to Si bipolar devices (27ps for the bipolar SST
(0.35um)). This data, however, was taken from ring oscillators with negligeble
wiring capacitances and only one fan-in and fan-out. Typical LSI environments
have 2 to 3 fan-ins and fan-outs and wiring lengths from 1 to 3mm.
Actual logic LSI delay times are shown in Fig.-2. All multipliers have a
simple array structure with ripple carry propagation(2)-(5). The dotted lines
representing slopes give the total delay time of a one stage add operation and
a one stage carry propagation. The gate delay times measured with ring
oscillators are 42ps for the GaAs MESFET(4) and 78ps for the bipolar SST(3).

As for LSI level, the SST multiplier LSI is more than twice as fast as the
GaAs multiplier LSI. This difference is caused by wiring capacitance delays,
fan-in and fan-out delays, and circuit configuration. Powerful drive
capability is a significant advantage for bipolar devices in actual LSI
circumstances.

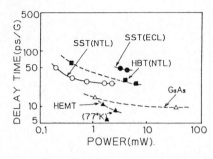

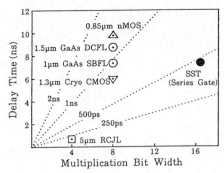

Fig.-1 Gate delay time versus power
       dissipation
       (ring oscillator level)

       (Ref.(2))

Fig.-2 Performances of parallel
       multipliers
       (LSI level)

3. ULTRA HIGH SPEED BIPOLAR TECHNOLOGY : SST

The structure of an integrated SST trasistor is shown in Fig.-3.

SST (Super Self-aligned Technology) was developed for the fabrication of smaller alignment shift free transistors. Small emitter and base structures are fabricated with a self-aligned technique using one optical mask pattern. The emitter can be reduced to a 0.35 to 0.5um, even using a 2um optical mask pattern. The narrow base contacts and base-emitter separation are uniformly and accurately fabricated. These are both approximately 0.3um. Furthermore, since margin areas are not needed, the base region of the SST transistor can be narrower than that of a planar transistor with a 0.5um rule. The SST transistor has extremely low base-collector capacitance and low base resistance. In addition, techniques for accurate ion implantation and for doped Poly-Si make shallow junctions possible . For example, estimated minimum base width is 80nm. The SST transistor with an emitter of 0.35um has a cut off frequency f_T=17GHz at V_{CE}=3V. The SST concept approaches the ultimate device structure of the bipolar transistor, challenging its physical limits.

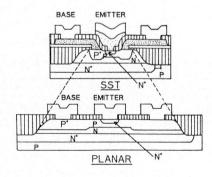

Fig.-3 Integrated bipolar SST
       transistor structure

       (Ref.(2))

4. CHARACTERISTICS OF SCALED DOWN DEVICES

Simulation techniques are used, to predict characteristics and circuit performance of scaled down devices. This is shown in Fig.-4. The simple scale-down model was assumed for the devices and wirings.

Simulated dimensions and f_T of the bipolar SST transistor are shown in Fig.-5. To scale down the transistor dimensions further, it will be necessary to develop a new device structure, for example, the HBT structure. Simulation data correlates with experimental data on a transistor with a 0.5um emitter width. This transistor was realized using SST. The other scaled down transistors are prospective devices. Simulation results for scaled down GaAs MESFETs are shown in Fig.-6. Velocity overshort effects were considered in this simulation for FETs with a gate length equal to or less than 0.5um. Simulated cut off frequencies of GaAs FETs are higher than that of bipolar transistors in devices with approximately the same dimensions.

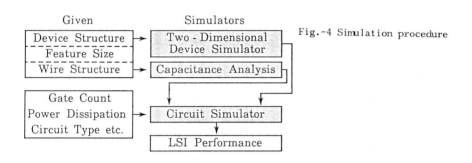

Fig.-4 Simulation procedure

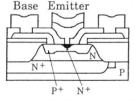

Terms	Scalings		
Le (µm)	0.5	0.35	0.2
Xje (nm)	80	40	20
WB (nm)	80	40	20
fT (GHz)	10	24	42

Fig.-5 Scaled-down bipolar device model
f_T: simulated values

Le : Emitter Length , Xje : Emitter Depth
WB : Base Width , fT : Cut off Frequency

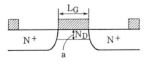

Terms	Scalings		
LG (µm)	1	0.5	0.2
a (nm)	100	71	45
ND(10^16cm-3)	8.5	16	40
fT(GHZ)	15	30	85

Fig.-6 Scaled-down GaAs MESFET device model
f_T: simulated values

LG : Gate Length
a : Thickness of Active Layer
ND : Impurity Density

$$a \propto L_G^{-1/2}$$

5. COMPARISON STUDY OF BIPOLAR SST LSI VS GaAs MESFET LSI.

To examine LSI performance using the scaled down devices, basic circuits were chosen according to specific criteria. This selection criteria was based on high speed or low power dissipation factors. Selected basic circuit configurations and supply voltages are listed in Table-1. These approach the operating voltage lower limit of each circuit.

Device	Bipolar		GaAs MESFET	
Circuit Name	NTL	LCML	DCFL	SCFL
Basic Circuit Configuration	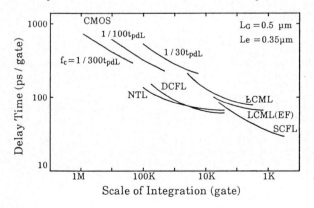			
Function	NOR	OR/NOR	NOR	OR/NOR
Power Supply	-1.1V	-2.3V	0.6V	-1.8V

Table-1
Basic circuits employed
Fan-in=3 was used in the
simulation

The calculated relationship between gate delay time and scale of integration is shown in Fig.-7. This simulation assumes a 3 fan-in and 3 fan-out logic gate, and to have a loaded wiring capacitance. The power dissipation was limited to 3W. To even the level of technological difficulty in LSI fabrication, bipolar transistor emitter width is 0.35um, while the GaAs MESFET and the Si CMOS transistor gate lengths are 0.5um. The 3K gate LSI propagation delay time is broken down for each type of gate to unloaded and loaded delay times, as shown in Fig.-8. The average gate delay time of a LSI FET circuit using GaAs and CMOS devices is approximately 4 times as long as the unloaded gate delay time of each. Average gate delay time for bipolar circuits with an emitter follower is less than twice as long.

These trends continue even for a feature size of 0.2um. The simulation in this feature size predicts that the gate delay may be less than 20 to 30ps for both bipolar and GaAs. The GaAs SCFL has the potential to go below 10ps/gate.

Fig.-7
Logic gate delay time
versus complexity

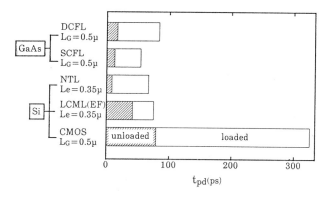

Fig.-8 Unloaded and loaded gate delay times

The followings are predictions for future LSI operation speeds.

(1) CMOS VLSI will prevail in very large scale integration over 100K gates per chip.
(2) GaAs LSI will compete with the Si bipolar LSI in the 2 to 3K to around 50K gate range.
(3) GaAs SCFL circuits show promise below the 2 to 3K gate range.

   In the above analysis, a simple scaling principle was used in the range to 0.2um for device structure and the line and space of wirings. This will probably cause many serious problems, especially in the fabrication process. Fabricating these small devices within the allowed tolerance of the mask alignment is one example. Achieving and assuring device characteristic uniformity is another. Reducing the device size in GaAs is even more problematic, because its threshold voltage depends on the impurity profile, geometrical channel structure and the defect density.
   The results of a statistical analysis of a 16Kb RAM is shown in Fig.-9. The RAM consisted of DCFL circuits. The gate length was 0.55um, designed V_{th} was 100mV and gm was 176mS/mm. Access time depends on the extent of dispersion of V_{th}. If σV_{th} exceeds 16mV, access time dispersion rapidly increases. Precise control of V_{th} is essential for ultra high speed LSIs using GaAs devices, especially in RAM applications. Currently, that control is not adequate for even a 1um feature size, in practical applications. Though V_{th} variation induced from crystal defects is being improved significantly by defect-free GaAs crystal growth technology, shorter channel lengths still cause serious short channel effect problems.
   There are no problems, however, with the V_{th} controllability of bipolar devices. This is because the main factor controlling switch in a bipolar transistor is the built-in potential which is determined by an intrinsic physical mechanism. Moreover, the bipolar SST concept will enable the easy fabrication of a transistor with a 0.2um wide emitter through a practical photolithography technology of 1um. For this reason, the SST bipolar LSI offers the best prospects for ultra high speed LSI applications in the near future.

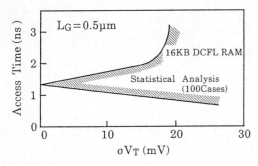

Fig.-9

Relationship between access
time and V_T standard deviation
(σV_T)

(Ref.(1))

6. CONCLUSIONS

This paper has described the current status of ultra high speed LSIs and
the future scaled down devices from the results of simulation techniques.
Comparisons of bipolar SST LSI vs GaAs LSI show that the bipolar LSI will hold
a dominant position in digital LSI applications.

A 2 to 3K gates bipolar masterslice with an average loaded gate delay
under 50ps and a 1Kb RAM with an access time under 0.4ns will be realized in
the near future.

ACKNOWLEGEMENTS

The authors would like to thank Drs. T. Sudo, M. Fujimoto, T.
Sakai and T. Sugeta, for their technical guidance.

REFERENCES

(1) T. Sugeta et al "High Speed Technology Comparison -GaAs VS Si-" GaAs IC
    Symp. Tech. Dig., Nov. 1986.
(2) T. Sakai et al "Prospects of SST Technology For High Speed LSI" IEDM Tech.
    Dig., Dec. 1985.
(3) S. Horiguchi et al "An 80ps 2500-Gate Bipolar Macrocell Array" ISSCC Tech.
    Dig., Feb. 1985.
(4) N. Toyoda et al "A 42ps 2K-Gate GaAs Gate Array" ISSCC Tech. Dig., Feb.
    1985.
(5) S. Hanamura et al "Low Temperature CMOS 8x8b Multipliers with Sub 10ns
    Speeds" ISSCC Tech. Dig., Feb. 1985.

VLSI '87, C.H. Séquin (editor)
Elsevier Science Publishers B.V. (North-Holland)
© IFIP, 1988

GaAs DIGITAL IC's FOR COMPUTER APPLICATIONS

Marc ROCCHI

LEP : Laboratoires d'Electronique et de Physique Appliquée
      A member of the Philips Research Organization
      3, avenue Descartes, 94451 LIMEIL-BREVANNES, FRANCE

Superfast computers with subnanosecond cycle times, multigigabit's
telecommunication and instrumentation systems are some of the main
applications that forces microelectronics into the submicron age. It
is now generally taken for granted that more than one technology is
needed to meet these goals. GaAs IC's after a long infancy, are thus
emerging as being complementary to fast submicron bipolar and MOSFET
IC's. Based on normally-off MESFET's, hetero FET's (HEMT's, undoped
HEMT's), or HBT's, they are becoming of age thanks to major
breakthroughs such as high uniformity material, improved surface
processing and more flexible and refined designs.
In terms of LSI performances, GaAs digital IC's have been extensively demonstrated up to a few thousand gates to exhibit a 2 to 3
times higher speed or a 3 to 5 times lower power consumption than
their silicon counterparts with equivalent feature sizes[1]. Nevertheless, there is still a lot of room for improvement, especially in
memory design and interconnect technology, before achieving ultimate
performances with GaAs digital IC's.

1. INTRODUCTION

GaAs digital IC's have long been regarded as a short-lived intruder into the
silicon world of microelectronics. However, the physical and electrical
advantages of GaAs devices over silicon ones (high electron velocity,
semi-insulating substrate...) still hold water as long as equivalent features
sizes are considered. Because of high speed and low power LSI requirements,
circuits based on N-OFF MESFET's or HEMT's will be mainly considered.

They are the first generation of GaAs LSI IC's being industrially developed.
Complementary JFET logic has been used successfully for low power, radiation
hard SRAM's[2]. N-OFF JFET's are however difficult to scale down below 1 μm gate
length. Heterobipolar IC's are so far in a very early demonstration phase, but
MSI performances are already outstanding[3].

More recently GaAs CMOS like gates have been demonstrated using p and n
channel hetero MISFET's (undoped HEMT's)[4]. This new logic approach is also in
a very early demonstration phase, but this is certainly the most promising for
a 2nd generation of GaAs (V) LSI circuits with subhalf micron feature sizes.
We will successively discuss the high frequency performances of GaAs FET's for
digital applications, evaluate how mature and uniform normally-off processes
are, then review the design of general purpose LSI IC's and SRAM's. Finally a
realistic comparison between silicon and GaAs IC's will be presented.

2. HIGH FREQUENCY PERFORMANCES OF GaAs FET's FOR DIGITAL APPLICATIONS

The performances of digital circuits depend on material properties and intrinsic device parameters, but also on circuit considerations. We will first consider, the intrinsic performances of FET's for digital applications.

Low dislocation density or/and annealed substrates have enabled to greatly improve the electrical uniformity of GaAs ion implanted active layers. Consequently, N-OFF MESFET's can now extensively be used for LSI applications[5-6-7]. Recently, HEMT's have also been shown to be a direct replacement and improvement of MESFET's[8]. Their development is essentially based on MBE and more recently on MO-VPE heterostructures[9]. MBE heterostructures may be as uniform as ion implanted layers for MESFET's, but MBE systems have so far exhibited a lower throughput and produced wafers with a poorer surface quality.

The high frequency response of normally-off and normally-on GaAs FET's are similar and can be characterized by the switching time $\overline{\tau}$ of the device. $\overline{\tau}$ can be approximated by $C_G/G_m = 1/\pi \, f_{Tmax}$ where C_G and G_m are the transistor gate capacitance (including the miller effect) and the transistor transconductance averaged over the logic swing (Δ V). f_{Tmax} is the maximum current gain cut-off frequency. It depends on the transport properties of carriers, but also on the size of the control electrode (gate length : Lg) and the distance between the other two electrodes (drain to source spacing : L_{DS}). Because of non stationary transport properties in GaAs over subhalf micron distances, the saturated velocity v_{sat} of electrons increases as Lg is decreased. This effect is much more pronounced than in silicon. The dependence of $\overline{\tau}$ on Lg is shown in fig. 1. For a 0.2 µm recessed gate MESFET's, $\overline{\tau}$ can be as short as 5 ps which is about 2.5 times shorter than for silicon BJT's with 0.2 µm base to emitter spacing[10],[11]. For ultimate self aligned MESFET's with $L_{DS} \lesssim 0.7$ µm and Lg $\lesssim 0.3$ µm, $\overline{\tau}$ can be expected to be as short as 4 ps which corresponds to transconductance as high as 500 ms/mm. Switching times between 2 and 4 ps can be expected with HEMT's and HBT's with similar feature sizes.

3. N-OFF MSI/LSI PROCESSES

N-OFF MESFET processes are based on highly uniform ion implanted 2" or 3" wafers. This electrical uniformity is mainly characterized by the local and overall variation of the transistor threshold voltage V_{th} across the wafer[5]. The local standard deviation $\sigma (V_{th})$ over 1 mm^2 for N-OFF MESFET's with Lg = 1 µm and V_{th} = 100 mV is typically 30 mV with defect free pre-annealed material as shown in fig. 2. Such good results have also been reported for HEMT's and HBT's fabricated on MBE heterostructures[12-13].

Down to 0.7 µm, standard aligned processes can be used. Depending on the gate configuratons, N-OFF MESFET's are associated with resistive or N-ON MESFET loads. The whole process typically requires 8 mask levels including 2 metal levels for interconnects.

Below 0.7 µm and in order to reduce L_{DS} as well as L_G, self-aligned processes are mandatory (fig. 3). They are usually based on refractory metal gates[14], but substitutional gate processes have also been reported[15].

The threshold voltage of submicron FET's is dependent on Lg due to short channel effects, and to surface stresses which are themselves dependent on the orientation of the gate[16]. Optimisation of the thickness and doping level ($N_D \geq 10^{18}$ cm^{-2}) of the active layer but also reduction of the surface stresses by proper dielectric deposition, enable to reduce $\Delta V_{th}/\Delta L_g$ down to less than 50 mV/μm.

Present development of the first generation of N-OFF LSI IC's is now leading to high fabrication yield by applying the methods and facilities used for silicon processes.

3. GaAs IC APPLICATIONS

GaAs digital IC's appear now as being complementary to fast silicon IC's, either to reach higher speed or to save power. The main field of applications where GaAs IC's can be used and have been demonstrated (table 1) are :
- telecommunication systems : (multiplexers, demultiplexers, decision circuits, switch matrixes, etc...)
- instrumentation systems (counters, A to D and D to A converters, sample and hold circuit)
- fast signal processors (parallel multipliers, dedicated bit slices...)
- supercomputers (gate arrays for fast data paths, SRAM's...)

There is practically no application that could not be addressed with GaAs digital IC's. We will however restrict this review paper to circuits for fast signal processors or (super) computers.

4. GaAs IC DESIGN

GaAs MSI/LSI IC's up to a few thousand gates (6 K gate arrays, 16 x 16 bit multipliers) and SRAM's (1K, 4K, 16Kbit) are designed and laid out using standard CAD tools developed for silicon IC's. Yet, some specific features have to be considered.
- CAD models for N-OFF and N-ON MESFET's used as amplifying transistors or as pass transistors[17-18].
- modelling of interconnect capacitances including cross-talk which is a 3D problem because of the semi-insulating substrate[19]. The various labs and foundries dedicated to GaAs digital IC's have developed their own models. Some standardziation will however be required in the near future if only to promote second sourcing.

4.1. Logic gate optimisation

The overall performance of an FET logic gate results from a trade-off between speed, power, design flexibility, temperature behaviour, capability to drive large capacitive loads, and small signal gain (G) which is directly related to the noise margins and therefore to the fabrication yield. The relationship between the performance of the inverting transistor and the propagation delay time (tpd) per gate is of the form :
$$tpd = \tau [\alpha + \beta \ FI + \gamma FO \ ] + \text{metal delay}$$
where FI is the gate fan-in, FO the gate fan-out and α, β, γ are fit parameters which depend on the gate configuration (buffered or unbuffered),

and the gate linear gain. For sufficient noise margins it is necessary that
$G \gtrsim 2$. Typical values for α , β and γ are :
α = 1-1.5 ; β = 0.7-0.2 and γ = 1-1.5 for unbuffered gates (DCFL)
α = 2   ; β = γ = 0.3 for buffered gates (SCFL).

The metal delay (τ_w) depends directly on the output resistance of the logic
gate (R_0) and the loading capacitance (C_w). τ_w = $R_0 C_w$. In GaAs processes with
two true metal levels on SiO_2 or polyimide dielectric interlayers ($\varepsilon_r \lesssim 4$),
C_w is much lower than in silicon processes. Even in densely packed bus, the
line interwiring capacitance is always $\lesssim 100$ fF/mm.

To drive long lines, buffered gates are used and :

$$\tau_w = \frac{C_w \, V_{supply}}{k}$$

where V_{supply} is the buffer stage supply voltage, P the gate power consumption
and k is design parameter quasi independent of the transistor used.
τ_w as low as 15 ps/mm can thus be achieved with 3 mW logic gates.

The best ring oscillator results usually correspond to G = 1 to 2, C_w = 0, FI
= FO = 1. Consequently, tpd (RO) $\approx$ 2 to 3 $\overline{\tau}$.
         The associated power consumption P per gate is of the form : P =
$C_L \, \Delta \, V^2 \, f + V_{DD} \, \Delta \, I$, where V_{DD} is the gate supply voltage, f the
system clock frequency, C_L the total capacitance on the gate output node,
I the gate DC supply current.
         In N-off gates, logic swings of about 0.6 V are used and similar
speed but much lower power consumption than with N-on gates can be achieved.

         The gate power consumption P is roughly proportional to ΔV^2 and
V_{DD} which results in a 10 times lower power consumption for N-OFF gates than
for N-ON gate with equivalent speed. In N-OFF IC's, N-ON FET's are utilized as
active loads (E/D gates) and wherever large current drive is needed.

4.2. Design flexibility logic approaches

         N-OFF GaAs FET's are mainly used to implement 3 types of logic
approaches (Fig. 4) :
- DCFL (Direct Coupled FET Logic) or BDCFL (Buffered Direct Coupled FET Logic)
which is equivalent to Si NMOS.
To improve the low noise margins of DCFL, many alternatives have been
proposed (series input diodes, capacitive feed back,...), but with degraded
speed-power performances.
- SCFL (Source Coupled FET Logic) which is equivalent to Si ECL.
- Pass transistors for transfer logic or dynamic logic design.
         NOR and wired OR functions are easily implemented with BDCFL, while
series gating is possible with SCFL[20].
         Very low power can be achieved with DCFL gates ($\lesssim 0.1$ mW/gate).
BDCFL gates are much more insensitive to Fan-out and finally SCFL gates will
be preferred when very large Fan-in and Fan-out are required as well as
complementary outputs.
         All these approaches can be used together in the same circuit,
producing a very high design flexibility (table 2).
The transition width ΔT between the 0 and 1 logic levels is about 120 mV for
BDCFL gate with V_{DD} = 1.2 V and V_T = 50 mV
This ensures a high fabrication yield when high uniformity material
(σ (V_{th}) $\lesssim 30$ mV) is used.

4.3. Design of LSI IC's

GaAs gate arrays may be a good way to get acceptance of GaAs IC's through foundries in the high speed IC market.

(B)DCFL gate arrays are mainly attractive because of the low power consumption which is the limiting factor of silicon ECL gate arrays. Excellent performances have thus been reported[21] for a 2K DCFL gate array with a loaded gate delay (FO = 3, FI = 3, 1.5 mm metal) of 185 ps for a power consumption pergate of 0.5 mW - table 3.

Yet it is obvious that ultimate performances will only be achieved with full custom of even semi-custom design using high performance standard cells. To minimize C_w, appropriate chip partitioning is required such as systolic arrays.

Using gate arrays or a custom design, many combinational circuits such as parallel multipliers, adders and ALU's have been implemented[1]. Some multiplier performances are summarized in table 4.

The performances of arithmetic circuits depend a lot on the algorithm and the architecture used. Nevertheless, a few conclusions can be drawn :
- HEMT IC's are marginally faster than standard MESFET's at 300 K, for they are 2 times faster at 77 K.
- N-OFF gates have a 5 to 10 times better speed power products than N-ON gates with equivalent design rules[22].
- 2 μ N-OFF DCFL gates have a similar speed power product to that of 0.3 μm CML gates in silicon.

5. SRAM's

In computer systems GaAs IC's could be best used to implement data paths, processors and fast cache-memories (SRAM's).
Early results on 1K, 4K are more than encouraging, but are far from being ultimate results because of poor packing density.

The power consumption per bit can be as low as 0.1 mW/bit (100 mW/bit with JFET's) but the speed performance (access time - cycle time) is still suffering from inadequate interconnect design rules to make the most of GaAs FET's - table 5.
1.5 ns/200 mW ECL compatible 1K SRAM's have thus been fabricated with a 0.7 μm process, and a 1200 μm^2 memory cell[27].
Further scaling down is necessary to achieve subnanosecond access times. A self-aligned MESFET process with 3 interconnect levels, 0.8 x 1.3 μm via holes 0.8 μm gate length has thus been proposed[29] and result in a 455 μm^2 memory cell.

To obtain a reasonable fabrication yield (10 % for 1K SRAM's) stability, local σ (V_{th}) have to be better than 30 mV. This can be achieved with the best 2" wafers available today. Moreover, further work is still needed to reduce the access time variation in a memory[30]. Excellent uniformity of the access time of HEMT SRAM's (a few %) has already been reported[8].

6. COMPARISON WITH FAST SILICON IC's

Recent scaling down of fast silicon processes (NMOS or ECL)[23,31] and the impressive performances achieved have raised the question of the real advantage of GaAs over Si for digital applications.

6.1. Switching performances of Silicon and GaAs transistors

Today's fast Si bipolar and MOSFET IC's are fabricated with self-aligned, fully implanted, polysilicon processes with trench isolation and submicron feature sizes.
Silicon bipolar transistors with less than 0.3 μm base to emitter spacing have thus exhibited switching time $\bar{\tau}$ of 12 ps which is equivalent to a 0.7 μm recessed gate MESFET. As shown in fig. 1, self-aligned 0.2 μm MESFET's and HEMT's are about 3 and 4 times faster respectively. 1.2 μm HBT's are equivalent to 0.5 μm MESFET's.

6.2. Gate performances

Gate performances are dependent on the transistor switching time, but also on electrical considerations such as sensitivity to capacitive loading, i.e. : metal delay, noise margins, design flexibiltiy. For instance full adders implemented with BDCFL or SCFL gates exhibit speed power products of 8 tpd x P and 6 tpd x P respectively. This shows the advantage of series gating over standard NOR or wired-OR gates.
The performances of loaded gates (FI = FO = 2) with a linear gain $\geqslant$ 2, agree rather well with the transistor performances (fig. 5). Because of lower interconnect capacitances and lower supply voltages, the metal delay in GaAs IC's is two to three times shorter than that in Si bipolar IC's with equivalent power consumption/gate. In conclusion, GaAs N-OFF gates are at least 2 to 3 times faster or 3 to 5 times less power consuming than silicon gates with equivalent feature sizes.

6.3. Circuit performances

To extend the comparison to circuits such as SRAM's and fast multipliers, similar circuit arrangements (algorithms, architecture..) but also similar design rules (memory cell area, feature sizes, logic swings...) have to be considered. A direct comparison between submicron NMOS and GaAs using a 3 bit adder vehicle has thus confirmed the speed and power advantages of GaAs IC's over equivalent Si IC's[32].

The experimental performances of SRAM's and multipliers (fig. 6 and 7) also indicate that 0.3 μm bipolar IC's can be as fast as 1 μm DCFL IC's, but with a 3 times higher power consumption. 0.8 μm NMOS is definitely at least 2 times slower.

7. CONCLUSION

N-OFF GaAs digital IC's are emerging as a 1st generation GaAs technology capable of breaking the 1 mW, 100 ps/gate barrier in real LSI environment. Comparisons with silicon IC's, assuming equivalent feature sizes, clearly establish a significant low power advantage at the fastest speed of silicon IC's. Further scaling down and improved interconnects are still needed before achieving ultimate speed performances with GaAs IC's.

BIBLIOGRAPHY

1 M. Rocchi, "N-OFF GaAs digital MESFET IC's", GaAs IC Seminar, London, (June 3, 1985)

2 R. Zuleeg, J.K.Notthoff and G.L. Troeger
"Double-Implanted GaAs Complementary JFET's", IEEE ED Lett., EDL-5, 1, January 1984

3 K. Wang, P. Asbeck, M. Chang, D. Miller, and G. Sullivan, "High speed MSI current-mode logic circuits implemented with heterojunction bipolar transistors, Rockwell International, Thousands Oaks, CA, GaAs IC Symposium Digest 1986

4 T. Mizutani, S. Fujita, M. Hirano, and N. Kondo, "Circuit performance of complementary heterostructure MISFET inverter using high mobilitiy 2 DEG and 2 DHG, NTT, Atsugi, Japan
GaAs IC Symposium Digest, 1986

5 J. Maluenda, G.M. Martin, "Homogeneity qualification of GaAs substrates for LSI applications", APL 48, (1986), p. 715

6 C. Rocher, J. Maluenda, B. Gabillard, T. Ducourant, M. Prost, M. Rocchi, "Evaluation of the theoretical maximum fabrication yield of GaAs 1Kbit SRAM's", 1986 Int. Symp. on GaAs and Rel. Comp., Las Vegas, Sept. 28 - October 1, 86

7 Y. Ishii, M. Ino, M. Idda, M. Hirayama and M. Ohmori, "Processing technologies for GaAs memory LSIs", Proc. GaAs IC Symp. 1984, p. 121

8 N. Kobayashi, S. Notomi, M. Suzuki, T. Tsuchiya, K. Nishiuchi, K.Odani, A. Shibatomi,
T. Mimura, M. Abe, "A fully operational 1Kbit HEMT static RAM, IEEE ED33, 5, 1986, pp. 548

9 J.P. André, M. Wolny, M. Rocchi, "MOVPE versus MBE for III/V heterostructure devices and IC's", Inst. Phys. Conf. Ser. n° 79, chapt. 7, Presented at Int. Symp. GaAs and Related Comp., Karuizawa, Japan 1985

10 M. Suzuki, K. Hagimoto, H. Ichino and S. Konaka
"A 9 GHz frequency divider using Si bipolar super self-aligned process technology", IEEE EDL-6, n° 4, pp. 181-183, April 1985

11 K. Washio and al., "A ' ps ECL in a self-aligned bipolar technology", ISSCC Digest, pp. 58-59, Feb. 1987.

12 S. Kuroda, T. Mimura, M. Suzuki, N. Kobayashi, K. Nishiuchi, A. Shibatomi and M. Abe "New device structure for 4Kb HEMT SRAM", Proc. GaAs IC Symp, Boston, MA, Oct. 23-25, 1984

13 P. Ashbeck, D. Miller, R. Anderson, R. Deming, R. Chen, C. Liechti, and F. Eisen, "Application of heterojunction bipolar transistors to high speed, small-scale digital integrated circuits" Proc. GaAs IC Symp. 1984, Boston, MA, Oct. 23-25

14 U. Kazuyoshi, T. Furutsuka, H. Toyoshima, M. Kanamori and A. Higashisaka,"A high transconductance GaAs MESFET with reduced short channel effect characteristics, Proc. IEDM 85, p. 4.2

15 K. Yamasaki, N. Kato, and M. Hirayama, "Below 10 ps/gate operation with buried P-layer SAINT FET's, Electron. Lett. 20, n° 25/26, pp. 1029-1031, Dec. 1984

16 P.M. Asbeck, C.P. Lee, M.F. Chang
IEEE Trans. ED, ED-31, p. 1377, 1984

17 M. Rocchi, B. Gabillard, "GaAs digital dynamic IC's for applications up to 10 GHz" IEEE Jl of SSC, SC-18, n°3, june 83

18 B. Gabillard, C. Rocher, M. Rocchi, "Theoretical and experimental temperature dependence of GaAs N-OFF IC's over 120 K to 400 K" Physical 129B (1985),403-407, presented at ESSDERC 84

19 JA. Maupin, PT. Greiling, NG. Alexopoulos
"Speed power tradeoff in GaAs FET integrated circuits, 1st specialty conference on Gigabit Logic for microwave systems", Orlando, FL, 3-4 may 1979

20 T. Takada, Y. Shimazu, M. Togashi, K. Yamasaki, K Hoshikawa and M. Idda
   "A 2 Gbs throughput GaAs digital time switch LSI using LSCFL", IEEE 1985
   Microwave and Millimeter-Wave Monolithic Circuits Symp. Dig.
21 N. Toyoda, N. Uchitomi, Y. Kitaura, M. Mochizuki, K. Kanazawa, T. Terada,
   Y. Ikawa, A. Hojo, "A 42 ps 2K gate GaAs gate array"ISSCC 85, Feb. 85
22 H. Singh, R. Sadler, A. Geissberger and D. Fisher, ITT Roanoke, VA, J.
   Irvine and G. Gorder, ITT, Nutley, NJ., "A comparative study of GaAs logic
   families using universal shift registers and self-aligned gate technology",
   GaAs IC Symposium Digest, 1986.
23 S.Horiguchi, M. Suzuki, H. Ichino, S. Konaka, T. Sakai, "An 80 ps 2500 gate
   bipolar macrocell array" ISSCC 85, Feb. 85
24 D.K. Arch, B.K. Betz, P.J. Vold, J.K.   Abrokwah, N.C. Cirillo, "A
   self-aligned gate superlattice (Al-Ga)As/n+ - GaAs MODFET 5 x 5 bit
   parallel multiplier", IEEE ED Letters, vol. EDL-7, n°12, december 1986.
25 H. Chung, G. Lee, K. Tan, K. Betz and P. Vold, Honeywell Bloomington, MN,
   "High speed and ultra-low power GaAs MESFET 5 x 5 multipliers", GaAs IC
   Symposium Digest 1986
26 E. Delhaye, C. Rocher, JM. Gibereau, M. Rocchi
   "A 2.5 ns, 40 mW, 4 x 4 GaAs multiplier in 2' s complement mode" Submitted
   to ESSCIRC'86, Delft (NL), Sept. 16-18, 1986
27 B. Gabillard and al, "A GaAs 1K SRAM with 2 ns cycle time, ISSCC Digest,
   p. 136, Feb. 1987
28 H. Hanaka and al, "A 4 K GaAs SRAM with 1 ns access time", ISSCC Digest,
   p. 138, Feb. 1987
29 N. Kato, M.Hirayama, K. Asai, Y. Matsuoka, K. Yamasaki, T. Ogino, "A high
   density GaAs Static RAM process using MASFET", IEDM 85
30 T. Hayashi, H. Tanaka, H. Yamashita, N. Masuda, T. Doi, J. Shigeta, N.
   Kotera, A. Masaki and N.Hashimoto, "Small access time scattering GaAs SRAM
   technology using boots-trap circuits", GaAs IC Symposium, Monterey, CA
   (November 12-14, 1985)
31 W. Fichtner, EA. Hofstatter, RK. Watts, RJ. Bayruns, PF. Bechtold, RL.
   Johnston and DM. Boulin, "A submicron NMOS technology suitable for low
   power high speed circuits", IEDM 85
32 A. Mitonneau, M. Rocchi, I. Talmud, JC. Mauduit, M. Henry, "Direct
   experimental comparison of submicron GaAs and Si NMOS MSI digital IC's",
   Proc 1984 GaAS IC Symposium
33 T. Terada and al, "A 6K GaAs gate array", ISSCC, p. 144, Feb. 1987

Applications	Function	Characteristics	Performances
Instrumentation systems	prescalers counters	: 2 : 8	20.2 GHz, 350 mW 9.4 GHz, 100 mW
Telecommunication systems	multiplexer converters	4 --> 1 4 bit ADC 8 bit DAC	4 Gb/s 200 mW 2 GHz 150 mW (6 bit) 1 GHz (0.025 % linearity)
Fast signal processing computers	ALU multipliers	4 bit 8 x 8 (")	3 ns 15 mW 3 ns 350 mW
	SRAM's	1 x 1 K 1 x 4 k	1.5 ns 200 mW 1 ns 1600 mW
	µprocessors	8 bit/RISC (23 instructions)	3 ns/4 x (256 x 4) SRAM's 10 ns/cycle time ; 840 mW

Table 1 : Significant applications and performances of GaAs digital IC's

	Logic	gate count	packing density gate/mm²	tpd(ps) (FI=FO = 1)	FO delay (ps)	FI delay (ps)	metal delay ps/mm	P(mW) gate
TOSHIBA (21)	DCFL 1.5 µ	2K	500	42	16	11	59	0.5
NTT (23)	Si ECL .5 µm	2.5 K (7 K)	250	78	19	14	64	2.6
FUJITSU	HEMT 1.2 µm	1.5 K	100	85 53 (77 K)	66 29 (77 K)		44 14 (77 K)	2.5
LEP	SCFL 0.7 µm			40	6	5	15	7.5
T.I.	HBT I²L	4 K		FO = 4 400				1
TRIQUINT	BDCFL 1 µm	3 K		120	19.5	10	41	1
TOSHIBA (33)		6 K		76	45	10	45	1.2

Table 3 : Performances of GaAs and Si gate arrays

	LPBFL/CDFL SDFL	DCFL	BDCFL	SCFL
V_t	- 0.5/-1 V	0.1 V/0.2 V	0.1 V/0.2 V	0.1 V/0.2 V
Supply voltages	V_{dd} - V_{ss} = 3 V	V_{dd} = 1-2 V	V_{dd} = 2 V	V_{dd} - V_{ss} = 3V
P (mW)	2 - 10	0.2 - 0.5	1 - 3	2 - 10
tpd (ps)	100 - 50	150 - 50	80 - 50	80 - 50
(FI = FO = 2)				
Logic swing (V)	0.8 - 1 V	0.5 V	0.6 V	0.4 - 0.8 V
Functions	OR NOR, NAND	NOR	WIRED OR, NOR	OR, NOR
				series gating
tpd/ T		0.2 ps/°C		
Packing density (gate/mm^2)	100 - 200	500 - 1000	100 - 500	10 - 100

Table 2 : Performances of GaAs logic gates   (Lg = 0.8 μm)

		Bit nbr	Logic	gate count	t_m (ns)	P (mW)	tpd (ps)	P/gate (mW)
LEP/RTC (26)	C	4x4	DCFL 1 μm	213	2.5	40	120	.2
BELL Labs	C	4x4	HEMT 1 μm	162	1.6	55	114	.34
HONEYWELL (24)	C	5x5	MESFET 1 μm	343	2.6	79	87	.23
HONEYWELL (25)	C	5x5	HEMT 1 μm	350	1.8	150	72	.43
FUJITSU	GA	8x8	HEMT 1.2μm	888	4.9 3.1 (77 K)	5800 3200		
LEP	C	8x8	DCFL 0.8 μm	800	3	325	90	0.3
ROCKWELL	C	8x8	SDFL 1 μm	1008	5.25	1000	160	1
HUGHES	C	8x8	NMOS 0.8 μm	400	9.5	600	244	1.5
FUJITSU	C	16x16	DCFL 2 μm	3168	10.5	950	162	0.3
MATSUSHITA	C	8x8	ECL-Si 2 μm		5	1400	160	
NTT	GA	16x16	ECL-Si 0.35μm	1750	6	2050		

Table 4 : Performances of GaAs and Si parallel multipliers
(C = custom, GA = gate array)

	N(bits)	t_{access} min. (ns)	P (mW)	Cell area (μm^2)	Logic	Design rules
LEP / RTC	16 x 4	0.7	200 *	55x45	DCFL 0.8 μ	3
FUJITSU	1K	1	300	1400	DCFL 1 μm	2
ROCKWELL	1K	0.8 (0.6)	450	47x46	HEMT 1 μm	2
LEP / RTC (27)	1K	1.5	2000	30x40	DCFL 0.8 μ	3
HITACHI (28)	4K	1	1600	1200	DCFL 0.7 μ	
FUJITSU	4K	2.7	700	1400	DCFL 0.8 μ	2
MITSUBISHI	4K	2.5	200	36x29	DCFL 1 μm	2/3
FUJITSU	4K	2 (77K)	1540	1600	HEMT 1.2 μ	3
NTT	16K	4.1	1460	41x32.5	DCFL 1 μ	1.5
NEC	16K	4	1600	700	SiECL 0.5 μ	

*including eight output buffers
Table 5 : Performances of GaAs SRAM's

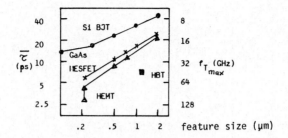

Figure 1
Switching time $\overline{\tau} = 1/\pi\, f_T$ versus feature size
for Si and GaAs transistors (L_G for FET's and
emitter/base spacing for BJT's)

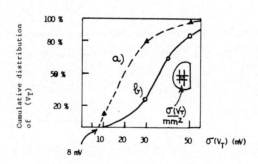

Figure 2
Cumulative distribution of the local standard
deviation of FET's threshold voltage over 2"
wafers :
a) defect free preannealed material
b) standard material

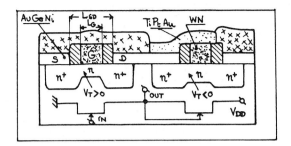

Figure 3
GaAs E/D inverter using a self-aligned gate
process with oxide spacers
(2 level of metal lines are used
and not shown here)

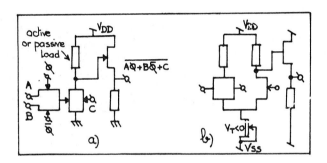

Figure 4
Main GaAs N-OFF gates
a) BDCFL gate + pass transistors
b) SCFL gate

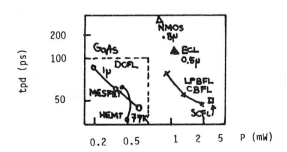

Figure 5
Loaded gate performances (FI = FO = 2)

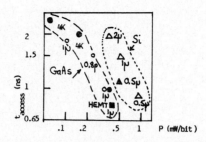

Figure 6
Performances of GaAs and Si SRAM's
GaAs (O 1K   ● 4K) ■ 1K HEMT
Si   (△ 256 x 4)
       (▲ 256 x 16)

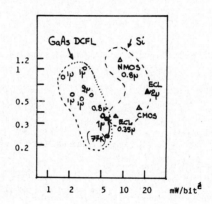

Figure 7
Performances of GaAs and Si parallel multipliers
O   MESFET   ●   HEMT

VLSI '87, C.H. Séquin (editor)
Elsevier Science Publishers B.V. (North-Holland)
© IFIP, 1988

CMOS TECHNOLOGY FOR HIGH SPEED VLSI

Tetsuya IIZUKA

Semiconductor Device Engineering Laboratory
TOSHIBA Corporation
Komukaitoshiba, Kawasaki 210 Japan

This paper reviews and demonstrates the impact of CMOS
device and circuit technologies on high speed system
VLSI's. CMOS does not necessarily provide the highest
gate level speed among many other alternatives.
However, it is the best device for high speed systems.
The system speed is strongly dependent on the scale of
integration, since the elimination of inter-chip
communication and implementation of parallel
processing are effective techniques for high speed
systems and require high potential of large scale
integration.

1. INTRODUCTION

The technical papers reported at an IEEE sponsored solid
state circuits conference during these fifteen years has become
dominantly based on CMOS technologies , 4 % in 1973, 11 % in
1980 and 69 % in 1987. Reason for this is clear: CMOS provides
density, power, speed and cost benefits for systems[1].
This paper will illustrate the impact of CMOS process and
circuit technology on the high speed VLSI and systems.

2. BENEFITS OF THE SCALE OF INTEGRATION

Basic advantage of CMOS technology lies in its high
potential of large scale integration.

2.1. Chip-to-Chip Interface Delay Reduction

Since the birth of classic CMOS technology, it has been
regarded as low power but low density technology. However, as
it enters into the VLSI era, the scale of integration is
strongly limited by power density. Reserving its inherent low
power characteristics, its circuit density has been improved by
structural innovation and new circuit techniques. By new
isolation structures and new scaling principles, high density
CMOS structure with high latch-up immunity has been developed.
New CMOS circuit schemes such as mixed CMOS, clocked CMOS (or
Domino CMOS), PN-CMOS and Zipper CMOS circuits, have been
developed to reduce transistor count per circuit function and
improved circuit density.

High density and low power consumption are essential
features for large scale integration. While, a system
performance (speed, cost and compactness) is a strong function
of the scale of circuit integration of chips used on the system
board. Since chip-to-chip interface delay time is not scalable,
speed of a system based on poorly scaled chips is mainly
determined by interface delay. Table 1 illustrates that the
number of chips composing system is more important than gate
delay itself. ECL gates, even NMOS gates have faster gate
switching speed compared CMOS gates, but this does not mean
that the system performance is automatically superior.

2.2. System on Chip and Parallel Processing

The age of "system on chip" has already started. Almost
all the newly reported 32bit-CPU's have embedded cache memories
and pipelining schemes. Many gate array suppliers are starting
to support the implementation of large macros such as memories
on chip. The "Super Integration" scheme has strong demands for
many applications including high speed systems. This means that
the elimination of chip-to-chip interface and implementation of
parallel data processing are key techniques for high speed
system performance. These schemes are possible only by using a
device technology that has very high potential of integration.

3. CMOS TECHNOLOGY TRENDS

3.1. Scaling

In spite of many non-technical obstacles, the rate of
device geometry miniaturization and growth of the scale of
integration shows no sign of saturation. Fig. 1 shows CMOS gate
speed improvement by device scaling.
A current CMOS mass-production technology has reached to
the level of two million elements on a chip. This is a 1.2um
geometry device and 250ps/gate technology.
A pilot CMOS line is now challenging eight to thirty
million elements integration on a single chip. This technology
uses 0.8 to 0.5um geometry and gate speed is reaching to
150ps/gate and 100ps/gate, respectively. Fig.2 shows a recent
achievement of 0.5um CMOS technology based 16x16bit multiplier
[2] with comparison to other technologies.
With regard to the manipulation of very large number of
gates on chip, CAD technology seems to have the casting vote
rather than the Si processing technology.

3.2. Technology Mixture

By adding some amount of cost overhead and process
complexity, CMOS can boost its speed, i.e. BiCMOS provides
switching speed up to 4-5 times faster than pure CMOS using the
same pattern size[3], apparently depending on the loading

condition. One of the big advantages of BiCMOS is that it inherits CMOS's low power characteristics in addition to non-saturation mode bipolar device speed. Another advantage of BiCMOS is that it is well suited for the ECL interface which is a good standard for high speed chip-to-chip communication.

4. CONCLUSION

For very small gate count IC's, GaAs and Si ECL devices may provide better chip performance. However, for predominant systems being composed of large size of circuitry, scaled CMOS technology with parallel processing scheme is the most promising approach to provide large systems with very high speed as well as low cost and compactness. As a higher end choice of technology, BiCMOS technology may be a possible solution.

ACKNOWLEDGEMENTS

The author should like to thank Y. Unno, H. Yamada, and O. Ozawa for their encourgement and discussions, as well as all colleagues in Semiconductor Device Engineering Laboratory of Toshiba Corporation.

Reference

[1] Iizuka,T, "A Review on CMOS -Circuits and Technologies for Digital VLSI-", 1983 Int. Symposium on VLSI Technology, Systems and Applications, Digest of Technical Papers, pp30-34.

[2] Tsuda, K., H.Takato, N.Takenouchi, K.Tsuchiya, Y.Oowaki, K.Numata,and A.Nitayama, "0.5um CMOS Technology for 5.6ns High Speed 16x16 bit Multiplier",1987 Symposium on VLSI Technology, Digest of Tech. Papers, pp109-110.

[3] Kubo, M., "Perspective to Bi-CMOS VLSIs", 1987 Symposium on VLSI Circuits, Digest of Tech. Papers, pp89-90.

DEVICE	PATH	2um TECH.	0.5um TECH.
ECL	LOGIC GATES	25.5ns	4.42ns
	PACKAGE INTERFACE CHARGE/DISCHARGE	10.8ns	5.4 ns
	LIGHT PROPAGATION	5.4ns	5.4 ns
	TOTAL	41.7ns	15.22ns
CMOS	LOGIC GATES	54.4ns	6.8 ns
	I/O BUFFERS	9.6ns	3.0 ns
	TOTAL	64.0ns	9.8 ns

TABLE 1. Critical path delay of 200Kgate systems
based on ECL and CMOS technologies.

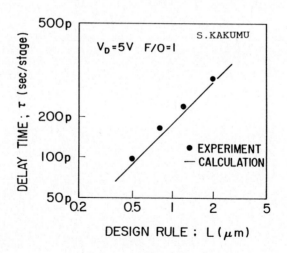

FIGURE 1
Propagation dely time as a
function of minimum geo-
metry.

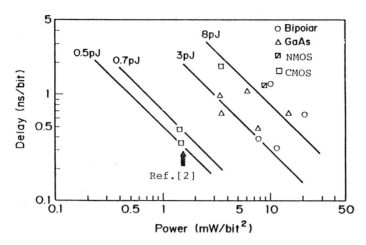

FIGURE 2
Multiplication time and
power consumption of
Bipolar, GaAs, and CMOS
based mutiplier IC's.

VLSI '87, C.H. Séquin (editor)
Elsevier Science Publishers B.V. (North-Holland)
© IFIP, 1988

LOW TEMPERATURE MOS MICROELECTRONICS

by

Fritz H. Gaensslen
IBM Thomas J. Watson Research Center
Yorktown Heights, NY 10598

Richard C. Jaeger
Electrical Engineering Department
Auburn University, AL 36849

The advantages of using MOS devices in a computer system operating at low temperature began to be explored in detail during the early 1970's, when it became clear that the high density and low power associated with future MOS technologies would result in a computer system packaged in a small, readily-cooled volume [1-3]. Recent advances in superconductors will increase this thrust toward low temperature systems, although radical changes are not expected to occur overnight.

The development of MOS device scaling theory [4] provided a methodology for systematic miniaturization of MOS devices. One important limitation to this theory is the lack of scaling of device turn-off in the subthreshold region. In order to reduce the threshold voltage, and at the same time maintain the off-current in scaled-down technologies, the subthreshold slope must be steepened. MOS scaling theory is isothermal in nature, but lowering the temperature provides an additional means to enhance the subthreshold slope. This fact provided the original impetus to look at low temperature MOS operation.

Direct proportionality between subthreshold slope and reciprocal temperature was subsequently demonstrated as shown in Fig. 1 from Ref. [3]. In the same paper it was also established that the classical threshold voltage theory still applies to enhancement-mode devices operating at low temperature. Figure 2 and Fig. 3 from [3] demonstrate for the linear and pinched-off regime of a n-type MOS-channel typical carrier mobility and current improvements obtained between 296K and 77K. Similar improvements are experienced by p-channel devices. As shown in Fig. 4 and Fig. 5, thermal and metallic interconnect conductivities increase substantially at low temperature. A reduction in junction leakage by several orders of magnitude is also demonstrated in [3]; this fact suggests a pseudo-static mode of circuit operation of otherwise dynamic circuitry. The improvements in mobility, subthreshold slope and other more subtle changes yield generically better MOS devices at liquid nitrogen temperature (LNT:77.3K). In addition, low-temperature operation of CMOS eliminates latchup as a concern [5, 6].

Operation at LNT yields a more tightly controlled temperature environment and hence tighter distributions of electrical parameters. Also, wear-out failure mechanisms usually follow an Arrhenius relationship and decrease exponentially with temperature. Therefore, low temperature operation should greatly reduce failure rates and improve reliability. However, this is yet to be substantiated in detail.

Work during the mid-70's discovered problems with freeze-out in common buried-channel depletion-mode devices [7, 8], obviating their use at low temperatures. Exactly the same effects, which are related to the parallel existence of a surface- and a buried-channel, occur in p-channel devices as currently fabricated in popular n-well CMOS technologies.

As we entered the decade of the 80's, it became clear that CMOS, because of its low power and high level of integration, would be the VLSI technology of the future, and the exploration of low temperature CMOS operation accelerated. LNT operation can directly yield a factor of 2.5-3 improvement in the switching speed of CMOS circuits, when compared to operation at 358K (85C). At any technology level, this performance improvement exceeds that achieved through down-scaling by a factor of 2. In the same sense, MOS technology limits are extended by one generation through LNT operation. Most performance data available so far present the results of cooling normal technologies to 77K; we expect that optimized LNT technologies will yield substantial performance improvements. A potential problem area is hot electron device degradation, but recent work has indicated that adequate design margins can be maintained in scaled devices of proper design [11-14].

ETA Systems Inc., a subsidiary of CDC, shipped the first LN cooled CMOS computer system called ETA 10 [9] at the end of 1986. Although large systems have used liquid cooling (water or freon) for a long time, there exists a widely perceived difficulty with cooling to LNT. It is frequently overlooked that cooling system technologies have also advanced through the last two decades, and economical cooling systems now exist for power levels of several hundred watts at LNT [10]. Such a cooling system, though certainly not small, occupies less volume than the water cooling systems of competitive ECL machines. As a coolant, liquid nitrogen is inert and inexpensive, and its boiling temperature provides an excellent compromise between improved system performance and cooling cost.

The main reason for not going to low temperature operation in the past, however, has probably been a simple lack of need. Throughout the past two decades, performance improvements have been achieved with relative ease through the continued miniaturization of device geometries. But, performance enhancement is becoming more and more difficult and expensive to achieve through feature size reduction as we attempt to reach below 1 μm. Therefore, low temperature operation is becoming increasingly attractive.

Low temperature operation of CMOS technology can more economically approach bipolar speeds with MOS yields, circuit densities and power levels, resulting in compact, power-efficient and fast systems [9, 15, 16]. Miniaturization and low temperature operation help each other in cooling, performance, parasitics etc. Functional and margin chip testing for low temperature can be done conveniently at room temperature to low temperature specifications. Low temperature CMOS technology allows to install more computing power per given volume, a most important consideration for end users. In summary liquid nitrogen cooled CMOS represents a strategic technology alternative for mainframe computers, an area which has traditionally been the exclusive domain of bipolar technology.

Recently, activities in low temperature electronics have greatly increased throughout the world. This increase is exhibited in many ways including an increased number of publications, panel sessions at major electronics conferences, publication of a reprint book on Low Temperature Electronics by the IEEE PRESS [17] and publication of the first Special Issue on Low Temperature Semiconductor Electronics by the IEEE Transactions on Electron Devices [18].

New results related to superconducting materials have also given an additional impetus to low temperature research. We do not expect these materials to have an immediate effect on chip technologies, but initially may have an important effect at the system packaging level. First, however, a number of questions must be resolved. These include understanding the influence of superconducting interconnections on system level performance, developing methods for deposition of thin films of the superconducting materials, and establishing that these films are stable and can support sufficient current density to be useful in microelectronic applications. In the absence of a superconducting three terminal switching device, high T_c materials have to be compatible with the technologies in place. The on-chip switching action of the assumed RC-network is still dominated by the non superconducting MOS device channel resistance.

Based on a liquid nitrogen cooled quarter micron MOS technology chips with several hundred thousand circuits and a gate delay of well below 100 ps will be available to design future digital systems. A summary of the advantages for MOS microelectronics operated at liquid nitrogen temperature is shown in Fig. 6.

References:

[1]   F. H. Gaensslen, V. L. Rideout and E. J. Walker, "Design and Characterization of Very Small MOSFETs for Low Temperature Operation", IEDM, Washington, DC, Technical Digest, pp. 43-46. December 1985.

[2]   R. L. Maddox, "P-MOSFET Parameters at Cryogenic Temperatures", IEEE Trans. Electron Devices, Vol. **ED-23**, pp. 16-21, January 1976.

[3]   F. H. Gaensslen, V. L. Rideout, E. J. Walker, and J. J. Walker, "Very Small MOSFETs for Low-Temperature Operation", IEEE Trans. Electron Devices, Vol. **ED-24**, pp. 218-229, March 1977.

[4]   R. H. Dennard, F. H. Gaensslen, L. Kuhn and H. N. Yu, "Design of Micron MOS Switching Devices", IEDM Digest, Talk No 24.3, p. 168, December 1972.

[5]   F. H. Gaensslen, "MOS Devices and Integrated Circuits at Liquid Nitrogen Temperature", 1980 IEEE ICCC Proceedings, pp. 450-452, October 1980.

[6]   J. G. Dooley and R. C. Jaeger, "Temperature Dependence of Latchup in CMOS Circuits", IEEE Electron Device Letters, Vol. **EDL-5**, pp. 41-43, February 1984.

[7]   F. H. Gaensslen and R. C. Jaeger, "Temperature Dependent Threshold Behavior of Depletion-Mode MOSFETs - Characterization and Simulation", Solid-State Electronics, Vol. **22**, pp. 423-430, April 1979.

[8]   R. C. Jaeger and F. H. Gaensslen, "Simple Analytical Models for the Temperature Dependent Threshold Behavior of Depletion-Mode MOSFETs", IEEE Trans. Electron Devices Joint Special Issue on VLSI, Vol. **ED-26**, pp. 501-508, April 1979.

[9]   T. Vacca, D. Resnick, D, Frankel, R. Bach, J. Kreilich and D. Carlson, "A Cryogenically Cooled CMOS VLSI Super Computer" VLSI Systems Design, pp. 80-88, June 1987.

[10] R. C. Longsworth and W. A. Steyert, "Technology for Liquid-Nitrogen-Cooled Computers", IEEE Trans. on Electron Devices, Vol. **ED-34**, pp. 4-7, January 1987.

[11] M. Itsumi, "Electron Trapping in Thin Films of Thermal SiO_2 at Temperatures Between 30 and 300K", J. Applied Physics, Vol. **54**., pp. 1930-1936, April 1983.

[12] D. Lau, G. Gildenblat, C. G. Sodini and D. E. Nelson, "Low-Temperature Substrate Current Characterization of N-Channel MOSFETs", IEDM Digest, pp. 565-568, December 1985.

[13]   A. K. Henning, N. Chan, and J. D. Plummer, "Substrate Current in N-Channel and P-Channel MOSFETs Between 77K and 300K: Characterization and Simulation", IEDM Digest, pp. 573-576, December 1985.

[14]   A. K. Henning, N. N. Chan, J. T. Watt and J. D. Plummer, "Substrate Current at Cryogenic Temperatures: Measurements and a Two-Dimensional Model for CMOS Technology", IEEE Trans. on Electron Devices, Vol. ED-34, pp. 64-74, January 1987.

[15]   S. Hanamura, M. Aoki, T. Masuhara, O. Minato, Y. Sakai, and T. Hayashida, "Operation of Bulk CMOS at Very Low Temperatures", IEEE Symposium on VLSI Technology, pp. 46-47, September 1983.

[16]   G. Gildenblat, L. Colonna-Romano, D. Lau and D. E. Nelson, "Investigation of Cryogenic CMOS Performance", IEDM Digest, pp. 268-271, December 1985.

[17]   R. K. Krischman, Editor, "Low Temperature Electronics", IEEE Press, 1986.

[18]   F. H. Gaensslen and R. C. Jaeger, Guest Editors, "Special Issue on Low Temperature Semiconductor Electronics", IEEE Trans. on Electron Devices, Vol. ED-34, January 1987.

Figures:

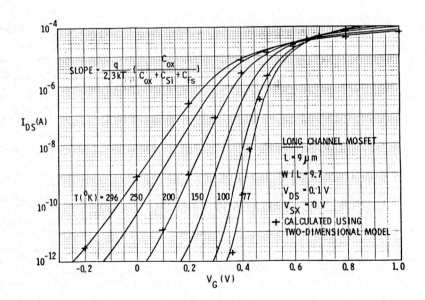

Fig. 1.   Semilogarithmic plots of transfer characteristics for a long channel device ($L = 9\ \mu$m) with temperature as a parameter. Discrete points (+) represent results of two-dimensional simulations for 296K, 200K and 77K.

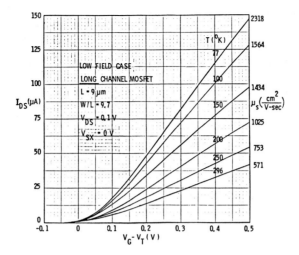

Fig. 2.   Drain current I_{DS} versus $V_G - V_T$ in the linear or below pinch-off regime ($V_{DS} < V_G - V_T$) for a long channel device ($L = 9 \mu m$) with temperature parameter. Right-hand scale lists surface mobility values calculated at a gate voltage of 0.5 V above threshold.

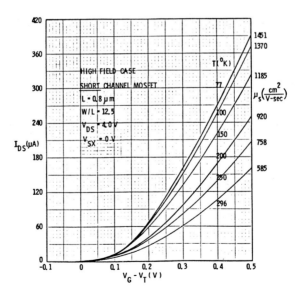

Fig. 3.   Drain current I_{DS} versus $V_G - V_T$ in the above-pinchoff regime ($V_{DS} > V_G - V_T$) for a short channel device ($L = 0.8 \mu m$) with temperature as parameter. The right-hand scale lists calculated effective surface mobility values calculated at a gate voltage of 0.5V above threshold.

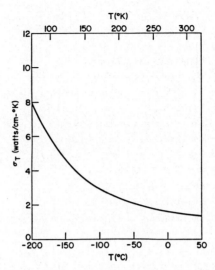

Fig. 4.   Thermal conductivity of 0.5 Ω • cm p-type silicon from "Thermal Conductivity of Metallic Elements and Alloys", Y. S. Touloukian et al. Eds., IFI, Plenum Press, 1970, New York.

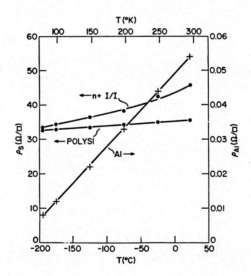

Fig. 5.   Measured sheet resistance versus temperature for aluminum, n+ polysilicon, and n+ ion implanted (I/I) lines with thicknesses of 1.0 μm, 0.35 μm, and 0.2 μm, respectively.

Advantages to Cooling

- Steeper subthreshold slope
- Higher transconductance
- Threshold voltage as function of temperature
- No degradation of geometry effects
- Dramatic junction leakage reduction
- Enhanced electrical line conductivity
- Improved thermal conductivity of silicon substrate
- Bulk CMOS latch-up suppression
- Better reliability
- Circuit improvements
- Miscellaneous

Fig. 6.   Summary of advantages for MOS microelectronics operated at liquid nitrogen temperature.

MACHINE ARCHITECTURES

VLSI '87, C.H. Séquin (editor)
Elsevier Science Publishers B.V. (North-Holland)
© IFIP, 1988

Inference Machines in FGCS Project

Shunichi UCHIDA

Institute for New Generation Computer Technology (ICOT)
Mita-Kokusai Building 21F., 4-28, Mita 1, Minato-ku, Tokyo

Abstract

In Japan's fifth generation computer systems (FGCS) project, logic programming is adopted for the base for software and hardware systems to be developed. As a primitive operation of logic programming is syllogistic inference, machines studied and built in the project are called **inference machines.**

One of the project's target machines is a parallel inference machine (PIM) having about 1000 processing elements. Smaller scale PIMs are also planned as intermediate targets. In addition to PIMs, sequential inference machines (SIMs) have been developed for a software development tool. A personal type SIM is called PSI which is a logic programming workstaion. For parallel software development, a multi-PSI system which consists of several CPUs of PSI connected with a high-speed network, is also under development.

In this paper, these sequential and parallel inference machines, some of which have already been developed, some are planned, shall be described with their languages and operating systems.

1 Introduction

Japan's fifth generation computer systems(FGCS) project aims at the research and development of new computer technology for knowledge information processing systems (KIPS) that will be required in 1990's. The project started from April 1982 as a ten year project. It is divided into three stages, namely, the initial stage (1982–1984), the intermediate stage (1985–1988) and the final stage (1989–1991).

The knowledge information processing systems are considered to have logical inference mechanisms using knowledge bases as their central functions. Logic programming is adopted as the base for software and hardware systems developed in this project. The final target computer system is generally considered to have two types of functions, namely, a high-speed inference function and a knowledge base management function. Two types of the machines have been studied, namely, parallel inference machines (PIM) and knowledge base machines (KBM). The target of PIM research and development is a highly parallel machine having about 1000 processing elements. In addition to these research and development items, software development support systems are also being developed. One of these systems is a personal sequential inference machine (PSI), a logic programming workstation.

The machine languages of all these inference machines are based on logic programming. These languages are called kernel languages (KLn, n=0,1 or 2). KL0 is a sequential language for PSI. KL1 is a parallel language for PIM. KL2 is for the final target machine.

In the initial stage, main research efforts of the inference machines were devoted more to the design of machine architectures than to the fast and compact implementation of machine hardware. From the intermediate stage, the implementation efforts using custom LSIs began with the development of the smaller version of PSI (PSI-II). Now, we plan to implement the intermediate stage PIM (PIM-I) containing about 100 processing elements. We have to use some custom VLSIs for this implementation.

In this paper, the inference machines, some of which have already been developed and others which are planned, shall be described with their languages and operating systems.

2   Sequential Inference Machine (SIM)

In the initial stage, we developed two types of sequential inference machine (SIM) as a software development tool. One was named PSI and the other was named the Cooperative High-speed Inference machine (CHI).

PSI was intended to be used as a common software development tool in the project. It was designed as a logic programming workstation having its programming and operating sytem on it. The development must be completed in a year and a half. Stable operation and smooth delivery were considered to be important. PSI adopted a rather conservative implementation technology using fast TTLs.

On the other hand, CHI could be designed more freely. We intended to design the fastest possible Prolog machine. It was designed as a backend high-speed processor and implemented using CML (Current Mode Logic). Its machine language was designed based on the abstract machine instruction set proposed by Tick and Warren [4] which is now widely known as WAM (Warren's Abstract Machine instruction set).

The SIM programming and operating system (SIMPOS) was developed on PSI. To describe SIMPOS, a new system description language, ESP (Extended Self-contained Prolog) was developed. SIMPOS is a personal OS having a multi-window based human interface and a programming environment for ESP like the LISP machine OS. SIMPOS has been continuously improved and extended. Its size is about 370K lines in ESP consisting of about 2100 class modules.

ESP is a new type of language combining object oriented language features and logic programming language features. It can be used not only for system description but also for knowledge representation. SIMPOS is fully written in ESP and its module structure is completely based on the object oriented concept. Thus, SIMPOS modules (class definitions) can be easily inherited and customarized by the user like the flavor system of the LISP machine OS. ESP is a higher level language than LISP, Prolog and Smalltalk. The productivity of software is very much improved, however, a variety of firmware and hardware support and compiling techniques are necessary to make execution speed satisfactory.

About 130 PSI machines have been distributed to ICOT, our cooperative companies, some universities and research institutes. All these PSI machines are connected by LAN and the public packet switching network.

From the beginning of the intermediate stage, we started the effort to develop a smaller version of PSI (PSI-II) and CHI (CHI-II) using custom LSIs. The CPU of the PSI-II is also intended to be used for the multi-PSI system which will be used for prallel software

Table 1: Main features of PSI-I and PSI-II

	PSI-I	PSI-II
Device	TTL (Fast)	CMOS-G.A., TTL
Cycle time	200 ns	200 ns
Word width	40 bits	40 bits
WCS	64b x 16KW	53b x 16KW
Cache memory	4KW x 2	4KW x 1
Main memory	16MW (Max)	64MW (MAX)
Memory chip	256 Kbit	1 Mbit
Max. No. of Process	64	S/W defined
Machine code	Table type	WAM type
Structure data	Sharing	Copying
Exe. speed(Average)	30 KLIPS	150 KLIPS
Exe. speed(Append)	35 KLIPS	333 KLIPS

Table 2: Performace of PSI-I and PSI-II

	PSI-I (KLIPS)	PSI-II (KLIPS)
Append	35	333
Naive Reverse	34	271
Quick Sort	40	132
Tree Traverse	41	100
8 Queens	60	162

development. We have almost completed the hardware development of PSI-II and CHI-II. They will be used from this fall in this project. Main features of these machines are shown in Tables 1, 2 and 3.

In the implementaion of these hardware and firmware systems, compilers and interpreters, multi-window systems and other parts of the operating systems, valuable experience and design criteria have been accumlated at ICOT. They are now being used for the development of PIM-I and its OS, PIMOS.

3   Parallel Inference Machine (PIM)

3.1   Outline of PIM research plan

The research target of PIM in the final stage was roughly described in the project plan that it would have about 1000 processing elements and attain 100 M to 1 G LIPS. We now feel that this target will be feasible in five years. As an intermediate stage target, we now plan to develop PIM-I which will have about 100 processing elements and attain about 10 to 20 MLIPS including some overhead caused by the operating system.

In the initial stage, we studied several PIM models such as reduction and dataflow for the parallel execution mechanisms of logic programming languages. In the beginning, we used pure Prolog and examind both OR-parallel and AND-parallel execution mechanisms. We built several software and hardware simulators. For dataflow, we designed a machine

Table 3: Main features of CHI-I and CHI-II

	CHI-I	CHI-II
Device	CML	CMOS-G.A., TTL
Cycle time	100 ns	170 ns
Word width	32 bits	40 bits
WCS	78b x 16KW	same
Cache memory	16KW x 2	same
Main memory	64MW (Max)	128MW (MAX)
Memory chip	256 Kbit	1 Mbit
Machine code	WA type	extended WAM
Structure data	Copying	same
Exe. speed(Append)	280 KLIPS	about 400 KLIPS

model and implemented a hardware simulator which was named PIM-D. It executed logic programs in a goal-diven manner. The hardware simulator consisted of 16 PEs and 15 structure memory modules. They were connected by a hierarchical bus network. Each PE was built using the AMD's 2900 series bit-sliced microprocesors and TTLs.

For the reduction, we designed and implemented a simulator, PIM-R. It consisted of 16 MC68K processors connected by a common bus and a shared memory. For the study of the hardware support of job division and allocation in a multiprocessor environment, we designed the Kabuwake-method and implemented it by software on a hardware simulator which consisted of 16 MC68K based computers connected by a switching network and a ring network.

Through this research, we learned many lessons on the parallel execution of logic programming:

1. We must have a simple and elegant language which enables us to introduce compiler optimization compiler effectively and also make the machine hardware simple and fast.

2. The machine language must have such features as to describe an operating system. Some features like process synchronization have to be included in the language model. Then, AND-parallel-type language features are necessary.

3. The amount of the hardware system can not be large for stable implementation of many PEs. For example, commercially available VLSI technology would not be sufficient to fully implement complex architectures such as a dataflow architecture.

In parallel with the PIM research, the design of the parallel logic programming language for PIM (KL1) was carried out. Considering the requirements imposed by the PIM design, a simple parallel logic programming language, GHC (Guarded Horn Clause) was designed. It is a committed-choice AND-parallel logic programming language. We decided to use it as the base for the PIM and PIMOS research in the intermediate stage.

In the beginning of the intermediate stage, we made the detailed plan for PIM research and development. We had realized the importance of the knowledge about parallel languages and parallel software systems, especially the parallel operating system, to design the efficient parallel hardware systems.

The functions of the software systems, for example, the optimization made by the compiler and the strategy of job division and allocation in the operating system greatly influence the optimal design of the machine language and architecture of PIM.

We decided to adopt a simple and fast architecture for the PE suited to the GHC execution mechanism and the cluster structure for the connection mechanism. In addition, we decided to make the hardware system fast and stable so that we could build larger scale parallel software systems like the experimental operating system.

To be able to design the practical hardware of the PIM, we decided to develop an experimental parallel operating system, PIMOS, in more systematic way. To provide the software researcher of PIMOS with a parallel hardware environment very quickly, we decided to develop the multi-PSI system. The second version of the multi-PSI system will be a multi-processor having up to 64 PEs being connected by two dimensional mesh network. The PE is the same as the CPU of PSI-II.

In the multi-PSI system (V.2), the KL1 interpreter will be implemented in the firmware of the PE. Its execution speed will be sufficient to actually support the large scale parallel software systems including PIMOS.

3.2   PIM-I, Intermediate stage target

As the intermediate stage targert of PIM, we now intend to build the experimental system as follows:

1. The number of PEs is About 100.

2. Target processing speed: For the total system, 10 to 20 MLIPS including some overhead caused by PIMOS. For each PE, 200 to 500 KLIPS for KL1.

3. Connection mechanism: In a cluster, a shared memory with parallel cache. Between clusters, a switching network.

4. Machine language: KL1-B based on GHC.

We decided to use the tag-architecture for the PE optimized to GHC (KL1-B). GHC can handle from very fine granularity to coarse granularity. The key problem of the PE architecture is how to make the process switching faster. The optimization by the compliler to reduce the frequency of process switching is also an important research item. Some support for garbage collection is necessary because GHC tends to consume much heap area.

For the connection mechanism, we introduce the cluster in which around 8 PEs are connected by a shared memory with a parallel cache system [12] [13] [14] to achieve fast communication among PEs. This mechanism is chosen because the language features of GHC require very quick responses for communications which are issued in unification operations. The granularity of GHC programs, namely the size of the processes, could be very small, and the synchronization of the parallel processes is made using shared variables. Then, the lock mechanism is also required. To deal with these difficult conditions, we decided to introduce the rather complex parallel cache system. For the connection among the clusters, we introduce a packet switching network. We have not yet decided its details, however, one example is the connection network of the multi-PSI system. The connection mechanism is very closely related to the strategy of job division and allocation among

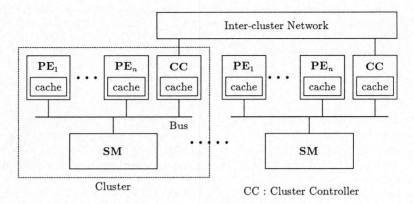

Cluster   CC : Cluster Controller

Figure 1: PIM Overview

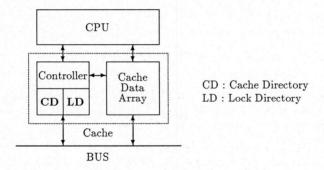

CD : Cache Directory
LD : Lock Directory

Figure 2: Cache and Lock Mechanism

clusters and PEs. Then we will design its detailed mechanisms considering the requirements
imposed by the PIMOS design.

We have not yet completed the implementation details of PIM-I. However, we roughly
plan to implement a PE on a printed circuit board the size of A4 paper using standard-cell
VLSIs and 2 to 4 clusters in a standard cabinet.

3.3   PIMOS and Multi-PSI system

The research and development of PIMOS started with the design of the KL1 language
system. The basic formal model of KL1 is given by GHC just as pure Prolog is a model
for practical logic programming languages such as DEC10 Prolog and Prolog-II.

We defined three language layers for a KL1 language system as shown in Fig. 3.
The core part of this system is KL1-C, namely GHC. KL1-U is the user language or
system description language which is now under design. KL1-P is a notation to permit
a programmer to explicitly specify the way of dividing a job into parallel processable
subjobs and also assign the amount of computational resources to each subjob. KL1-B is

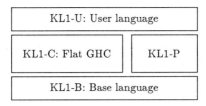

Figure 3: The KL1 Language Systems

the machine language which is directly executed by the PEs.

For KL1-U, we intend to introduce the object oriented concept for its modularization just as we sucessfully introduced it for ESP. KL1-B is now under design in parallel with the design of the architecture of the PE. We are designing KL1-B so that we can make full use of optimization by the compiler.

The experimental versions of the KL1 language sytem include a GHC compiler, and a KL1-B interpreter on such machines as PSI, multi-PSI(V1), VAX, DEC20 and Balance 21000. Several small parallel programs were written in KL1 and run on these machines to evaluate the KL1 execution method and also observe the effect of the job division and allocation strategy.

We have started to design PIMOS. Main design features of PIMOS are summarized as follows:

1. It is designed as a single unified operating system which controls the parallel hardware system just as one system. Main functions are the hardware resource management and the control of load distribution and balancing.

2. Basic functions for the programming environment are implemented on it. Debugging, man-machine interface, measurement and evaluation and exception handling are being considered.

3. It is fully written in KL1 and implemented on the Multi-PSI system. The interpreter for KL1-B is implemented in firmware, and will be moved to PIM-I after the PIM-I hardware system is completed.

PIMOS will be actually built on the multi-PSI system (V2) which will be developed in the end of 1987.

The multi-PSI system was planned to encourage the software researcher to actually make larger scale parallel programs in KL1. Especially, the development of PIMOS needs fast and stable parallel hardware. The multi-PSI is best suited to this purpose at ICOT.

As the key item of parallel software research is the job division and allocation problem and the mapping between software models and machine architectures, we adopted a simple topology for the inter-PE network for the multi-PSI, namely, two dimensional mesh structure.

We built the first version of the multi-PSI using 6 PSI-I systems. We made a specialized network hardware. Each node of the network has a simple routing control mechanism and 5 channels. One channel is connected to the PSI and others are connected to 4 neighbors. Each channel has two 8 bit-buses and two independent FIFO buffers which are used for read and write data transfers. The data transfer rate is 500 Kbytes per second.

The multi-PSI V2 is now under development. One PE consists of a CPU, 16 MW main memory and connection hardware for one node of the network. The connection hardware is improved to achieve faster data transfer and augment the routing function. Some hardware support for load balancing is added to the connection hardware. Two custom LSIs are included in the hardware. As one PE is not so small, 8 PEs will be implemented in one cabinet. Up to 8 cabinets, namely 64 PEs, can be connected.

The KL1-B interpreter will be implemented in the firmware of the PEs. The firmware interpreter is expected to attain 100 to 150 KLIPS for KL1. The communication delay between the two PEs of the multi-PSI is much longer than that of PIM-I which uses the shared memory with the cache system. The job division and allocation strategy must be more optimized on the multi-PSI than PIM. This means that we have to find better method for job division and allocation which makes full use the locality of communication in the given progrms. If this is successful, we can attain a few MLIPS for well organized parallel programs on the multi-PSI. Research results of this kind will be reflected in the network design of PIM.

4   Concluding Remarks

The research and development of inference machines is closely related to many other research fields. Inference machines are considered to be general purpose machines for AI applications. They need more general and powerful functions than conventional machines. Limitless symbol crunching jobs are apparently existing although many of them are not well formalized to be suited to existing parallel architectures. The implementation of sophisticated parallel architectures will require more advanced VLSI technology.

Considering this background, we have been making the best effort to combine current advanced knowledge in software, language, architecture, hardware, and VLSI. Our first effort was the development of PSI and SIMPOS where we combined a multi-window based personal operating system, a logic programming language and a tag architecture. We did not combine the most advanced VLSI technology because our project was planned to use commercially available LSI technology.

Our next effort is much more difficult than the first one. We are trying to combine a parallel software system, a parallel logic programming language and a parallel architecture. Naturally, we have to use the most advanced VLSI technology availabe to us.

We decided to combine the above elements in a step by step manner. The first step is to combine KL1 and PSI as the multi-PSI system, the PE of PIM-I and VLSI switch in the cluster, and, KL1 and a parallel OS as PIMOS. PIMOS is probably the most difficult job among the three because we have very little knowledge about parallelism in programming languages, operating systems, paradigms, algorithms and applications.

Finally, we intend to build fast, simple and stable hardware systems to allow software systems to be as large as possible. Advances in VLSI technology will enable us to make more sophisticated PEs and network systems in the near future. This will again enable us to build larger scale software systems. This bootstrapping development will be the most natural strategy for inference machines research.

Acknowledgment

The author would like to express his gratitude to the researchers of his laboratory, especially, Dr. Atsuhiro Goto, Dr. Kazuo Taki and Dr. Takashi Chikayama. He would like to thank Dr. Kazuhiro Fuchi, the director of the ICOT research center, for his encouragement.

References

[1] A. Goto and S. Uchida. *Toward a High Performance Parallel Inference Machine -The Intermediate Stage Plan of PIM-*. TR 201, ICOT, 1986.

[2] S. Uchida. *Toward a Parallel Inference Machine* TR 196, ICOT, 1986. Proc. of COMPAR 86, Sept. 1986.

[3] H. Nakashima, K. Taki and K. Nakajima *Performance and Architecture Evaluation of the PSI Machine* To appear in Proc. of ASPLOS-II, Oct. 1987.

[4] David H.D. Warren. *An Abstract Prolog Instruction Set*. Technical Note 309, Artificial Intelligence Center, SRI, 1983.

[5] K. Ueda. *Guarded Horn Clauses*. TR 103, ICOT, 1985.

[6] K. Taki. *The parallel software research and development tool : Multi-PSI system*. Technical Report No. 237, ICOT, 1986. Proc. of France-Japan Artificial Intelligence and Computer Science Symposium 86, October 1986.

[7] H. Nakashima, K. Nakajima *Hardware Architecture of the Sequential Inference Machine PSI-II* , To appear in Proc. of 4th Sympo. on Logic Programming, Aug. 1987.

[8] N. Ichiyoshi, T. Miyazaki and K. Taki. *A Distributed Implementation of Flat GHC on the Multi-PSI*. Technical Report No. 230, ICOT, 1986. To appear in Proc. of 4th International Conference on Logic Programming.

[9] S. Habata, et al *Co-operative High Performance Sequential Inference Machine: CHI* Proc. of IEEE International Conference on Computer Design: VLSI in Computer and Processors, Oct. 1987.

[10] Y. Kimura and T. Chikayama *An Abstract KL1 Machine and Its Instruction Set* Technical Report No. 246, ICOT, 1987. To appear in Proc. of 4th Sympo. on Logic Programming, Aug. 1987.

[11] T. Chikayama and Y. Kimura *Multiple Reference Management in Flat GHC*. Technical Report No. 248, ICOT, 1986. To appear in Proc. of 4th Internaltional Conference on Logic Programming, May, 1987.

[12] M. Sato et al. *KL1 Execution Model for PIM Cluster with Shared Memory*. Technical Report No. 250, ICOT, 1986. To appear in Proc. of 4th Internaltional Conference on Logic Programming, May, 1987.

[13] R. H. Katz et al. Implementing a cache consistency protocol. In *Proc. of the 12th Annual International Symposium on Computer Architecture*, June 1985.

[14] J. R. Goodman. Using cache memory to reduce processor-memory traffic. In *Proc. of the 10th Annual International Symposium on Computer Architecture*, 1983.

[15] P. Bitar and A. M. Despain. Multiprocessor cache sychronization. In *Proc. of the 13th Annual International Symposium on Computer Architecture*, June 1986.

VLSI '87, C.H. Séquin (editor)
Elsevier Science Publishers B.V. (North-Holland)
© IFIP, 1988

PEGASUS: A RISC PROCESSOR FOR
HIGH-PERFORMANCE EXECUTION OF PROLOG PROGRAMS

Kazuo SEO and Takashi YOKOTA

Central Research Laboratory
Mitsubishi Electric Corporation
Amagasaki, JAPAN 661

Pegasus is a Prolog-oriented RISC(Reduced Instruction Set Computer) processor. By making the best use of custom VLSI technology, it provides an efficient way of performing Prolog-oriented operations. The cost of backtracking especially is reduced by the use of a register-file partially composed of register pairs which can be copied into each other. Simulation results for a prototype Pegasus chip show a processing speed of $239KLIPS$ (Kilo Logical Inferences Per Second) for a deterministic append program and $149KLIPS$ for a non-deterministic quicksort program.

1. INTRODUCTION

Prolog is an excellent and powerful logic programming language which is becoming popular in the field of Artificial Intelligence. Execution of Prolog programs requires iterating two primitive operations: unification and backtracking. In spite of such a simple execution process, the non-numerical feature of these operations stands in the way of high-performance execution by conventional computers. To cope with this problem, many Prolog machines, most of which are based on Warren's work[1], have been developed[2-5]. The most popular approach is to build the *Warren Abstract Machine* (WAM) using microprogramming. However, taking Prolog's simple execution process into account, it seems to be more effective to construct a VLSI processor for Prolog based on the RISC (Reduced Instruction Set Computer) concept[6-11].

The RISC concept has been proposed to establish a new design criterion in the VLSI era. Based on analysis of application programs, the instruction set is reduced to essentials. This leads to a short machine cycle, and also simplifies the control logic, which usually occupies a large silicon area in commercial microprocessors. As the result, both total performance and design cycle time are improved. The architecture of RISC's greatly depends on the high-level language supported. In order to develop a high-performance RISC processor for Prolog, the following operations have to be supported:

  o manipulation of different kinds of stacks
  o save/restore operation of state/argument registers for backtracking
  o manipulation of tagged words to support the data types of Prolog

This paper presents a Prolog-oriented RISC processor named ***Pegasus***. Based on analysis of the WAM and Prolog application programs, its instruction set provides an efficient way to perform Prolog-oriented operations mentioned above. These instructions are realized by making the best use of custom VLSI technology. For example, the register-file is partially composed of register pairs which can be copied into each other. By virtue of this feature, the cost of backtracking is greatly reduced.

A prototype Pegasus chip is designed in 2-micron CMOS technology. This chip occupies a silicon area about 10mm by 10mm and its cycle time is estimated to be 200ns. Simulation results show a processing speed of 239$KLIPS$ (Kilo Logical Inferences Per Second) for a deterministic append program and 149$KLIPS$ for a non-deterministic quicksort program.

2. PROLOG-ORIENTED FEATURES

A Prolog program is a collection of *procedures*, each consisting of one or more *clauses*. Each *clause* consists of a *head*, which has a predicate and a collection of arguments, and a *body*, which is an ordered sequence of procedure calls. Thus, executing Prolog programs iterates procedure calls. The main distinction between Prolog and ordinary procedural languages is that Prolog supports backtracking. That is, in Prolog, on failure of any goal (procedure call), execution is backed up to the entry of the most recently invoked procedure which has unattempted clauses and is resumed at its next clause.

To execute Prolog programs efficiently, the WAM model provides a stack-oriented execution environment. In this section, we describe the Prolog-oriented features of Pegasus which are derived from analysis of the WAM model and Prolog application programs.

2.1 Support for Stack Access

The WAM model defines the following four stacks. These stacks are allocated in the main memory and frequently accessed during the execution of Prolog programs.

Heap(Global Stack) for global variables and structures
·Local Stack for control frames (choice-points and environments)
Trail Stack for information on variable bindings
Push Down List for unification of structures

The accessing rules to these stacks are not identical, especially for the local stack, which holds two types of variable-length control frames: environments and choice-points. A choice-point is used for backtracking, as is explained later. An environment holds local variables (called permanent variables in the WAM) used in a clause which has more than one procedure call in its body. Analyzing these accessing rules, it is found that they can be grouped into the following two types:

    o access to environment frames on the local stack
        register $\leftrightarrow$ memory(p+n)

    o others (ordinary stack access)
        register $\leftrightarrow$ memory(p); p=p$\pm$1
            (p: stack pointer; n: offset)

Pegasus implements both of these stack operations as its LOAD/STORE instructions. In other words, in Pegasus, all stack operations are executed in a single cycle. To implement the first type of stack access, an adder must be introduced on the memory-address calculation path to add an offset and the address held in the stack pointer. To implement the second type of stack access, the register-file must have a two-port reading/writing capability so that the stack pointer can be updated simultaneously.

2.2 Support for Backtracking

The backtracking mechanism makes Prolog a powerful logic programming language. However, necessity to save/restore the processing state held in system registers, makes backtracking operation costs very high. Pegasus makes the best use of custom VLSI technology to reduce backtracking operation costs. Before explaining the Pegasus backtracking operation, we describe the system registers defined in the WAM model.

The WAM model defines the following state and argument registers. The state registers are used to manage system resources: a program memory and data stacks. The argument registers are used to hold arguments for procedure calls. WAM's optimization technique of these argument registers is one of its superior features. In Pegasus, all of these registers are implemented on the register-file.

> E: current environment
> B: current choice-point
> H: heap pointer
> HB: heap backtrack pointer
> TR: trail pointer
> P: current program pointer
> CP: continuation program pointer
> S: heap structure pointer
> A0-An: argument registers

If more than one clause is unifiable during the execution of a Prolog program, a choice-point frame is created by saving the following registers on the local stack: E, B, H, CP, P, TR and A0-Ai (i: number of arguments). On the other hand, when backtracking occurs, almost all of these registers are restored to the register-file. Because the local stack is allocated in the main memory, both of these operations require a series of memory accesses. Execution stops during these memory accesses.

Pegasus's solution to this problem is a custom-made register-file partially composed of register pairs which can be copied into each other. One register of this register pair is called *the main register* and the other is called *the shadow register*. When creating a choice-point, the contents of the main registers are copied into the shadow registers. Conversely, when backtracking, the contents of the shadow registers are copied into the main registers. By virtue of full-custom implementation, both of these register copies are executed in a machine cycle (According to SPICE simulation results, this takes only about 10*ns*.). Moreover, to cope with consecutive choice-point creations or consecutive backtracking operations, data transfer between the shadow registers and the main memory is performed in parallel with the execution of an instruction which does not have access to the main memory. These operations are called *shadow operations* and are summarized in Figure 1.

Figure 2 shows the construction of the register-file which consists of **72 40**-bit registers:

> R0: a constant-zero register
> R1-R17: ordinary registers
> R20/R60-R37/R77: main/shadow register pairs
> (all register numbers are hexadecimal)

Register pairs are assigned for E, B, H, CP, P, TR and A0-An. Ordinary registers are assigned for the others, such as the other state registers and some constant registers. A two-port reading/writing capability is supported for efficient stack accesses, as mentioned in 2.1. The layout design of this register-file is done by modifying a typical two-port SRAM.

*Shadow Write Operation

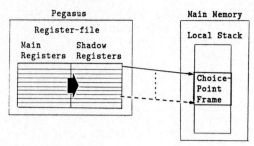

*Shadow Read Operation

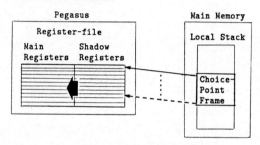

Figure 1. Shadow Operation

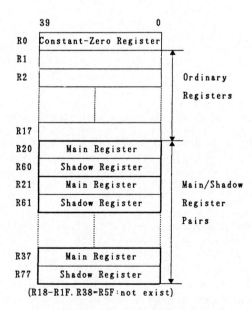

(R18-R1F, R38-R5F: not exist)

Figure 2. Construction of Register-File

2.3   Support for Prolog Data Types

There are four data types in Prolog. These are variable, constant, structure and list types. The unification procedure varies according to the data types of the two terms being unified. Therefore, for efficient unification execution, it is important to instantly recognize the data types of the terms to be unified.

Pegasus assigns two tag bits to distinguish the four Prolog data types and provides a 16-way branch instruction, branching according to these tag bits of two specified registers. Figure 3 shows the Pegasus tag assignment for data words. Each data word occupies 40 bits: 8 bits for tags and 32 bits for data. The highest two tag bits are assigned for garbage collection and the lowest two tag bits are assigned for the discrimination of the four Prolog data types.

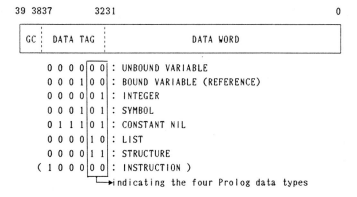

Figure 3. Tagged Data Word

3.   INSTRUCTION SET AND EXECUTION CONTROL

In this section, we describe the Pegasus instruction set and execution control. Having the Prolog-oriented features described in the previous section, the instruction set provides an efficient way of executing Prolog programs. Each instruction occupies a fixed-length word and takes a single machine cycle. A 6-stage pipeline with an instruction in every other stage is adopted for high-performance execution. A unique feature of the Pegasus architecture is a dynamic execution control using instruction tags for the shadow operations.

3.1   Shadow Operation Control

The execution of the shadow operations, explained in 2.2, requires a dynamic execution control. This is because both data transfer and register copy, between the shadow registers and the main memory and between the main registers and the shadow registers, respectively, are not always executable. The data transfer is executable only if the fetched instruction satisfies the following conditions:

  o it does not use the both ports of the register-file in its register-file read stage.
  o it does not access the main memory in its memory access stage.

The register copy is not executable if the same type of shadow operation is being executed. If this condition is not satisfied, some data in a choice-point frame may be lost. (However, in ordinary Prolog execution, a shadow-read (shadow-write) operation terminates before the next shadow-read (shadow-write) operation takes place.)

To control the execution of the shadow operations, Pegasus uses instruction tags. The Pegasus instruction tags are summarized in Figure 4. Among these instruction tags, SE, WS and RS play an important role for the shadow-operation control. Figure 5 shows a state transition diagram for the execution of the shadow operations based on the instruction tags. Instruction tags are automatically generated by the Pegasus compiler during the compilation process.

Instruction Tags

39	38	37	36	35	34	33	32
--	--	IN	SE	WS	RS	IM	--

IN(INstruction bit) distinguishes instructions from data words.

SE(Shadow operation Enable bit)

   enables data transfer between shadow registers and main memory.

WS(shadow-Write Synchronization bit)

   suspends execution while a shadow-write operation is being executed.

RS(shadow-Read Synchronization bit)

   suspends execution while a shadow-read operation is being executed.

IM(Interrupt Mask bit) disables interrupt requests.

(--: currently not used)

Instruction Format

39	3231	2423	1615	87	0
TAGS	OPCODE / MODIFIER	OPERAND1	OPERAND2	OPERAND3

Figure 4. Instruction Format

3.2   Instruction Set

As shown in Figure 4, each instruction occupies a 40-bit word which is composed of an 8-bit tag part, an 8-bit opcode/modifier part and three 8-bit operand parts. This instruction word format is compatible with the data word format and simplifies the memory interface.

Table 1 summarizes the Pegasus instruction set. The instructions are classified into the following six groups:

   1) Load/Store
   2) Register Transfer
   3) Arithmetic/Logical Operation

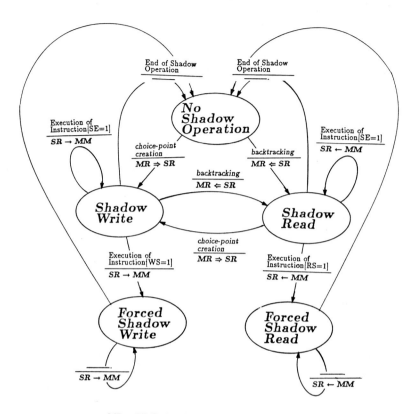

MR ⇔ SR: Register Copy between Main Registers and Shadow Registers
SR ↔ MM: Data Transfer between Shadow Registers and Main Memory

Figure 5. State Transition Diagram for Execution of Shadow Operation

4) Jump/Call
5) Shadow Operation
6) Miscellaneous

As mentioned in 2.1, the two stack-access types are implemented as a LOAD/STORE instruction. Such instructions have a modifier that indicates whether the register used as a stack pointer is updated or not.

Most of the instructions manipulating tags are as primitive as the instructions manipulating data. The only exception is the tag-dispatching instruction (JTD: *Jump Tag Dispatching*) which is explained in 2.3. Being followed by a dispatch table, JTD concatenates the lowest two tag bits of two specified registers and makes a 4-bit offset to look up the dispatch address in the dispatch table. The result is a 16-way branch according to the data type of the two terms held in the registers. In addition to this, if the constant-zero register (R0) is specified as the first operand, a 4-way branch based on the data type of a single term can be realized. The 16-way branch is useful for unification; the 4-way branch is useful for the WAM's indexing instruction.

Table 1. Pegasus Instruction Set Summary

OPcode	Modifier	OP1	OP2	OP3	Meaning
					Load/Store Group
LDP	.	R_{DST}	C_{OFF}		$R_{DST} \leftarrow M[PC + C_{OFF}]$
LDR	\<mdf\>	R_{DST}	R_{IDX}	C_{OFF}	$R_{DST} \leftarrow M[R_{IDX} + C_{OFF}]$
STP	.	R_{SRC}	C_{OFF}		$R_{SRC} \rightarrow M[PC + C_{OFF}]$
STR	\<mdf\>	R_{SRC}	R_{IDX}	C_{OFF}	$R_{SRC} \rightarrow M[R_{IDX} + C_{OFF}]$
SCP	.	C_{TAG}	R_{SRC}	C_{OFF}	$C_{TAG}\$R_{SRC} \rightarrow M[PC + C_{OFF}]$
SCR	\<mdf\>	C_{TAG}	R_{SRC}	R_{IDX}	$C_{TAG}\$R_{SRC} \rightarrow M[R_{IDX}]$
					Register Transfer Group
MCV	.	R_{DST}	C_{SRC}	R_{SRC}	$R_{DST} \leftarrow C_{SRC}\$R_{SRC(VAL)}$
MTV	.	R_{DST}	R_{S1}	R_{S2}	$R_{DST} \leftarrow R_{S1(TAG)}\$R_{S2(VAL)}$
MTT	.	R_{DST}	R_{S1}	R_{S2}	$R_{DST} \leftarrow R_{S1(TAG)}\$R_{S2(TAG)}$
MVV	.	R_{DST}	R_{S1}	R_{S2}	$R_{DST} \leftarrow R_{S1(VAL)}\$R_{S2(VAL)}$
MAD	.	R_{DST}	C_{OFF}		$R_{DST} \leftarrow PC + C_{OFF}$
					Arithmetic/Logical Operation Group
OVR	\<mdf\>	R_{DST}	R_{S1}	R_{S2}	$R_{DST(VAL)} \leftarrow R_{S1(VAL)}$ \<mdf\> $R_{S2(VAL)}$
OVC	\<mdf\>	R_{DST}	R_{SRC}	C_{SRC}	$R_{DST(VAL)} \leftarrow R_{SRC(VAL)}$ \<mdf\> C_{SRC}
OTR	\<mdf\>	R_{DST}	R_{S1}	R_{S2}	$R_{DST(TAG)} \leftarrow R_{S1(TAG)}$ \<mdf\> $R_{S2(TAG)}$
OTC	\<mdf\>	R_{DST}	R_{SRC}	C_{SRC}	$R_{DST(TAG)} \leftarrow R_{SRC(TAG)}$ \<mdf\> C_{SRC}
					Jump/Call Group
JPP	.	C_{OFF}			$PC \leftarrow PC + C_{OFF}$
JPR	.	R_{IDX}	C_{OFF}		$PC \leftarrow R_{IDX} + C_{OFF}$
JIP	.	C_{OFF}			$PC \leftarrow M[PC + C_{OFF}]$
JIR	.	R_{IDX}	C_{OFF}		$PC \leftarrow M[R_{IDX} + C_{OFF}]$
CAP	.	R_{DST}	C_{OFF}		$R_{DST} \leftarrow PC; PC \leftarrow PC + C_{OFF}$
CAR	.	R_{DST}	R_{IDX}	C_{OFF}	$R_{DST} \leftarrow PC; PC \leftarrow R_{IDX} + C_{OFF}$
CIP	.	R_{DST}	C_{OFF}		$R_{DST} \leftarrow PC; PC \leftarrow M[PC + C_{OFF}]$
CIR	.	R_{DST}	R_{IDX}	C_{OFF}	$R_{DST} \leftarrow PC; PC \leftarrow M[R_{IDX} + C_{OFF}]$
JCR JUR JSR	\<mdf\>	R_{rf1}	R_{rf2}	C_{OFF}	*if* R_{rf1} \<mdf\> R_{rf2} *then* $PC \leftarrow PC + C_{OFF}$
JCC JUC JSC	\<mdf\>	R_{ref}	C_{ref}	C_{OFF}	*if* R_{ref} \<mdf\> C_{ref} *then* $PC \leftarrow PC + C_{OFF}$
	Compare-and-Jump 　JCx for TAG part (as an unsigned integer) 　JUx for VAL part as an unsigned integer 　JSx for VAL part as a signed integer				
JTD	.	R_{S1}	R_{S2}		$PC \leftarrow M[PC + Dispatch(R_{S1}, R_{S2})]$
JTR	\<mdf\>	R_{S1}	R_{S2}	C_{OFF}	*if* $Trail(R_{S1}, R_{S2}, MAR)$ *then* $PC \leftarrow PC + C_{OFF}$
					Shadow Operation Group
SRR	.	R_N	R_{IDX}	C_{OFF}	ShadowRead $R_N$words
SRC	.	C_N	R_{IDX}	C_{OFF}	$C_N$words
SWR	.	R_N	R_{IDX}	C_{OFF}	ShadowWrite $R_N$words
SWC	.	C_N	R_{IDX}	C_{OFF}	$C_N$words
SGR	.	R_N	R_{IDX}	C_{OFF}	ShadowGet $R_N$words
SGC	.	C_N	R_{IDX}	C_{OFF}	$C_N$words
SPR	.	R_N	R_{IDX}	C_{OFF}	ShadowPut $R_N$words
SPC	.	C_N	R_{IDX}	C_{OFF}	$C_N$words
					Miscellaneous Instruction
NOP	.				No_Operation
HLT	.				Halt
CTT	\<mdf\>	R_{DST}	R_{S1}	R_{S2}	Compare TAG of R_{S1} and R_{S2}, Cause TRAP

Several types of shadow instructions are implemented. The shadow-read (shadow-write) instruction executes the shadow-read (shadow-write) operation explained in 2.2. Moreover, to select zero as the number of registers in these instructions, only register copy is executed. This is useful for *shallow backtracking*[12]. On the other hand, the shadow-get (shadow-put) instruction executes only data transfer between the shadow registers and the main memory. This is useful for the *cut* operation[12].

3.3   Pipeline Control

Pegasus employs a 6-stage pipeline with an instruction in every other stage. That is, a new instruction is fetched on every other pipestage and the machine cycle exactly occupies two pipestages. Each pipestage is controlled by a two-phase clock whose phases are called phase-1 and phase-2. Figure 6 shows each pipestage and its function.

In pipelining machines like Pegasus, two types of delays exist. The first one occurs because the result of a previous instruction is not available to the current instruction. For example, in Pegasus's pipelining, the R-stage of an instruction is executed before the execution of the W-stage of the previous instruction. Therefore, if the instruction accesses to the same register as the previous instruction is to write into, it is necessary to insert a NOP (NO-Operation) between these instructions to maintain consistency. This causes a delay. To eliminate this type of delay, Pegasus employs bypassing[9] which allows an instruction to use the result of a previous instruction before being written back to the register-file. Pegasus implements bypassing by having paths directly connecting the MRR(Memory Read Register) and the ALU output to the output buses of the register-file, as shown in Figure 7.

The other type of delay is caused by branch instructions. This comes from the fact that the instruction immediately after a branch instruction is always executed. Thus, for safety, a NOP is inserted after branch instructions. These NOP's are removed by the optimization method called delayed branch[7,8] in the compilation process.

A Prolog cross-compiler for Pegasus is being developed using DEC10 Prolog on a DEC System 20. The compilation process is divided into the following three stages. First, a Prolog program is translated into WAM-instruction-based intermediate instructions. Each of these intermediate instructions directly corresponds to a set of Pegasus instructions. Thus, secondly, non-optimized Pegasus instructions are generated by a macro-expansion-like technique. Last, optimization, such as the delayed branch, is performed.

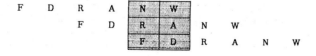

F-stage: Instruction Fetch
D-stage: Instruction Decode
R-stage: Register-file Read / Memory-address Calculation
A-stage: ALU Operation / Memory Access / PC Update for Branch
N-stage: No-operation
W-stage: Register-file Write

Figure 6. Pipeline Stages

4. FABRICATION OF A PROTOTYPE CHIP

A prototype Pegasus chip is designed in 2-micron CMOS technology. Figure 7 shows the data path of this prototype chip. To reduce the design time, each module except the register-file is designed by the standard-cell design approach. Figure 8 shows the prototype chip layout. (This is not the final layout; wiring-area compaction will be done.)

This chip occupies a silicon area about 10mm by 10mm and the total number of transistors is about 80,000 (40,000 transistors for the register-file and 10,000 gates for the others). The largest module, the register-file, occupies a silicon area about 4mm by 5mm, which is one fifth of the total chip area. The second largest module, the ALU, consists of an 8-bit ALU for tag manipulation and a 32-bit ALU for data operations. The address adder, a critical module, has a carry-lookahead circuit. The control logic consists of two ROM's and some random logic circuits. Although managing the shadow operations, in addition to ordinary instruction decoding and pipeline control, the control logic is rather small because of the instruction tags.

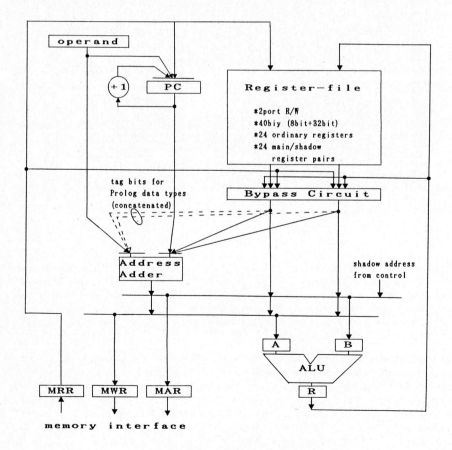

Figure 7. Pegasus Data Path

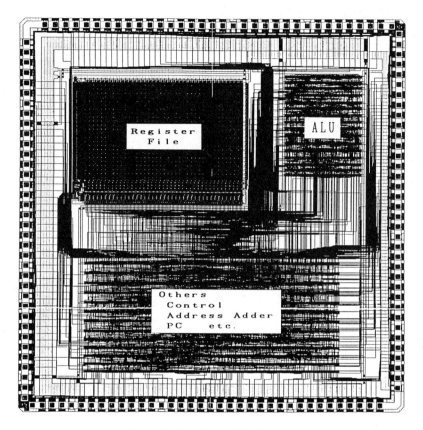

Figure 8. Prototype Chip Layout

The shadow operations are executed by the register-file and the control logic. If we remove these operations, the register-file size and the control-logic size can be reduced to 50 percent and to 80 percent, respectively. When using 2-micron CMOS technology, this area reduction may be effective in terms of yield. However, when using 1.2-micron or 0.8-micron technology in future, it is apparent that the execution speedup for non-deterministic programs is preferred.

The critical path of this chip is from the register-file to the ALU/MWR(Memory Write Register) via the address adder. The access time of the register-file is estimated to be about 25ns by SPICE simulation. The operation time of the address adder is estimated to be about 30ns due to the carry-lookahead circuit. The delay caused by buses and multiplexers is estimated to be less than 20ns. Thus, 75ns is a conservative estimate for the critical path, that is, for the phase-1 time. The phase-2 time, which is used to precharge some components, is estimated to be 25ns. This results in a clock cycle time estimated to be 100ns, making the machine cycle time 200ns.

5. PERFORMANCE EVALUATION

In order to evaluate the performance of the prototype Pegasus chip, an instruction-level
simulator is implemented. Given a Pegasus assembler program, the simulator interprets
it, including the effect of the shadow operations, and generates statistics. Using this simulator, two simple Prolog programs are simulated: a deterministic append program and
a non-deterministic quicksort program, as shown in Figure 9. The simulation results are
summarized in Table 2.

The processing speed is very high in both cases: $239KLIPS$ for a deterministic append program and $149KLIPS$ for a non-deterministic quicksort program. Table 2 also contains three
factors which contribute to performance improvement: optimization, shadow operation, and
bypassing. Optimization was mainly performed by the delayed branch which removed 80~90
percent of NOP's after jump instructions in each case. Bypassing, which also contributed
much in each case, seems to be essential for pipeline processors like Pegasus. When executing
the quicksort program, which requires non-deterministic processing, the shadow operations
contributed most: a 17 percent improvement in processing time.

The Pegasus processing speeds indicated are at least twice as fast as the Prolog machines
and systems appeared in the first Prolog contest[13]. However, the machine cycle time of
$200ns$ can be improved by employing a more sophisticated pipeline control. According to
the performance studies[4], Berkeley's PLM, which has a $100ns$ machine cycle time, requires
only $18.8\mu s$ for a deterministic append program on lists of five element, for which Pegasus
requires $25.0\mu s$. On the other hand, PLM requires about $3.95ms$ for the quicksort program
of Figure 9, for which Pegasus requires $4.03ms$ as shown in Table 2. (In each case, single
cycle memory reference is assumed.) This shows that Pegasus, which utilizes the shadow
operations, can execute non-deterministic programs efficiently.

Append Program

```
append([],L,L).
append([X|L1],L2,[X|L3])  :- append(L1,L2,L3).

:- append([1,2,3,4,5,6,7,8,9],[10],X).
```

Qsort Program

```
qsort([X|L],R,R0)  :- split(L,X,L1,L2), qsort(L2,R1,R0), qsort(L1,R,[X|R1]).
qsort([],R,R).

split([X|L],Y,[X|L1],L2)  :- X =< Y, !, split(L,Y,L1,L2).
split([X|L],Y,L1,[X|L2])  :- split(L,Y,L1,L2).
split([],_,[],[]).

list50 = [27,74,17,33,94,18,46,83,65, 2,
          32,53,28,85,99,47,28,82, 6,11,
          55,29,39,81,90,37,10, 0,66,51,
           7,21,85,27,31,63,75, 4,95,99,
          11,28,61,74,18,92,40,53,59, 8]

:- qsort(list50,X,[]).
```

Figure 9. Simulated Prolog Programs

Table 2. Simulation Results

		Append	Qsort
	Number of Instructions	6 6	Qsort 8 9 Split 2 5 8
	Processing Time	4 1 . 8 μ sec (2 3 9 KLIPS)	4 . 0 3 m sec (1 4 9 KLIPS)
C.	Optimization	1 7 . 9 %	1 1 . 2 %
T. P.	Shadow Operation	− − −	1 7 . 2 %
I.	Bypassing	1 7 . 9 %	1 2 . 7 %

(C. T. P. I. : Contribution To Performance Improvement)

The most serious problem of the Pegasus architecture is that the size of object programs increases as shown in Table 2. Some improvement might be obtained by reorganizing the instruction format. However, we believe that the cost of additional main memory is offset by the high-performance execution of Prolog programs.

6. CONCLUDING REMARKS

This paper presents a Prolog-oriented RISC processor named Pegasus. Based on analysis of the Warren Abstract Machine and Prolog application programs, Pegasus provides several unique features for high-performance execution of Prolog programs. The shadow operations, especially, realized by a custom-made register-file and the instruction-tag based dynamic execution control, makes it possible to efficiently execute, not only deterministic Prolog programs, but also non-deterministic Prolog programs.

A prototype Pegasus chip has been designed and is being fabricated. Further evaluation of the Pegasus architecture will continue using this prototype chip in parallel with machine-cycle improvement by employing a more sophisticated pipeline control.

ACKNOWLEDGMENTS

The authors would like to gratefully acknowledge Akira Fusaoka, Masaharu Hirayama, and many other colleagues of the Central Research Laboratory, Mitsubishi Electric Corporation, for their encouragement and valuable advice.

REFERENCES

[1] Warren, D.H., "An Abstract Prolog Instruction Set," Technical Note 309, Artificial Intelligence Center, SRI International, 1983.

[2] Uchida, S. and T. Yokoi, "Sequential Inference Machine: SIM Progress Report," Proceedings of FGCS'84, 1984.

[3] Nakazaki, R., et al., "Design of a High-Speed Prolog Machine (HPM)," Proceedings of the 12th International Symposium on Computer Architecture, pp.191-197, 1985.

[4] Dobry, T.P., et al., "Performance Studies of a Prolog Machine Architecture," Proceedings of the 12th International Symposium on Computer Architecture, pp.180-190, 1985.

[5] Tick, E. and D.H.D. Warren, "Towards a Pipelined Prolog Processor," Proc. of the International Symposium on Logic Programming, pp29-40, 1984.

[6] Colwell, R.P., et al., "Computers, Complexity, and Controversy," Computer, Vol.18, No.9, pp8-19, 1985.

[7] Patterson, D.A., "Reduced Instruction Set Computers," Communications of the ACM, Vol.28, No.1, pp8-21, 1985.

[8] Hennessy, J.L., "Design of a High Performance VLSI Processor," 3rd Caltech Conference on VLSI, pp33-54, 1983.

[9] Chow, P., "MIPS-X Instruction Set and Programmer's Manual," Technical Report No.CSL-86-289, Computer Systems Laboratory, Stanford University, 1986.

[10] Ungar, D., et al., "Architecture of SOAR: Smalltalk on a RISC," Proceedings of the 11th International Symposium on Computer Architecture, pp.188-197, 1984.

[11] Taylor, G.S., et al., "Evaluation of the SPUR Lisp Architecture," Proceedings of the 13th International Symposium on Computer Architecture, pp.444-452, 1986.

[12] Warren, D.H.D., "Applied Logic - Its Use and Implementation as Programming Tool," Technical Note 290, Artificial Intelligence Center, SRI International.

[13] Okuno, H.G., "The Report of the Third Lisp Contest and The First Prolog Contest," Information Processing Society of Japan WGSYM 33-4, 1985.

VLSI '87, C.H. Séquin (editor)
Elsevier Science Publishers B.V. (North-Holland)
© IFIP, 1988

Architecture of a 32 bit Fast Reduced Instruction Set Computer
(FRISC) for Implementation with Advanced Bipolar Differential
     Logic and Wafer Scale Hybrid Packaging Technology

H.J. Greub *, J.F. McDonald *, and T. Creedon **

*   Center for Integrated Electronics
    Rensselaer Polytechnic Institute

** Electronic Systems Laboratory
    Tektronix, Inc.

Abstract

The architecture of a 32 bit Fast-RISC for the implementation
with LSI bipolar circuits is described. The architecture will be
implemented with bitslices using a wafer scale hybrid with micro-
transmission lines to obtain low interconnect delays. The high
speed circuit technology and the dense wafer scale hybrid
packaging reduce the I/O delay penalties introduced by the
partioning of the architecture significantly, resulting in a high
peak throughput rate of 125 MIPS.

1. Introduction

          New high speed digital circuit technologies like GaAs or
Advanced Bipolar provide logic circuits with subnanosecond gate
propagation delays. However, these new technologies still have
löw processing yields compared to mature CMOS or NMOS processes.
The low yield of GaAs or the high power dissipation of advanced
bipolar circuits currently limit the number of gates that can be
integrated on a chip to medium or large scale integration levels.
Yet high speed MSI or LSI circuits have applications only in the
front end stages of high speed data acquisition or communication
systems. The full speed potential of these new technologies can
only be exploited if complete processing systems can be
implemented. The implementation of high speed systems generally
requires VLSI circuits or I/O pipelining since the data
communication between chips introduces long delays if
conventional packaging methods are used. However, the processing
yield or the high power dissipation currently prohibit the
implementation of VLSI circuits. Thus only two alternatives are
available: partitioning of the system into small integrated
circuits, or waiting for significant processing or packaging
improvements.

          The implementation of high speed systems with small
subcircuits introduces several problems. First, the system must
be partitioned into small blocks such that each one can be
fabricated with good yield and has an acceptable power
dissipation for the given packaging and cooling technology. In
addition the partitioning must be optimized with respect to the

critical delay paths in the system since these paths limit the operating speed. Further, the number of I/O pins of each die must be below the maximum number of I/O pins given by the test equipment or the maximal chip area for I/O bound circuits. The pin limitations and the high I/O pin number in partitioned systems can make optimal partitioning very difficult.

The die interconnect must have a very high bandwidth to allow high speed data transfers between chips. Further, the distance between the dies must be small to keep the inherent delay of the interconnect low. The assembled system must ,therefore, be very dense. Traditional packaging approaches do not result in dense systems. The density of circuits is very low if each chip is packaged individually and then mounted on a printed circuit board. This approach leads, therefore, to long interconnect delays. Even if the printed circuit boards and the chip packages are modified to allow the transmission of high frequency signals, the device density will still be too low to exploit the speed of the new circuit technologies.

On the other hand, hybrid packaging provides a high surface density [1]. A Wafer Scale Hybrid like the WTM (Wafer Transmission Module [2]). allows dense system implementation and provides the high bandwidth and high density die interconnect that are necessary to keep the penalties for partioning low. The interdie connections on the WTM must be designed so that low loss transmission lines are obtained [3]. Otherwise, slow RC line charging behavior with a low bandwidth is obtained if the lines are just a few millimeters long. The micro-transmission lines on the WTM have a polyimide dielectric that provides fast wave propagation (17cm/ns for er=3), low wiring capacitance, and high bandwidth if the geometry of the wires is chosen properly [4].   The direct mounting of the chips onto the WTM substrate results in a very high surface density. This density can be further increased by using flip chip mounting instead of wire bonding like on IBM's Thermal-Conduction Module [5]. The Wafer Scale Hybrid is thus a packaging concept that allows to implement high speed systems, even with new circuit technologies that require extensive partioning due to low yield or high power dissipation.

Typically transmission lines have   a characteristic impedance that is much lower than the input impedance of internal gates and require thus special I/O drivers with a high drive capability and special line receivers. Further, the loading of the transmission lines must be very light and the lines must be terminated at one end in order to avoid reflections.

The total delay inflicted by a die interconnection is the sum of the I/O driver and receiver delay plus the signal propagation delay which is proportional to the length for ideal transmission lines. Generally I/O drivers have high propagation delays compared to internal gates due to the high output current required for driving transmission lines. Many interdie delays will be on the critical signal paths if a data processing system has to be implemented with MSI or LSI circuits . The gain in speed expected from high speed circuit technologiescan, therefore, be completely lost in the interdie delays introduced by partioning. For this reason dense packaging and fast I/O drivers and receivers are essential to minimize the effect of partioning on the operating speed. Unfortunately, the high circuit density increases the power dissipation problem considerably so that only forced cooling can remove the dissipated power.

As circuit technologies become more mature and the fabrication of dies of higher complexity become feasible, the speed of a system can be increased by partitioning the system into bigger subcircuits with fewer die interconnections. However, this will only be the case if the chip size does not increase significantly since the signal propagation on a die is much slower than on a transmission line with a polyimide dielectric. Monolithic systems are only faster than a partitioned system because of the small die size of conventional integrated circuits and the fact that no special drivers and receivers must be used for on chip interconnections.

Reduced Instruction Set Computers [6] can be implemented with a relatively low hardware cost. This and the high performance achievable with this processor type make it the only feasible choice for circuit technologies with low yield or high power dissipation [7,8,9]. Therefore, a RISC architecture was chosen for the implementation with an advanced bipolar process developed by the Tektronix Research Laboratory. The devices built with this process have a high transit frequency of 15GHz resulting in gate propagation delays as low as 55ps [10].

2. Architecture

The architecture of the 32 bit RISC is shown in figure 1. The separate data and instruction buses allow the processor to execute a data I/O operation in parallel with an instruction fetch. Address and Data are multiplexed on the external buses to save I/O pins. A dual port read/write register file with 30 registers allows parallel access to the two operands of an ALU operation. The dual port write feature gives the CPU the capability to perform data I/O and datapath operations without interlocks. The register file must have a low access time (2ns) since two read and two write operations can occur in a system cycle. It has recently been shown [11] that 12 general purpose registers are sufficient for most applications. The register file is ,therefore, divided into two banks of 16 registers with two global registers. One bank is reserved for fast interrupt service to avoid the saving of the register file contents before serving an interrupt. Fast interrupt service is important since many system functions must be performed by software in high speed systems due to the high cost of their hardware implementation [7].

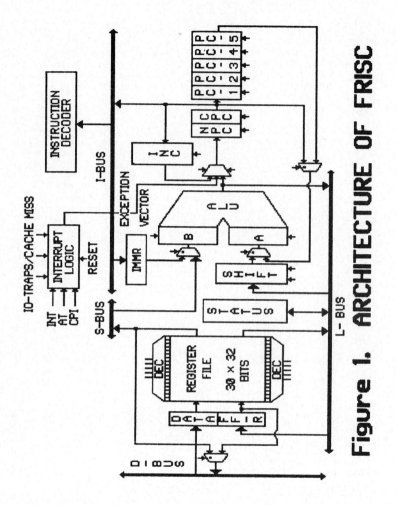

Figure 1. ARCHITECTURE OF FRISC

The two operands read from the register file are sent on the two internal data buses, the L-BUS and S-Bus, to the ALU. The L-Bus operand is sent through a shifter to the ALU input register. The shifter has only four functions: pass, shift left, shift right, and shift left by 4 since the lack of pass transitors in bipolar circuits increases the cost for barrel shifter implementations considerably. The ALU has four functions; ADD, EXOR, OR, and AND. A subtraction can be performed by executing an ADD and negating the S-Bus operand. The ALU output is sent on the L-Bus to its destination register or it is transferred to the program counter (PC) in case of a branch instruction.

The program counter logic consists of a 32 bit incrementer and five registers that save the addresses of the last instructions executed. These addresses are necessary to restart an instruction after an interrupt or trap has occurred. If an exception like cache miss occurs the PC is loaded with an exception vector from the interrupt logic and the register bank as well as the status are switched to the interrupt mode. The CPU will branch to a different exception vector if the processor was already in the interrupt mode when the exception occurred. The following traps and interrupts are implemented: nonmaskable interrupt, maskable interrupt, arithmetic trap, cache miss data, cache miss instruction, system-error, and reset.

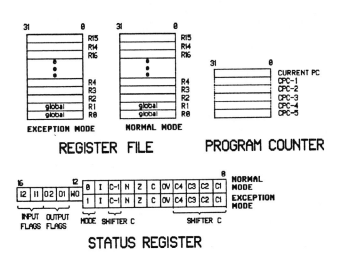

Figure 2. USER VISIBLE STATE

The two status registers contain the following flags: Negative, Zero, Overflow, ALU Carry, Interrupt Enable and five Shifter Carry flags. The Mode Flag determines which register bank and which status register is active. It is set whenever an interrupt or trap is serviced. In addition the status includes two user input and two user output flags. Figure 2 shows the registers that are visible at the user level. Figure 3 shows the instruction format and figure 4 shows the basic instruction set that can be implemented with the given format. Each arithmetic instruction specifies an L-BUS operand, an S-Bus operand, and a destination register. The S-Bus operand can be replaced with a 12 bit immediate constant. The S-operand can be negated and the L-operand can be shifted left, right ,or four bits left. The only I/O instructions provided are the Load and Store instructions with 3 basic addressing modes (register , register + 12 bit offset, register indexed) and the stack operations PUSH and POP. Any of the registers in the active register bank can be used as stack pointer. A 20 bit constant (or its negative value) can be loaded into a register with the LOAD# instruction. The BRANCH instruction allows conditional branches within an address range of +- 2^{20}. The condition codes include the testing of signed and unsigned integers as well a the testing of the Negative, Zero, Carry, Overflow and user input flags.

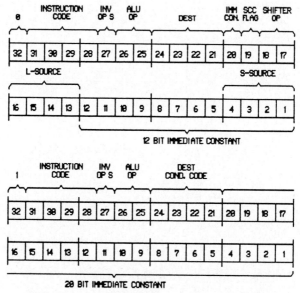

Figure 3. INSTRUCTION FORMAT

<u>INSTRUCTION SET OF FRISC</u>

Arithmetic Instructions

C = Carry, AT = Arithmetic Trap Enable , SHEX = Shift
extended: bits are shifted in from the status register
and are shifted out to the status register

```
ALUOP                   ALUOP = ADD ¦ EXOR ¦ OR ¦ AND
ALUOP C                 Operand A can be shifted :
ALUOP C AT              one bit left,  one bit right
ALUOP SHEX              or four bits left
ALUOP SHEX C            Operand B and the Carry can
ALUOP SHEX C AT         be inverted
```

I/O Instructions

Addressing Modes: register, register +- 12bit offset,
                     register + indexed

```
LOAD
LOAD# +- 20bit Constant
STORE
PUSH
POP
```

Control Instructions

RTI = Return from Interrupt Mode, CC = Condition Code,
PC = Program Counter

```
JMP
JMPI jump and return to normal mode
BRANCH CC
SETSTATUS
GETSTATUS
MODIFYSTATUS
GETPC
GETPC-5
NOOP
CLRI   clear interrupt service mode
RETURN
RETURNI return from interrupt
```

Figure 4. Instruction Set

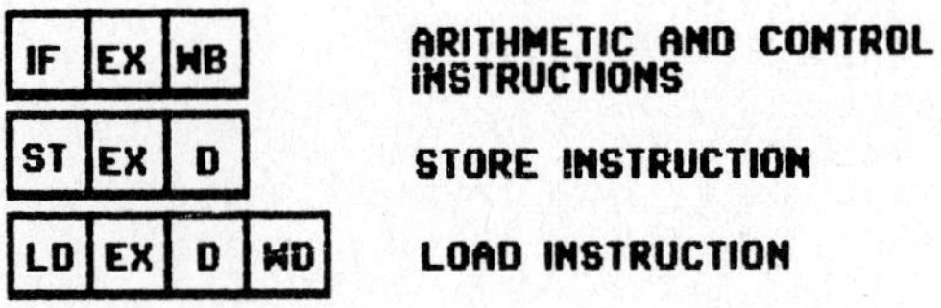

| IF | EX | WB |

ARITHMETIC AND CONTROL
INSTRUCTIONS

| ST | EX | D |

STORE INSTRUCTION

| LD | EX | D | WD |

LOAD INSTRUCTION

```
IF = Instruction Fetch
EX = Execution Cycle on Datapath
WB = Write ALU result into register file
D  = Data I/O
WD = Write data into register file
```

The WB and WD cycles are not
visible to the user.

INSTRUCTION EXECUTION

1	2	3	4	5	SYSTEM CYCLE
ST	EX	D			
	LD	EX	D		
		IF	EX		
			IF	EX	

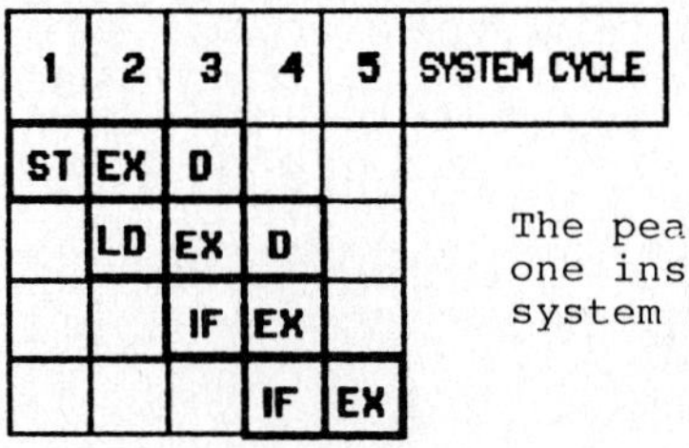

The peak throughput is
one instruction per
system cycle.

INSTRUCTION PIPELINING

Figure 5a. PIPELINED INSTRUCTION EXECUTION

The system architecture is shown in figure 6. Two separate cache memories are used to reduce the main memory bandwidth. In one system cycle the FRISC can access one instruction and one data word. Thus the two cache memories must be able to provide data at a rate of 1 Giga Byte per second. This high data rate can only be achieved by using static high speed GaAs or ECL memories since an access time of 4ns is necessary. The caching schemes used in most current systems require a monolithic implementation and therefore very high levels of integration to obtain a reasonable cache size. Thus, an implementation of a monolithic cache of sufficient size is impossible in advanced bipolar logic. Fast ECL or GaAs memories built with processes optimized for memory implementation must be used to implement a fast block associative cache. The cache should allow static block prefetches without stopping the CPU since the main memory access time in GaAs or advanced bipolar systems is much higher than the cache access time [7]. This high speed difference makes even the insertion of a large intermediate bipolar memory between the main memory and the cache desirable. However, such a memory would consume considerable amounts of power and money. A cache memory as shown in figure 6 could be implemented with small memory modules storing a page from the main memory. Each module has a specific I/O address in the system. A memory module with currently available high speed ECL memories would have a size of 256 words (1 kbyte).

The cache controller needs to be implemented in a high speed circuit technology. The controller checks if the addresses on the data and instruction buses match the tags for the data stored in the memory modules. All modules that are not being accessed through the system bus monitor the (index) address on the bus and decode the address. The cache controller will then enable the transceiver of the memory module that stores the memory page with the matching address tag. Further, the controller updates status information about each memory module (Empty, Sticky, Dirty) and stores information about the least recent use of each module (LRU) which is important for effective cache management. If the data address is not stored in one of the memory modules the controller interrupts the CPU. The interrupt software determines which cache page is best overwritten or copied back if dirty. All page transfers between the cache modules and the main memory are executed by the DMA unit that provides a DMA channel for the instruction cache modules and a DMA channel for the data cache modules.

No instructions are provided for subroutine calls and returns with the exception of the instruction RETURN which transfers the S-operand to the PC and the L-operand to the Status Register. Complex instructions like 'save register file ' can not be implemented in a RISC since these instructions require several system cycles. Subroutines that perform frequently used system functions like 'swap the register file' must be stored in a resident local memory. This memory can be considered as a writable control store.

The FRISC can perform an instruction fetch, a data I/O operation, and an execution cycle on the datapath in parallel. See figure 5. One instruction leaves the three stage pipeline per system cycle resulting in a peak instruction rate of 125 MIPS. However, the pipelining also inflicts certain penalties. Data dependencies and branch delays are caused by the pipelined instruction execution. Increasing the pipelining to 5 stages would allow the use of slower memory by pipelining the memory access, but this also would increase the load latency and the branch delay from one cycle (one instruction) to two cycles and hence reduce the throughput and increase the code size.

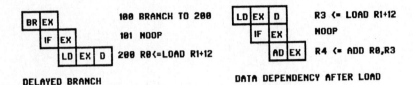

DELAYED BRANCH

The instruction following a BRANCH will always be executed before the BRANCH takes effect.

DATA DEPENDENCY AFTER LOAD

Data loaded from memory will be available after a load latency of one instruction.

Figure 5b. LATENCIES DUE TO PIPELINING

The NOOP slots can be filled in most cases with a usefull instruction by a code reorganizer.

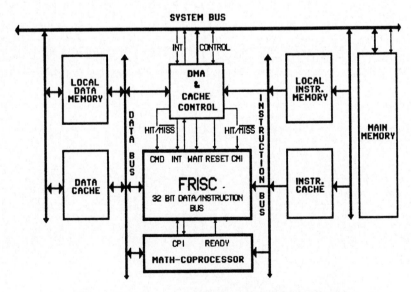

Figure 6. SYSTEM ARCHITECTURE

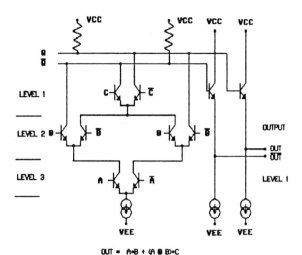

OUT = A·B + (A ⊕ B)·C

Figure 7. DIFFERENTIAL CIRCUIT FOR A BIPOLAR CARRY PROPAGATION GATE

3. Circuits

The high speed logic circuits are implemented using bipolar current trees with three level of series gating [12,13]. Figure 7 shows the circuit for the carry propagation gate. The output ECL buffer is necessary to reduce the sensitivity to interconnect capacitance. The interconnect capacitance is 2 to 4 times higher for silicon circuits than for GaAs circuits since the semi-insulating GaAs bulk material lowers the capacitance of metal runs. The advanced bipolar devices have about the same transit frequency as 1 µm MESFETs. However, the same speed performance as with a 1 µm GaAs MESFET circuit can only be achieved if the effect of the higher interconnect capacitance is reduced. This can be achieved by using output buffers for each gate which unfortunately increases the power dissipation and by using lower logic swings than GaAs MESFET circuits (0.7-1.0V).

The logic swing can be reduced to (250mV) half the single ended logic swing of bipolar gates by using fully differential logic. In addition differential logic reduces the high frequency switching transients on the power supply significantly. The increase in chip area for routing two lines for each signal is insignificant for circuits with a high degree of regularity like ALU bitslices. This is especially true when the chip area is I/O bound due to the need for many internal interconnections in partioned systems. An increase in area of 10 to 20% will not increase the wiring capacitance significantly. The testing of differential circuits is ,however, a severe problem since stuck at faults can not be detected by functional tests, if one of the two differential signal lines is stuck at a voltage that lies within its nominal range. The gates that are driven by the signal that has become single ended through the fault will switch quite unreliably since the logic swing is too low.

Figure 8 shows the ALU circuit and the delays obtained from TSPICE simulations. A worst case transmission line delay of 100ps (length=17mm) is assumed for the carry propagation between the ALU bitslices. An ALU delay of 3ns or less is necessary to achieve a system cycle time of 8ns.

The FRISC architecture is partioned into 10 LSI chips and a clock generator / skew control chip. They will be mounted after testing together with the cache memories on a WTM. The high power dissipation of about 36 Watts for the FRISC requires forced cooling. The heat can be removed through thermal columns since the dies are only a few mils away from the aluminium substrate that will be kept at a constant temperature. Figure 9 shows the minimal WTM structure. An additional ground plane between the two signal layers would be desirable to reduce cross coupling between the x and y signals. However, adding layers reduces the fabrication yield of the wafer scale hybrid.

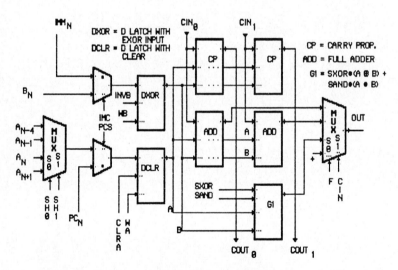

Figure 8a.   ALU BIT-SLICE

Worst case :   carry propagation from bit 1 to bit 32
                during an addition

First Stage

```
Receiver                                                70ps
4 input Multiplexer of Shifter                         100ps
2 input Multiplexer                                     70ps
D-Latch with EXOR input                                 70ps
Carry Propagation Gate (2nd level input)               140ps
7 * Carry Propagation Delays(1st level input)          490ps
I/O Driver (differential)                              170ps
                                                      ------
                                                      1180ps
```

Second Stage & Third Stage

```
Transmission Delay for Carry (17mm)                    100ps
Receiver                                                70ps
2 input Multiplexer with Enable                         70ps
Driver                                                 170ps
                                                      ------
                                                       410ps
```

Fourth Stage

```
Transmission Delay for Carry (17mm)                    100ps
Receiver                                                70ps
Buffer for Carry In Signal                              70ps
4 input Multiplexer                                    100ps
Driver                                                 170ps
                                                      ------
                                                       510ps
```

```
                                                 -----------
Maximum Delay till ALU outputs valid                 2510ps
                                                 ===========
```

Figure 8b.   ALU and Shifter Delays

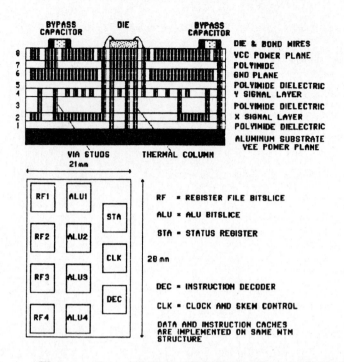

Figure 9. WAFER TRANSMISSION MODULE

4. Conclusions

The architecture of a FRISC for general purpose or fast
control applications has been presented. The dual port/read write
register file and the separate instruction and data buses allow
the instruction fetch, execution, and data I/O units to operate
without interlocks. Further, by using only three pipeline stages,
the load and branch latencies are kept minimal.

Wafer scale hybrid packaging promises to allow the
implementation of a bipolar FRISC architecture that has a high
throughput rate of 125 MIPS. The dense packaging and the high
bandwidth of the interconnect reduce the I/O delays introduced by
the partioning of the architecture into bitslices significantly
such that the inherent high speed of the advanced bipolar circuit
technology can be exploited.

References

[1]   C. A. Neugebauer, " Comparison of VLSI Packaging
      Approaches to Wafer Scale Integration", CICC, 1985.

[2]   Brian J. Donlan et al. , " The Wafer Transmission
      Module ", VLSI Systems Design, January 1986.

[3]   Jack F. McDonald et al., " Wafer Scale Interconnections
      for GaAs Packaging -Applications to RISC architecture",
      IEEE Computer, vol. 20, no. 4, 1987.

[4]   Jack F. McDonald et al., " Fabrication and Performance
      Considerations for GaAs Wafer Scale Integration ",
      CICC, 1985.

[5]   C. W. Ho et al., " The Thin-Film Module as a High-
      Performance Semiconductor Package ", IBM Journal of
      Research and Development, vol. 26, no. 3, May 1982.

[6]   D. A. Patterson and C. H. Sequin, " A VLSI RISC ",
      Computer, vol. 15, no. 9, September 1982.

[7]   Veljko Milutinovic et al. , " Issues of Importance in
      Designing GaAs Microcomputer Systems", Computer,
      October 1986.

[8]   Veljko Milutinovic et al. , " Impacts of GaAs on
      Microprocessor Architecture ", Proceedings of the 1985
      International Conference on Computer Design.

[9]   Barry K. Gilbert et al. , " The Need for a Wholistic
      Design Approach ", Computer, October 1986.

[10] H. K. Park et al. , " High Speed Polysilicon Emitter-
      Base Bipolar Transistor ", Bipolar Circuits and
      Technology Meeting, 1986.

[11] Manolis G. H. Katevenis," Reduced Instruction Set
      Computer Architectures for VLSI ", The MIT Press,
      1985.

[12] Michael Cooperman, " High Speed Current Mode Logic for
      LSI ", IEEE Transactions on Circuits and Systems,
      vol. CAS-27, no. 7, July 1980.

[13] R. J. M. Verbeek, " Low-Power Current Mode Logic ",
      Philips Telecommunication Review, vol. 31, no. 4,
      December 1973.

Session 8
HIGH-SPEED SYSTEMS

VLSI '87, C.H. Séquin (editor)
Elsevier Science Publishers B.V. (North-Holland)
© IFIP, 1988

A EUROPEAN PROGRAM ON WAFER SCALE INTEGRATION

Jacques TRILHE

THOMSON-SEMICONDUCTEURS
BP 217
38019 GRENOBLE CEDEX, FRANCE

Six european organizations : Thomson-Semiconducteurs (F), British Telecom (UK), Laboratoire d'Electronique et de Technologie de l'Informatique (F), Institut National Polytechnique de Grenoble (F), Technische Hoschule Darmstadt (FRG), National Microelectronic Research Centre (IR) are cooperating in a European program on WAFER SCALE INTEGRATION : Esprit 824. The main problem being addressed is the yield of a 100 cm2 device.

The first step has been the realization of a test mask in order to introduce the switches necessary to discard faulty elements and to replace them by spares into the Thomson 1.2 um CMOS technology.
The switches can then be programmed either by laser or by e-beam (floating gate FETs). Three WSI products will then be designed and manufactured : a 4.5 Mbits static RAM, a systolic array for image processing and a 16 bits microprocessor tolerant to end of manufacturing defects.

The 4.5 Mbit static RAM is organized as 256 kwords of 18 bits. The basic cell used to build it is the MK 4187 (64 kword of 1 bit). Four cells, with an extra one among four decoder, have been put together to implement a 256 K block. The wafer scale memory will be powered with 5 volts and will have an access time of 100 ns.

The systolic array has an SIMD architecture and the fundamental problem being addressed is the configuration of the wafer. A virtual array of 128 x 128 processors consisting of a one bit adder and 128 bits of RAM is to be built on the 4" wafer.

The 16 bits microprocessor tolerant to end of manufacturing defects is the first block in a family. The goal is to build custom system on a wafer by putting together the microprocessor, ROM, RAM, PIA, ACIA, UART, ... and making customized interconnection with a sea of gates.

The program started in May 1986 for a duration of 4 years.

1. INTRODUCTION

It is clear that the increase in complexity of IC in the forthcoming years will be obtained by the decrease of minimum features down to 1 or .8 µm and the increase of chip size (IBM claims 2cm2).

In the nineties the rate of decrease of minimum features will stagnate due to the fundamental limit of the silicon device and the increase of chip size, perhaps up to WSI level, will become a necessity.

The need for the increase in complexity of the component is economic. If we consider that packaging costs of a system is higher than marketing cost plus design cost plus silicon manufacturing cost plus testing cost, it becomes obvious that putting several dies in a single chip will drastically decrease the cost of a system.

In addition, the increase of integration goes with a decrease of pin-count, leading to an extra decrease in packaging cost ; as predicted by Landman and Russo rent's rule (1971).

This increase of integration leads to other major advances of Wafer Scale Integration : higher speed due to shorter interconnection length and better reliability due to less inter-level interconnection.

The decrease of cost of a system while it is getting smaller, more powerful and more reliable is a general phenomenon : see for instance the Personal Computers. WSI will probably be the next step, at the hardware level conti- nuing this trend.

Possibilities of Wafer Scale Integration (WSI), are being evaluated in the form of a European project : ESPRIT 824. Partners involved in this project are British Telecom (UK), Laboratoire d'Electronique et de Technologie de l'Informatique (F), Institut National Polytechnique de Grenoble (F), Technische Hoschule Darmstadt (FRG), University College Cork (IR), with the leadership of Thomson-Semiconducteurs (F). The project started on May 15th 1986 and will last four years. The first step has been the study on the various wafer scale products that have been announced (J. Trilhe, Revue Technique Thomson) and the evaluation of products needed by industrial partners : "Thomson Branche Equipement et Système" and British Telecom. Then a test mask has been processed and is presently under test to evaluate switches programmed by e-beam or laser and the compatibility of a field as large as a wafer with state of the art CMOS photolithography. Three WSI demonstrators will be processed within ESPRIT 824 : a 4.5 Mbit static RAM, a 128 x 128 systolic array and a 16 bits microprocessor tolerant to end of manufacturing defects. The four parts of this paper will describe the test chip and the three demonstrators.

2. TEST CHIP FOR WSI

Wafer Scale Integration will lead to zero yield if there is no possibility of discarding faulty elements and replacing them by spares. This point must be taken into account at the architecture and testability level as well as at the technology level. Our test mask is dedicated to the optimization of switches programmed either by e-beam or by laser. It can be advantageous for reconfiguring the wafer to have both switches that are normally on and switches that are normally off. If they are reversible, it is a major help for test. Copper tracking after passivation of the device is also being studied within project 824 and will be used to power the good parts of the wafer.

2.1. Switches

2.1.1. Floating gate FETs

The floating gate FET is a very attractive switch for the following reasons :
. possibility of having a test configuration at end of manufacturing as normally on and normally off switches are possible for a CMOS process,
. increased testability : possibility of programming and erasing the switch
  as many time as necessary,

. low cost : in a CMOS process, only an N channel depletion implant has to be added,
. high density due to the small dimension of the active element on one hand and on the other hand no extra pins are needed to control the switch (e-beam in a Scanning Electron Microscope, SEM, is used to charge the gate).

The only limitation is the low retention time in military conditions |2|. Floating gate FETs are illustrated on Fig. 1.

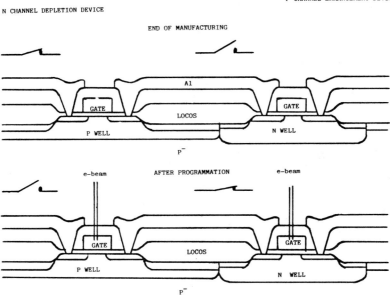

FIGURE 1
Schematic of operation of a floating gate FET.

With e-beam irradiation, a N-channel depletion device is turned on and a P-channel enhancement device is turned off.
For 1nA incident beam, typically 120 us is needed to charge a 7 x 2 um2 gate. For erasing, standard UV techniques can be used to eliminate the charge of the floating gate by photoinjection through the gate oxide. The UV can be either given by a flood lamp or localized with the use of a laser beam (in order to erase a single floating gate selectively).

It is more attractive to use an e-beam to erase the floating gate as programming and erasing can be done in the same machine (SEM). The physics involved are for very low energy beam, a secondary emission higher than the primary incident beam. With a high energy electron beam, the gate is discharged by injection of electrons in the substrate through the gate oxide. One can question then the reliability of the gate oxide and surrounding junctions after the high energy treatment.

In our test chip, the width of the gate has varied from 1.2 to 25 um in order to be able to drive different currents. The parasitic effects on neighbouring MOS can be measured for separation ranging from 1.5 to 20 um.

For programming the floating gate FETs we will use an ISI/SS40 SEM connected to a system of control of the beam ABT/IL200.

2.1.2. Laser switches

Cutting aluminium or polysilicon fuses is widespread in the Integrated Circuit (IC) business, in particular for memories. Using a laser switch for WSI requires high reliability of the laser machine, due to the large number of flashes required on a wafer which have to be all at the good location and at the right energy. In this project, we will use all the refinement hardware and software of the ESI 8000C laser machine. The yield of laser shooting can be measured on our test mask on a 16 K aluminium ROM, each cell of the memory is programmed with a laser shot. The efficiency of the laser machine will be checked by the comparison of the result of test of the 16 K ROM with the good results, assuming a high yield of the decoder.

There is no widespread technology available to connect with laser. MIT |3| has proposed melting a gap between two aluminiums tracks in order to obtain an electrical connection. They obtained resistance in the range of 1Ω. Another approach from MIT requires minor modifications of CMOS process. They add between the two layers of Al-Si-Cu a deposit of amorphous silicon and two very thin, 100 Å, silicon oxide barriers |4|. A laser shot on this structure makes a conduction between the two aluminium layers with a resistance $< 10\Omega$ (99.5% of measurements for a 25 x 25 um2 laser link). This work was stopped in MIT in 1986.

The poly resistor-dopant redistribution method of O.Minuto and al. |5| affords a conduction from 10exp10 to a few $k\Omega$ by heating with a laser an intrinsic poly film between two N+ doped areas. Such an high on resistance is a problem for power lines and buses.

With our WSI test mask we will evaluate the technique of connection with direct laser writing on the wafer and lift off of an additional aluminium deposit. The resistance of this switch is typically the contact resistance to aluminium (1Ω).

2.2. Connection through the wafer

2.2.1. Aluminium lines running through the wafer

Our target is to use a state of the art, CMOS, 1.2 um fabrication line to process our WSI parts. This means that we want to use a single reticle for each level, except for the last aluminium level which will be exposed with a reduction stepper for the central area of the wafer and with a 1:1 projection aligner for bonding pads on the periphery of the wafer. In this way, there will be little extra cost for WSI wafer, unlike the case if e-beam direct writing on the wafer has been used or if 4 reticles per level are used, as in MIT |4| or Brunel |6|.

2.2.2. Copper tracking

Copper tracking technology has been developed at the University College Cork (IR) within ESPRIT 544. A description of the process can be found in the book Wafer Scale Integration edited by G. Saucier and J. Trilhe, published by North-Holland 1986 |1|. The copper tracking technique is a method in which low cost, high conductivity copper patterns are formed on top of the passivation layer of a semiconductor wafer.

The copper is deposited by electroplating through photoresist and is an additive process with resultant economical use of materials. Copper patterns of varying thickness can be deposited on the same wafer allowing different applications of the technique to be used simultaneously. Contact is made to the wafer metallization via contact windows in the glass passivation layer. Typically for power distribution, a 3 um copper track is deposited, leading to a factor of 3 decrease of resistivity in comparison to an aluminium line and with negligible increase in capacitance.

Copper tracking for discretionary wiring can also be used to repair a break in an aluminium line.

3. THE FIRST DEMONSTRATOR : A 4.5 Mbit STATIC RAM

Due to its high repetivity memory architecture is the easiest wafer scale product to implement. The initial goal of the 4.5 Mbit static RAM memory was to check the reliability of the switches mentionned above. The discussion with people building electronic systems (CIMSA-SINTRA) has indicated that the most useful format was a byte + a parity bit. So we have organized our memory in 2 x (8+1) bits. In doing so, the memory is not only a vehicle to evaluate the yield of our switches, but also a usuable product.

The cell used is the TS 41 87, organized as 64 Kword of 1 bit. On a 4" wafer we will implement 256 Kwords of 18 bits, or 18 blocks of 256 x 1 bit (Fig. 2).

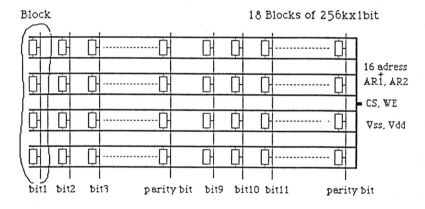

FIGURE 2
Virtual organization of the memory-WSI.

A block is defined by a set of 4 basic 64 K cells. These 4 cells will be chosen as close as possible and will be connected to the same bit line (Fig. 3). Doing this we will optimize the use of connecting bit lines and their floor space on the wafer.

For each 64 K basic cell this organization requires a programmable decoder (1 among 4) which will be able to select one 64 K in a block of 256 K. This decoder powers only the quarter of the 4.5 Mbits (i.e. 64 K x 18 bits) during operating conditions. So static and dynamic current are reduced. The decoders of the four 64 K of a same block are all different and are programmed with one of the switches described in part 1.

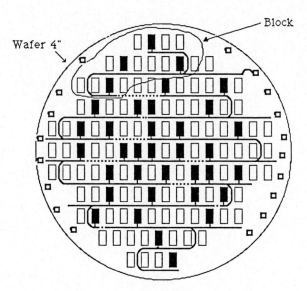

FIGURE 3
Reconfiguration model for Data network.

The interconnection network must provide : for each 64 K
. power supply : Vdd, Vss
. addresses : 16 lines
. write enable : 1 line
. cell selection : 2 addresses and chip selection.

This interconnection latice must allow connecting and disconnecting of cells
(to discard faulty 64 K) and to be reconfigurable (to discard faulty connection
lines). This will be done by the use of floating gate FETs and/or laser fuse-
antifuse.

In addition 4 defects can be repaired in each 64 K cell by blowing fuses.

4.   THE SECOND DEMONSTRATOR : A SYSTOLIC ARRAY

Systolic arrays are well suited to WSI because all communications are between
nearest neighbours and thus connection length is very short with the integration on a wafer. Applications in the field of image processing in particular,
are numerous.

The BT application is in the field of block matching |7|. When processing
video images, in an attempt to reduce the amount of information to be trans-
mitted to a receiving station, it would be nice to be able to spot blocks
that had moved. Hence, it should be possible to define an arm as a block,
and transmit that the arm had moved up, down, etc. This is impossible at the
current time, but a first approximation to this is to split a picture into
blocks (say 9 x 9 pixels) and try and predict where these blocks have moved
to. To do this, a processor is required that can compute an 9 x 9 convolution
for the 9 x 9 blocks, in all positions in the search area.

This leads to a requirement for a processor that can compute approx 289 9 x 9 convolutions, for every position in the image in real time.

The Thomson application is in the field of advanced display graphics. Thomson wish to be able to do geometric transformations on a high resolution colour image in real time. The actual problem is to be able to do a 4 x 4 interpolation on 1024 x 1024 12 bit pixels, in 1/30th of a second. In order words, it is necessary to be able to do 31.5 million 4 x 4 interpolations every second.

The Darmstadt application is in the field of advanced memory devices, for computer applications. Their requirement is for a serial associative memory, in which a memory value can be accessed by name, rather than by address. In this application the computer would send the required search name to the array and each memory element (processor) would search its memory to try and match it. This type of Associative memory would be very expensive, and very slow using standard RAM techniques.

Our approach has been to choose an architecture that was not only capable of solving the above applications but likely to be of value for many other applications.

The rational behind this was that the design development and realization of any product as complex as a wafer scale systolic array involved a level of investment and resource commitment that could only show a satisfactory return by being manufactured in relatively large volumes, and no single application was identified that would require high volumes.

Furthermore the use of a circuit of this scale requires software compilation and emulation tools to manage and understand the complexity of the processing and data flow and these tools can aid the speed with which new problems can be tackled using general purpose hardware. The reasons for this approach are similar to those that fueled the development of microprocessors but the existence of a powerful general purpose parallel processing engine capable of performing at a rate of many thousands MIPs opens up a whole new range of exciting applications. Our demonstrator is an SIMD machine, every processor performs the same operation at the same time. Communications is achieved by 4 way connectivity each PE connects to North, South, East and West neighbours. Each PE is a simple 1 bit adder/subtractor with 128 bits of local memory. A flag resister is included in the PE to enable local modification of the instruction according to the register content.

A schematic of the architecture of the basic cell is shown in Fig. 4 and the proposed interconnect architecture is shown in Fig. 5.

The configuration of a systolic array on a wafer raises many problems. All nearest neighbours of a cell may be faulty and yet a cell must be connected to the nearest good cell. The length of the wires is, therefore, longer than the minimal distance between 2 PEs.

Of course, as the number of faulty PEs increases, the maximum wire length will increase too. The connection length depends on the configuration method as well as on the yield. Therefore, among the many possible ways in which the good cells of the wafer can be connected to form a systolic array, some of them are more desirable than others according to the spare material required for reconfiguration ot to the wire length. The PE previously described has about 900 transistors, 84% of which are in the RAM. The area of the PE is in the range of .2 mm2 with the 1.2 μm CMOS technology used. Reconfiguration at the PE level is, therefore, not attractive since the PE yield will already be very high. So the reconfiguration will be achieved at the "chip" level (block of 8 x 9 PEs), using a decoder to discard faulty PEs.

J. Trilhe

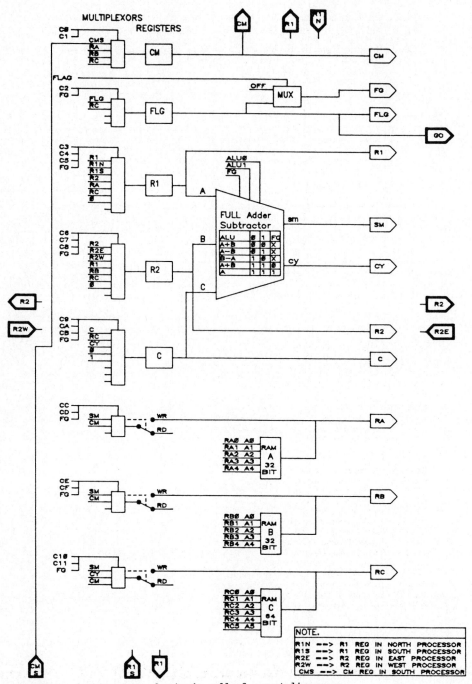

FIGURE 4 : Architecture of a basic cell of a systolic array.

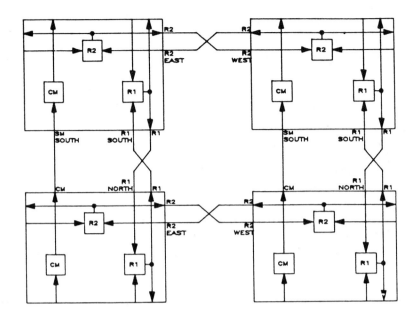

Inputs
CMS — CM Reg from the Processor to the South
R1S — R1 Reg from the Processor to the South
R1N — R1 Reg from the Processor to the North
R2E — R2 Reg from the Processor to the East
R2W — R2 Reg form the Processor to the West

Outputs
R1 — R1 Reg to the North and South Processors
R2 — R2 Reg to the East and West Processors
CM — CM Reg to the North Processor

Control
C0–1 — CM Input Multiplexor
C2 — FLG Input Multiplexor
C3–5 — R1 Input Multiplexor
C6–8 — R2 Input Multiplexor
C9–B — C Input Multiplexor
CC–D — RAM A Input Multiplexor
CE–F — RAM B Input Multiplexor
C10–11 — RAM C Input Multiplexor
FLAG — Flag Enable/Disable Input (If On then use FLG, else ignore)

RAM Address Lines
RA0–4 — RAM A Address Lines (32 Bits)
RB0–4 — RAM B Address Lines (32 Bits)
RC0–5 — RAM C Address Lines (64 Bits)

FIGURE 5
Architecture of the interconnection of a systolic array.

5. THE THIRD DEMONSTRATOR : A MICROPROCESSOR BASED SYSTEM ON WAFER

5.1. Principle

The goal is to integrate a complete dedicated system, usually including several printed circuit boards (PCBs), on a single chip by using the MegaPIL (*) approach.

The method consists of using pre-defined (and tailorable) blocks embedded in a flexible interconnection structure to implement a specific system. It is obvious that different applications like signal processing or real time controllers cannot be implemented with the same set of blocks. The approach therefore consists in providing tailorable blocks adapted to different sets of applications. This means, for example, that for each set of applications, a structure including all the blocks required by the application will be used. The global system uses the flexible connection structure (sea of gates) to connect the blocks and to implement some random logic, with the possibility of tailoring the blocks to the particular application requirements.

5.2. Flexible interconnection structure

As mentioned above, the flexible connection structure is implemented with a sea of gates. This allows both the realization of interconnections between the blocks and the implementation of interface random logic which cannot be included inside the blocks. The general structure for a set of applications will therefore consists of several "hard" blocks embedded in a sea of gates used to interconnect them (Fig. 6).

5.3. Predefined blocks

Since the goal is to integrate a microprocessor based system, the blocks that will be used are the usual microprocessor and peripheral circuits. The first block is the microprocessor itself.

5.3.1. ASIC microprocessor

Being the master block, the microprocessor has to be particularly adapted to the application, i.e. its instruction set must be defined according to the application specifications. It is obvious that in our approach, such a circuit cannot be designed as a full custom chip. This would take too long. A fast microprocessor design is based on fast design of its two blocks : the data processing part and the controller.

Since the circuit must be perfectly adapted to the application, an approach based on using standard bit-slice circuits such as 2901 and 2909 (as in the WSI Inc. products) cannot offer the specialized operators required by some applications. On the other hand, some area may be wasted because of unused possibilities of such blocks.

5.3.1.1. Data processing part design

The DPP is made up of several elements (registers, operators) which must be chosen to fit the application requirements. Since a short design time does not allow full custom design, these blocks are chosen from a library of pre-defined and parameterized elements. In order to optimize the design, the library will contain blocks that are adapted to the type of application for which the circuit is to be designed.

(*) MegaPIL is a trademark of Thomson Semiconducteurs.

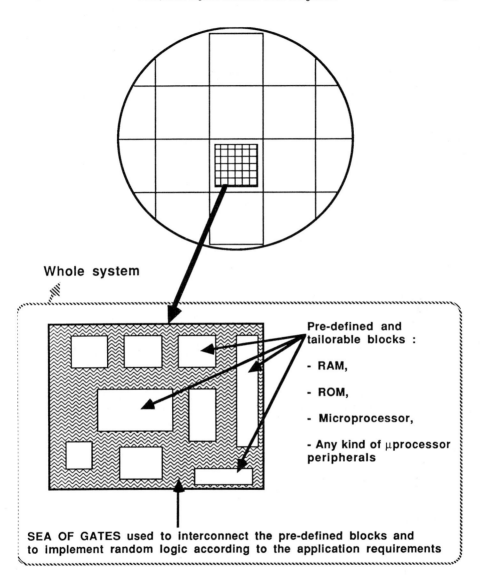

Whole system

Pre-defined and tailorable blocks :

- RAM,

- ROM,

- Microprocessor,

- Any kind of μprocessor peripherals

SEA OF GATES used to interconnect the pre-defined blocks and to implement random logic according to the application requirements

FIGURE 6
Example of hard blocks in a sea of gates.

This leads to several DPP block libraries adapted for example to 8, 16 or 32 bits DPPs, signal processing applications, real time controllers and so on. Such an approach guarantees a DPP perfectly adapted to the application constraints in both terms of functionality and speed. The design process includes several steps. The first one is to choose the DPP general structure, i.e. to determine in which library the blocks will be taken. Then, a first DPP is obtained according to the circuit specifications. The following steps consist of modifying the DPP architecture to optimize both the control algorithm and the DPP use.

These modifications are guided by the results of functional simulations of the whole circuit. The DPP description for these simulations is obtained from the library block description for these simulations is obtained from the library block descriptions. Finally, once the DPP elements are defined, a silicon assembler is used to generate the DPP layout.

5.3.1.2. Controller design |8|

Even if the choice of DPP elements cannot be neglected when designing a tailored microprocessor ; the controller is far more important because it implements the instruction set interpretation. The same DPP can be used to execute several instruction sets, each one implemented by a specific controller. Two points need to be considered when designing the controller : the control algorithm and the target architecture.

There are many kinds of architectures : single PLA, multiple PLA, microprogrammed, ... each one with its own advantages and drawbacks. The choice is made by taking into account such different parameters as the overall silicon area, the maximum size of a controller block, the synchronization system, etc.

Once the architecture has been chosen, from several possibilities using automatic controller generation tools, the control algorithm can be optimized interactively together with the DPP. This optimization is made by performing functional simulations of the whole circuit with the controller description issued from the commands required by the DPP blocks and from the register transfer operations used in the control algorithm.

After several iterations of this process of optimization both the control algorithm and the data path, a controller generation tool is used to produce the controller layout. This tool performs the following operations :
. determination of an optimal encoding of the controller states.
. generation of the equations of both internal and external command variables, which also depends on the target architecture.
. boolean minimization of these equations, at first locally (the functions are processed separately) and then globally by reducing the number of product terms required to generate these functions.
. partition of the "virtual" PLA generated in the previous step into a set of PLAs.
. layout generation for the controller elements are made with usual PLA generation tools.

The final step is the design of interfaces and the remaining random logic, before integrating them with the DPP and controller layouts to obtain the final microprocessor layout.

5.3.2. Other blocks

The other blocks consist of all existing peripheral circuits for microprocessors. A first set includes memories. Several types of RAM and ROM memories must be available as blocks to implement a system. These blocks must be tailorable which means that the system designer can choose exactly the memory size and access procedure he needs to fulfill the application requirements. A second set includes interface devices such as PIA, ACIA, UART, DMA, A/D and D/A converters and so on. These circuits may be tailorable too by allowing the user to choose the number of I/O lines on a device, for example.

A third group consists of all the special operators such as arithmetical processors, specialized multipliers, ... These circuits are mainly unmodifiable ones and just have to be used as they are.

5.4. Advantages of the MegaPIL approach

The first one is the system size which decreases from several PCBs to nearly one chip. This has other advantages such as a reduction of the power consumption because there are fewer buffers to power in the system. Another advantage is the reduction of connections between chips (and between boards) which implies fewer weldings and therefore fewer bad contacts. This improves the mechanical reliability. The latter coming from the fact that having all the functions on a single chip which reduces the number of PCBs, also reduces the probability of mechanical failures.

This is particularly important for systems working in harsh environments like in planes, space... These three first advantages are particularly interesting in the case of on-board systems where space, power consumtpion and reliability are critical points.

Also a consequence of the reduction of interconnections length at the system level, the increased speed possibilities for chip-based systems are an important point for realizing powerful and compact computers.

5.5. Design constraints - Yield

Added to the fact that the design of very big circuits using new design tools may bring some changes to usual design methods, the yield of big chips is the most critical problem. Since the big chip obtained when integrating full systems are made up of blocks which size (more than 50 000 transistors) is as great as their yield is low, it becomes obvious that the yield of such circuits will be nearly 0 if nothing is done to improve it.

The way to improve the overall circuits yield since the sea of gates yield is very good (because of the small cell size) is to improve the yield of "hard blocks".

It has been shown that reconfiguration must be performed at two levels |9| :
. big chip level : at this level, spare blocks are provided to replace those destroyed by big defects. This is mostly used for interface circuits which are generally smaller than microprocessors and memories. This requires adequate bypass and replacement strategies to be defined.
. block level : in order to raise the yield values for large blocks and to tolerate small defects, redundancy is provided within the block.

Since the biggest blocks are those requiring the most important yield increase we had focused our attention on their problems. Two kinds of big blocks structures can be encountered : memories and microprocessors like circuits.

Reconfiguration of memories has been studied and used at an industrial level |10|. The reconfiguration strategy mainly consists in providing spare pages to replace faulty ones.

The microprocessor like blocks include a DPP and a controller. The reconfiguration of these two parts present different requirements and constraints but is based on the same principle. The basic point is that one cannot correct easily more than one defect at a time.

The circuit therefore has to be partitioned into sub-blocks where no more than one defect may appear. Starting from there, both the partitioning and the reconfiguration strategy differ for the DPP and for the controller. They have been presented in |11|.

5.6. Application example

In the following section, we present an application example which illustrates the above points. This application is an automatic railway control system. Its structure is shown in Fig. 7.

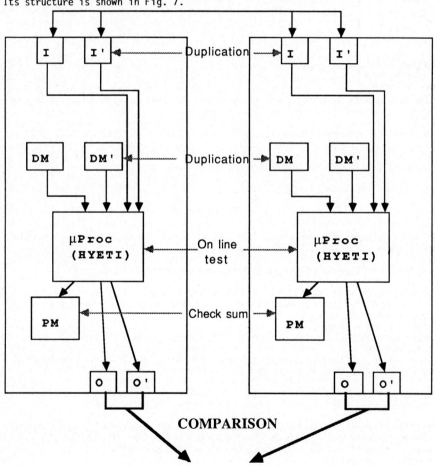

COMPARISON

(High safety hybrid comparator)

FIGURE 7

Automatic railway control system

Its realisation requires 7 to 9 PCBs for input, 1 processor board, 1 security link board, one service link board. This involves the number of chips and the power consumption summarized in Table 1.

	Processor	Inputs	Outputs	Service link	Safety link
Boards Nb	1	7 to 9	4 to 6	1	1
ICs Nb in a board	75	42	72	35	40
Power consumption for 1 board (Watt)	≈ 9.5	≈ 5.5	≈ 9.5	≈ 4.5	≈ 5

TABLE 1
Comparison of different realizations for the automatic railway control system.

The total number of ICs is 875. This leads to a 110 watt power consumption for an estimated 1 300 000 logical gates system.

A big chip realization of the system has the following features :
- it is a single chip system
- the type of pre-defined elements to implement allows several similar application to use this circuit (the application specificity is taken into account when designing the inter-blocks connection)
- size : 50 mm x 50 mm
- power consumption reduced to less than 20 watts
- reduced cost
-fewer sources of failures :fewer PCBs, simple power and clock distributions.
This clearly shows the interest of such an approach.

6. CONCLUSION

The ESPRIT project on wafer scale integration brings together efforts of six european partners to investigate three types of architectures which have a good chance of success : a memory, a systolic architecture, a micro-processor based system.

Strong cooperation between technology experts and designers has been the characteristics of the first step of the project. Starting from user defined products, companies and universities have put together design tools and metho-dologies to cope with the challenge of wafer scale integration.

ACKNOWLEDGEMENTS

We acknowledge CEC for support of this work under grant ESPRIT 824.
This paper is a compilation of results obtained through the cooperation of
teams in British Telecom, LETI, Darmstadt University, Cork University,
Grenoble University and Thomson.
Many thanks to all of them.
Part of this work has been published in "revue technique Thomson".

REFERENCES

|1| Wafer Scale Integration. Editors : G. Saucier, J. Trilhe.
    North-Holland. 1986
|2| D.C. Shaver, Solid-State Technology, February 1984, p. 135
|3| J.Y. Asaitis, G. Chapman, J. Raffel, IEEE Electron Device Letters,
    Vol. EDL 9 n° 7, July 1982, p. 184
|4| P.W. Wyatt, J.I. Raffel, G.H. Chapman, B. Mathur, J.A. Burns,
    T.O. Herdon, IEDM 1984
|5| O. Minuto and al IEEE Journal of Solid State Circuits, Vol. SC 17, n° 5,
    October 1982, p. 193
|6| S.R. Jones, K.D. Warren, R.M. Lea, Silicon Design Conference,
    Wembley, UK, July 1986
|7| D. Hein, IEEE Trans. on Electromagnetic Compatibility, Vol. EMC 26,
    n° 3, August 1984, p. 134
|8| A Computer Aided System for Logic Synthesis using Artificial Intelligence
    S. Hanria, E. Dupont, G. Saucier, ICTC Conference Limerick, Ireland,
    September 1986
|9| Reconfiguration strategies for yield improvement of complex nodes in
    WSI of 2D processors arrays, P. Genestier, G. Saucier,
    ICTC Conference, Limerick, Ireland, September 1986
|10| Yield enhancement of large memories, Will Moore, IFIP Workshop on WSI,
    Grenoble, March 1986
|11| A reconfigurable microprocessor for Wafer Scale Integration,
    P. Genestier, C. Jay, G. Saucier, IFIP workshop on WSI, Grenoble,
    March 1986

VLSI '87, C.H. Séquin (editor)
Elsevier Science Publishers B.V. (North-Holland)
© IFIP, 1988

Self-Timed Iteration

M.R. Greenstreet[1], T.E. Williams[2], and J. Staunstrup
Computer Science Department, Aarhus University
Ny Munkegade, DK-8000 Århus C, Denmark

This paper describes a technique for specifying, analyzing and implementing a series of computations using iterative, self-timed circuits. Even though the circuits iterate, they operate without clocking. The circuits do not require arbiters, have no possibility of synchronization failure, and function correctly independent of time delays. Each computation in the iteration can be a general function and is implemented using asynchronous, delay-independent logic which indicates its completion. A general implementation for self-timed iteration is presented; then, simplifying assumptions for specific implementations are shown which can reduce the amount of hardware required.

1 Introduction

Self-timed circuits operate without external clocking and perform their operations as fast as the technology, temperature, and specific data inputs allow. These circuits indicate their completion along with an output value by either providing a signal from a matching worst case path or encoding completion as part of the result[6]. However, most previous usages of self-timing techniques in integrated circuits have been very localized and have not performed iteration (cycling) within the self-timed domain. For example, though the self-timed PLA[9] has become common, it is typically embedded in a synchronous system, and though it operates repeatedly, the self-timing does not extend beyond one evaluation of the PLA; the iteration is controlled by clocked circuitry. Although iterative asynchronous designs are presented in [1], those circuits perform synchronization with arbiters. This paper shows that it is possible to build a system which iterates within the self-timed domain, and without any external clocking, arbiters, timing hazards, or constraints on propagation delays.

The analysis of self-timed iterations was inspired by, and is a generalization of, the technique used to implement a division chip in [10]. Using self-timed iterations is particularly attractive and practical for arithmetic processors, such as the divider, because they involve a long sequence of calculations which can proceed without further external inputs after initialization. The self-timed iterations can provide a performance advantage over a system whose iterations are controlled by an external clock because each iteration can begin as soon as the previous is finished; whereas, a clocked design must wait for the worst possible delays in each cycle.

In order to specify and analyze communication in an asynchronous environment, a notation called "Synchronized Transitions" [7] is used. After introducing the notation, a self-timed iterative algorithm is given and shown to operate correctly independent of delays. A general hardware implementation for the self-timed algorithm is shown which corresponds directly to the specification. This is followed by a discussion of optimizations which can be performed based on bounds for relative timing in specific implementations.

[1]Supported by the Danish Research Council
[2]Supported by Jydsk Telefon A/S; on leave from Center for Integrated Systems, Stanford University, USA

2   Synchronized Transitions

A system is typically constructed by hierarchically partitioning it into smaller blocks of circuitry with defined communication between the blocks. In synchronous designs, this communication is based on clocks which are common to the communicating circuits. In self-timed designs, communication between blocks must be asynchronous because there are no common clocks to control communication actions.

State changes are modeled as **transitions**. Transitions are described using an imperative notation similar to what is found in many high-level programming languages. For example,

```
TRANSITION evaluate(s:  state; z:  BOOLEAN)
< s.x → s.x, s.y := FALSE, f(z) >
```

The transition `evaluate` is performed only in a state satisfying `s.x` and leads to a state where `s.y = f(z)` and `s.x = FALSE`. The transition is atomic, which means that it *appears* to be indivisible. Asynchronous blocks communicate by participating in the same transition. This is expressed by including state variables from two or more blocks as actual parameters to the same transition. The general form for a transition is:

```
TRANSITION name(n1, n2 ...  )
< C(n1, n2 ...) → A(n1, n2 ...) >
```

- `n1, n2 ...` are the state variables used by the transition.

- `C(n1, n2 ...)` is the **precondition** of the transition; it is a boolean condition on the values of `n1, n2 ...` The transition can only be performed when its precondition is satisfied.

- `A(n1, n2 ...)` is the **action** of the transition. This is an assignment which specifies the **state transformation** made by this transition. It may only change the values of `n1, n2 ...`

It is not required that a transition is performed immediately after its precondition has been satisfied, and there is no upper bound on when it takes place. The precondition may become **false** again without the transition having been performed; however, restrictions presented in section 2.1 prevent this in the self-timed implementations we are considering. The execution order and duration of enabled transitions is unspecified. A transition is atomic as indicated by the notation `< ... >`. This means that the transition appears to be executed indivisibly; this may, however, not be the way it is implemented.

Initiation of a transition is written as a procedure call, e.g. `invert(a, b)`. Transitions are repeated indefinitely once they are initiated. Usually, many transitions must be initiated to describe the desired computation. This is done by giving a list of transition initiations separated by | | (to indicate concurrent executing of the transitions):

```
invert(ready, reset) || evaluate(si, input) || evaluate(so, yi) ...
```

This type of description gives an abstract model (specification) for the behavior of a design. A more detailed description of "Synchronized Transitions" and their applications is given in [7]. A similar notation using "Production Rules" for the synthesis of self-timed circuits is presented in [5].

2.1 Implementation rules

The "Synchronized Transitions" notation provides a **specification** of a system in terms of atomic actions (transitions). However, it is not required that an **implementation** perform *only* one transition at a time. To do so would be both impractical and inefficient. Therefore, the implementation should perform many transitions simultaneously, while preserving the appearance of atomicity.

This section presents criteria for correspondence between a specification using the "Synchronized Transitions" notation and an implementation where the transitions are non-atomic. Sufficient conditions for a non-atomic implementation to be correct are given, and some relationships between these conditions and the physical behavior of circuits are described. This presentation is informal; a rigorous derivation is beyond the scope of this paper.

In a non-atomic implementation of a transition, $< C \rightarrow A >$, the appearance of atomicity must be maintained locally, since there are no global synchronization signals to enforce indivisible operations. This means that the condition C must be strong enough (together with all other preconditions) to prevent inconsistent executions, and that some restrictions must be imposed on the allowable collections of transitions.

Executions where two transitions simultaneously write the same state variable must be prohibited. Such writing could result in variables with undefined values. We do not use arbiters to resolve these conflicts, because an arbiter cannot be both error free and guaranteed to decide in bounded time[4]. By observing the following restriction, simultaneous writing is avoided:

> *Exclusive Write*: Each state variable must only be written by a single transition.

This is a very strong condition; weaker conditions could be sufficient. However, this condition is simple, and it is satisfied by the algorithms presented in this paper.

The values of variables must be stable while a transition is (possibly) using them. If the value of a variable read by a transition were to be changed while the transition was modifying another variable, the write variable of the transition could receive an undefined value. For example, a transition could be disabled when it had half-way changed the value of its write variable. Thus, we further restrict the allowable set of transitions with the following condition:

> *Stable Read*: Let **t1** and **t2** be two transitions such that **t1** writes a variable which **t2** reads, then **t1** and **t2** may not be simultaneously **active**.

A transition, $t, (< C_t \rightarrow l_t := f(r_t) >)$ is defined to be **active** if $C_t \wedge (l_t \neq f(r_t))$. Like exclusive-write, this condition is stronger than necessary.

"Synchronized Transitions" descriptions which meet the above conditions can be implemented by hardware which never produces metastable values. Metastability occurs when an intermediate value (neither **true** nor **false**) is written into a storage element. This can occur either by attempting to concurrently write different values, or by inhibiting a write before the stored value has been completely changed. The first situation is prevented by the exclusive-write condition. The stable-read condition prevents the second.

Furthermore, "Synchronized Transitions" descriptions which meet the above two restrictions can be implemented by hardware which functions correctly independently of delays in logic elements and wires. Arbitrary delays in logic elements are modeled by the property that enabling a transition *allows* the transition to execute, but an arbitrary delay

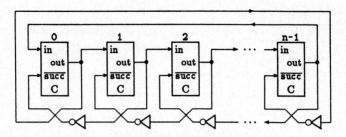

Figure 1: Ring-Oscillator

may elapse before it actually does. Wire delays influence the order in which inputs arrive to a transition. This is equivalent to altering the order in which the other transitions wrote these variables. The stable read condition guarantees that the values assigned by a transition are independent of the order in which enabled transitions were executed. Thus, hardware implementations satisfying these conditions are independent of both wire and logic element delays.

3   Iterative Self-timed Algorithms

In this section, two algorithms will be presented for self-timed iteration. The first algorithm is for a simple **ring-oscillator**, but it demonstrates many of the key features of more complex iterations. The second algorithm is a generalization of the ring-oscillator; arbitrary functions can be computed, yet the algorithm retains the simple underlying structure of the ring-oscillator. The correctness of both algorithms is demonstrated by establishing invariants which they maintain.

In an iterative design, computation progresses as a wave traveling around the loop of stages. The rising edge of the wave corresponds to computing a new result, the falling edge corresponds to resetting the hardware element in preparation for the next computation. The wave can be represented by a single bit, in which case the circuit oscillates, but computes no other result. By representing the wave with more than one bit, data-values can be encoded into the wave, and useful computation can be performed as the wave progresses. For proper computation, it must be ensured that *the rising edge of the wave never overtakes the falling edge* (i.e. attempting to perform a computation on a stage which is not reset from the previous computation), and *that the falling edge never overtakes the rising edge* (i.e. resetting all stages and entering a dead-state).

3.1   Simple Iteration

In the case of a simple ring-oscillator, a single bit circulates around the loop. Such a ring-oscillator is shown in figure 1. This oscillator differs from traditional ring-oscillators in that it is built from Muller-C elements (see figure 2) instead of inverters. The forward path along which a pulse progresses around the oscillator results in no overall inversion; thus, the number of stages, n, can be either even or odd.

The operation of the oscillator can be understood by, initially, assuming that the lower ($\overline{succ}$) input of each C element is always the same as the upper input. In this case, the C element functions as a buffer; thus, the oscillator works as a ring of buffers. The C

Truth Table

in	s̄ūc̄c̄	out
L	L	L
L	H	Unchanged
H	L	Unchanged
H	H	H

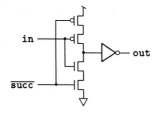

Figure 2: The Muller-C Element

elements are divided into two non-empty, contiguous groups: those whose outputs are true (the crest of the wave) and those whose outputs are false (the trough of the wave). The wave progresses around the ring as the buffers on the boundary between the crest and the trough transfer a true value forward and by the complement action at the other boundary.

If the circuit was simply a ring of buffers, the oscillation would eventually die out. In real circuits, propagation delays are different for rising and falling values and for different instances of the same circuit. Thus, in a ring of buffers, either the trough will eventually overtake the crest, or the crest will overtake the trough, and the circuit will enter a dead-state. The ring of C elements avoids this problem. This is the purpose of the lower ($\overline{succ}$) input to the C elements. This input ensures that the output of one element can only become true when the output of the successor element is false. This guarantees that the crest cannot overtake the trough. Likewise, the output of an element can only become false when the output of the successor element is true.

The preceding arguments assumed that the delays of the wires and inverters were insignificant in comparison to the delays of the C elements. In particular, it was assumed that the value of the lower input to a C element was the complement of the value of the output from the successor stage. To account for arbitrary delays, we can only assume that the value at an input is a value which the supplying output had *sometime in the past*. To consider this more general case, it is useful to employ the "Synchronized Transitions" notation. This will also be useful when the algorithm is generalized by replacing the C elements with circuits which compute a useful result in the course of the oscillation. A program for the ring-oscillator using "Synchronized Transitions" notation is shown in figure 3.

This program satisfies the restrictions given in section 2.1 and can be expected to function correctly independently of the delays of wires or logic elements. Since each state variable is written by exactly one transition, the program satisfies the exclusive-write condition. The dynamic behavior of the program must be considered to show that the stable-read condition is satisfied.

In the self-timed paradigm, there is no global time reference (such as a clock) to allow reasoning about the state of the entire system. Instead, we can reason about individual transitions, and show that certain pairs of transitions cannot be simultaneously active. This allows us to reason about the values of variables in *local* sets of transitions, and from this, *global* properties of the system can be demonstrated.

Invariant 1 *The stages whose outputs are* true *form a non-empty set of adjacent stages. The stages whose outputs are* false *form a non-empty set of adjacent stages.*

```
ringosc(n:  3..∞)  (* n is the number of stages in the loop *)
   VAR y:  ARRAY [0..n-1] OF BOOLEAN
   TRANSITION C(in, out, succ:  BOOLEAN)
   (* C-element with one input inverted *)
   < in <> succ → out := in >
BEGIN
   ||ⁿ⁻¹ᵢ₌₀ C(y[i⊖1], y[i], y[i⊕1]);
END ringosc.
```

Where: $i \oplus 1 = (i + 1) \bmod n$ and $i \ominus 1 = (i - 1) \bmod n$.

Figure 3: "Synchronized Transitions" Program for the Ring-Oscillator

To see that this is an invariant, assume that it holds at some point of the execution. This means that there exists a stage y[i] such that:

$$(\text{in} = \text{true}) \wedge (\text{out} = \text{succ} = \text{false}) \quad \text{or} \quad (\text{in} = \text{false}) \wedge (\text{out} = \text{succ} = \text{true})$$

In both cases, performing out := in maintains the invariant. [3]

From the invariant and the requirement that $n \geq 3$, it follows that the stable read condition is satisfied. Observe that, if there is an element whose output is true followed by two elements whose outputs are false, there must be an active transition (to set the middle output to true). A similar argument applies for an element whose output is false followed by two elements whose outputs is true. This leads to one more invariant, which shows that the ring-oscillator never enters into a dead-state.

Invariant 2 *If there are at least three C elements in the loop, then there exists an active transition.*

In this section, we have shown how a description using "Synchronized Transitions" may be used to demonstrate the correctness of a self-timed design. This was done by checking the implementation rules of section 2.1 and establishing invariants, which we believe is a much more reliable way of demonstrating properties of a design than simulation or exhaustive case analysis.

3.2   A General Algorithm for Iteration

A tail-recursive function can be computed by repeatedly applying a simpler kernel to the result of the previous application (or input). A direct implementation of such a function, $\mathcal{F}$, uses a separate instance of the hardware for each application of the kernel. This is shown in figure 4. Such implementations are used, for example, in fully-combinatorial multipliers, where the kernel is a shift and a conditional addition. Given an input value y_0, the circuit computes a sequence of values $y_1, y_2, ..., y_k$. Each stage computes a new value, y_i, of the sequence by applying some fixed function $\mathcal{F}$ on the value received from its predecessor, y_{i-1}. The exact nature of $\mathcal{F}$ is not important for our analysis. In the divider [10], which inspired this work, $\mathcal{F}$ is a function which given a divisor and a partial remainder computes a quotient digit and a new partial remainder.

Iteration allows the computation of the desired sequence $(y_1, y_2, ..., y_k)$ by looping the evaluation around a small, fixed number of stages arranged in a ring. This is possible

---

[3] Strictly speaking, it should also be demonstrated that the initial state satisfies the invariant.

$$y_i = \begin{cases} \text{input} & i = 0 \\ \mathcal{F}(y_{i-1}) = \mathcal{F}^i(\text{input}) & k \geq i > 0 \end{cases}$$

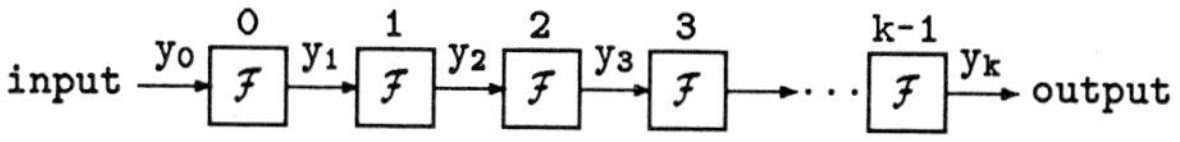

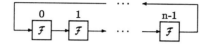

Figure 4: Fully-Combinatorial Implementation

Figure 5: Iterative Implementation

because it is the same function $\mathcal{F}$ which is used repeatedly. Such an implementation is shown in figure 5. For simplicity, issues of input to and output from such a loop are deferred to section 5.

In this paper, we are concerned with self-timed implementations. Let F be a physical (self-timed) implementation of $\mathcal{F}$. Let in and out be the input and output of a stage, and let succ be the output of the succeeding stage (as in figure 1). The circuit F may require some time to compute a new output given a new input. During this time, it may be the case that $F(y_{in}) \neq \mathcal{F}(y_{in})$. The output is said to be **invalid** during this time. To use F in a self-timed system, it must be possible to determine if the output is **valid**, from the value of $F(y_{in})$. This can be done by adding one or more **reset** values to the range of F. Such representations of values are called **self-completion-indicating**. A completely delay-independent implementation requires self-completion-indicating signals; sending a separate completion signal would introduce a timing dependency into the design. In particular, the delays of the wires carrying the actual data and the wire(s) carrying the completion signal would have to be matched.

The block F can be used in an iterative system as follows. First, the input of F is set to a reset value. When the output of F becomes reset, we know that the circuit is ready to begin a new computation. Second, the input of F is set to a valid value. When the output of F becomes valid, we know that the circuit has computed a new result. These operations can be performed repeatedly as required by the iterative algorithm. The computation progresses like the wave in a ring-oscillator. A valid value represents the crest of the wave, and a reset value represents the trough. This is a generalization of the simple oscillator in section 3.1.

The "Synchronized Transitions" program for such a system is shown in figure 6. The predicate valid(X) is true if the value of the signal X is valid, and the predicate reset(X) is true if it is reset. During the time a signal X is transitioning due to the resetting or evaluation of its source, neither reset(X) nor valid(X) will be true. The validity of this program can be verified using invariants analogous to those presented with the simple oscillator.

Invariant 3 *The stages whose outputs are* valid *form a non-empty set of adjacent stages. The stages whose outputs are* reset *form a non-empty set of adjacent stages.*

```
iteration(n:  3..∞)   (* n is the number of stages in the loop *)
   VAR y:  ARRAY[0..n-1] OF alphabet;
          (* alphabet is a self-completion-indicating signal *)
   TRANSITION C'(in, out, succ:  alphabet)
   <(valid(in) ∧ reset(succ)) ∨ (reset(in) ∧ valid(succ)) → out := F(in)>
BEGIN
   ‖ⁿ⁻¹_{i=0} C'(y[i ⊖ 1], y[i], y[i ⊕ 1]);
END iteration.
```

It is assumed that F will produce a reset output when reset(in).

Figure 6: "Synchronized Transitions" Program for Iteration

Invariant 4 *If there are at least three C' elements in the loop, then there exists an active transition.*

Furthermore, the program in figure 6 computes the desired sequence of values as demonstrated by the next invariant. Let j be an index for the stages $(0 \leq j < n)$ and i be an index for the values $(0 \leq i \leq k)$. Because each stage computes many values, i increases as the computation progresses.

Invariant 5 $y[j] = \mathcal{F}^i(input) \lor reset(y[j])$

Assume that the invariant holds before performing an instance of a C' transition writing to y[j]. There are two cases to consider depending on which clause of the precondition is satisfied. If valid(in) ∧ reset(succ), it follows from the invariant that there is an i such that in = y[j⊖1] = $\mathcal{F}^{i-1}(input)$; hence, performing out := F(in) establishes y[j] = $\mathcal{F}^i(input)$. Otherwise, reset(in) ∧ valid(succ), and performing out := F(in) establishes reset(y[j]).

4   Hardware Implementation

Self-timed hardware can be designed which corresponds to the algorithm described in the previous section. First, designs are presented which are technology independent and preserve all the properties of the algorithm. In particular, they function correctly regardless of the delays of logic elements or wires. Next, simplifications for specific implementations are suggested. Then, it is shown how more efficient designs can be derived when some timing relationships are known.

4.1   Direct Implementation

Figure 7 shows a block diagram corresponding directly to the self-timed iteration algorithm presented above. The function F computes a new value for out from the value of in when the **enable** input is **true** (corresponding to the precondition of a transition enabling the action); otherwise, the old value of out is retained. The enabling can be implemented with a transparent latch on the output of a purely combinational function which produces a reset value for out when in is reset, and out = $\mathcal{F}$(in) when in is valid.

The signals for **in**, **out**, and **succ** to the function F are self-completion-indicating. A simple encoding is to let each bit, X, in such a signal be represented on two wires, X^T and

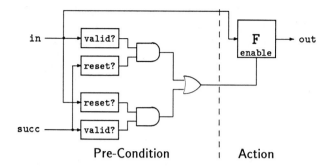

Figure 7: Direct Implementation of an Iteration Stage

X^F. When both wires are low, the value is reset (e.g. not yet valid), and when either of the wires becomes high, the boolean value encoded on the pair is valid. The value for X is indicated by the superscript on whichever of the two wires X^T and X^F is high. The wire pair must return to the reset condition before the transmission of another value; so, there is never a high on both wires simultaneously. The two wires can be OR'ed together to produce the status of the signal: high if the pair represents a valid value, and low for a reset value. This representation of a boolean value can be generalized to a multi-bit representation. A multi-bit value is valid if each of its bits is valid (i.e. the AND of the status of all the bits) and reset if each bit is reset (i.e. the complement of the OR of the status of all the bits). These are the functions performed by the boxes labeled valid? and reset? in figure 7.

4.2 CMOS Implementation

Figure 8 shows a CMOS two-input NAND gate which uses the encoding described above. If both inputs are reset (A^T, A^F, B^T, and B^F are low), the stacks of P-channel transistors will pull the internal nodes (I and J) to vdd resulting in both Y^T and Y^F being low (i.e. a reset value on the output). If either A^F or B^F goes high, node J will be pulled to gnd by the corresponding N-channel transistor, resulting in the Y^T output going high. This implements the function of the NAND gate that if either input is **false** the output is **true**. A similar analysis of the other half of the circuit shows that, if both inputs are **true**, the output is **false**. Arbitrary logic functions can be implemented by these techniques to implement the function, F, for the iteration algorithm. As both the **true** and **false** signals are available from every logic element, appropriate networks of N-channel devices can be designed to implement whatever function is desired. Furthermore, logic implemented as the NAND gate above makes *monotonic* transitions. If each bit of the input remains stable after transitioning from a reset value to a valid value (or valid to reset), each bit of the output will also make a single transition from a reset value to a valid (or valid to reset).

This form of logic implementation has properties which allow simplification of the hardware design. It is possible for neither the pull-up network nor the pull-down network of such logic networks to be active. In this situation, the old value of the output is retained by the capacitance of nodes I and J. This dynamic storage can be utilized to merge the hardware for F and the transparent-latch.

The monotonicity of all circuitry makes it possible to implement the tests for valid(in)

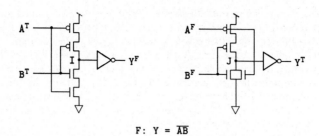

F : Y = $\overline{AB}$

Figure 8: Self-Completion Indicating Two-input NAND Gate

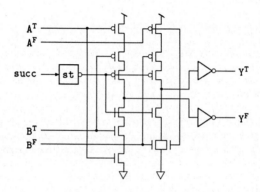

Figure 9: A CMOS Implementation of an Iteration Stage

and **reset(in)** implicitly, within the the hardware for F. Such tests do not need to be separately implemented for the pre-condition. Moreover, the tests for **valid(succ)** and **reset(succ)** can be combined into a single test, **status**, which has memory as to whether **valid(succ)** or **reset(succ)** were last true:

$$\text{status}(X) \quad = \text{TRUE} \quad \text{if X were last valid}$$
$$= \text{FALSE} \quad \text{if X were last reset}$$

Figure 9 shows a single stage for the iterative algorithm simplified by the observations above. The function F is a two-input NAND gate to provide a simple example. The transparent-latch is combined with the hardware for computing F by adding an extra N-channel and an extra P-channel transistor to each stack. Tests for **valid(in)** and **reset(in)** are implicitly performed by the logic implementing the NAND gate, and the tests for **valid(succ)** and **reset(succ)** are replaced by the single test for **status(succ)** as above.

The "Synchronized Transitions" algorithm guarantees that the stages interact correctly independently of any timing delays. Each stage corresponds to an atomic transition. This requires that inputs to F have sufficiently short rise and fall times that the various transistors connected to the signal interpret it as the same boolean value. Furthermore, when an output changes, it must be guaranteed that it makes a complete change between voltage levels corresponding to the logical values so that, if the value is used by more than one stage, it will be interpreted consistently. Schmidt-triggers[3] can be used to buffer the inputs and output of each stage such that these conditions are met. The Schmidt-trigger can be designed such that, for a monotonically changing input, once the output enters the undefined region (voltages between high and low), the output is guaranteed to complete the transition in bounded time.[4] The Schmidt-triggers isolate the internal nodes to guarantee bounded wiring delays and rise and fall times within each stage regardless of the properties of the other stages and the inter-stage wiring.

These observations are made to show that truly time-delay independent circuits can be built for self-timed iteration (the largest isochronic region is a Schmidt-trigger and the internal node to which it is connected). However, it is often possible to derive reasonable bounds for timing delays. Thus, much more efficient implementations are possible as described in the next section.

4.3 Optimization

Optimization seeks to simplify the hardware and lessen the execution delay and silicon area. If adequate relations are known about relative time delays, more efficient designs can be produced than those described in the previous section. When an implementation is fabricated on a single integrated circuit, reliable delay judgements can usually be made based on transistor sizing and the similarities of transistors fabricated on the same chip. If such is the case, then it can be assumed that faster paths have already finished when a known slower path is observed to finish. This assumption means that the hardware to explicitly check such conditions can be removed, yielding a simpler design.

In the case of the CMOS implementation of figure 9, the P-channel transistors controlled by A^T, A^F, B^T, and B^F serve to confirm that the reset value on all of a stage's input wires is received from its predecessor before the stage itself can reset. If it is known that one particular input wire is the slowest, then these stacks of transistors can each be replaced by a single transistor.

The generation of status(out) can be simplified in a similar manner. If a particular bit of out, represented on the wire pair out.slowV, is known to be the last to become valid, and another wire pair, out.slowR, is known to be the last to become reset then:

$$\text{status(out)} = \left(\text{out.slowV}^T \vee \text{out.slowV}^F \right) \copyright \left(\text{out.slowR}^T \vee \text{out.slowR}^F \right)$$

where the symbol $\copyright$ denotes the Muller-C function. If out.slowV and out.slowR are the same wire pair (e.g. the pair driving the largest capacitance), denoted out.slow, then this relation reduces to

$$\text{status(out)} = \text{out.slow}^T \vee \text{out.slow}^F$$

Thus, the circuit which computed status in the previous implementation (which required logic elements for each wire in out) can be replaced by just a NOR gate to sense the completion of the slowest wire pair.

Further optimizations are possible when the stages are the same and they can be reset faster than they evaluate. This is often the case because evaluation may require several levels of logic, whereas resetting can be done in parallel to all of the nodes within a stage. If resetting and the associated wire propagation is always faster than evaluation, then all of the P-channel transistors which confirm the reception of the reset inputs from a stage's

---

[4]Note that this is not using a Schmidt-trigger to solve a decision or arbitration problem. There can be input voltages for which the Schmidt-trigger takes unbounded time to change; however, once the output has changed far enough to enter the undefined region, the time to complete the transition is bounded.

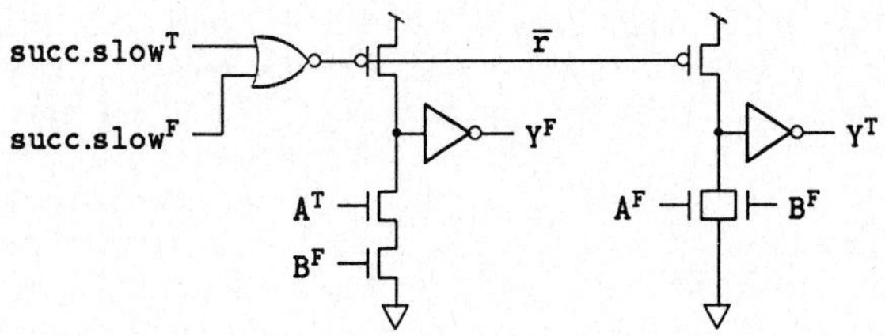

Figure 10: Optimization of an Iteration Stage Based on Known Timing Relations

predecessor can be eliminated. Similarly, the N-channel transistors connected to the **st** box delay the evaluation of the stage until the reception of the status that the next stage has been reset. If resetting is always faster than evaluation, then these N-channel transistors are unnecessary because the successor to a stage will have had plenty of time to reset. The resulting circuit is shown in figure 10. It is noted that in this implementation that the invariants of the algorithm are maintained as a consequence of known time-delays in the circuit and are not explicitly enforced by the logic.

The iteration algorithm concurrently performs the resetting of one stage and the evaluation of another when there are more than three stages. However, there is no concurrency with only the minimum of three stages. When resetting is known to be faster than evaluation for similar stages, concurrency can be achieved for the three stage case as well. In figure 10, a stage was actively reset as long as the output of the successor stage is valid. This can be expressed as:

r = valid(succ)

Hence, the signal r̄ to reset a stage is low (active) throughout the time it takes for the second successor to evaluate and then for the successor to reset. If resetting is assumed to be faster than evaluation, the reset signal for a stage can be removed as soon as the stage's second successor finishes evaluation. This is because it is known that the resetting of a stage will be already done by the time the second successor has finished evaluating. Since the successor begins resetting after the second successor finishes evaluating, the reset control for a stage can be changed to:

r = valid(succ) ∧ ¬succ.r

By thus removing the reset signal of a stage sooner, the evaluation of that stage may proceed concurrently with the resetting of its successor. This modification, shown in figure 11 for the CMOS implementation, is the circuit used in [10] which achieves the execution speed improvement from concurrent reset and evaluate even with three stages.

5   Generalizations

In the simplest form of the algorithm, only limited concurrency is realized (e.g. one stage can compute a new valid value while another resets). Greater concurrency is possible by implementing several parallel data-paths or several communicating loops. Diagrams for these configurations are shown in figure 12.

As shown in the left half of figure 12, parallel data-paths may be implemented with the addition of **split** and **join** operators. The split operator, **s**, sends data from **p** to both a

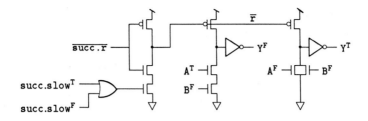

Figure 11: Modifications to Achieve Concurrency with only Three Stages

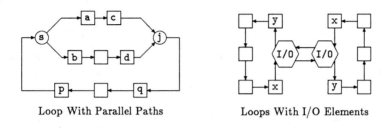

Loop With Parallel Paths   Loops With I/O Elements

Figure 12: Systems With Increased Concurrency

and b and combines the status signals from a and b to send back to p. In particular, s indicates a valid (reset) successor when *both* a and b have valid (reset) outputs as shown below:

    valid(s) = valid(a) ∧ valid(b)
    reset(s) = reset(a) ∧ reset(b)

The join operator, j, performs the complementary function of the split. The data values from c and d are concatenated to provide the input for q, and valid(q) and reset(q) are sent to both c and d.

The right half of figure 12 shows two communicating loops. Each loop implements the iteration algorithm. The I/O element can perform one of two operations based upon the value of its input (e.g. a particular bit of the value may specify the operation). One operation is to copy the input (from x) to the output (i.e. to y). This allows the two loops to iterate independently. The other operation exchanges a pair of values between the two loops. In this operation, the I/O element sends its input to the I/O element of the other loop, waits to receive a value from the other I/O element, and then sends this value to y. Because each element waits to receive a valid input before performing its next action, the exchange can be performed without arbitration[2]. This provides a mechanism for I/O operations within the self-timed domain without any possibility of synchronization failure. This also provides a method for communicating with circuits designed by other (e.g. synchronous) methods; however, the other system may be susceptible to timing hazards if adequate precautions are not taken.

The algorithms presented in this paper provide a basis for self-timed iteration which is independent of the function performed by each stage. Different functions may be implemented for different applications. Iteration is well suited for dedicated co-processors such as chips for multiplication, division[10], transcendental functions (e.g. the CORDIC algorithm[8]), and data encryption/decryption. Using the generalizations presented in this section, self-timed iteration could be applied to arrays of processors or cellular automata, where individual cells can operate at much higher rates than it is practical to distribute a global clock.

6 Conclusions

We have presented an algorithm for iteration in the self-timed domain using only asynchronous circuits. Fabricated and tested VLSI arithmetic chips [10] using these circuits have previously verified and demonstrated the usefulness of self-timed iterations. The algorithm in this paper can be applied to systems of any size independent of communication and processor delays. Because it is self-timed, particular hardware implementations will operate as fast as the technology, temperature, and data values allow.

References

[1] T.S. Anantharaman, E.M. Clarke, et. al., "Compiling path expressions into VLSI circuits," Distributed Computing, vol. 1, no. 3, pp. 150-166, 1986.

[2] D.M. Chapiro, "Globally-Asynchronous, Locally-Synchronous Systems," Ph.D. thesis, Department of Computer Science, Stanford University, October 1984.

[3] L.A. Glasser and D.W. Dobberpuhl, **The Design and Analysis of VLSI Circuits**, pp. 280-282, Addison-Wesley, 1985.

[4] L.R. Marino, "General Theory of Metastable Operation," IEEE Transaction on Computers, vol. 30, no. 2, pp. 107-115, February 1981.

[5] A.J. Martin, "Compiling communicating processes into delay-insensitive VLSI circuits," Distributed Computing, vol. 1, pp. 226-234, 1986.

[6] C.L. Seitz, "System Timing," Chapter 7 of **Introduction to VLSI Systems** by C. Mead and L. Conway, Addison-Wesley, 1978.

[7] J. Staunstrup and A.P. Ravn, "Synchronized Transitions," DAIMI PB-219, Computer Science Department, Aarhus University, Denmark, (submitted for publication) January 1987.

[8] J.S. Walther, "A Unified Algorithm for Elementary Functions," 1971 Spring Joint Computer Conference, AFIPS Proceedings, vol. 38, pp. 379-385, 1971.

[9] N. Weste and K. Eshraghian, **Principles of CMOS VLSI Design, A Systems Perspective**, p. 372, Addison-Wesley, 1985.

[10] T.E. Williams, M. Horowitz, et. al., "A Self-Timed Chip for Division," Proceedings of the Conference on Advanced Research in VLSI, Stanford University, March 1987.

VLSI '87, C.H. Séquin (editor)
Elsevier Science Publishers B.V. (North-Holland)
© IFIP, 1988

Functional Simulation for the CRISP Microprocessor

Alan Berenbaum
Robert Heaton

AT&T-Information Systems
Holmdel, NJ 07733

The CRISP Functional Simulator is a multi-level simulation system, written in the C programming language, that models a complex VLSI part, the CRISP Microprocessor. It provides for functional design and documentation, functional verification and logic verification as well as test vector generation for physical testing of completed parts. It also provides statistics which are useful for architectural evaluation and runs quickly enough to enable pre-silicon software debugging and benchmarking. The simulator features an interactive interface with screen-oriented output, which conveys a large amount of information about the state of the processor in an concise manner as well as providing a logic analyzer-like ability to view internal signals. In several areas the simulator was less detailed, or used more shortcuts, then previous functional simulators used in AT&T-Bell Laboratories, but precision was only relaxed if another step would ultimately correct any inaccuracy. The result was a simulator that ran more quickly and was easier to use than previous implementations.

1. Introduction

Turning a specification for a microprocessor into a working piece of silicon requires a series of refinements that begin with broad concepts and end with the specifics of IC layout. The Functional Simulator (FSIM) was the principle tool used in performing this refinement and verifying correctness of the CRISP Microprocessor[1] [2], a 32-bit CMOS microprocessor, with six pipeline stages and about 170,000 transistors. This simulator enabled us to

— Determine a feasible functional partition of the processor,

— Verify the correctness of the logic design,

— Generate test vectors for physical testing of the final silicon, and

— Document the design.

The CRISP Functional Simulator went beyond previous simulators used in Bell Labs in several areas. The most important extensions were:

— An interactive interface, which enabled a designer to step through a program and query individual signals. The state of the system was apparent at a glance without the need to decode dumps and log files.

— Verification without log files. The Functional Simulator can be run in parallel with a program which defines the correct chip behavior, and the FSIM will stop when the two deviate. Log files of events or signal traces are not needed, so file space and system I/O is minimized.

— A switch-level simulator, integrated into the Functional Simulator, so any part or all parts of the chip model could be simulated at the transistor level instead of the functional level.

— A philosophy of maximizing the speed of simulation, possibly at the expense of strict accuracy in the modeling of component behavior. For example, rather than mimic a complex combination of Nands, Nors and inverters, a simple C expression would be used to generate a signal. This relaxation of constraints was only allowed if any errors introduced would be caught in a later, more detailed level of simulation. By increasing the speed of the simulator, we could make more simulation runs and cover a larger set of test sequences.

2. Development of the Functional Simulator

The Functional Simulator is a phase-accurate representation, in program form, of the data paths and all control signals in the target microprocessor. It is unclear what datapath elements are required when a design is beginning, so the Functional Simulator was not the first representation of the CRISP architecture. Two simulators preceded it, called the Interpreter and the Architectural Simulator. The Interpreter was done without much knowledge of an implementation and the Architectural Simulator somewhere in between. With the first, it was possible to refine such details of the architecture as instruction encoding and address mode selection. With the second, details of the pipeline structure were resolved.

2.1 Interpreter

The CRISP interpreter interprets programs on an instruction by instruction basis. The Interpreter has no knowledge of implementation, so it has no concept of the number of cycles required to execute an instruction. Because it deals so directly with the target machine instructions, the actual simulation step is very simple; the relevant C code requires only about 1500 lines. This simplicity makes the program run quickly, and it is easy to modify. The basic program loop is to execute one instruction, and on an IBM 3081, the Interpreter can simulate about 5,000 instructions per second. The CRISP architecture was refined using the Interpreter. Many variations of instructions, address modes and encodings were tried in order to see how they affected data traffic and instruction counts. When the instruction set architecture settled, the Interpreter remained an accurate way to execute a CRISP object file, and so it was used in verification in later steps of the design process.

2.2 Architectural Simulator

The Architectural Simulator modeled the pipeline structure of CRISP, unlike the interpreter, which only modeled instructions. It could count cycles with a reasonable degree of accuracy. The Architectural Simulator was used to evaluate various implementation options. Several perturbations of the architecture were tried, such as varying cache sizes, alternate mechanisms for conditional branches, prefetch strategies and so on. The procedures of the Architectural Simulator represent pipeline stages, and the basic loop runs once for every cycle (exercising every pipeline element). The Architectural Simulator contains about 3,000 lines of C code in the machine description sections, and it runs about 1,000 cycles a second on a 3081.

2.3 Functional Simulator

The Functional Simulator for CRISP evolved from the Architectural Simulator, along with a silicon floor plan. Instead of being organized by pipeline stages, each module represents a major block in the floor plan. Control blocks, including PLA's, are explicitly modeled. This organization is the key to the utility of the functional simulator. Since each module accurately reflects a corresponding hardware block, a high-level description of a block could be replaced by a low-level one, down to individual transistors, without perturbing the rest of the model. This enabled piecewise verification of our logic design.

The Functional Simulator was written for efficient execution as well as portability. Early in its design we decided to sacrifice some potential modeling accuracy in the interests of executing more cycles per second on our host machines. The assumption was the faster the simulator ran, the more code we could run through it, and when bugs were detected, we could try more variations to fix them. Whatever inaccuracy that occurred because of shortcuts we would eventually correct when the model was running at its most refined level, at the cost of slower debugging. We routinely ran simulations of 500,000 to 1,000,000 cycles at a time. FSIM contains about 10,000 lines of C code for the chip model and runs about 500 cycles per second of CPU time on an IBM 3081.

3. Organization

The Functional Simulator is separated into sets of modules; one set to simulate logic, and another set to provide an environment which allows the model to run, as well as provide verification, statistics and a debugging interface. Each function was written as a separate code file, which made it easy to maintain the system. Most of the time, two people worked on the FSIM, and each file was the responsibility of one or the other. Various systems developed within Bell Labs were also added, such as a screen interface, a test-vector interface and the switch-level simulator, which will be described later.

The FSIM was written entirely in C, with the exception of a special C-like language for the PLA's. We had considered using special simulation systems, either using ones already available in Bell Labs, or writing one specifically for the CRISP project. We rejected the latter course on the basis of time, and the available simulation systems were rejected because they were too slow. Using C also made it easy to exploit the Unix system: it took little time to integrate existing packages into the FSIM if we wanted them (such as the screen management interface). The C model is adequately fast (in fact, it is about twice as fast as similar simulators written for other chips developed in AT&T). The drawback of C is that it allows the designer *too much* flexibility, to the extent that it is easy to code something that may be impossible to implement with real transistors. We tried to avoid problems by adopting a strict coding style, but generally we relied on the designers to adhere to the convention. Problems that remained were eventually eliminated during a full-chip switch-level simulation.

3.1 Superblock Modules

The chip layout is divided into "superblocks," a relatively large collection of logic that is laid out together. Each superblock was represented by two files. One file contained C code for a single function which represented the superblock, and another file contained declarations which provided the superblock I/O list. Each one-bit signal was represented by an 8-bit *char* variable, while multi-bit signals were represented by 32-bit *int*s.

The module was responsible for providing accurate 0-1 values for all of its outputs at the end of each phase. It was not necessary that every internal signal in the final logic design be represented in the simulator, so the coding of a signal in the FSIM emphasized clarity, while the schematics minimized transistors, or constraints forced by layout considerations. Previous functional simulators tried to match the schematics identically, and the resulting increase in terms and signal names made it more difficult to comprehend the *intent* of an expression, although it was easier to turn the C code into schematics. Again, we found our short cut saved simulation time, and any transcription errors were discovered during the switch level simulation.

Standard C operators performed the function of logic gates, so the C && operator represented a logical AND, the | | a logical OR, and latches were emulated with simple assignment statements, suitably conditioned (via an *if*) with a clock signal. Using the && and | | operators assures values of 0 or 1, which keeps errors or undefined values (represented as a 2 by the switch level simulator) from propagating. Multi-bit signals were assembled with the C logical or (|), while individual bits were extracted with the logical and (&). We did not use C bit-fields for this purpose. With masks defined as manifest constants, multiplexors or decoders are easily implemented as C *switch*es, and the default case neatly checks for illegal bit patterns.

Figures 1, 2 and 3 show some examples of functional modules from the FSIM. Figure 1 is a fragment from a control block of the Execution Unit. Names in upper case are manifest constants; Figure 2 contains signal definitions for the example in Figure 1. One set defines the decoding of a two bit register number field, and another defines the four control wires that go to the datapath to control the register bus. Most of the signals are from one of the major pipeline stages (*i.e.*, they are outputs of phase 1 static latches), and are indicated by leading upper case letters. Irlop and Irrop are 32-bit signals, and only the two lowest bits are needed for the register code; these bits are extracted with the REGMASK mask. Figure 3 is a fragment of code from the Execution Unit datapath. The bus multiplexor is modeled with a C *switch*, which guarantees that only one bit of the mux control can be on at a time. A diagnostic is generated if any illegal bit pattern is detected. Also, the bus is driven during phase 3, so the entire *switch* is contained with a conditional expression, depending on one of the clocks.

The two PLA's in the CRISP Microprocessor were modeled with a special PLA language developed in Bell Labs and used in the design of several earlier chips. Tools are provided that translate the description into a C language subroutine, or directly generate layout for the PLA. The PLA system is described elsewhere[3].

Every functional C module has an accompanying header file, which provides an I/O list for the superblock as well as defining variables for the module. Almost every signal is a C *extern*, so all signals are globally known in the simulator environment. Every input and output wire in a superblock is declared in the header file. Using the C pre-processor, several keywords were defined to describe all signals, and the syntax requires one signal definition per line. Signals could be declared as inputs, outputs or both (ioput). Signals that did not leave a superblock could be typed internal or *layout* if the signal would be used for display or debugging purposes. Multibit signals could be specified with a range of bit numbers.

Figure 4 lists a few examples of signal declarations.

3.2 Simulation Environment Modules

The Functional Simulator has about 5,000 lines devoted to the simulation environment. The files in this part of the simulator provide the main simulation driver, and do   the usual necessary and interesting tasks:

— processing command line arguments
— maintaining a memory model to drive the chip
— providing an interactive interface for single stepping
— debugging and display of internal information
— verification
— gathering and displaying statistics

The I/O module of the simulator has all the chip output pins listed as inputs and outputs in its I/O list. The memory model portion of the simulator reads its inputs every phase and adjusts its outputs appropriately, simulating a real memory. The memory itself covers the full 32-bit address space of the processor; actual addresses are hashed into whatever space is available on the computer. For simple tests, the memory can be adjusted for different numbers of wait states, and it can assert faults and interrupts at particular times. For more complex I/O interactions, a protocol model is available, which is described below.

In combination with the CRISP assembler, there is a hook to emulate Unix system calls and library functions. Certain system calls are recognized as "special" and the simulator intercepts the logic modules and hands control over to the host Unix system. These can be low-level system calls like *read* or *write*, or they can be C library functions like *printf*. With this mechanism, it becomes possible to run large benchmark programs on the Functional Simulator without having to implement a full Unix System. Programs like *nroff* and *cc* have been simulated on the FSIM.

4. Converting the FSIM to Logic

The conversion of the Functional Simulator to schematics, which represent the actual transistors to be laid out, is a manual process. Ultimately, it would be desirable to have an automatic process which converts a functional specification to logic gates without manual intervention, but we did not have such a tool available. Such automatic conversion, however, could not be done unless the source included buffering, local signal inversion, and all intermediate subexpressions. Each module would have to be written at least twice, once to get the sense of the operation right, and when that was understood, expanded into a final, logical form. The final form would most likely run slower, as well.

Schematics were entered with the UNIX Circuit Design System[4]. Figure 5 is a schematic representation of the code in Figure 1. Active low signals appear with a "_L" suffix, and the pl wires are buffered with inverter chains to increase their drive. It is not immediately clear from the schematics that the read enable for register VB (rgselr3), is decoded register number 7.

Furthermore, if it became necessary to change the control wire from 3 to 6, or the encoding from 7 to 2, several terms would probably have to be changed. In the FSIM, this change can be done by changing the manifest constants. In addition, there are many intermediate signals in the schematics that do not appear in the simulator, like `usell1` and `usir`.

5. Verification

In the past, we have verified complex microprocessors and associated chips primarily with vectors. One simulator, believed to be reliable, would output a set of vectors, or traces of various signals on a phase, cycle or event basis, as a result of a test. Then these vectors would be compared to the output of the simulator under test. This methodology assumes that one simulator is correct, or at least that two do not make the same error in the same way. If the two simulators disagreed, a designer would scan long columns of hexadecimal numbers to determine where the discrepancy lay. Although this method is feasible, and in fact is the way physical chip testers work, it can get very tedious for designers as they daily ferret out bugs, as well as consuming large amounts of file space to store the vectors and large amounts of computer time to read, write and format them. We used a mechanism that did not trap errors on a cycle-by-cycle basis, but would report an error "soon" after it occurred. This turned out to be sufficient for most testing, and relieved the designers of the task of pouring over large quantities of data.

We used a two-level simulation technique to trap errors in the FSIM. The CRISP Interpreter was modified to report every time a memory location, either on or off chip, was modified. In this mode, the interpreter would write a three word packet on its standard output for every instruction which did a store, consisting of the data to be stored, the address of the memory location, and the address of the instruction which was doing the store. When put into verification mode, the FSIM would initiate the Interpreter as a background process, and every time the FSIM updated memory, either on-chip or off-chip, it would read the packet from the Interpreter. If the data matched, the process continued, but if there was a discrepancy, an error condition was raised.

Since the Interpreter runs two orders of magnitude faster than the Functional Simulator, running it as a background process makes a minimal impact on the execution of the simulator. This has the effect of generating vectors "on the fly." Because the Interpreter is so simple, it is likely that it implements CRISP instructions correctly. Although very few control or data path signals are actually checked with this mechanism, the side effects (updating memory) are accurately tracked. Since almost every instruction does a store, either on-chip or off-chip, the error would be flagged no more than two or three cycles from the source of the problem on most occasions.

The Simulator also has a mechanism for running regressions. By pointing to a directory and a list of files, a set of several hundred tests could be run with one invocation of the simulator. The result of a regression is a file with just a couple of lines per test, instead of megabytes of vector files. A full regression of the FSIM through 200-odd tests takes about an hour and a half on an IBM 3081.

6. Backporting

The mechanism used to prove that the logic drawn in schematic form is correct is called backporting. One by one, C-coded modules in the Functional Simulator are replaced by switch level simulations of the schematics for each module. Eventually the entire chip is modeled at the switch level by SOISIM, and the FSIM is a skeleton which provides an operating environment, verification and debugging facilities. The result is an efficient mixed mode simulation capability.

When backporting a module, the module's FSIM C code is replaced by special C code that binds a module's inputs to variables, issues a call to SOISIM to settle the circuit, then maps the appropriate SOISIM variables back to C variables for the module's outputs. The binding, settling and mapping function is handled automatically from the module's header file and the netlist file generated from the schematics.

The tool which generates the linking module automatically translates between the FSIM naming convention and the schematics naming convention. (The distinction exists primarily so the simulator can represent multi-bit signals as C integers, instead of a collection of 1-bit variables.)

In addition, the tool provided another level of verification, since it complained if the inputs and outputs specified in the C header file do not agree precisely in number with the inputs and outputs specified in the schematics.

Backporting more than one module at a time is a simple extension of the procedure to backport individual modules. All that is required is an I/O list (which is in the form of a C header file) for the union of all the modules in question, and a netlist, which could be generated either by hand in schematic form or automatically from the constituent modules. For backporting the full chip, the I/O list was the specification of the chip's I/O.

All facilities of the Functional Simulator are available to the backported simulator, so that the interactive debugging interface and all verification mechanisms function. All FSIM variables are available for inspection by the debugger, including signals being simulated by SOISIM. In addition, all nodes internal to the SOISIM model can be examined or traced. The debugging paradigm is the same as the stand-alone FSIM: run a test while comparing its results with the background interpreter, and when a conflict occurs, inspect signals until the problem is revealed. Usually, once a bug was known, its cause could be uncovered in a few minutes. As a result, we did not use any vector files until just before the chip mask date, when vector files were necessary for detailed I/O protocol verification as well as for the silicon wafer testing machines.

The speed of a backported Functional Simulator depends on the size and the nature of the circuit being simulated by SOISIM. A small block of a couple of hundred transistors runs in nearly the same time as the bare FSIM. A full CRISP model, which comprises about 170,000 real transistors, runs *very* slowly, on the order of two cycles per second of IBM 3081 CPU time. This is about two orders of magnitude slower than the bare FSIM. The process, even with the hierarchical names in the SOISIM netlist flattened to save space, takes about 7 Megabytes of virtual memory space. Therefore, we ran a full-chip model infrequently, and only after we were reasonably certain that all of its sub-modules backported successfully. A full regression of the full-chip model through 200-odd tests takes about 3 3081-CPU-days.

7. Debugging

Once the verification procedure detects an error, it is necessary to determine what caused it. Once again, we avoided the use of vector files as much as possible. Instead, we provided an interactive screen-oriented interface, and a debugging mechanism that gave us much of the power of a logic analyzer.

7.1 Screen Interface

The screen-oriented interface we used for the FSIM turned out to be easy to use, and has been adapted to a number of other chip projects within AT&T. When the simulator was run in interactive mode, it would come up with a window of useful information, using a terminal-independent screen management system (Curses[5]). Space on the screen was allocated to the principle regions of the chip. One block displayed data associated with the Prefetch Unit, one with the Execution Unit, and another displayed the I/O. All the major pipeline registers, as well as various internal registers, were displayed as hexadecimal numbers. Interesting control signals were displayed in various encoded ways, placed in the window so it was clear to the relevant designer what was happening. It was simple for a designer to step through a program and instantly see the entire state of the machine, as well as watch instructions flow down the pipeline.

Every cycle (or phase if the simulator was stepping one phase at a time) the entire screen image was stored in a circular buffer. Only displayed signals are saved, not the entire state of the simulator. With this buffer in place, it is possible to "step back" in time and see what caused a particular event to happen. Figure 6 is an example of the screen interface.

7.2 Interactive Interface

When the Simulator is invoked interactively, it comes up with an interactive interface that allows a designer to step through a program in a number of ways: advance a number of phases, cycles, or instructions, until a error is detected by the verification mechanism, or until a breakpoint occurs. Breakpoints could be set on instruction addresses or store addresses. When the simulator is run for multiple cycles, the screen is only updated at the end of the set, although a cycle counter is updated every 100 cycles to inform the designer that the program is still running. Like a logic analyzer, the last n cycles are saved in the window buffer, so when a breakpoint or error stops the simulator, the designer can back up and see what happened just before the simulator stopped.

7.3 Debugger

An extensive debugging interface is provided as well. All memory locations, on and off chip, can be examined, and data memory can be altered. In addition, it is possible to "probe" any signal in the model. Since every signal is a C global variable, the FSIM can look in its own symbol table and find the address in its memory of every signal. The signal can then be displayed or altered. Furthermore, there is space allocated on the screen for up to 18 signals to be actively displayed every cycle. These signals are stored in the screen buffer along with all the others, so one can attach "probes" to a number of interesting signals, run the simulator up to a breakpoint, and then back up and observe how they behaved. This mechanism went a long way towards eliminating the need for vector files to do routine debugging.

8. Protocol

To test the functional simulator, an environment had to be developed to apply test stimuli to the model. The environment had to serve 4 basic functions

1. provide a simulated program memory into which code could be "downloaded" and executed by the functional simulator.

2. provide correct I/O protocol responses to requests by the CPU.

3. enable the user to assert desired events, such as interrupts, bus faults, etc at specific points in the simulation.

4. provide a mechanism for continuously checking the pins of the functional simulator to ensure that the model did not violate the defined inter-chip I/O protocol.

To accomplish this an environment generator called PWB (Protocol WorkBench) was used. PWB was written to enable designers to develop a protocol testing environment for chips. PWB allows the user to write an event generator and protocol checker as a collection of state machines. Typically, each device input has a state machine that generates the correct pin stimuli. In turn, each output has a state machine that checks that the pin is always asserted in a "protocol correct" fashion. Sample input and output state machines are shown in Figures 7 and 8.

State machines can also be built on top of lower level state machines. These state machines can then check that the CPU performs higher level sequences or transactions correctly. For example, "when an interrupt is asserted the CPU should respond with an interrupt acknowledge cycle", or "upon reset the CPU will request the bus from the external arbiter." The set of state machines embodies the definition of the protocol and enables the CRISP protocol environment to produce any correct protocol sequence in response to requests by the CPU.

The PWB generator also allows the designer to define a low level user command interface. Commands are "compiled" from a script file and are then read and executed by the protocol environment. Commands were provided in the CRISP environment to control the handshaking with the CPU model. The user is capable of triggering on events such as addresses, and access types and asserting events like faults, interrupts, and retries. The command interface also lets the user directly control inputs so that the CRISP model's response to incorrect protocol scenarios can be tested. A sample protocol script is shown in Figure 9.

The environment was used to verify almost 600 protocol scenarios and supported the design verification testing as well.

9. Conclusion

The CRISP Functional Simulator has proved to be a useful tool in designing, debugging and documenting a complex VLSI microprocessor. With a little care on the part of the designers, it was straightforward to transfer ideas into logic. By using standard C code the simulator could run fast enough that it was natural to run a test twice, rather than running it once along with a core dump or vector dump for later perusal. In effect, we treated simulation as a time-shared or personal computer activity, rather than the usual batch activity. Bugs could be identified and repaired quickly, and perhaps most importantly, our offices did not become filled with huge mounds of computer listings of log files. One of the best indications of the value of the ideas in the CRISP FSIM is that several other chips developed in AT&T have been developed with functional simulators adapted in part from the CRISP FSIM.

10. Acknowledgements

The design of the CRISP Architectural Simulator, which inspired much of the flavor of the Functional Simulator, was written by Dave Ditzel and Rae McLellan. Kerry Maletsky was one of the original authors of the FSIM and wrote several sections. Walter Roper provided an I/O model. R. F. Cmelik wrote several tools that performed the mapping from LSL into the simulator. Tom Szymanski helped to integrate SOISIM into the FSIM.

REFERENCES

1. A. D. Berenbaum, D. R. Ditzel, H. R. McLellan, *Introduction to the CRISP Microprocessor*, IEEE Compcon, Spring 1987

2. A. D. Berenbaum, B. W. Colbry, D. R. Ditzel, R. D. Freeman, K. J. O'Connor, H. R. McLellan, M. Shoji, *A 32b CMOS Microprocessor with 13kb of RAM*, ISSCC, February, 1987

3. P. Agrawal, M. J. Meyer, "Automation in the Design of Finite-State Machines," *VLSI Design*, September, 1984, pp. 74-84.

4. A. G. Fraser, "Circuit Design Aids," *The Bell System Technical Journal* **57**(6, part 2), pp. 2233-2249 (July-August 1978).

5. Mark R. Horton, *The New Curses and Terminfo Package*, AT&T-Bell Laboratories Internal Memorandum, August 2, 1982.

```
if( clk1)
     Prgser = prgser;
pl = 0;
if(Irnop || ( Prgser != NO_REG ))
     pl = Prgser;
else if(Irrreg)
     pl = Irrop & REGMASK;
else if(Irlreg)
     pl = Irlop & REGMASK;
switch(pl) {
     case MSP: rgselr = R_MSP; break;
     case PSW: rgselr = R_PSW; break;
     case ISP: rgselr = R_ISP; break;
     default:  rgselr = R_RRA;
}
```

Figure 1. Multibit Decoder-Encoder

```
/* register numbers, in encoded form */
#define NO_REG          0
#define MSP             1
#define ISP             2
#define SP              3
#define REGMASK         3
/* Register bus mux control */
#define R_SP            0x1
#define R_MSP           0x2
#define R_ISP           0x4
#define R_RRA           0x8
```

Figure 2. Register Control Bit Position Definitions

```
if (clk3){
    switch( rgselr ) {      /* select a source */
    case R_SP:
        rgbus = sp;     /* put SP register on the bus */
        break;
    case R_ISP:
        rgbus = isp;    /* put ISP register on the bus */
        break;
    case R_MSP:
        rgbus = msp;    /* put MSP register on the bus */
        break;
    case R_RRA:
        rgbus = Rra & ~0xf; /* use upper 28 bits only */
        break;
    default:
        error("Bad rgselr value (%x)",rgselr,ticks);
    }
```

Figure 3. Datapath Multiplexor

```
/* inputs from CLOCK */
input       clk1;

/* control inputs */
input   Irnop;          /* instruction is not valid (no-op) */
input   Irlreg;         /* lop is a register */
input   Irrreg;         /* rop is a register */
inputi prgser; /* 2  register select for reads */

/* data path inputs */
inputi Irrop;   /* 00,01  low bits of rop for reg number */
inputi Irlop;   /* 00,01  low bits of lop for reg number */

/* register control outputs */
outputi rgselr;     /* 4  source control for Register bus */

/* internal signals */
internal Prgser;        /* slave version of prgser */
internal p1;            /* intermediate for decode */
```

Figure 4. Input/Output Declarations

Register Select Read Control Lines.

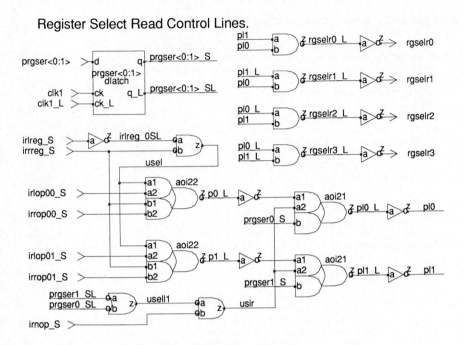

Figure 5. Schematic Equivalent of Figure 1

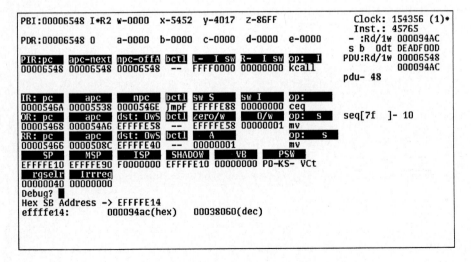

Figure 6. Screen Interface Example

```
STATE_MACHINE: DTACK CLOCK(perphase)
{
    /* this state machine is called every clock phase
    /* this state machine waits until it receives a signal(trans_beg)
    /* from a higher level state machine that an access has  started.

    START_STATE: WAIT_TRANS;
    STATE: WAIT_TRANS
    {
        /* wait_states is a user definable variable that sets the
        /* number of wait states.
        (trans_beg == 1 && phase==3) {
            cyc_to_wait = wait_states;
        } GOTO PHASE4;
    }
    STATE: PHASE
    {   /* always negate dtack in phase 4
        ALWAYS: { dtack_pin = 1; } GOTO WAIT_END;
    }
    STATE: WAIT_END
    {
        (cyc_to_wait == 0 && phase == 2);
        {
            /* The user can set assert_dtack to terminate an access.
            /* The state machine will set dtack active during phase2
            /* and deassert it in phase 3, according to the protocol
            /* trans_end signals the end of a transaction.
            /* Fault and retry are also "wire ored" in

            if(assert_dtack) { trans_end = 1; dtack_pin = 0; }
        } GOTO END_DTACK;
        (cyc_to_wait != 0 && phase == 2): {
            cyc_to_wait--;
        }GOTO WAIT_END;
    }
    /* enter this state after dtack has been asserted and wait until
    /* phase 3 to deassert it.
    STATE: END_DTACK
    {
        (phase == 3): {
            dtack_pin = 1;       /* clear trans_end as well as return
            trans_end = 0;       /* to the top of the state machine
        } GOTO WAIT_TRANS;       /* and wait for the next transaction
    }
}
```

Figure 7. Input state machine

```
/* the STC state machine monitors and checks the assertion
/* of the start of cyclepin (STC).  The pin should be asserted
/* at the beginning of phase 3 for only one cycle at the
/* beginning of an access.

STATE_MACHINE: STC CLOCK(perphase)
{
    START_STATE: WAIT_STC;
    STATE: WAIT_STC {
        (start_pin == 0 && phase == 3): {} GOTO CHECK_STC;
        (start_pin == 0): {
            error("STC incorrectly asserted on phase %d",phase);
        } GOTO CHECK_STC;
    }
    STATE: CHECK_STC {
        (start_pin == 1 && phase == 2): {} GOTO END_STC;
        (start_pin == 1): {
            error("STC incorrectly deasserted on phase %d",phase);
        } GOTO END_STC;
    }
    STATE: END_STC {
        (trans_end == 1): {
            if(start_pin == 0) error("STC asserted >1 cycle");
        } GOTO WAIT_STC;
        (start_pin == 0): { error("STC asserted >1 cycle"); }
    }
}
```

Figure 8. Output state machine

```
MEMPARM: wait_states,3;        /* environment will insert 3 wait
                               /* states on all accesses
RESET:  3;                     /* assert reset for 3 cycles
WAITFOR: address,0xeeee0000;   /* wait for address == 0xeeee0000
HANDSHAKE: nodtack,buserror;   /* Assert fault instead of dtack.
WAITFOR: stc;                  /* wait for next access
HANDSHAKE: nobuserror,dtack;   /* return to handshaking with dtack
WAITFOR: prefetch;             /* wait for a prefetch
HANDSHAKE: nodtack;
WAITFOR: cycle;                /* wait one cycle
WAITFOR: phase2;               /* wait until the start of phase 2
ASSERT: retry;                 /* assert the retry pin
WAITFOR: phase;                /* wait one phase
DEASSERT: retry;               /* deassert retry
CONTINUE: NULL;
```

Figure 9. Protocol command script.

TIMING VERIFICATION
AND ELECTRICAL SIMULATION

VLSI '87, C.H. Séquin (editor)
Elsevier Science Publishers B.V. (North-Holland)
© IFIP, 1988

Simulating MOS VLSI Circuits Using SuperCrystal

Romy L. Bauer
Antony P-C Ng
Arvind Raghunathan
Mark W. Saake

Computer Science Division
573 Evans Hall
University of California
Berkeley, CA 94720.

Clark D. Thompson

Department of Computer Science
University of Minnesota, Duluth
Duluth, MN 55812

ABSTRACT

This paper describes SuperCrystal, a computer program for quick yet reasonably accurate simulation of MOS VLSI circuits.

SuperCrystal divides the time axis into time steps. In each time step, a transistor circuit maps to a linear RC network for the purpose of waveform estimation. Single exponential approximations to node waveforms in the RC network are then calculated using an algorithm due to Raghunathan and Thompson.

Unlike several other timing analyzers based on the linear RC model, SuperCrystal approximates transistor resistances as functions of the voltage waveforms at the gate, source, and drain nodes, after distinguishing between the triode and pinchoff modes of operation. An iterative algorithm is presented for the calculation of a transistor's average resistance over a given time period.

Preliminary tests using SuperCrystal are highly encouraging. Several MOS circuits are analyzed in this paper using Crystal, SuperCrystal and SPICE, and the resulting outputs and CPU times are compared.

1. Introduction

Giant leaps in technology over the last several years have made possible the routine production and use of MOS VLSI chips with hundreds of thousands of transistors. SPICE [7], a popular circuit simulator, provides detailed and highly accurate voltage waveforms. Unfortunately, SPICE is much too slow to analyze VLSI chips directly. It is useful only on isolated subcircuits of tens or hundreds of transistors.

This work was supported in part by National Science Foundation through its Computer Engineering Program, under grant DMC-8406408. Author Ng is also supported by a Regent's Fellowship; author Saake is also supported by the Golden Nugget Scholarship Fund.

Relaxation-based simulators, such as SPLICE [16], ELOGIC [5] and WASIM [8], and waveform-relaxation based simulators, such as RELAX2.1 [22], offer potentially faster runtimes while retaining the accuracy of SPICE.

At the other end of the speed-accuracy spectrum are timing analyzers such as Crystal [12], MOS-SIM [2], SDS [6], and TV [4]. These analyzers are fast enough to process entire VLSI chips, but are sometimes woefully inaccurate.

SuperCrystal is a new circuit simulator suitable for full-custom VLSI. Our intention was to build a simulator that is nearly as fast as Crystal, but much more accurate. SuperCrystal is implemented in the C programming language, and runs under Berkeley UNIX.

Conventional circuit simulators attempt to find the exact voltage waveforms at nodes in a MOS circuit. Since these circuits are in general non-linear, waveform estimation is time consuming [9]. In an attempt to get around this problem, SuperCrystal restricts circuit elements to be MOS transistors, linear resistors, and linear grounded capacitors. Voltage waveforms of nodes in the circuit are approximated as first-order exponentials.

SuperCrystal is most closely akin to the waveform estimators which model a digital MOS circuit by a linear RC network. This approach, described initially by Bryant [2], has been used in a number of timing analyzers [4,6,12,15,19]. Raghunathan and Thompson [13,14] extend Bryant's model by incorporating leakage resistors in RC trees. SuperCrystal currently uses the Raghunathan Thompson algorithm for waveform estimation.

This paper is organized as follows: In Section 2, we review classical circuit simulation techniques. Section 3 gives an outline and organization of SuperCrystal. The Raghunathan Thompson algorithm is detailed in section 4. Section 5 shows how the transistor model is incorporated into the Raghunathan Thompson algorithm. Section 6 describes how SuperCrystal schedules the simulation of different parts of the circuit. Discretization of the simulation into time steps is discussed in section 7. Section 8 details the comparative results of running Crystal, SuperCrystal, and SPICE on various circuit examples. Our conclusions and directions for future work are presented in section 9.

2. A Brief Overview of Circuit Simulation

For the purpose of waveform estimation, a MOS circuit maps to an LCR network. Such an LCR network is modeled by a system of non-linear, first-order differential equations which is in general impossible to solve exactly. This motivates the discretization of the time axis into *time points*. An approximate solution to the system of equations is obtained for each time point. Information from previous time points is used to predict the solution for the current time point.

2.1. Standard Circuit Simulation

Standard circuit simulators like SPICE [7] apply stiffly stable integration formulas (e.g. Backward Euler) at each time point to the non-linear system of nodal equations to yield a set of non-linear algebraic difference equations. These equations are solved iteratively using a damped Newton-Raphson algorithm. Each iteration produces a sparse linear system, which is solved by sparse LU decomposition or Gaussian Elimination. Experimental evidence indicate runtimes of $O(n^{1.1-1.5})$ to solve the sparse linear system.

Newton-Raphson approximation techniques are preferred in practice because the rate of convergence is quadratic and convergence is guaranteed if the initial guess is sufficiently close to the solution.

2.2. Relaxation-Based Methods

Relaxation-based methods do not require the direct solution of a large non-linear system of equations. They also permit the simulator to only solve for the nodes whose waveforms are actually changing. The two most common techniques used to solve the system of nodal equations are the Gauss-Jacobi and the Gauss-Seidel methods [11, 20].

Both the Gauss-Jacobi and the Gauss-Seidel methods are iterative methods. If the circuit is restricted to have a grounded capacitor at each node, then convergence of both methods is guaranteed, and the rate of convergence is at least linear. This compares unfavorably with the provable quadratic convergence rate of the Newton-Raphson algorithm.

One advantage of relaxation-based methods is that they involve solving a set of decoupled equations, while Newton-Raphson methods involve solving a set of simultaneous equations. Therefore the computational cost of each iteration of relaxation-based methods is $O(n)$. This compares well with the sparse LU decomposition runtimes if the number of iterations is small.

Examples of relaxation-based circuit simulators are SPLICE [16], and WASIM [8].

3. The SuperCrystal Approach

SuperCrystal restricts circuit elements to be MOS transistors, linear resistors, and linear grounded capacitors. SuperCrystal models such a circuit as a *control graph* where each control graph node is a *transistor group*.

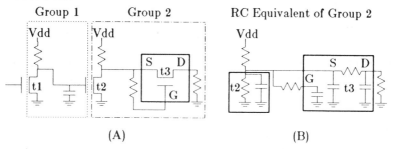

Figure 1: Transistor Groups

Definition 1: A *transistor group* is a collection of circuit elements that are electrically connected by wires or by transistor channels. Notice that under this definition, the gate of a transistor is not in the same transistor group as the source and drain unless explicitly connected, as in transistor *t3* in figure 1A.

For the purposes of waveform estimation, a transistor group maps to an RC network. Figure 1B shows the such a mapping. In this mapping, a MOS transistor is modeled by a non-linear resistor. However, the Raghunathan Thompson algorithm expects linear resistors. Our solution is to partition the time axis into *time steps* and determine a linear approximation to the non-linear resistor within each time step.

Definition 2: The *Control Graph* of a circuit is a digraph where the nodes are transistor groups and where a directed edge (u,v) exists between distinct nodes u and v iff the gate node of some transistor t is in transistor group u, and the source and drain nodes of t are in transistor group v.

The decomposition of the circuit into transistor groups is motivated by the fact that the voltages of the nodes in a transistor group are heavily interdependent, and have to be solved as a simultaneous system of equations. On the other hand, transistor groups interact by modulating the effective resistance of transistors. Note that this is "unidirectional"; if the gate of a transistor belongs in a different transistor group from its source and drain, the voltage at the gate of a transistor affects its source-drain resistance, but not vice versa. So it suffices to ensure that the gate waveforms of transistors in a transistor group are valid before simulating it.

The naive approach of simulating the entire circuit can be improved by exploiting *latency*. We say a transistor group v is *latent* with respect to some input transient applied to a node in another transistor group u, iff there **doesn't** exist a directed path from node u to v in the control graph. Intuitively, this means that a transient applied to a node in transitor group u cannot affect transistor group v. SuperCrystal only simulates transistor groups that are not latent with respect to the applied transient.

4. The RC Model

This section introduces the model of Raghunathan and Thompson for their waveform estimation algorithm.

Definition 3: An *RC network* is a tree on n nodes. With each edge i is associated a nonnegative resistance r_i. With each node k is associated a positive resistance R_k, a positive capacitance C_k, a nonnegative charge Q_k, and a voltage source $v_k \in \{ V_{DD}, GND, \phi \}$, where ϕ indicates no connection.

In the above definition, circuit elements associated with a node exist between the node and GND in the network. Note that this definition does not allow for floating capacitors (capacitors associated with the edges of the graph) in the network.

The incorporation of leakage resistors in the RC network has a twofold effect:

1   Node capacitors need not have to charge to V_{DD}, or discharge to GND, but could take on intermediate voltage values.

2   RC networks can now be driven by more than one source.

When the edges and nodes are all labeled with numbers, these parameters can be grouped together as vectors. An RC network is then denoted by $N(n, r, R, C, Q, V)$, where n is the number of nodes, r is a vector of edge resistances, R is a vector of leakage resistances, C is a vector of node capacitances, Q is a vector of capacitance charges, and V is a vector of node voltage sources. When an RC network is driven by exactly one source, it is called a standard RC network.

4.1. Modeling Voltage Waveforms in an RC Network

The Raghunathan Thompson algorithm defines the approximate time constant of the voltage waveform at node k in an RC network to be

$$\tau_k = \frac{\int_0^\infty [v_k(\infty) - v_k(t)]\, dt}{v_k(\infty) - v_k(0)}$$

We now have the following exponential waveform with time constant τ_k,

$$\bar{v}_k(t) = v_k(\infty) + [v_k(0) - v_k(\infty)] e^{-t/\tau_k}$$

where $v_k(t)$ represents the actual voltage waveform at node k.

Theorem 1. The exponential waveform $\bar{v}_k(t)$ of node k in an RC network satisfies the property

$$\int_0^\infty [v_k(t) - \bar{v}_k(t)] dt = 0$$

In other words, the average error over time is 0.

In an RC network with no input or only step inputs, the Laplace transform [3] of the voltage waveform of a node can be written as

$$V_k(s) = \frac{1}{s} \left[v_k(0) + \frac{c_{1,k}}{1 + t_{1,k}s} + \cdots + \frac{c_{n,k}}{1 + t_{n,k}s} \right]$$

Stated more simply, the voltage waveform can be expressed as a sum of exponentials. This leads to one further property of τ_k, namely that it is a weighted average of the individual time constants.

Theorem 2. τ_k can be expressed as

$$\tau_k = \frac{c_{1,k} t_{1,k} + \cdots + c_{n,k} t_{n,k}}{c_{1,k} + \cdots + c_{n,k}}$$

Although τ_k has many interesting properties, it is not a linear function in the sense that the time constant of the sum of two voltage waveforms is not the sum of the individual time constants. This leads us to define the following parameter.

Definition 4: The parameter D_k is defined as the product of $(v_k(\infty) - v_k(0))$ and τ_k.

$$D_k = [v_k(\infty) - v_k(0)] \cdot \tau_k$$

It can easily be shown that D_k is a linear function.

When the context is not obvious, we will refer to D_k in a network $N(n, r, R, C, Q, V)$ as $D_k(n, r, R, C, Q, V)$.

We need another important result from network theory, the **Superposition Theorem** [3], which can be stated as follows for the purpose of this paper.

Theorem 3. $D_k(n, r, R, C, Q, V)$ is obtained as the sum of the D_k in each network obtained from $N(n, r, R, C, Q, V)$ by setting all but one source to GND.

$$\begin{aligned}
D_k(n, r, R, C, Q, V) = \quad & D_k(n, r, R, C, Q, [v_1]) \\
& + D_k(n, r, R, C, Q, [v_2]) \\
& + \cdots \\
& + D_k(n, r, R, C, Q, [v_n])
\end{aligned} \tag{5}$$

where $[v_i]$ represents the vector V with all driven sources other than v_i set to GND.

Since the Raghunathan Thompson algorithm provides $v_k(0)$, $v_k(\infty)$, and D_k for RC networks driven by a single source, we can use the superposition theorem for estimating waveforms in RC networks driven by several sources.

4.2. Waveform Estimation In Standard RC Networks

Prior to any further discussion, a more constructive definition of standard RC networks is given. A standard RC network is recursively defined to be one of the following:

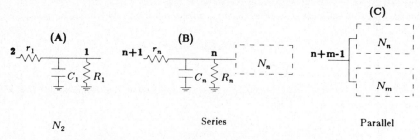

Figure 2: Primitive Element, Series Connection, and Parallel Connection

1   A resistor in series with a nonideal capacitor. The free end of the resistor is the input, labeled 2, and its other end is the output, labeled 1. The other end of the capacitor is grounded. This is shown in figure 2(A). This network will also be referred to as the primitive element or N_2 in the rest of the paper.

2   A series connection of the primitive element and an RC network with n nodes, N_n, to give N_{n+1}. The input of N_{n+1} is the input of N_2, with the input of N_n connected to the output of N_2. The nodes in N_{n+1} are renumbered as follows: The node numbers in N_n remain unchanged. Node 2 of N_2 is relabeled $n+1$. This is shown in figure 2(B).

3   A parallel composition of an n-node network N_n with an m-node network N_m, forming a network N_{n+m-1}. The input of N_{n+m-1} is the input of N_n, as shown in figure 2(C). The nodes in N_{n+m-1} are renumbered as follows: The node numbers in one of them, say N_n, remain the same except for the input node, while the node numbers in N_m get incremented by $n-1$. The input node of N_{n+m-1} gets the label $n+m-1$.

In all three cases, the input node is connected to V_{DD}.

Any N_n has a set of twelve parameters associated with it. While it is beyond the scope of this paper to define them all in detail, some of the more important parameters are defined below.

Parameter	Dimension	Remark
$\rho^{(n)}$	resistance	Effective Resistance between input and GND.
$v_k^{(n)}(\infty)$	voltage	Final voltage of node k.
$D_k^{(n)}$	time $\times$ voltage	Time-Voltage product at node k.
$Q^{(n)}$	charge	Total initial charge in the network.
$\overline{C}^{(n)}$	charge	Total final charge in the network.

From definition 4, the time constant of the voltage waveform at node k is given by

$$\tau_k^{(n)} = \frac{D_k^{(n)}}{v_k^{(n)}(\infty) - v_k^{(n)}(0)}$$

The Raghunathan Thompson algorithm provides simple equations involving only additions and multiplications for the three separate cases: (A) calculating the parameters for N_2, (B) deriving the parameters for N_{n+1} from the parameters for N_2 and N_n, and (C) deriving the parameters for

N_{n+m-1} from the parameters for N_n and N_m. Some of these equations are listed below:

Parameter	Primitive $k=2$	Series $k=n+1$	Parallel $k=n+m-1$
$\rho^{(k)}$	$r_1 + R_1$	$r_n + \dfrac{R_n\,\rho^{(n)}}{R_n + \rho^{(n)}}$	$\dfrac{\rho^{(n)} \cdot \rho^{(m)}}{\rho^{(n)} + \rho^{(m)}}$
$v_i^{(k)}(\infty)$	$V_{DD}\left[\dfrac{R_1}{r_1 + R_1}\right]$	$V_{DD}\left[1 - \dfrac{r_i}{\rho^{(i+1)}}\right] \quad i=n$ $\left[\dfrac{v_n^{(n+1)}(\infty)}{V_{DD}}\right] v_i^{(n)}(\infty) \quad \text{otherwise}$	$v_i^{(n)}(\infty) \qquad 1 \le i < n$ $v_{i-n+1}^{(m)}(\infty) \quad n \le i < n+m-1$
$Q^{(k)}$	$v_1(0) \cdot C_1$	$v_n(0) \cdot C_n + Q^{(n)}$	$Q^{(n)} + Q^{(m)}$
$\overline{C}^{(k)}$	$v_1^{(2)}(\infty) \cdot C_1$	$v_n^{(n+1)}(\infty)\left[C_n + \dfrac{\overline{C}^{(n)}}{V_{DD}}\right]$	$\overline{C}^{(n)} + \overline{C}^{(m)}$

Table 1: Some Equations from the Raghunathan Thompson Algorithm

The set of equations given in [13] provides us with the following simple linear time algorithm for estimating the waveform at a node in the RC network:

> Starting off from the leaf nodes of the tree, build the tree using the serial and parallel connections described earlier, until the entire tree is built. At each stage of tree construction, update the relevant parameters using the equations of [13].

The node waveform can now be approximated as

$$\bar{v}_i(t) = v_i(\infty) + \left[v_i(0) - v_i(\infty)\right] e^{-t/\tau_i}$$

5. Transistor Model

SuperCrystal supports any transistor model that satisfies the following requirements:

1   The transistor model must define a finite set of states. A transistor is required to be in exactly one of these states at a given time. The *final* state is the state that a transistor assumes at $t = \infty$. A transistor has *triggered* when it enters its final state permanently. The transistor model must be able to determine when a transistor triggers.

2   The transistor model must provide the effective resistance as a function of the voltages at its gate, source, and drain nodes and other technology dependent process parameters.

Although there are several models for the MOS transistor in the literature, SuperCrystal currently supports the second-order Shichman-Hodges model [18, 21]. The Shichman-Hodges model defines three states: OFF, TRIODE, and PINCHOFF.

Let $\mathbf{r}(t)$ denote the effective source-drain resistance of transistor k. Using the Shichman-Hodges model, we have:

$$\mathbf{r}(t) = \begin{cases} \infty & v_{gs}(t) < v_t(t) & \text{OFF} \\[2mm] \dfrac{1}{K(v_{gs}(t) - v_t(t))} & v_{gs}(t) \ge v_t(t) \quad v_{gd}(t) \ge v_t(t) & \text{TRIODE} \\[2mm] \dfrac{2v_{ds}(t)}{K(v_{gs}(t) - v_t(t))^2} & v_{gs}(t) \ge v_t(t) \quad v_{gd}(t) < v_t(t) & \text{PINCHOFF} \end{cases} \qquad (1)$$

where K is a constant dependent on the geometry of the transistor and other technology dependent process parameters, and $v_t(t)$ is the transistor threshold voltage, given by:

$$v_t(t) = \begin{cases} v_{to} + \gamma[(v_{sb}(t) + 2_{\phi f})^{1/2} + (2_{\phi f})^{1/2}] & \text{N-Channel} \\ v_{to} - \gamma[(v_{sb}(t) + 2_{\phi f})^{1/2} + (2_{\phi f})^{1/2}] & \text{P-Channel} \end{cases}$$

where v_{to}, γ, and $2_{\phi f}$ are process parameters.

5.1. The Iterative RC Network Algorithm

There are two difficulties to be overcome in modeling a transistor as a linear resistor. Firstly, the equation for $r(t)$ is dependent on the voltages at the source and drain nodes, $v_s(t)$ and $v_d(t)$, which are in turn dependent on $r(t)$. This interdependence motivates the iterative RC network algorithm, described below. Secondly, $r(t)$ is non-linear. We overcome the non-linearity of equation (1) by simulating a transistor group over some small time interval $[\alpha, \beta]$. The average effective resistance, $\bar{r}$ is approximated by an integrating average:

$$\bar{r} = \frac{\int_\beta^\alpha r(t)\, dt}{\beta - \alpha}$$

Notation: $X^{(i)}$ denotes the quantity X during the ith iteration of the iterative RC network algorithm.

The iterative RC network algorithm makes an initial guess, $\bar{r}_k^{(0)}$, for each transistor k using the transistor model and the initial voltages at the nodes of the RC network. The node voltages are then approximated with the Raghunathan Thompson algorithm. The transistor model is then run again on the updated node voltages. This iterative process continues until the effective resistances of the transistors have "stabilized".

Formally, at the ith iteration, we have $\bar{r}_k^{(i)}$. We then run the RC network algorithm to get $v_{s,k}^{(i+1)}(t)$, and $v_{d,k}^{(i+1)}(t)$, the source and drain voltages for each transistor k. These voltage waveforms then give a value for $r_k^{(i+1)}(t)$ which we integrate by the above equation to get a value for $\bar{r}_k^{(i+1)}$.

Definition 5: δ_{trans} is defined as:

$$\delta_{trans}^{(i)} = \frac{\sum_{k \in T} \left[\dfrac{\bar{r}_k^{(i+1)} - \bar{r}_k^{(i)}}{\bar{r}_k^{(i)}} \right]^2}{|T|}$$

where T denotes the set of transistors in the transistor group under consideration. $\delta_{trans}^{(i)}$ is the mean of the squares of the normalized difference between iterations of the effective resistance. Intuitively, $\delta_{trans}^{(i)}$ is a measure of how much the transistor resistances have changed. The algorithm converges when $\delta_{trans}^{(i)}$ falls below some threshold value.

Further details can be found in [10].

6. Transistor Group Firing Sequence

We have seen how a transistor group g is simulated within a time interval. Ideally, the voltage waveforms at the gates of transistors in g should have been computed prior to the simulation of g – in other words, the parents of g in the control graph should, as far as possible, be simulated before g.

Consider the simulation of a circuit for which a transient is applied to some node n in a transistor group g. The following tasks are performed:

1 Cycles in the control graph are detected by running a depth-first search algorithm [1] starting from g. Back edges (edges that complete cycles) are marked.

2 The control graph, minus the marked edges, is then a DAG. A breadth-first search [1] is done on the DAG to decide the order in which the transistor groups are processed by the iterative RC network algorithm.

We note that the DAG defines a partial order on the firing sequence. The breadth-first search algorithm finds a total order compatible with the partial order such that a transistor group is processed only after all ancestor groups in the DAG are processed.

3 The breadth-first search will only process groups that are affected by the input exponential – i.e. groups which can be reached by a directed path from the root group. This way, unaffected groups are not re-computed.

7. Time Steps

As mentioned previously, the resistance of a transistor, $\mathbf{r}(t)$, is a time varying quantity, and cannot be used directly in the corresponding RC network for waveform estimation. Instead, we partition the time axis into small enough intervals so that $\mathbf{r}(t)$ can be assumed to be constant over that time interval.

Notation: $[T_{j-1}, T_j]$ denotes the jth time interval. $X^{[j]}$ denotes the quantity X in the jth time interval.

The iterative RC network algorithm provides us with $v_k{}^{[j]}(t)$ for the jth time interval. Since this is valid for the jth time interval only, we set the voltage at the beginning of the $(j+1)$th time interval to be the voltage reached at the end of the jth time interval:

$$v_k{}^{[j+1]}(0) = v_k{}^{[j]}(T_j - T_{j-1})$$

We then rerun the iterative RC network algorithm.

This iterative process gives us waveforms $v_k{}^{[j]}(t)$ for all $j = 1,2,...$, which we put together piecewise to obtain $v_k(t)$.

7.1. Triggering of Transistors

Although it is theoretically feasible to find $v_k{}^{[j]}(t)$ for $j = 1, 2, \ldots, \infty$, in practice, we need to stop at some finite value for j. This section describes the criterion SuperCrystal uses to determine this value.

Since any transistor changing state can potentially change the topology of the RC network, any measure of convergence can only be applied after all transistors have *triggered*. Once all transistors have triggered, the measure of convergence is the mean of the squares of the difference between iterations of the $v(\infty)$ terms of each node:

Definition 6: $\delta_\tau{}^{[j]}$ is defined as:

$$\delta_\tau{}^{[j]} = \frac{\sum\limits_{k \in N} (v_k{}^{[j]}(\infty) - v_k{}^{[j-1]}(\infty))^2}{|N|}$$

where N is the set of the nodes of the RC network under consideration.

Convergence is reported when $\delta_\tau^{[j]}$ falls below some threshold. Let convergence be reported at the f th time interval. We then define $v_k(t)$ to be:

$$v_k(t) = \begin{cases} v_k^{[j]}(t - \tau_{j-1}) & \tau_{j-1} \leq t < \tau_j \leq \tau_{f-1} \\ v_k^{[f]}(t - \tau_{f-1}) & t > \tau_{f-1} \end{cases}$$

7.2. The Firing Sequence and Time Steps

A naive approach to simulating a circuit would be to run the iterative RC network algorithm on each transistor group in a given firing sequence for each time step. However, empirical evidence [9] has shown that not all transistor groups need to be simulated for each time step. SuperCrystal uses the above time step convergence criterion to determine dynamically if a transistor group needs to be simulated for the next time step. If a transistor group needs to be simulated, then all descendents of that group in the control graph will also be simulated. If there exists descendents of the current group that preceed it in the firing sequence, then simulation is backed up to the earliest such descendent. Otherwise, simulation continues with the next group in the firing sequence.

8. Experimental Results

Contrived Examples				
Circuit	Description	# Nodes	# Fets	# Transistor Groups
osc	3-inverter ring oscillator	5	6	3
nand4	4-input NAND driving pass-gate	12	9	6
Real-Life Examples				
Circuit	Description	# Nodes	# Fets	# Transistor Groups
rsff	1-bit clocked static RS flip-flop	13	16	7
bit	1-bit static register	23	18	13
eq0	16-bit equal-0 comparator	38	40	21
decode	4 to 16 decoder	74	136	24
decrem	16-bit parallel-prefix decrementer	499	932	317

Table 2: Circuit Sizes

Table 2 gives the seven circuits that were simulated using SuperCrystal and SPICE. In addition, the real-life circuits were analyzed by Crystal. For the simulations, SuperCrystal used a subset of the SPICE parameters for the transistor model. In all the experiments, the parameters for the transistor models for both SuperCrystal and SPICE were identical. The Crystal parameters were derived from these SPICE parameters [17]. In addition, SuperCrystal and SPICE simulated the circuits with the same time steps and time intervals.

8.1. Contrived Examples

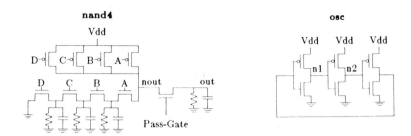

Figure 3: Circuit Diagrams for *nand4* and *osc*.

Figure 3 gives the circuit diagrams for two circuits that demonstrate SuperCrystal's ability to handle "difficult" simulations. For *nand4*, the n-channel transistors on the D, C, and B inputs and the pass transistor have varying voltages at the source terminals. In addition, loading the nodes with parasitic capacitances and leakage resistances "slows" the waveforms.

Steady-state analysis was performed with Input A held at 0V, inputs B, C, and D held at 5V, and the Pass-Gate held at 3V. A 0V→5V step was applied to input A for transient analysis.

The ring oscillator *osc* demonstrates SuperCrystal's ability to handle astable sequential circuits. In addition, there are no load capacitances on the nodes, thus the method by which SuperCrystal estimates the source and drain capacitances on the transistors determines the delay through the inverter and thus the frequency of oscillation. Since *osc* has no steady-state, the initial transient solution was specified with $N1 = 5V$.

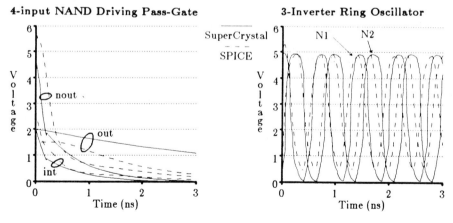

Figure 4: Simulation Waveforms for *nand4* and *osc*.

Figure 4 shows the results from SPICE and SuperCrystal for the *nand4* and *osc* circuits. Super-Crystal models the waveforms in *nand4* quite accurately, despite the fact that the end points of the waveforms are not V_{DD} or GND. In *osc*, SuperCrystal is acceptably close to SPICE even though we do not allow floating capacitors between the gate-source and gate-drain terminals of each transistor in our transistor model.

8.2. Real-life Examples

Simulations were run using Crystal, SuperCrystal, and SPICE on real-life circuit examples. *eq0*, *decode*, and *decrem* are combinational circuits, and *rsff* and *bit* are sequential circuits.

Two simulation runs were performed on *eq0*. In the first run, all inputs were held at 0V for the steady-state analysis. A rising 0V→5V step was applied to least-significant bit for transient analysis. In the second run, steady-state analysis was done with all inputs except for the least significant bit, which was held at 5V. A falling 5V→0V step was applied to the least-significant bit during transient analysis.

For *decode* and *decrem*, the steady-state analysis was done with all inputs at 0V. A rising 0V→5V step was then applied to the least significant bit of the input during transient analysis.

16-bit Equal-0 Comparator

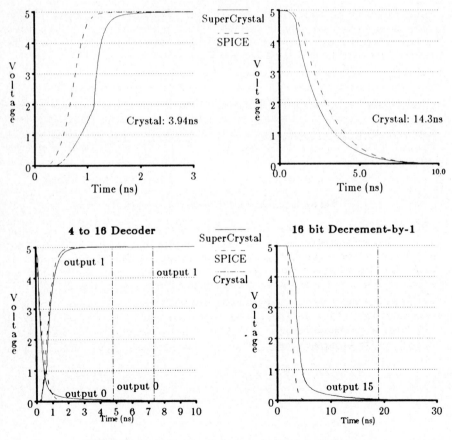

Figure 5: Simulation Waveforms for *eq0*, *decode*, and *decrem*

Figure 5 shows the Crystal delay values, and SuperCrystal and SPICE simulation waveforms for the three combinational circuits. In each case, the SuperCrystal waveform closely tracks the SPICE waveform.

The disparity in the delay for *eq0* arises from the way the circuit is implemented. The inputs to the circuit drive 4-input CMOS NOR gates, with the least significant bit driving the topmost p-transistor in the series chain. It therefore takes longer to pull the output of the NOR gate to V_{DD} through 4 p-transistors, than it takes to pull in to GND through 1 n-transistor.

Single-bit Clocked RS Flip-Flop   **1-bit register**

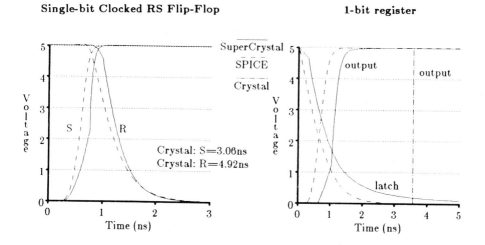

Figure 6: Simulation Waveforms for *rsff* and *bit*.

For *rsff* the steady-state was computed with the flip-flop in its "reset" state and both inputs inactive. A 5V step was applied to the Set input for transient analysis, causing the flip-flop to change state. For *bit* the steady-state was computed with the register storing 0V and input held at 5V, with the register-load disabled. A 0V→5V rising step was applied to *ld* and 5V→0V falling step was simultaneously applied to $\overline{ld}$, thus loading the register with the input value, i.e. 5V.

These two examples were chosen to demostrate SuperCrystal's ability to handle different types of sequential circuits. *rsff* is a pair of back-to-back NAND gates, so that the actual loading and storage functions are realized digitally. *bit* realizes the storage mechanism by a pair of inverters of different strength driving the same node. This node waveform is plotted as *latch*.

8.3. RunTimes

Circuit	Crystal	SPICE	SuperCrystal			SPICE/SuperCrystal Ratio
			Steady-State	Transient	Total	
osc	-	74.0	-	13.2	13.2	5.6
nand4	-	79.7	5.1	2.0	7.1	11.3
bit	0.1	168.3	0.3	20.3	20.6	8.2
rsff	0.1	122.4	0.3	10.0	10.3	11.9
eq0 – up	0.1	296.5	0.6	17.7	18.3	16.2
decode	1.0	1478.4	1.5	31.3	32.8	45.1
eq0 – down	0.1	342.2	0.6	3.3	3.9	87.7
decrem	1.0	19940.3	12.2	33.0	45.2	441.2

Table 3: SuperCrystal and SPICE Runtimes.

Table 3 shows the runtimes of Crystal, SuperCrystal, and SPICE. Note that the SuperCrystal runtimes scale more favorably than SPICE.

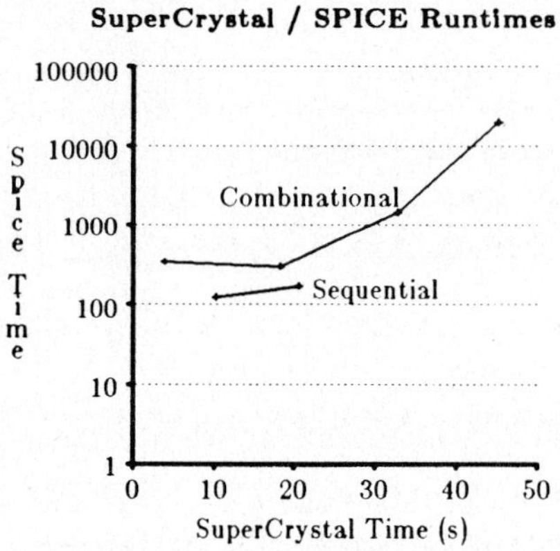

SuperCrystal / SPICE Runtimes

Figure 7: Comparison Plot of SuperCrystal and SPICE Runtimes.

Figure 7 is a comparison plot of SuperCrystal and SPICE runtimes. Note that the SPICE scale is logarithmic. These results show that SuperCrystal is more than just a constant factor faster than SPICE. The gains in runtime appear to increase non-trivially as circuits get larger. In addition, whereas the SPICE runtimes appear in be a function of the size and not the topology of the circuit, the SuperCrystal runtimes appear to depend on both size and topology. In particular, the distinction between combinational and sequential circuits is more pronounced in the SuperCrystal case as is evident from the figure.

9. Conclusions and Future Work

This paper described SuperCrystal, a computer program for the simulation of full-custom VLSI chips. The highlights of SuperCrystal are briefly listed below:

1   The time axis is divided into time steps.

2   In each time step, a transistor circuit maps to a linear RC network for the purpose of waveform estimation.

3   Node voltage waveforms are single time constant exponentials.

4   Node capacitors need not charge all the way to V_{DD}, or discharge all the way to GND, but could take on any real number between V_{DD} and GND.

5   Node waveforms are speedily calculated in the equivalent RC network.

6   Transistor channel resistances are not independent of gate waveforms; instead, SuperCrystal distinguishes between the TRIODE and PINCHOFF modes of operation, and arrives at an effective resistance over a given time step that is a function of the gate, source and drain waveforms.

7   SuperCrystal allows the introduction of other transistor models. In particular, models used by the various levels of SPICE can be incorporated. Table-lookup models can also be incorporated.

A version of SuperCrystal has been coded and is running on Berkeley 4.3 UNIX. The program has been distributed to various on-campus test-sites. We expect a version available for external users shortly.

Further work is required in the following areas. Empirical evidence indicates that the iterative RC network algorithm converges quickly for the MOS circuits analyzed. It still remains to be shown that it will converge in all cases.

Further studies are required on the effect of varying the length of timesteps. The relationship between the convergence criteria, δ_τ and δ_{trans}, and the length of the timestep needs careful investigation.

We are currently developing a new algorithm to obtain exponential approximations to the waveforms for all n nodes in a transistor group in $O(n)$ time.

Finally, extensive code optimization needs to be done to achieve faster running times.

10. Acknowledgements

The authors would like to thank Prof. John Ousterhout for graciously allowing us to look at the Crystal source code. Thanks are also due to Prof. Alberto Sangiovanni-Vincentelli for many useful comments, and Prof. Eugene Lawler for his helpful support throughout the course of this project.

References

1.   A. Aho, J. E. Hopcroft, and J. D. Ullman, *The Design and Analysis of Computer Algorithms,* Addison-Wesley, Reading, Mass., 1974.

2.   R.E. Bryant, "A Switch-Level Simulation Model for Integrated Logic Circuits," *MIT/LCS/TR-259,* Doctoral Thesis, MIT, Mar. 1981.

3.   C.A. Desoer and E.S. Kuh, *Basic Circuit Theory,* McGraw Hill, New York, 1969.

4.   N.P. Jouppi, "TV: An nMOS Timing Analyzer," *Proc. 3rd CalTech Conf. VLSI,* pp. 71-86, Mar. 1983.

5.   Young Hwan Kim, "ELOGIC: A Relaxation-Based Switch-Level Simulation Technique," *UCB/ERL M86/2,* UC Berkeley, 3 Dec 1985.

6.   T. Lin and C.A. Mead, "Signal Delay in General RC Networks," *IEEE Trans. CAD*, vol. CAD-3, pp. 331-349, Oct. 1984.

7.   L.W. Nagel, "SPICE2: A Computer Program to Simulate Semiconductor Circuits," *ERL Memo ERL-M520*, UC Berkeley, May 1975.

8.   Sani R. Nassif and Stephen W. Director, "WASIM: A Waveform Based Simulator for VLSICs," *Proc. ICCAD*, pp. 29-31, 1985.

9.   A.R. Newton and A.L. Sangiovanni-Vincentelli, "Relaxation-Based Electrical Simulation," *IEEE Transactions on Computer-Aided Design*, vol. CAD-3, pp. 308-330, Oct. 1984.

10. Antony P-C Ng, A. Raghunathan, and Clark D. Thompson, "Incorporating Input Slopes in the Linear RC Model for MOS VLSI Signal Delays," *Technical Report (in preparation)*.

11. J.M. Ortega and W.C. Rheinboldt, *Iterative Solution of Nonlinear Equations in Several Variables*, New York Academic Press, 1970.

12. J.K. Ousterhout, "Crystal: A Timing Analyzer for nMOS VLSI Circuits," *Report No. UCB/CSD 83/115*, Computer Sciences Division, UC Berkeley, Jan. 1983.

13. A. Raghunathan and C.D. Thompson, "Signal Delay in RC Trees with Charge Sharing or Leakage," *Report No. UCB/CSD 85/243*, Computer Science Division, UC Berkeley, June 1985.

14. A. Raghunathan and C.D. Thompson, "Signal Delay in RC Trees with Charge Sharing or Leakage," *Proc. Nineteenth Asilomar Conference on Circuits, Systems and Computers*, Nov. 6-8, 1985.

15. J. Rubinstein, P. Penfield, and M. Horowitz, "Signal Delays in RC Tree Networks," *IEEE Transactions on Computer-Aided Design*, vol. CAD-2, pp. 202-211, July 1983.

16. Resve A. Saleh, "Iterated Timing Analysis and SPLICE1," *UCB/ERL M84/2*, University of California, Berkeley, Jan 1984.

17. W.S. Scott, R.N. Mayo, G. Hamachi, and J.K. Ousterhout, "1986 VLSI Tools: Still More Works by the Original Artists," *Report No. UCB/CSD 86/272*, Computer Science Division, UC Berkeley, December 1985.

18. H. Shichman and D. A. Hodges, "Modeling and simulation of insulated gate field-effect transistor switching circuits," *IEEE J. Solid-State Circuits*, vol. SC-3, pp. 285-289, Sept., 1968.

19. E. Tamura, K. Ogawa, and T. Nakano, "Path Delay Analysis for Hierarchical Building Block Layout System," *Proc. 20th Design Automation Conf.*, pp. 403-410, 1983.

20. J. Varga, *Matrix Iterative Analysis*, Prentice Hall, 1969.

21. A. Vladimirescu and S Liu, "The Simulation of MOS Integrated Circuits Using SPICE2," *UCB/ERL M80/7*, University of California, Berkeley, Oct 1980.

22. J. White and A.L. Sangiovanni-Vincentelli, "Relax2.1: A Waveform Relaxation Based Circuit Simulation Program," *Proc. 1984 Custom Integrated Circuits Conference*, pp. 232-236, May 1984.

VLSI '87, C.H. Séquin (editor)
Elsevier Science Publishers B.V. (North-Holland)
© IFIP, 1988

A CLOSED-FORM EXPRESSION FOR SIGNAL DELAY IN CMOS-DRIVEN BRANCHED
TRANSMISSION LINES

Ernst-Helmut Horneber and Wolfgang Mathis

Institut für Allgemeine Elektrotechnik, Technische Universität
Braunschweig, Postfach 3329, 3300 Braunschweig, FRG

In this paper an expression is given which allows a fairly accurate
calculation of the signal propagation delay of interconnections in
LSI cell designs. It takes account of the delay of CMOS gates driving
the branched transmission line and the driven gate loading the line.
Some simulation results are presented which show the accuracy and
efficiency of this approach.

1. INTRODUCTION

In order to achieve a correct design of semicustom MOS LSI circuits, not only
logical and geometrical correctness of a layout has to be verified but also
signal delays of lines connecting layout cells have to be considered to ascer-
tain the desired functions. Typically an aluminium layer is preferred for long
lines but branching and crossing of lines force to layout parts of a line in
high-resistive polysilicon layer. Also the gates loading a branched line and
the nonlinear characteristic of the gate driving the line have to be taken into
account in order to obtain accurate timing informations. It would be possible
to calculate these signal propagation delays by appropriate modelling of the
transmission lines and applying circuit simulation. But this approach is not
feasible with integrated semicustom design systems which demand fast timing
verification to enable an interactive improvement of cell placement and routing.

Commonly the signal delay is estimated. For that purpose a transmission line is
usually substituted by a RC line or a RC tree in the case of a branched line.
Sakurai [1] has shown that this modelling has to be done with care to achieve
acceptable results. Depending on the driving and load conditions suitable T or
π ladder circuit models have to be chosen. The widely used one-step L ladder
circuit was found to be a poor approximation. On the other hand application of
better models with three to five-step T or π ladder circuits requires considerable computational effort. Another method proposed by Penfield and Rubinstein
[2] is the calculation of upper and lower bounds for the signal waveforms at
the load terminals of a RC tree network driven by an independent voltage source.
Application of this approach has shown that the bounds can differ for more than
30% from the exact step response so that it is scarcely possible to deduce a
measure for transmission delay which is sufficiently close to the exact results
to be used in an interactive semicustom design system.

In this paper a closed form expression for signal propagation delay is developed. It is based on a delay approximation for a capacitively loaded straight interconnection line as given by Sakurai [1] for a limited range of loading. Numerical results show that the linear delay estimation is valid for the entire range of capacitive loading. Furthermore this approach is extended to branched transmission lines. The nonlinear characteristic of the driving gate is taken into account by applying a first order transistor model. This results in a formula for signal delay estimation which allows fairly accurate predictions using two to three orders of magnitude less computer time than SPICE simulations.

2. DEFINITION OF DELAY

Most investigations of signal propagation delays use either Elmore's delay definition or the definition of rise and fall time, i.e. the time a signal needs to change between 10% and 90% of the maximum signal value. Elmore [3] has defined a delay T_D as the first moment of the impulse response. This measure may be efficient for theoretical investigations but it does not provide a good prediction of the timing behaviour of interconnected MOS circuits. Another delay definition is the time required for a response to reach the threshold voltage of a MOS transistor. This kind of definition causes some problems due to threshold voltage shift in NMOS circuits with back gate bias. In most applications acceptable delay definitions can be found by simulating typical driver-gate/ line/ receiver-gate combinations. By this approach Carter and Guise defined the delay time as 62% criterion of the average of pulling-up and pulling-down [4].

By similar simulations of interconnected CMOS gates a delay time definition corresponding to a change of the output signal of 0.7 VDD has shown to give reasonable results. In the case of different pull-up and pull-down times the worst case is taken. If necessary, this definition can easily be changed which only results in a change of the weighting factors in the delay time formula given below.

3. TRANSMISSION LINE MODEL

In [1] Sakurai modelled a single MOSFET driven transmission line by a step voltage source with resistance R_T, a distributed RC line with total resistance R and capacitance C and a load capacitor C_T (Fig. 1).

The output step response in Laplace domain can be written as

$$V_0(s')/V_{DD} = H(s')/s' \qquad (1)$$

with the voltage transfer function

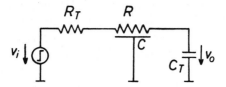

FIGURE 1

Distributed RC line model.

$$H(s') = [\cos(jg)(1+s'r_Tc_T) - j \sin(jg)(s')^{1/2}(r_T+c_T)]^{-1} \tag{2}$$

where

$$g = (s')^{1/2} \tag{3}$$

is the normalized transfer constant and

$$r_T = R_T/R$$

$$c_T = C_T/C$$

$$s' = sRC = sT \tag{4}$$

$$t' = t/T$$

are the normalized driver resistance, load capacitance, frequency, and time.

Applying Heaviside's second expansion theorem [5] the time domain response can be written as [1]

$$v_o(t')/V_{DD} = 1 + \sum_{n=1}^{\infty} K_n e^{-\sigma_n t} \tag{5}$$

where

$$K_n = \frac{(-1)^n \cdot 2[(1+r_T^2\sigma_n^2)(1+c_T^2\sigma_n^2)]^{1/2}}{(\sigma_n)^{1/2}[(1+r_T^2\sigma_n^2)(1+c_T^2\sigma_n^2)+(r_T+c_T)(1+r_Tc_T\sigma_n)]} \tag{6}$$

and the poles of (1) : $0,\sigma_1,\sigma_2,\ldots,\sigma_n$ can be determined from

$$\tan\left[(\sigma_n)^{1/2}\right] = \frac{1 - \sigma_n c_T r_T}{(r_T + c_T)\sigma_n^{1/2}} \quad , \qquad n - \frac{3}{2} < \frac{\sigma_n}{\pi} < n - \frac{1}{2} \ . \tag{7}$$

Sakurai has solved equation (7) numerically. He suggested to neglect the third and higher terms of (5) to get an excellent approximation for the step response in the range of r_T and $c_T < 1$

$$v_o(t')/V_{DD} = 1 + K_1 e^{-\sigma_1 t} \ . \tag{8}$$

Introducing the delay time $t_{0.7} = t(v_o = 0.7\ V_{DD})$ as stated above, calculation of $t_{0.7}$ from (8) as function of r_T or c_T shows that it depends nearly linear on both r_T and c_T in the range $r_T, c_T \leq 1$.

Consequently, delay can be written as

$$t'_{0.7} \approx \alpha_1 + \alpha_2 c_T + \alpha_3 r_T + \alpha_4 r_T c_T \tag{9}$$

where α_3 is equal to α_2 because [8] is symmetric in r_T and c_T. Taking into account that the influence of the driving gate shall be considered separately, equ. (9) reduces to

$$t'_{0.7} = \alpha_1 + \alpha_2 c_T \ . \tag{10}$$

Weighting factor α_1 can be determined from (8) setting $c_T = 0$ to

$$\alpha_1 = 0.59 \ ,$$

factor α_2 depends on c_T and increases by 7% between $c_T = 0.1$ and $c_T = 1$. To simplify the analysis the maximum value

$$\alpha_2 = 1.21$$

is taken resulting in an error for $t'_{0.7}$ which is smaller than 1.5% in the range $0 \leq c_T \leq 1$. Thus we get the approximation

$$t_{0.7} = 0.59 \ RC + 1.21 \ RC_T \qquad (11)$$

for the signal delay of a single transmission line.

In order to model a transmission line with tree structure the branched line is now decomposed into single sections with no side branches. Each section shall be placed either in polysilicon or in aluminium layer. Interconnections layed out in aluminium will be modelled as capacitances. They can be considered as node capacitances at the nodes between sections in poly layer. For each of these sections a delay time can be calculated using (11). However, for each single section the load capacitance C_T does now consist of all capacitances between the output node of the actual section and all succeeding nodes loading this section. This follows from applying a theorem of Lin and Mead ([6], Corollary 10). Unfortunately we move into the range $c_T>1$ where $|K_1|$ decreases rapidly as shown in fig. 2. Hence $|K_1| \cdot \exp(-\sigma_1 t'_{0.7})$ deviates from the value 0.3, so that (8) is no longer a valid approximation of (5). On the other hand, the numerical results fig. 3 obtained from solving the partial differential equations show a linear dependence of $t_{0.7}$ from c_T. Thus, the above approximation can be continued in the range of $c_T>1$ but K_1 can no longer be understood as the variable defined in (6). Rather it is interpreted as the constant value $\overline{K}_1 = K_1(c_T=1) = -1.14$. This leads to the new approximation

$$v_0(t')/V_{DD} = 1 - 1.14 \ e^{-\sigma_1(c_T) \cdot t'} \qquad (12)$$

which allows to understand α_2 to be constant. Thus, equ. (11) remains valid. The resulting estimation for the delay $t'_{0.7}$ can be seen in fig. 2 showing that $|\overline{K}_1| \cdot \exp(-\sigma_1 t'_{0.7})$ is slightly smaller than 0.3 for $c_T \leq 1$ and increases up to 0.34 for $c_T \gg 1$. As consequence, equ. (12) can be expected to give reasonable results for all possible values of c_T.

Furthermore, equ. (12) can be interpreted as the step response of a suitable RC circuit with an initially charged capacitor. This allows to apply a theorem of Lin and Mead ([6], Theorem 9) which states that the total delay of a path in a tree network is given by the sum of the delays of the single portions of the unique path between the input and the actual output. Therefore the total delay of a path with k sections between the input node of the branched transmission line and an output node can be written as

$$t_{0.7} = \sum_{\nu=1}^{k} R_\nu (0.59 \ C_\nu + 1.21 \sum_\mu C_\mu) \qquad (13)$$

where C_ν is the capacitance of transmission line section ν and C_μ denotes the capacitances between the output node of section ν and all succeeding branches loading this section.

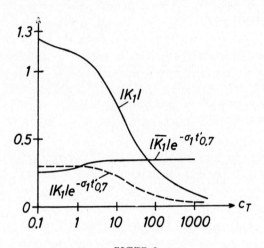

FIGURE 2

Effect of pole σ_1 and its approximation.

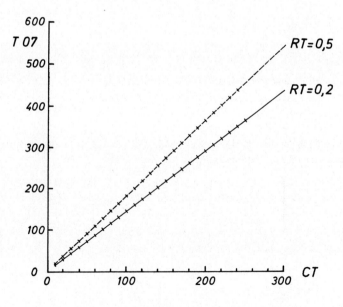

FIGURE 3

Influence of capacitiv load on delay.

4. LOAD AND DRIVER MODEL

The load of each branch of the transmission line is effected by the input capacitance of the driven gate. Albeit of the nonlinearity of the MOS gate capacitance depending on the gate voltage, the load can be modelled with sufficient accuracy by a constant capacitance

$$C_o = (W_p L_p + W_n L_n) \; C_{ox}' \tag{14}$$

where W, L are the width and length of the gates of the p-load and n-driver transistor of the driven CMOS gate. C_{ox}' denotes the oxide capacitance per unit square. Load capacitance C_o can be included in (13), thus it is taken as a term of C_μ.

To model the influence of the driving gate on the total delay, this gate is interpreted as an additional RC circuit which represents the first portion of the transmission network. That implies that the effective load capacitance C_L which is needed to calculate the gate delay includes not only the gate output capacitance C_D but also the total capacitance C_{tot} of the remaining part of the transmission network. As in most practical cases C_{tot} is much larger than C_D the nonlinear portion of the resulting capacitance can be ignored without significant capacitance errors.

Hence

$$C_L = C_{tot} + A_{Dp} C_{Ap} + P_{Dp} C_{Pp} + A_{Dn} C_{An} + P_{Dn} C_{Pn} \tag{15}$$

where A_D and P_D denote the drain area and length of drain junction perimeter, C_A/C_P are the drain junction capacitance per unit area/perimeter each for the PMOS and NMOS transistor.

To calculate the driver delay a first order model is used for the drain-source current i_{DS} in the triode region and in saturation

$$i_{DS} = \begin{cases} \pm \; \beta [\, (v_{GS} - V_T) v_{DS} - v_{DS}^2/2] \, , & \text{triode region} \\[2mm] \pm \; \beta (v_{GS} - V_T)^2/2 \; , & \text{saturation} \end{cases} \tag{16}$$

where the positive sign is valid for NMOS, the negative for PMOS. With μ denoting the carrier mobility

$$\beta = \mu C_{ox}' W/L \tag{17}$$

which gives different values for NMOS and PMOS transistors.

Using the models fig. 4 which represent the pull-up phase of a CMOS inverter
with input $v_G=0$ we get

$$C_L \frac{dv_o}{dt} = \text{ß}_p (V_{DD} + V_{Tp})^2/2 \tag{18}$$

in saturation and

$$C_L \frac{dv_o}{dt} = \text{ß}_p [(V_{DD} + V_{Tp})(V_{DD} - v_o) - (v_o - V_{DD})^2/2] \tag{19}$$

in the triode region. Integrating (17) from $v_o=0$ to $v_o=-V_{Tp}$ (limit of saturation region) and (18) from $v_o = -V_{Tp}$ to $v_o=0.7\ V_{DD}$ (triode region) yields the
driver delay time

$$T_{Ip} = \frac{C_L}{\text{ß}_p} \left[\frac{|V_{Tp}|}{(V_{DD}-|V_{Tp}|)^2} + \frac{\ln(\frac{17}{3} - \frac{20}{3}|V_{Tp}|/V_{DD})}{2(V_{DD}-|V_{Tp}|)} \right] . \tag{20}$$

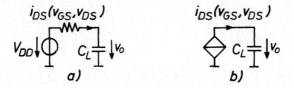

FIGURE 4
Driver models for

a) pull-up   b) pull-down

The same equation holds for the pull-down phase $(V_{DD} \geq v_o \geq 0.3\ V_{DD})$ if ß_p is substituted by ß_n and V_{Tp} by V_{Tn}. Generally, a driver circuit is designed to generate a symmetric signal with $T_{Ip}=T_{In}$. If not, the maximum driver delay should
be taken to get a worst case estimation. Thus the total delay of the driver/
branched transmission line/load combination is given by

$$T_{0.7} = t_{0.7} + \max\{T_{Ip}, T_{In}\} . \tag{21}$$

5. RESULTS

To evaluate (20) the program DECADE (Delay Calculation of Driven Lines) was written and verified by comparing its results with SPICE2 simulations of the wiring of gate array and standard cell layouts. To get reliable results each poly section of a line was modelled by a five step π ladder circuit for the SPICE2 simulation. Portions of the line layed out in aluminium layer were modelled as capacitance.

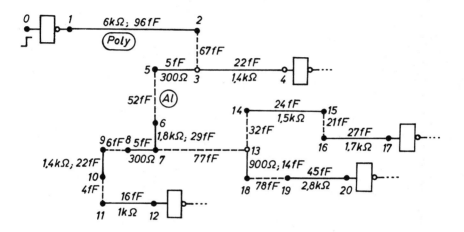

FIGURE 5   Example of a transmission line.

A typical example for a branched transmission line is shown in fig. 5. It consists of 11 sections in poly layer and 8 sections in aluminium layer. A comparison of the calculated delays between node 0 and the driven gates is shown in table 1.

Table 1. Calculated delay between node 0 and load

node	DECADE	SPICE2	error
4	9.51 ns	9.70 ns	-1.96%
12	11.84 ns	11.84 ns	0%
17	11.95 ns	11.93 ns	+0.17%
20	12.15 ns	12.10 ns	-0.41%

In spite of the wide range of c_T from 3.6 up to a value of 178.4 for the section between nodes 3 and 5, the total error is smaller than 2% of the actual delay. As it can be expected from the approximation, the delay estimation has a negative error for short lines which includes that c_T is in the lower range.

For long transmission lines the average c_T exceeds 1 which results in a positive error. For this example the run time was reduced by a factor of 150 compared with SPICE2. Other examples have shown that for larger nets a reduction of the run time up to three orders of magnitude can be attained while the maximum absolute error for delay time is smaller than 5%.

ACKNOWLEGDEMENTS

The authors would like to thank Rolf Leppin for his help in this project and the implementation of the program.

REFERENCES

[1] Sakurai, T., Approximation of Wiring Delay in MOSFET LSI, IEEE J. Solid-State Circuits, vol. SC-18, no. 4, Aug. 1983, pp. 418-426
[2] Penfield, P. and Rubinstein, J., Signal Delay in RC Tree Networks, Proc. 2nd Caltech Conf. VLSI, March 1981, pp. 169-283
[3] Elmore, W.C., The transient response of damped linear networks with partial regard to wideband amplifiers, J. App. Phys., vol. 19, no. 1, Jan. 1948, pp. 55-63
[4] Carter, D.L. and Guise, D.F., Effects of Interconnections on Submicron Chip Performance, VLSI Design, Jan. 1984, pp. 63-68
[5] Van der Pol, B. and Bremmer, H., Operational Calculus Based on the Two-sided Laplace Integral (Cambrigde University Press, 1950), Chap. VII.10
[6] Lin, T.-M. and Mead, C.A., Signal Delay in General RC Networks, IEEE Trans. CAD, vol. 3, no. 4, Oct. 1984, pp. 331-349

VLSI '87, C.H. Séquin (editor)
Elsevier Science Publishers B.V. (North-Holland)
© IFIP, 1988

VECTORIZATION OF THE LU-DECOMPOSITION FOR CIRCUIT SIMULATION

L. K. Steger

Siemens AG, Corporate Research and Technology,
Otto-Hahn-Ring 6, D-8000 Munich 83, FRG §

An algorithm is presented for the efficient LU-decomposition of sparse matrices with a highly irregular sparseness structure on vector processors.The algorithm is based on the MVA algorithm proposed by Yamamoto and Takahashi [2]. The algorithm is numerically equivalent to the classical Gauss algorithm. The improved performance is achieved by reordering the sequence of operations.

The algorithm was developed for application to circuit simulation. Some examples are presented from the analysis of highly integrated electrical circuits.

1. INTRODUCTION

The development of large-scale integrated circuits relies on software tools for design and verification. For the full-custom design, the simulation of the electrical behaviour of circuits is one of the most challenging tasks. E.g. the design of memory chips that are state-of-the-art affords at present a circuit simulator that is capable of producing reliable results for circuits with up to ten thousand transistors within reasonable time. In the future, the size of the circuits that have to be analyzed will increase considerably.

The classical program for circuit simulation is SPICE2 [1] whose first version was published in 1975. Many efforts have been made since then to improve the algorithms and their implementations used in SPICE2, but the basic ideas are still competitive with alternative approaches because of their general applicability. Like our simulator SPICE2-S, many circuit simulation programs of our day are based on this program. To meet the requirements of progressing technology, the physical models and the user interface have been exchanged in SPICE2-S, but the basic numerical algorithms and the data structures have not been modified substantially.

The analysis of circuits composed of several thousand transistors consumes such an amount of computer resources, especially CPU-time, that the use of the most high performance computer systems is justified. So it was decided to run SPICE2-S on our vectorprocessor VP200 [3]. The first experiences have shown that there would be no speedup without a thorough revision of the time consuming parts of SPICE2-S. The kind of simulation that is most time consuming is the transient analysis of circuits. Mathematically this is equivalent to the solution of an initial value problem for an algebro-differential system of equations [1]. After discretizing the time variable, a nonlinear system of equations has to be solved for every time step. The solution of this system is approximated by performing some iterations of Newtons method. For every iteration a system of linear equations has to be solved. The structure of this linear system is invariant throughout the whole analysis, whereas the values of the entries change with every Newton iteration. Most of the computing time is spent

§ Work supported in part by Bundesministerium für Forschung und Technologie under contract number NT 269.

calculating the entries of this linear equation system and in solving it. For small circuits up to one thousand transistors, the computation of the matrix is more time consuming than the solution. Whereas for large circuits with more than two thousand transistors, the solution time becomes dominant. In the following, our efforts to speedup the solution of the linear systems will be described.

2. TEST EXAMPLES

All the algorithms presented in the following will be tested by running four example problems. All these examples stem from the development of integrated circuits in MOS-technology.

Table 1 : Test examples

circuit	ex1	ex2	ex3	ex4
number of transistors	642	828	1895	4822
number of equations	342	376	1040	2027
sparsity	97%	97%	99%	99%

Different transistor models were used. Example ex3 is computed with the well-known MOS transistor model level 3 of SPICE2.G5 [5] , example ex1 with an improved version of the level 3 model developped at the Siemens laboratories. For the examples ex2 and ex4 a pseudo-physical model with local iteration of an internal 'channel node' [6] was chosen.

In the original version the loading of the matrix and the solution of the linear systems took the following percentages of the computing time for the transient analysis.

Table 2 : Relative CPU-times for load and solve

circuit	ex1	ex2	ex3	ex4
load	72%	80%	51%	29%
solve	16%	18%	43%	71%
overhead	12%	2%	6%	0.3%

3. DATA STRUCTURE

Before discussing the algorithms, the data structure [1] used to store the matrix will be considered. Our efforts to speedup the algorithm for the LU-decomposition were made under the assumption that this data structure should not be changed so that the modifications of the program would be local to the subroutines performing the LU-decomposition.

Let N be the dimension of the linear system, NUT the number of nonzero elements in the upper triangle and NLT the number of nonzero elements in the lower triangle. There are five arrays used for storing the matrix :

INTEGER IUR(N), IUC(NUT), ILC(N), ILR(NLT)
REAL*8 VALUE(N + NUT + NLT)

The four arrays IUR, IUC, ILC, ILR are storing the structure of the matrix. They are computed once at the beginning of the transient analysis and kept constant afterwards.

IUR(I)	gives the index from where on the elements of the I-th row and above the diagonal are stored within the arrays IUC and VALUE
IUC	gives the column indices of the elements of the upper triangle grouped by consecutive rows
ILC(I)	gives the index from where on the elements of the I-th column and below the diagonal are stored within the arrays ILR and VALUE
ILR	gives the row indices of the elements of the lower triangle grouped by consecutive columns

The values of the matrix entries are stored in the array VALUE. The first N places are occupied by the diagonal, followed by the elements of the upper triangle and finally of the lower triangle.

4. THE ORIGINAL ALGORITHM

The algorithm used in SPICE2-S followed the lines of the classical LU-decomposition by Gauss. For a matrix in full storage mode this algorithm works like

```
for I = 1 to N-1 do
   for J = I + 1 to N do
      A(J,I) = A(J,I)/A(I,I) ;
      for K = I + 1 to N do
         A(J,K) = A(J,K)-A(J,I)*A(I,K)          (*)
      end
   end
end
```

The problem in adapting this algorithm to the case of sparse matrices represented by a data structure like described above is in the formulation of the statement marked by (*). The access to all the elements of a column below the diagonal and to all the elements of a row above the diagonal can be accomplished easily. The problem results from the need to compute the index of the element A(J,K) within the array VALUE in statement (*).

This problem was solved within SPICE2 by searching explicitly for the index one is looking for. This solution is well suited for machines with rather small main memory, say less than eight megabytes, so that storage for temporary variables is rare. The CPU-time spent searching for the unknown index is acceptable because the lengths of the search loops are very small, reflecting the high sparsity of the matrices that are typically encountered in circuit simulation.The CPU-times measured for one LU-decomposition on the VP200 using the original algorithm of SPICE2 are given in table 3. The table includes the CPU-times for scalar execution i.e. execution without any use of vector instructions and for vector execution i.e. with vector instructions included in the code generated by the FORTRAN77-compiler of the VP200 system.

On the vectorprocessor VP200 this algorithm is unacceptable for two reasons. First, the available vector instructions are used in a very inefficient manner. Although the

L.K. Steger

Table 3 : CPU-times [ms] for one LU-decomposition

circuit	ex1	ex2	ex3	ex4
original (scalar)	26.9	58.2	298.2	2947.9
original (vector)	27.8	60.2	307.8	3043.1

search loops are vectorized by the compiler, the vectorized version is slower than the scalar version because of the extremely short vector lengths of the search loops and the overhead necessary to perform the search operation by vector instructions. The arithmetical operations are not executed by vector instructions at all because these operations are done in the surrounding loops of the innermost loops. Second, the big main memory of the vector processor is not used for shortening the CPU-time. In the well-known trade-off between memory and CPU-time, the above solution favours small memory needs. This strategy seems unreasonable for the efficient use of a vectorprocessor.

5. VECTORIZATION OF THE ORIGINAL ALGORITHM

In a first attempt to achieve a positive vectorization effect, some index lists were introduced to eliminate the index calculation. By introducing three arrays

INTEGER IUPD(NUPD), IUPDL(NUPD), IUPDU(NUPD)

to store the indices for the operands of the update-operations (*), where NUPD is the total number of update-operations, the operations (*) can be written as

VALUE(IUPD(J)) = VALUE(IUPD(J)) - VALUE(IUPDL(J))*VALUE(IUPDU(J))

The index lists IUPD, IUPDL and IUPDU are calculated in a preprocessing routine and are invariant throughout the entire time analysis. The advantages of these modifications are twofold. First, the number of operations is reduced by eliminating the search loops. This should result in a shorter execution time independent of the vector unit just by using the big main memory. Second, the arithmetical operations are executed by vector instructions. This can be achieved by the compiler in a straightforward manner because the instruction set of the VP200 includes indirect load and store instructions. So we expect also a considerable positive vectorization effect. Some care has to be taken to reduce conflicting accesses to the memory banks of the vectorprocessor. In our context this means that subsequences of identical indices within the arrays IUPDL and IUPDU should be avoided. This can be achieved by sequencing the update-operations of one elimination step not row by row but by diagonals.

Table 4 : CPU-times [ms] for one LU-decomposition

circuit	ex1	ex2	ex3	ex4
COA (scalar)	8.69	12.7	50.4	311.8
COA (vector)	5.08	4.70	13.1	43.4

In the following we shall call this algorithm the conventional order algorithm COA.This name pronounces the fact that the order of the arithmetical operations is still the order of the classical Gauss algorithm.The CPU-times for this algorithm are given in table 4.The speedup was achieved by increasing the memory need. There has to be supplied memory for the index lists IUPD, IUPDU and IUPDL as given by table 5.

Table 5 : Additional memory for algorithm COA

circuit	ex1	ex2	ex3	ex4
Additional memory (MB)	0.09	0.13	0.56	3.71

6. THE MAXIMAL VECTORIZATION ALGORITHM

Most of the work that has to be done for a LU-decomposition consists of the update operations (*). These update operations can be executed in parallel for each step of the Gauss algorithm. This inherent parallelism of the Gauss algorithm is used by the vectorization method described in section 5.

The sparseness of the matrices from circuit simulation is so extreme that the number of updates in one step of the Gauss algorithm is in most cases just some ten operations. These blocks of update operations are interspersed with multiplications of the rest column which can also be performed in parallel, but with an even shorter vectorlength. To raise the vectorization effect, a modification of the algorithm has to be found that works with a higher degree of parallelism i.e. with longer vectors. In Yamamoto/Takahashi [2] the so called maximal vectorization algorithm MVA was proposed for this purpose.

The basic idea of this algorithm is the data flow principle: 'An operation is executed as soon as all its operands are available'. To every multiplication and every update operation, a level of execution is assigned. The level is defined as the first level upon which all the operands are available.

To determine the levels of the operations, the preprocessing has to be extended. A temporary matrix M is introduced which is identical in structure to the circuit matrix. The entries of M represent the actual level of execution of the corresponding matrix component. The determination of the levels runs as follows:

```
clear M ;
for I = 1 to N-1
    for all { J | A(J,I) ≠ 0 and J > I }
        M(J,I) = 1 + max{M(J,I),M(I,I)} ;
        M(J,I) is assigned as level to the operation A(J,I) = A(J,I)/A(I,I) ;
        for all { K | A(I,K) ≠ 0 and K > I }
            M(J,K) = 1 + max{M(J,K),M(J,I)-1,M(I,K)} ;
            M(J,K) is assigned as level to the operation
                            A(J,K) = A(J,K)-A(J,I)*A(I,K) ;
        end ;
    end ;
end ;
```

All the operations with the same level of execution can be executed in parallel. The multiplications and update operations of the same level are put together to form a 'stage'.

The classical Gauss algorithm can be interpreted as ordering the operations in N-1 stages. By reducing the number of stages the number of operations per stage should increase on the average, and thereby the effect of vectorization should be improved since the arithmetic operations are executed by vector instructions of greater vectorlength.

The number of stages that will result from the MVA preprocessing depends in such an intricate way on the structure of the matrix that no estimation can be computed in advance. The only proposition that can be given a priori is that the number of stages will be less or equal to N-1 i.e. to the number of stages given by the classical Gauss algorithm. In the case of a full matrix for example, the MVA preprocessing will give the same ordering of the operations as the Gauss algorithm.

For the test problems the number of stages computed by the MVA preprocessing are given in table 6.

Table 6 : Number of stages given by MVA preprocessing

circuit	ex1	ex2	ex3	ex4
dimension	342	376	1040	2027
number of stages	239	213	742	1771

The CPU-times have been reduced by the MVA preprocessing to :

Table 7 : CPU-times [ms]. for one LU-decomposition

circuit	ex1	ex2	ex3	ex4
MVA (vector)	3.25	3.3	11.0	43.3

The memory needed for storing the index lists is approximately the same as for the algorithm COA.

7. THE MAXIMAL VECTORIZATION ALGORITHM WITH STAGE REDUCTION

The improvement obtained with the MVA preprocessing has been disappointing. The explanation for the poor results was found to be the 'scalar tail'. Typically the first stages are filled satisfactorily i.e. the number of operations is considerably increased in comparison with the Gauss algorithm, but more than half of the final stages are only including less than ten update operations. This means that most of the work is done within some few stages at the beginning by vector instructions of sufficient vectorlength to give the desired improvement of the vectorization effect, but part of this gain is lost with the execution of more than half of the stages at the end where only scalar performance can be expected. The reason for this distribution of operations lies in the presence of matrix components that are updated significantly more times than the majority of the matrix components. Electrically this fact reflects the existence of nodes within the circuit that have many more connections to other nodes than the average node of the circuit. Examples of these kind of nodes are power supplies, bulk supplies, clock lines,etc. .

To avoid the 'scalar tail' a way has to be found to transform the weakly occupied final stages into operations that are better suited for vector processing. The reason for the 'scalar tail' was found in the existence of elements that are updated many times. Since by definition of the MVA preprocessing, a matrix component can be updated at least one time on a single stage, the number of stages must be at least as great as the maximal number of update operations on a single matrix component. One can hope to eliminate this drawback of the MVA preprocessing by collecting the update operations of those matrix components that are updated many times and by executing them simultaneously in a multiple update operation. This multiple update operation is executed at the highest level upon which the matrix component under consideration is updated. A multiple update operation can be considered as a scalar product whose result has to be subtracted from a given matrix component. As scalar products are vectorizable on modern vector processors [3] the execution will be efficient if the multiple update operation is long enough.

In Yamamoto/Takahashi [2] multiple update operations are proposed for the so called Block Vectorization Algorithm BVA. They introduce 'short' multiple update operations to assure the vectorizability of the BVA and to enhance the performance. Vectorization is achieved by executing the update operations of different matrix components in parallel. In Yamamoto/Takahashi [2] it is stated that this concept of multiple update operations is inapplicable to the MVA preprocessing. Our concept of multiple update operations differs from theirs in that we are proposing 'long' multiple update operations that are vectorized by executing the single update operations making up the multiple updating of one matrix component in parallel.This concept contradicts the strict data flow principle in that the collection of the update operations can be interpreted as retarding the update operations of a specific matrix component until the level of execution is reached upon which the last update of that component is done. It is justified only if it succeeds in transforming the weakly occupied final stages into multiple update operations of sufficient length. Also it is well suited to be added upon the MVA preprocessing.

To implement the proposed concept, a criterion has to be given for the determination of those update operations that are to be transformed into multiple update operations. Experience has shown that in the case of matrix structures that are typically encountered in circuit analysis, the diagonal elements are finished at a rather early stage and that this stage marks rather reliably the beginning of the 'scalar tail'. So it was decided to take this stage as the last stage and to transform the update operations of all the higher stages into multiple update operations. This strategy can be implemented by adding the following operations to the MVA preprocessing :

/* Let MS be the number of stages as given by the MVA preprocessing */

```
MSR = MS ;
while (number of updates of diagonal elements at stage MSR is zero) do
    MSR = MSR-1
end ;
MP = 0 ;
for M = MSR + 1 to MS do
    for all elements that are finished on stage M do
        Make a multiple update operation out of all the update operations
        acting on the chosen element since stage MSR + 1 ;
        MP = MP + 1
    end ;
end ;
```

MSR gives the reduced number of stages, MP the number of multiple update operations. In executing the multiple update operations, a certain ordering has to be observed. They have to be executed in the order they are generated by the above algorithm.The final algorithm is called maximal vectorization algorithm with stage reduction MVAR.

With a more sophisticated postprocessing, the transformation of single update operations to multiple update operations could be extended to a larger class of operations e.g. all those update operations acting on matrix elements that are updated more often than a fixed lower bound. Since the results of the above algorithm have been satisfying we have made no efforts to improve upon it.

Application of MVAR to the test problems gave the reduction of stages as given in Table 8.

Table 8 : Number of stages given by the MVA resp. MVAR preprocessing

circuit	ex1	ex2	ex3	ex4
dimension	342	376	1040	2027
MVA : stages	239	213	742	1771
MVAR : stages mult. updates	47 9	62 14	106 4	418 4

Table 9 gives the final CPU-times. Table 9 contains also the scalar times for COA as for all examples the algorithm COA was the fastest one in scalar mode among the considered algorithms. There is a speedup factor of 3-5 for the scalar execution of the small examples and of 6-10 for the large examples. This speedup of the scalar execution has to be paid for by additional memory needs. The ratio of fastest scalar execution to fastest vector execution is about 6 for the small examples and about 10 for the large examples.

Table 9 : CPU-times [ms] for one LU-decomposition

circuit	ex1	ex2	ex3	ex4
Original (scalar)	26.87	58.2	298.2	2947.9
COA (scalar)	8.69	12.7	50.4	311.8
COA (vector)	5.08	4.7	13.1	43.4
MVA (vector)	3.25	3.3	11.0	43.3
MVAR (vector)	1.28	1.9	5.2	30.6

The memory needs for MVAR are not increased in comparison to MVA. Just some additional temporary memory space has to be delivered that can be released after completion of the MVAR preprocessing.

8. EXAMPLE

Consider the 9x9 matrix structure :

	1	2	3	4	5	6	7	8	9
1	x					x			
2		x		x		x		x	
3			x			x			x
4				x		x			
5	x				x	x			x
6						x			
7					x	x	x		
8	x	x	x	x	x	x		x	x
9			x			x			x

The algorithms COA, MVA and MVAR will give the following sequences of operations. The operations for COA are succeeded by the level of execution.

COA

$A_{51} = A_{51}/A_{11}$ (1)
$A_{81} = A_{81}/A_{11}$ (1)
$A_{56} = A_{56}-A_{51}*A_{16}$ (1)
$A_{86} = A_{86}-A_{81}*A_{16}$ (1)

$A_{82} = A_{82}/A_{22}$ (1)
$A_{84} = A_{84}-A_{82}*A_{24}$ (1)
$A_{86} = A_{86}-A_{82}*A_{26}$ (2)
$A_{88} = A_{88}-A_{82}*A_{28}$ (1)

$A_{83} = A_{83}/A_{33}$ (1)
$A_{93} = A_{93}/A_{33}$ (1)
$A_{86} = A_{86}-A_{83}*A_{36}$ (3)
$A_{89} = A_{89}-A_{83}*A_{39}$ (1)
$A_{96} = A_{96}-A_{93}*A_{36}$ (1)
$A_{99} = A_{99}-A_{93}*A_{39}$ (1)

$A_{74} = A_{74}/A_{44}$ (1)
$A_{84} = A_{84}/A_{44}$ (2)
$A_{76} = A_{76}-A_{74}*A_{46}$ (1)
$A_{86} = A_{86}-A_{84}*A_{46}$ (4)

$A_{85} = A_{85}/A_{55}$ (1)
$A_{86} = A_{86}-A_{85}*A_{56}$ (5)
$A_{89} = A_{89}-A_{85}*A_{59}$ (2)

$A_{76} = A_{76}/A_{66}$ (2)
$A_{86} = A_{86}/A_{66}$ (6)
$A_{96} = A_{96}/A_{66}$ (2)

MVA

$A_{51} = A_{51}/A_{11}$
$A_{81} = A_{81}/A_{11}$
$A_{82} = A_{82}/A_{22}$
$A_{83} = A_{83}/A_{33}$
$A_{93} = A_{93}/A_{33}$
$A_{74} = A_{74}/A_{44}$
$A_{85} = A_{85}/A_{55}$
$A_{56} = A_{56}-A_{51}*A_{16}$
$A_{86} = A_{86}-A_{81}*A_{16}$
$A_{84} = A_{84}-A_{82}*A_{24}$
$A_{88} = A_{88}-A_{82}*A_{28}$
$A_{89} = A_{89}-A_{83}*A_{39}$
$A_{96} = A_{96}-A_{93}*A_{36}$
$A_{99} = A_{99}-A_{93}*A_{39}$
$A_{76} = A_{76}-A_{74}*A_{46}$

$A_{84} = A_{84}/A_{44}$
$A_{76} = A_{76}/A_{66}$
$A_{96} = A_{96}/A_{66}$
$A_{86} = A_{86}-A_{82}*A_{26}$
$A_{89} = A_{89}-A_{85}*A_{59}$

$A_{86} = A_{86}-A_{83}*A_{36}$

$A_{86} = A_{86}-A_{84}*A_{46}$

$A_{86} = A_{86}-A_{85}*A_{56}$

$A_{86} = A_{86}/A_{66}$

MVAR

$A_{51} = A_{51}/A_{11}$
$A_{81} = A_{81}/A_{11}$
$A_{82} = A_{82}/A_{22}$
$A_{83} = A_{83}/A_{33}$
$A_{93} = A_{93}/A_{33}$
$A_{74} = A_{74}/A_{44}$
$A_{85} = A_{85}/A_{55}$
$A_{56} = A_{56}-A_{51}*A_{16}$
$A_{86} = A_{86}-A_{81}*A_{16}$
$A_{84} = A_{84}-A_{82}*A_{24}$
$A_{88} = A_{88}-A_{82}*A_{28}$
$A_{89} = A_{89}-A_{83}*A_{39}$
$A_{96} = A_{96}-A_{93}*A_{36}$
$A_{99} = A_{99}-A_{93}*A_{39}$
$A_{76} = A_{76}-A_{74}*A_{46}$

$A_{84} = A_{84}/A_{44}$
$A_{76} = A_{76}/A_{66}$
$A_{96} = A_{96}/A_{66}$

$A_{89} = A_{89}-A_{85}*A_{59}$

$A_{86} = A_{86}-A_{82}*A_{26}$
      $-A_{83}*A_{36}$
      $-A_{84}*A_{46}$
      $-A_{85}*A_{56}$

$A_{86} = A_{86}/A_{66}$

9. CONCLUSION

An algorithm for LU-decomposition has been developped that gives a speedup factor of almost 100 for large circuits on the vector processor VP200. For medium sized circuits of about 500 to 1000 transistors the algorithm is still about 20 to 30 times as fast on the VP200 as the original algorithm. The algorithm can be implemented efficiently without changing the original data structure for storing the matrix in SPICE2. There has to be supported additional memory to store some index lists. For large circuits of about 5000 transistors these lists will occupy up to 4 Megabytes. For still larger circuits the additional memory need may exceed practically available resources. This may be one of the problems one has to face in the future.

REFERENCES

[1]   L.W.Nagel,'SPICE2-A computer program to simulate semiconductor circuits',University of California, Berkeley, ERL Memo ERL-M520 (1975).

[2]   F.Yamamoto,S.Takahashi,'Vectorized LU-decomposition algorithms for large-scale circuit simulation',IEEE Trans. Cad., Vol.4, No.3, pp 232-239 (1985).

[3]   M.Motegi,K.Uchida,and T.Tsuchimoto,'The architecture of the FACOM vector processor',in *Parallel Computing '83*, ed. by M.Feilmeier,J.Joubert and U.Schendel, North-Holland, Amsterdam, pp. 541-546 (1984).

[4]   U.Feldmann,K.-G. Rauh, K.Steger,'Circuit Simulation on Vectorprocessors', to be published.

[5]   A.Vladimirescu,S.Liu,'The simulation of MOS integrated circuits using SPICE2',University of California, Berkeley, ERL Memo ERL-M80/7 (1980).

[6]   B.Rehn,R.Mitterer,'Ein MOS-Modell mit "pseudophysikalischen" Parametern', Nachrichtentechn. Fachberichte, Bd. 51,pp.162-167 (1975).

VLSI '87, C.H. Séquin (editor)
Elsevier Science Publishers B.V. (North-Holland)
© IFIP, 1988

SYSTEMATIC DESIGN OF MOS CELLS

G. SAUCIER, G. THUAU
Circuits and Systems Laboratory
46 Avenue Félix Viallet
38031 GRENOBLE Cedex FRANCE

Abstract

The aim of the research described here is to present systematic logical and topological synthesis for MOS circuitry. Synthesis of one function by a complex gate or by a set of interconnected gates (multilayer synthesis) is addressed as well as synthesis of independent functions. Regular layout capabilities are considered as a prime optimization factor.

Introduction

Optimized logic synthesis leads to worthwhile trade-offs between classical optimization criteria such as area, performance and systematic layout capabilities. PLA implementation relies on highly efficient NOR/NOR or NAND/NAND logic synthesis which basically minimizes the number of product terms and is a good example of a straightforward systematic layout. Complex MOS gates offer a larger variety of logic primitives but lead to difficult synthesis methods as well as to thorny layout problems.

Logical synthesis involves firstly, a decomposition procedure, [MUR82], [ELZ77] as the Boolean functions have to be partitioned into subfunctions or complex gates meeting the requirements of MOS circuitry (limited number of transistors in series). An optimized [UEH81] and systematic [ELC82] [KUB83] [YOF85] topological arrangement of these complex gates then has to be generated. This paper suggests solutions to both problems and looks at how far optimized synthesis and systematic layout may be used for four types of cells (switching cells, MOS basic gates implementing one Boolean function, interconnected gates implementing one Boolean function, set of basic gates implementing a set of independent functions). The important point is that logical and topological design are considered together, thus giving rise to efficient solutions.

1. DESIGN OF WELL STRUCTURED SWITCHING CELLS

A switching cell implements a Boolean function by a network of transistors receiving fixed values (0 or 1) on one side, the input variables in a given order (figure 1) on another side.

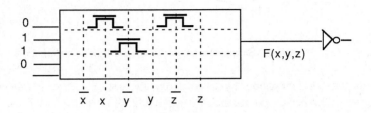

Figure 1 : A Switching Cell

The starting point may be an expression of F as a sum of minterms [MEA80]. The input values on the left are then the 2^n values of the inputs. A better starting point is a canonical lexicographic tree [KUN68] (figure 2) or a simplified lexicographic tree created by using the Shannon formula for the successive variables (figure 3).

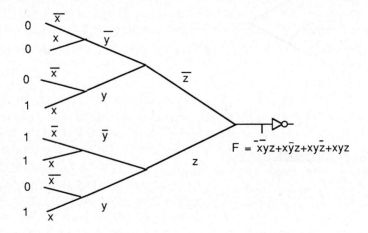

Figure 2 : Canonical tree representing a three variable function

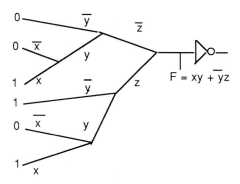

Figure 3 : Simplified tree representing a Boolean function

This tree is simplified by considering a set of rules ; three rules are given below for purposes of illustration.

(i) <u>First rule : edge elimination</u>
Two edges x_i and $\bar{x}_i$ having the same origin and root of identical subtrees can be eliminated. The subtree is reconnected to the initial point (fig.4).

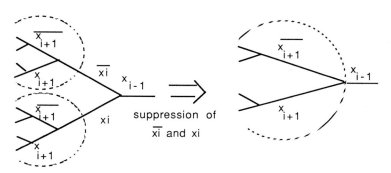

Figure 4 : Edge suppression

(ii) <u>Second rule : edge merging</u>
Two partial paths made up of two edges, having the same origin, labelled respectively by $x_i \, x_{i+1}$ and $\bar{x}_i x_{i+1}$, whose ends are roots of two identical subtrees can be replaced by one edge, having the same origin, labelled by x_{i+1} (figure 3).

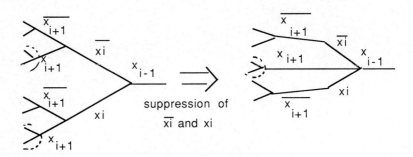

Figure 5 : Edge merging

(iii) <u>Third rule : node merging</u>

Consider two partial paths, consisting of two edges of the tree, having the same origin, labelled respectively by $\overline{x}_i x_{i+1}$ and $x_i \overline{x}_{i+1}$ which are the roots of two identical subtrees. The ends of these two paths can be merged (figure 6).

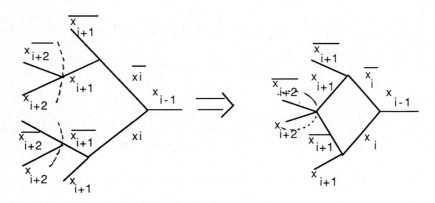

Figure 6 : Nodes merging

<u>Remark</u> :

The parasitic paths created are deleted as $x_{i+1} . \widetilde{x}_{i+1}$ appear on them. Let us consider the canonical tree of figure 1. The first and second rules are applicable ; they lead to the tree of figure 7.

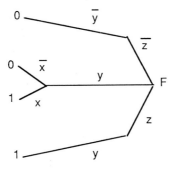

Figure 7 : Simplified tree of figure 1

Let us consider the simplified tree of figure 8. Its implementation gives the circuit diagram of figure 9 which is a lexicographic network with the variables in the following order : x,y,z,t (given by the tree).

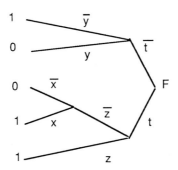

Figure 8 : Simplified tree of a four variable function t,z,y,x

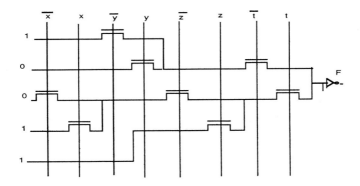

Figure 9 : Circuit diagram obtained from the simplified tree of figure 6

Remark :

The variables crossing the array (columns), may come either from the top or from the bottom of it, according to the external wiring.

2. DESIGN OF A WELL-STRUCTURED COMPLEX MOS GATE

An NMOS complex gate implementing a function F(x,y...) is made up of an N-transistor network implementing $\overline{F}$(x,y...). A CMOS complex gate is made up of an N-transistor network implementing $\overline{F}$(x,y...) and a P-transistor network implementing the dual function $\overline{F}$*(x,y...). A systematic layout is possible if these networks are "well-structured networks" i.e networks in which the input variables appear in the same order [SAU85]. Two cases are considered according to whether the ordering of the input variables is predefined or not. In the first case, this ordering is a consequence of a global floorplanning and a top-down layout approach. The global wiring has been planned and some random logic or glue has to be designed with fixed input (wires) ordering. In the second case, this ordering is still free and is a parameter of the optimization. If the number of transistors put in series is too large (in excess of 3 or 4 for instance), a decomposition into interconnected basic gates is carried out (section III).

2.1. Design of an optimized well-structured complex MOS gate with a fixed ordering of the input variables

The starting point here is an irredundant sum of prime implicants of the function. The initial network associates with each prime implicant a path in a transistor network.

Consider the function :

$$\overline{F} = x_1 x_3 + \overline{x}_2 x_4 + \overline{x}_1 x_2 \overline{x}_3 + \overline{x}_1 \overline{x}_3 x_4$$

The network is given in figure 10.

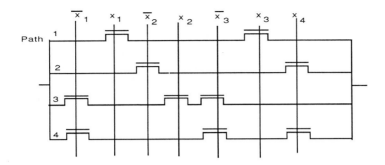

Figure 10 : initial network

If the ordering of the variables is fixed, transistor mergings are performed by a factorization process between the different product terms starting from one end of the network. This leads to a rooted tree structure. A second step minimization begins at the other end of the network, looks for a satisfactory path ordering, and allows more transistor mergings.

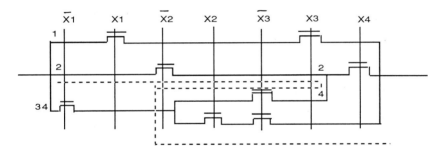

Figure 11

In the example of figure 11, the transistors controlled by x_1 are merged on the left, the transistors controlled by x_4 are merged on the right side. It should be observed that the dotted parasitic path does not introduce any erroneous product term.

2.2. Design of an optimized well-structured complex MOS gate with a free ordering of the input variables

The optimization procedure looks first for an ordering of the input variables leading to a maximal number of transistor mergings by a factorization procedure. The algorithm is explained in [SAU85] and leads for the previous example to the network of figure 12.

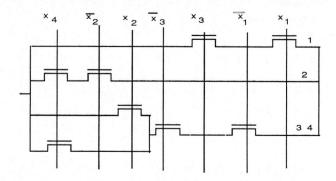

Figure 12 : Network with best ordering of the input variables

The second step of the optimization is similar to the previous one as the order of input variables is now fixed. A reordering of the paths leads to a supplementary merging of the transistors controlled by x_4 (figure 13).

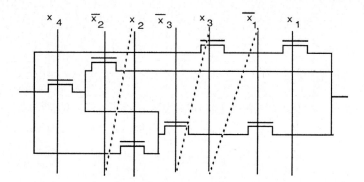

Figure 13 : Non series-parallel network

We have now a gain of 3 transistors (10 to 7 transistors). For NMOS gates, the starting point may be taken to be the paths of $\overline{F}$. For CMOS gates, the paths of $\overline{F}$ and $\overline{F}^*$ are considered as a whole set of paths.

2.3. Systematic layout

Systematic layout is obtained by translating the previous circuit diagram in either a diffusion string layout or a diffusion block layout. The systematic layout is possible because the input ordering allows a regular array of two sets of appropriate physical lines. Consider the non-series network in figure 13. Two diffusion string layouts are given in figure 14 with the following legends :

—— aluminium

- - - polysilicon

.... N diffusion

▨ ion implantation

⊠ contacts

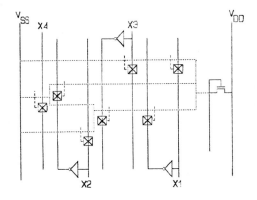

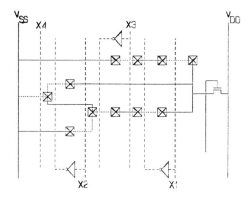

Figure 14 : Two diffusion strings layout for an NMOS gate

The diffusion block layout relies on a partitioning of the diffusion lines into a set of paths (see the dotted lines in figure 13), where each path is associated with a silicon block crossed by the corresponding input lines (figure 15).

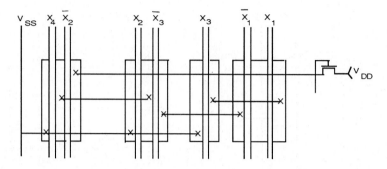

Figure 15 : Diffusion blocks layout for an NMOS gate

3. WELL STRUCTURED MULTILAYER SYNTHESIS OF A BOOLEAN FUNCTION

3.1. General principles

Consider a function whose prime implicants have a number of variables which is higher than the number of transistors which can be put in series in MOS gates.

A decomposition will be performed, while respecting the systematic topological structure. This will be illustrated using NMOS logic but may be translated into CMOS logic. The approach is decomposed into 4 steps.

Step 1 : synthesis of the global function by a well structured complex gate.
This step finds an optimal ordering of the input variables, allowing a maximal number of transistor mergings as in the previous section. This ordering of the variables is definitive. The function is synthesized by a set of paths ; each path corresponding to a prime implicant.

Step 2 : definition of cut points
If the maximal number of transistors which can be input in series is equal to N : a cut point is defined on each path having more than N

transistors in series after, at most, N-1 transistors.
Let us consider the example of the gate on figure
where $\overline{F}$ = abc + $\overline{a}\overline{b}\overline{c}$d + $\overline{a}\overline{b}$cd
The first step has led to the well-structured gate of figure

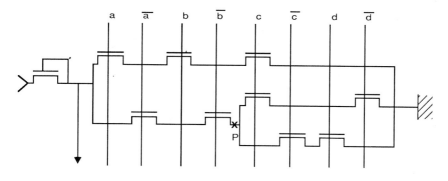

Figure 16

Two paths having more than 3 transistors are cut at the point P.

<u>Step 3</u> : computation of the subfunctions associated with the cut points.
A subfunction associated with a point P is the transfer function between
P and the ground.
In the example of figure 16 : F_P = c$\overline{d}$ + $\overline{c}$d

<u>Step 4</u> : synthesis of the complementary subfunctions respecting the
input variable ordering.
The subfunctions will be generated by an NMOS gate and thus have to be
complemented. In the previous example F_P = cd+$\overline{c}\overline{d}$ becomes the output of
an NMOS gate as indicated in figure 17.

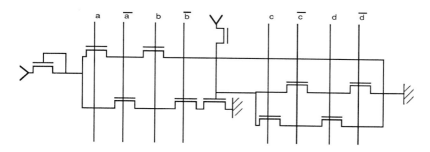

Figure17

Of course, the regularity is somewhat disturbed by the introduction of the new V_{dd} line between the b and c lines. But this is a minor modification. The number of transistors has not significantly increased. There are a number of important points here. The set of cut points is placed in a minimal set of vertical rows (one if possible) so that a minimal number of power supply lines has to be introduced. CMOS technology leads to the same logical synthesis problem. The load transistor is replaced by a precharge transistor. If necessary an inverter is introduced between the two layers in order to avoid precharge losses.

4. DESIGN OF A SET OF INDEPENDENT BOOLEAN FUNCTIONS

4.1. General organizations

Let us consider a set of independent functions $\{F_i\}$, each expressed by an irredundant sum of prime implicants of the complementary function $\overline{F}_i$ and of the dual complementary function $\overline{F}^{*}_i$. Two types of organizations are defined in NMOS and four types in CMOS [THU 87]. The approach is illustrated on a two band structure where the functions are partitioned into two subsets in order to reach a PLA-like area and to allow comparison. In practise, this shape depends essentially on the floorplanning requirements. A bipartitioning looks for reduced dependency of the functions towards input variables. Functions depending on the same reduced set of input variables are put together. As the final shape of the circuit is a rectangle, the numbers of transistors have to be nearly the same in the two bands. In each band an optimal ordering of the input variables is obtained with regard to the global set of functions of the band as for an isolated function. This allows an initial transistor gain. Further optimization in a band is obtained by merging transistors between paths belonging to two adjacent functions. An ordering of the functions is looked for. Two functions are put adjacent if they allow the merging of supplementary transistors. This means that the two functions both have a path with at least one transistor controlled by the same input variable. This transistor will be put in common at one end. To provide protection against parasitic paths, these two paths both have to contain another transistor controlled by x_i and $\overline{x}_i$ respectively. Figure 15 shows that the functions F_1 and F_2 can share the transistor controlled by variable d, and that this merging does not introduce any parasitic paths as there exists a pair of transistors controlled at F_1 and F_2 respectively by a and $\overline{a}$.

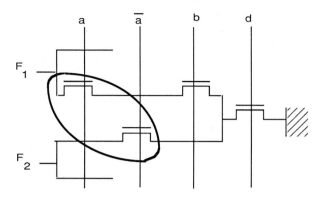

Figure 18 : Transistors merging between two functions

4.2. Example

The BCD to seven segments decoder (figure 19) is again taken as an example since its implementation allows comparisons with PLA.

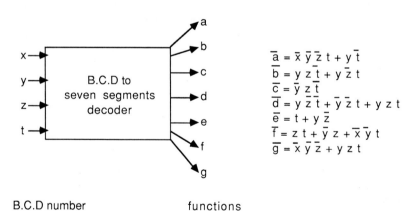

$$\overline{a} = \overline{x}\,\overline{y}\,\overline{z}\,t + y\,\overline{t}$$
$$\overline{b} = y\,z\,\overline{t} + y\,\overline{z}\,t$$
$$\overline{c} = \overline{y}\,z\,t$$
$$\overline{d} = y\,\overline{z}\,t + \overline{y}\,\overline{z}\,t + y\,z\,t$$
$$\overline{e} = t + y\,\overline{z}$$
$$\overline{f} = z\,t + \overline{y}\,z + \overline{x}\,\overline{y}\,t$$
$$\overline{g} = x\,\overline{y}\,\overline{z} + y\,z\,t$$

B.C.D number   functions

Figure 19 : BCD to seven segments decoder

An example of two band organization in NMOS technology is given. The functions are partitioned into two subsets $\{\overline{b},\overline{c},\overline{d},\overline{e}\}$ $\{\overline{f},\overline{a},\overline{g}\}$, as the first subset does not depend on the variable x. The ordering of the input variables are optimized for each subset, as well as the ordering of the functions to allow mergings of transistors between functions. The results are shown in figure 20. The parasitic paths between distinct functions are equal to zero because of the existence of the circled pairs indicated in figure 20.

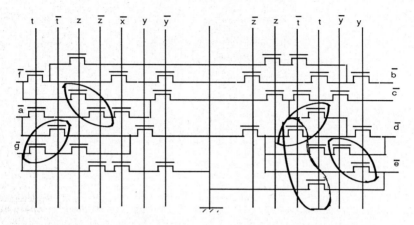

Figure 20 : Global optimization of the two subsets (NMOS)

The diffusion string layout, the diffusion block layout and the PLA layout are given in figure 21, 22 and 23.

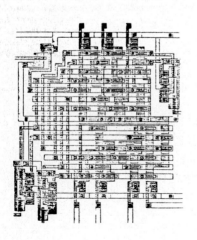
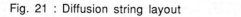

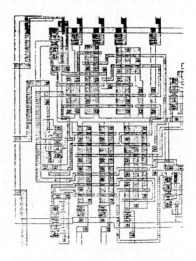

Fig. 21 : Diffusion string layout   Fig. 22 : Diffusion block layout

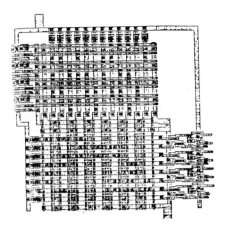

Figure 23 : PLA layout

The comparison with PLA is shown in the table below ; electrical characteristics and areas for one function of the decoder (with the French MCP parameters and $\lambda = 2\,\mu$) are indicated.

Layout types	Propagation delay (ns)	Rising time (ns)	Falling time (ns)	Global power	Global area
PLA	13	5	4	890	$(170{\times}190)\lambda^2$ $= 32300\,\lambda^2$
Diffusion strings	7,5	6,5	4,5	390	$(150{\times}130)\,\lambda^2$ $= 19500\,\lambda^2$
Diffusion blocks	6,5	4	3	390	$(160{\times}130)\,\lambda^2$ $= 208000\,\lambda^2$

The previous results show that area and propagation delay are better with complex MOS gates than with PLA.

CONCLUSION

Systematic design with MOS complex gates has to cope with a difficult Boolean decomposition problem and with irregular topological structures. To overcome these two major problems elegant synthesis primitives are proposed for basic MOS cells as well as for multilayer synthesis and several independent function synthesis.

BIBLIOGRAPHY

[EIC82]   **P. EICHENBERGER, R. MATHEWS, J. NEWKIRK**
             "A target language for silicon compilers"
             COMPCON SPRING, February 1982.

[EL-Z77]   **Y.M. EL-ZIQ**
             "Logic design automation of MOS combinational with fan-in, fan-out constraints"
             14th Design Automation Conference, pp.240-249, June 1977

[KUB83]   **W.J. KUBITZ, J.F.P. LUHUKAY, F.L. WONG**
             "An automatic NMOS cell synthesis system"
             ICCAD, Santa Clara, pp.190-191, Septembre 1983.

[KUN68]   **J. KUNTZMANN**
             "Algèbre de Boole"
             Editions Dunod, Paris 1968.

[MUR82]   **S. MUROGA**
             "VLSI system design"
             John Wiley & Sons, 1982, Chapter 4.

[SAU85]   **G. SAUCIER, G. THUAU**
             "Systematic and optimized layout of MOS cells"
             22nd Design Automation Conference, pp.53-61, June 1985.

[UEH81]   **T. UEHARA, W.M. VAN CLEEMPUT**
             "Optimal layout of CMOS functional arrays"
             IEEE Transactions on computers, vol.C30, pp.304-312, n°5, May 1981.

[YOF85]   **E.J. YOFFA, P.S. HAUGE**
             "ACORN : A local customization approach to DCVS physical design"
             22nd Design Automation Conference, pp.32-38, June 1985.

VLSI '87, C.H. Séquin (editor)
Elsevier Science Publishers B.V. (North-Holland)
© IFIP, 1988

A New Bucketing Technique for Automatic/Interactive Layout Design

Masato EDAHIRO

Application System Research Laboratory
C&C Systems Research Laboratories
NEC CORPORATION
4-1-1, Miyazaki, Miyamae-ku
Kawasaki   213
JAPAN

ABSTRACT

In the current status of VLSI CAD technologies, the cooperation between automatic and interactive algorithms is indispensable in layout verification. Although the bucketing technique is applicable to both algorithms, this technique becomes less efficient when there are many long edges in layouts. The paper proposes a new bucketing technique, where the long edges are stored in a special data structure called the "Window List". Automatic and interactive algorithms based on the new method are also proposed. It was confirmed that the computation time and the required memory size of the new method are on average linear with respect to the number of edges in the layout.

I. Introduction

The circuit scale of IC's has increased tremendously in recent years. The utilization of VLSI is being examined in various fields, and many design-automation tools have been developed. However, it is more difficult for the improvement of design tools to catch up with the expansion of the demand. The design by these tools is still of poorer quality than manual designs. Therefore, it is common to divide the design of VLSI chips into manual and automatic parts. The essential part of design is done manually and routine tasks (which may have some heuristic rules) such as automatic design rule checks for a whole chip are assigned to mainframe computers. Manual designs may contain many errors, and consequently designers use mainframe computers repeatedly to correct all of them. This design method becomes less efficient as the scale of the circuit becomes larger because mainframe computers are shared by many designers, and designers are forced to wait a long time for responses from the computers.

One way to solve this problem is to use both interactive algorithms and automatic algorithms. In interactive designs on workstations, designers create layout data, and repeat local modifications or checks (e.g. design rule checks) on a small part of the layout data. The whole layout data that results from the interactive designs are managed by mainframe computers. After the interactive designs, mainframe computers perform automatic verifications for the whole chip in order to check conflicts among local modifications. If any error is detected in the automatic verifications, the chip is modified interactively and then the automatic verification continues. Automatic verifications are performed only a few times because chips are mostly designed interactively. Therefore, both automatic and interactive algorithms are important for design methods using mainframe computers and workstations. In addition, it is indispensable for an efficient design that both these algorithms, automatic and interactive, work on the same databases.

The interactive algorithms must have a strong ability to manipulate the data of a region specified by the designer. Polygons intersecting the specified region must be found efficiently by the interactive algorithm. On the other hand, the automatic algorithms must guarantee high-speed design for global chip layouts. Since very large-scale layout data is dealt with, it is desirable that the algorithms have $O(n)$ processing time using $O(n)$ memory space, where n denotes the number of edges of the polygons.

Computational geometry [9,11] has provided many techniques for problems in VLSI layout verification. The plane-sweep technique, the quad trees and the bucketing technique are typical. The plane-sweep technique [3,12] is the most popular for automatic algorithms in VLSI layout verification. However, the plane-sweep technique is not efficient for use in interactive algorithms, because the data structure of the plane-sweep technique is not suitable for "local designs" in a specified region. The Quad-CIF tree [8] is a technique for interactive algorithms, which is based on quad trees [4]. It is an efficient data structure for localized data, but the special data structure excludes it from automatic algorithms.

The bucketing technique [2,6] is applicable to both automatic and interactive algorithms. Still, it has not been utilized in VLSI layout design algorithms, because it is not very efficient when there are many polygons with long edges, such as the wiring in VLSI layouts.

In this paper, a new bucketing technique is proposed. The bucketing technique is improved by storing the long horizontal or vertical edges separately in a special data structure. The other edges are stored in buckets. In order to achieve operations by the bucketing technique, it is necessary to efficiently find the edges intersecting a given bucket. However, this is not a trivial problem for horizontal or vertical long edges. We propose a technique to formulate the problem into the "segment-overlapping problem" in computational geometry, for which a simple and efficient algorithm with a data structure called "window list" is known. The horizontal or vertical long edges are efficiently stored in the window list. By using the new bucketing technique, linear-time and linear-space algorithms, in the average sense, for automatic and interactive processes are obtained. This was confirmed in computational experiments.

In the next section, the VLSI layout design problems are defined, and existing algorithms are summarized. The bucketing technique is introduced in Section III and the new method is described in Section IV. Section V and VI describe the data structures and automatic/interactive algorithms, respectively. In Section VII, the results of computational experiments are reported.

II. VLSI Layout Design Problems and Existing Algorithms

In VLSI layout design, there are many problems in dealing with polygons in physical layouts. By solving these problems, various characteristics of a given VLSI layout can be examined. These include the following:

1) design rule check
2) circuit extraction
3) extraction of circuit parameters for electrical performance.

We call these problems "*VLSI layout design problems*." Such geometric operations for polygons as shown in Fig. 1, are fundamental to solve the problems. In order to efficiently perform these operations, it is important to find the "near-by" polygons of a specified polygon. Plane-sweep techniques and quad-trees are well-known methods for doing this.

Plane-sweep techniques [3,12] are the most popular algorithms for automatic designs. The main characteristic of the plane-sweep technique is that the plane on which polygons lie is divided into $O(n)$ *slabs* by drawing parallel lines through all the vertices of polygons and all the intersections of edges (Fig. 2). The worst-case complexity of processing time is $O(n \log n)$, which is the most efficient of existing algorithms. The average case complexity is of the same order of magnitude as in the worst case, because of the management of the tree structure and the sorting of n vertices. In the plane-sweep technique, polygons in the same slab are processed together (Fig. 3), even if they are distant. For

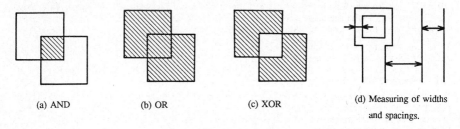

(a) AND   (b) OR   (c) XOR   (d) Measuring of widths
                                                              and spacings.

Fig. 1   LSI layout design problems.

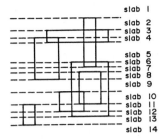

Fig. 2   Plane-sweep technique.

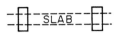

Fig. 3   Distant polygons.

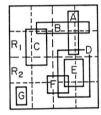

(a) Subdivisions and rectangles.

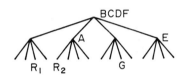

(b) Quad tree.

Fig. 4   Quad trees.

larger-scale layouts, each edge of the polygons belongs to more slabs, so that the searching processes increase. To prevent this shortcoming, some improvements have been proposed [13,14], but the complexity has not been reduced. As for the interactive designs, the plane-sweep technique is not suitable, because it is inefficient to calculate the data in a specified region from a layout database consisting of sorted vertices.

The *quad tree* [4,8] is quite popular as a data structure for interactive designs. It is a quaternary tree whose nodes are recursively associated with rectangular regions (Fig. 4). Each polygon is associated with the farthest node from the root in the nodes whose rectangle include the polygon. The interactive design can be easily performed with the quad trees. For a design in a specified region, all the nodes whose rectangle intersect the region, are examined while tracing the quad trees from the root to the leaves. Geometric operations are performed on data associated with the relevant nodes in the region. However, it is a costly operation to change the viewpoint on a layout if the quad tree is used for large-scale layouts. This is because the operation often requires another trace of the tree. The operation is necessary in the automatic design as well as in the interactive design. Therefore, the automatic algorithm based on the quad tree does not seem to be efficient.

Consequently, it is difficult for existing algorithms to design automatically/interactively on the same database. However, the bucketing technique is capable of doing this.

III. Bucketing Technique

The *bucketing technique* [2] is in a class of methods in which the *objective region,* covering the whole layout, is divided into many regular subregions, and geometric operations are performed on localized data in each subregion. This class of methods based on localization are attractive because we only need to investigate around a polygon in order to resolve VLSI layout design problems. In other words, operations can be done locally in the pertaining buckets.

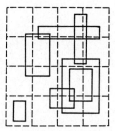

Fig. 5   Bucketing technique.

The basic idea of the bucketing technique is as follows. The objective region is divided into $O(n)$ congruent rectangles called *buckets*, independent of the density of polygons (Fig. 5). Since each bucket includes on average $O(1)$ vertices, it is expected that a local operation in a bucket will be carried out in $O(1)$ time, resulting in $O(n)$ processing time as a whole. Therefore, if data structures and algorithms for local operations are carefully chosen, it is possible to obtain linear-time VLSI layout design algorithms. The algorithm is faster than typical existing algorithms based on the plane-sweep technique, in the sense that the plane-sweep algorithm takes at least $O(n \log n)$ processing time.

In order to evaluate the superiority of the bucketing technique to the plane-sweep technique, the author has made preliminary computational experiments for the range-search problem, which is one of the fundamental problems in VLSI layout verification [6]. The problem is stated as follows. When a set of points and a set of polygonal regions are given on a two-dimensional region, the range-search problem is to enumerate the points within the closed shapes. For example, for the point-set and region-set depicted in Fig. 6(a), the range-search problem enumerates the circles and dots.

In the experiment, the algorithms were applied to more complex figures that had the polygons of Fig. 6(a) juxtapositioned many times. They were arranged in a grid-like fashion (Fig. 6(b)). A comparison between the bucket algorithm and the plane-sweep algorithm is illustrated in Fig. 6(c). It shows that although these two algorithms are comparable for a small number of vertices, the bucket algorithm is much faster than the plane-sweep algorithm as the number of vertices becomes large.

As shown throughout the experiments, the bucketing technique has a good potential for efficient calculations in VLSI layout verification. However, existing systems based on the bucketing technique are not successful in actual implementations. The reason is that, in VLSI layouts, edges whose lengths are comparable to the length or breadth of the chip frequently appear in polygons used for wiring. The "long" edges are divided into more than one piece by buckets, resulting in a rapid growth of edge sections. The bucketing technique becomes less efficient when there are many edges of comparable length to the height or width of the objective region. Even if the objective region is cut into $O(\sqrt{n}) \times O(\sqrt{n})$ buckets, such an edge is cut off into $O(\sqrt{n})$ pieces by buckets. Therefore, $O(n\sqrt{n})$ memory area is required, and consequently, a geometrical operation takes $O(n\sqrt{n})$ time. Unfortunately, in VLSI design, many horizontal and vertical edges which pass through $O(\sqrt{n})$ buckets appear frequently.

IV. The New Bucketing Technique with the Window-List Algorithm

As mentioned in the last section, the bucketing technique has the shortcoming that it becomes less efficient when many edges have $O(\sqrt{n})$ intersections with buckets. In order to improve the bucketing technique, the number of intersections must be reduced, while keeping the efficiency of enumerating the edges of a given bucket. Hence, we introduce another data structure called a *"strip"*, which corresponds to the rows (columns) of buckets (Fig. 7(a)). A strip data structure is used as described below.

Each horizontal (vertical) edge which belongs to more than two buckets is divided into three parts, two End segments (A) and one Middle segment (B) (Fig. 7(b)). Then, the Middle segment is stored in a strip instead of buckets, while the End segments are stored in buckets. It should be noted here that a horizontal or vertical edge is divided into at most three parts even if it is long. Since most of the edges in VLSI layout are horizontal or vertical, the data structure substantially reduces the required memory area. The effect of the new data structure is shown in Fig. 8. The figure shows that only 16 edges need be used by the new method, while 24 are needed by the original method.

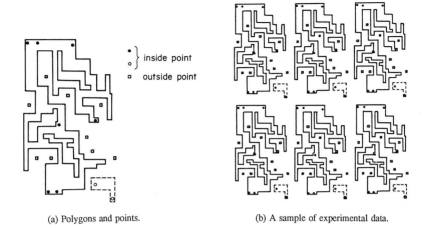

(a) Polygons and points.　　　　　　　(b) A sample of experimental data.

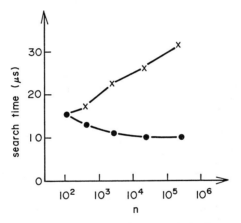

(c) Processing time (CPU time) per vertex in the plane-sweep
method (x——x) and the bucket method (●—●).

Fig. 6　Range-search problem.

Now, the problem is how to enumerate middle segments (which are stored in a strip) as if they are stored in ordinary buckets. That is, we have to solve the following problem:

Problem A:　Given a set of horizontal and vertical edges, enumerate all edges in the set which pass completely through a query bucket.

In order to solve the problem A, we will propose a formulation of problem A into the "*segment-overlapping problem*" in computational geometry, for which a simple and efficient algorithm called the *window-list algorithm* is known. Before describing our method, the segment-overlapping problem and the window-list algorithm are explained.

The *one-dimensional segment-overlapping problem* may be stated as follows. Given a set of n' overlapping segments on a line, then the segment-overlapping problem is to enumerate the segments that contain a prescribed query point (Fig. 9). The problem is said to be *discrete*, if the vertices of

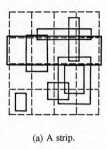

(a) A strip.

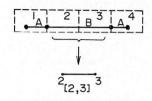

(b) A strip and a segment.

Fig. 7   Improvement of Problem A.

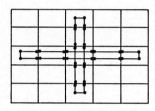

(a) Original bucketing technique.

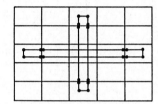

(b) New bucketing technique.

Fig. 8   Edge sections by two kinds of bucketing techniques.

each line segment and the query point have integer coordinates within the range of 0 to $O(n')$. As described later, the complexity of the algorithm for the segment-overlapping problem can be reduced, if the problem is discrete.

The *window-list algorithm* [5] has been proposed for the segment-overlapping problem. The algorithm consists of a set-up phase and an enumeration phase. In the set-up phase, the interval including all segments is divided into p subintervals $I_j (j=1, \cdots ,p)$, called *windows* (Fig. 10). In each window, all the segments intersecting the window are stored. This data structure is called the *window list*. Each window satisfies the condition that the number of segments intersecting the window is 1 or less than twice the number of segments overlapping any query point in the window. For example, in Fig. 9, the query point Q is overlapped by four segments, while in Fig. 10 six segments intersect the window I_2 which involves the point Q. In the enumeration phase, segments are enumerated by determining the window which involves the query point and by investigating all the edges stored in the window. The enumeration is performed in $O(\log n' + k')$ time, where k' is the number of segments enumerated. This is because the number of enumerated edges is more than half the number of investigated edges. To construct the window list, a simple and efficient algorithm was proposed [5]. Chazelle proved that the algorithm runs in $O(n' \log n')$ time and using $O(n')$ memory. In the case of the discrete problem, the set-up time and enumeration time can be reduced to $O(n')$ and $O(k')$, respectively. This is because sorting is not needed.

Now, we propose a technique to formulate Problem A into the discrete segment-overlapping problem. For simplification, we consider only horizontal edges. A strip which stores long edges is defined as a row of buckets (Fig. 7(a)). In each strip, buckets are associated with an integer coordinate with 1 at the left-most end and N_x at the right-most end, where N_x is the number of buckets in the strip. As explained before, an edge in a strip is divided into at most three parts, two End segments (A) and one Middle segment (B) (Fig. 7(b)). The Middle segment of an edge can be considered as a segment between vertices at integer coordinates on a straight line. Namely, the Middle segment which begins at the j-th bucket and ends at the k-th bucket is represented by the interval [j,k]. In Fig. 7(b), the Middle segment which passes through bucket numbered by 2 and 3 is represented by the interval [2,3].

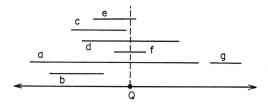

Fig. 9   Segment-overlapping problem.

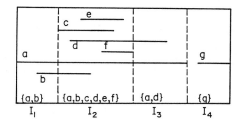

Fig. 10   Window list.

Clearly, problem A can be solved by enumerating all Middle segments which pass through a query bucket. A Middle segment passes through the query bucket, if and only if, the coordinate assigned to the bucket is overlapped by the interval corresponding to the Middle segment of the edge. Moreover, the query bucket is associated with an integer coordinate, and Middle segments are represented as intervals between vertices of integer coordinates. Thus, Problem A is reduced to the discrete segment-overlapping problem in the strip containing the bucket.

Here, the complexity of the new bucketing technique is examined. The technique has two types of data structures. The End segments are stored in each bucket. The Middle segments are structured into a window list for each strip. We can find out edges intersecting a given bucket in $O(k)$ time, where k is the number of segments in a given bucket. Namely, we take out the End segments stored in the bucket, and Middle segments stored in the window list for the strip that includes the bucket. It takes on average $O(1)$ time to take out End segments and $O(k)$ time to enumerate Middle segments, giving a total time of $O(k)$. The time complexity to set up the data structure as well as the space complexity of memory area is $O(n)$, because there are $O(n)$ buckets, $O(n)$ End segments, and the window list for Middle segments needs $O(n)$ memory area.

V. Data Structures for the New Bucketing Technique

We have described the new bucketing technique theoretically. In this and the next section, we will state some further considerations to apply the technique to practical algorithms.

5-1) Size of a Bucket and a Window

The size of a bucket and a window should be tuned in order that the new bucket algorithm attains good performance. Large buckets result in longer processing time to search for a point in each bucket, while small buckets result in more memory space required to store the data of each bucket. It is not easy to determine the size of buckets in general.

However, in the case of VLSI layouts, the bucket size is easily calculated. The height and width of a bucket can be assigned independent of n in order that the number of edges intersecting a bucket is a constant in the average sense. This is because design rules restrict the maximum number of polygons in a bucket, and consequently, the average number of vertices in a bucket is independent of the size of layouts. A typical value of the height and width of a bucket is 10λ, where λ is the length-unit defined in Mead and Conway [10]. Therefore, the size of a bucket need not be updated when layouts are edited. The length of a window can be calculated easily in the case of VLSI layouts for the same reason. A typical value of the length of a window is 100λ.

5-2) Data Structures for the New Bucket Algorithm

As explained in preceding sections, the data structures of the bucketing technique are simple. All points in every bucket are stored in the bucket and all edges through a bucket are stored in the window including the bucket. The size of a bucket or a window is automatically calculated from the size of the objective region and design rules. The objective region is defined by the minimum rectangle which includes all the given polygons.

Since we can enumerate all edges in a bucket from the bucket or the window including the bucket, geometric operations in layout design problems can be solved by using the data structure.

In VLSI layouts, there are "large" rectangles which intersect many buckets, e.g. pads or function blocks. We store such a rectangle in all windows that intersect the rectangle so as to get the rectangle from any bucket completely included in the rectangle. The data structure requires more memory space for such rectangles, but fortunately, there are only a few polygons on such rectangles in VLSI layouts. Therefore, those buckets intersecting such rectangles do not have many polygons and the bucketing technique does not become less efficient.

VI. Automatic/Interactive Algorithms based on the New Bucketing Technique and a Comparison with Existing Algorithms

The plane-sweep algorithm is good for automatic designs but not for interactive designs. The opposite is true for the quad trees. The new bucket algorithm is not only applicable to both designs, but also more efficient than the other algorithms. In this section, the algorithms based on the new bucketing technique are proposed and comparisons with other algorithms are discussed from two points of view, automatic and interactive.

6-1) Automatic Algorithm

We propose an automatic algorithm for layout design problems based on the new bucketing technique.

Phase 1 Calculate an objective region from the layout data. Partition the objective region into buckets whose length and breadth are a certain constant.

Phase 2 Assign all End segments to the bucket containing the vertex of each segment. Construct window lists of horizontal and vertical Middle segments for each strip.

Phase 3 Repeat geometric operations for all polygons in each buckets. Collect the results of the operations. Store the results of the automatic process in the database.

In the above algorithm, the computation time is dominated by the geometric operations in phase 3. Therefore, it is important to choose efficient algorithms for the geometric operations. In order to perform a geometric operation with respect to a polygon, we first find polygons "related" to the polygon (polygons which intersect, include, or is included by the polygon, or which lie within a certain distance to the polygon). This is achieved by examining the buckets and window lists that intersect the polygon. Then the geometric operation is performed for these polygons. The algorithms for the operation can be simple and fast because the problem size for which we apply the operations to the polygons will be very small. Consequently, the automatic algorithm becomes faster by the new bucketing technique.

After all geometric operations in the buckets have been performed, the results are collected. For example, the circuits in the whole chip are extracted by combining transistors with wires, where the transistors and the wires are recognized by the geometrie operations.

Its time complexity is on average $O(n)$. One may point out that the time complexity can be $O(n\sqrt{n})$, because many edges in window lists pass through $O(\sqrt{n})$ buckets. However, in VLSI design an edge is not needed by all geometric operations in the buckets intersecting the edge. It is empirically known that all the edges which take part in all geometric operations, is $O(n)$. So the bucket algorithm takes $O(n)$ time in the automatic design.

On the other hand, the plane-sweep algorithm takes theoretically $O(n \log n)$ time, because of the sorting of $O(n)$ vertices and finding out $O(n)$ segments which take part in $O(n)$ geometric operations. This theoretical time complexity also holds in the average case. Therefore, although the plane-sweep algorithm is the most efficient in the theoretical sense, the bucket algorithm is more efficient in practical cases such as in VLSI design.

The space complexity is $O(n)$ in both the new bucketing technique and the plane-sweep tech-

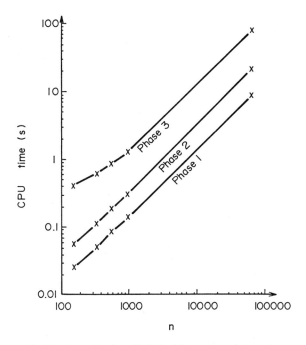

Fig. 11   Processing time (CPU time) for an automatic operation.

nique. In the new bucketing technique, more memory space is needed than the plane-sweep technique, because every polygon must be stored in all the buckets or window lists that the polygon intersects. Moreover, these data are managed in random-access files because of the two-dimensional structure of buckets. This may seem to cause an increase in the I/O time in the bucketing technique. However, a virtual memory space with which the algorithms are carefully implemented instead of explicitly using random-access files, can reduce the I/O time.

If the quad tree is used for the automatic designs, the algorithm requires a lot of tree traversing. Therefore, the quad tree is rarely used for automatic processes.

6-2) Interactive Algorithm

We propose an interactive algorithm for layout design problems based on the new bucketing technique.

Phase 1   Read the layout data, managed in a database, consisting of the minimum number of buckets covering the layout data to be modified. If creating new data, then input the size of the objective region and partition it into buckets whose length and breadth are a certain constant.

Phase 2   Edit the layout data or perform geometric operations for the layout data. Modify the sets of End segments and the window lists, if necessary.

Phase 3   Restore the layout data and the results of the geometric operations to the database.

One of the critical points for the interactive design is to bring data from a database efficiently. The bucketing technique is also efficient because its two-dimensional array structure eases the random access of the data in a specified region from databases.

Although both the bucketing technique and the plane-sweep technique partition an objective region into $O(n)$ rectangular subregions, the length-breadth ratio of a subregion is nearly equal to unity in the bucketing technique, while very large or small ratios exist in the plane-sweep technique. Since users frequently request nearly square regions in which they modify data, the bucket is suitable for the

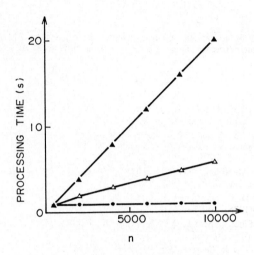

Fig. 12   Processing time for interactive operation
(time to construct the bucket structure ($\triangle - \triangle$), to display
all polygons ($\blacktriangle - \blacktriangle$), and to display 100 polygons in the
specified region ($\bullet - \bullet$)).

required region. On the other hand, the slab in the plane-sweep technique does not seem to be suit-able, because much of the data may be not used.

As for the quad tree, the region associated with a leaf of the tree is nearly equal to the size of the buckets, so that both techniques can get data from a database efficiently. The bucketing techniques use more memory space than the quad trees because a polygon is stored many times in the buckets or window lists. However, the two-dimensional structure of the buckets enables us to approach the region directly. This allows users to conveniently shift their viewpoint on a layout in the new bucket-ing technique.

VII. Computational Experiments

The new bucketing technique has been evaluated in two kinds of experiments. One is a geometric operation in order to estimate the efficiency of the bucketing technique for automatic design processes. The other is to display a specified region, which is a fundamental operation in interactive design processes.

The first experiment is the OR operation in each layer. The tested data have 13 layers. The change of CPU time is shown in Fig. 11. In Fig. 11, it is shown that the new bucketing technique per-forms bucket decomposition and geometric boolean operations in $O(n)$ time.

The second experiment is the operation to take data out of a specified region from a large data-base. Fig. 12 shows that the time to find the required data is proportional to the data size required and independent of the size of the whole data. This operation is a basic function of the interactive part of our layout design system that is under development.

VIII. Conclusions

A new bucketing technique has been proposed for VLSI layout design problems. It enables the design of an VLSI layout from the same database for both automatic and interactive design. More-over, both design processes are expected to be performed in linear time, and this is confirmed by two experiments. These tools show that the bucketing technique is more efficient and promising than the existing techniques.

IX. Acknowledgment

The author would like to express his sincere gratitude to Dr. S. Goto and Mr. T. Yoshimura of NEC Corporation for their constant guidance and valuable suggestions, discussions and comments on this paper.

REFERENCES

[1]   A. V. Aho, J. E. Hopcroft and J. D. Ullman: *The Design and Analysis of Computer Algorithms.* Addison-Wesley, Reading, Massachusetts, 1974.

[2]   T. Asano, M. Edahiro, H. Imai, M. Iri and K. Murota: Practical Use of Bucketing Techniques in Computational Geometry. *Computational Geometry* (G. T. Toussaint, ed.), North-Holland, Amsterdam, pp.153-195, 1985.

[3]   H. S. Baird: Fast Algorithms for LSI Artwork Analysis. *Proc. 14th Design Automation Conference,* New Orleans, Louisiana, pp.303-311, 1977.

[4]   J. L. Bentley and D. F. Stanat: Analysis of Range Searches in Quad Trees. *Information Processing Letters,* Vol.3(1975), pp.170-173.

[5]   B. M. Chazelle: Filtering Search: A New Approach to Query-Answering. *SIAM J. Computing,* Vol.15(1986), No.4, pp.703-724.

[6]   M. Edahiro: *Geometric Search Algorithms* (in Japanese). Master's Thesis, Department of Mathematical Engineering and Instrumentation Physics of the Faculty of Engineering of University of Tokyo, March, 1985.

[7]   M. Edahiro, I. Kokubo and T. Asano: A New Point-Location Algorithm and Its Practical Efficiency --- Comparison with Existing Algorithms. *ACM Trans. Graphics,* Vol.3(1984), No.2, pp.86-109.

[8]   G. Kedem: The Quad-CIF Tree: A Data Structure for Hierarchical On-Line Algorithms. *Proc. 19th Design Automation Conference,* pp.352-357, 1982.

[9]   D. T. Lee and F. P. Preparata: Computational Geometry - A Survey. *IEEE Trans. Computers,* Vol.C-33, pp.1072-1101, 1984.

[10] C. Mead and L. Conway: *Introduction to VLSI Systems.* Addison-Wesley, Reading, Massachusetts, 1980.

[11] F. P. Preparata and M. I. Shamos: *Computational Geometry.* Springer-Verlag, New York, 1985.

[12] M. I. Shamos: Geometric Complexity. *Proc. 7th ACM Annual Symp. Theory Comput.,* Albuquerque, New Mexico, pp.224-233, 1975.

[13] A. Tsukizoe, J. Sakemi, T. Kozawa and H. Fukuda: MACH: A High-Hitting Pattern Checker for VLSI Mask Data. *Proc. 20th Design Automation Conference,* pp.726-731, 1983.

[14] M. T. Yin: Layout Verification of VLSI Designs. *VLSI DESIGN,* Vol.6(1985), No.7, pp.30-38.

VLSI '87, C.H. Séquin (editor)
Elsevier Science Publishers B.V. (North-Holland)
© IFIP, 1988

Synthesizing Transducers from Interface Specifications
(or How to Get Chips Into Systems)

Gaetano Borriello and Randy H. Katz

Computer Science Division/Dept. of EECS
University of California at Berkeley
Berkeley, CA 94720, USA[†]

Circuit interfaces are worthy of careful design in their own right, yet few CAD tools directly support interface design. We have developed a new methodology for abstract specification of interfaces based on timing diagrams. This forms the foundation for reasoning about interface design, synthesis, evaluation, and testing. We describe, in detail, a synthesis tool for interface transducers, that is being implemented using this methodology. A transducer is a collection of logic circuitry that connects two compatible circuit interfaces. We present a practical example that demonstrates that the synthesized circuitry is comparable in performance to human-generated designs while using only 11% more gates.

1. Introduction

Circuit interfaces are an important design abstraction. They describe the communication between a digital circuit and its surrounding environment. A circuit interface can be viewed as a collection of signal wires and the constraints on these signals. The constraints are a contract between the circuit and its environment; if they are not satisfied, then the circuit will be unusable. In general, interface constraints exist in the physical, electrical, logical, and behavioral domains. For example, physical constraints include the formfactor of circuit boards, and the positioning and size restrictions of chip packages and signal traces. Logic levels, current requirements, and input/output capacitances are examples of the electrical concerns. In this paper, we will concentrate on the logical and behavioral constraints on interfaces. These consist of the event sequences on interface signals, indicated by changes in logic level, and their proper separation in time.

The design of *interface circuitry* (i.e., that portion of the design concerned with implementing the interface in accordance with the constraints) is an important aspect

---

[†]Research supported by the University of California under a Microelectronics Fellowship and the Defense Advanced Research Projects Agency under Contract No. N00039-83-C-0107.

of system design requiring careful attention. Considerable design effort must ensure that interface constraints are satisfied. An interface achieves good performance if its bandwidth comes close to the maximum allowed under the constraints.

Circuit interface design has largely been ignored by CAD tool developers. Specification, synthesis, analysis, and optimization tools exist for the data path and control portions of a design, but not for its interface. Design description languages concentrate on circuit logic, not interface constraints. Some of these have been extended to include some interface information, but this is always within a textual description of the overall circuit logic [Nestor86]. Without interface details explicitly factored out, it is difficult, if not impossible, to exploit interface descriptions for design.

Interface abstractions are especially important when connecting a digital system with a communication medium, such as a system bus. A system bus specification is nothing more than an interface in the sense we have described above: a collection of constraints on signal wires. System bus interfaces must be independent of logic specification, since there is no logic circuitry to describe their behavior. Thus, they are described in terms of waveform diagrams augmented with timing constraints, electrical requirements for currents and capacitances, and a set of operations supported by the bus (e.g., read data). In general, interfaces support a variety of methods for transferring data across the interface boundary. We call these methods *semantic operations*. Examples include the memory reads and writes across the interface between a custom microprocessor and a commercial system bus.

Independent *interface specifications* provide a basis for an entire new set of CAD tools that reason about and manipulate interface information. We will highlight a new kind of synthesis tool that takes two interface specifications and generates the circuitry for a *transducer* that connects them (see Figure 1). An interface transducer generator can dramatically reduce the time required to integrate a custom circuit into a computer system. It allows an application designer to ignore the many interfacing

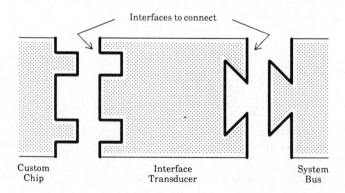

Interfaces to connect

Custom   Interface   System
Chip   Transducer   Bus

Figure 1. An interface transducer is the "adaptor" circuitry that makes two interfaces compatible. Transducers are especially useful when integrating a custom VLSI chip with a system bus.

details of a specific system bus. The designer specifies the interface for the custom circuit and selects the appropriate system bus description from a library. The generator creates the interface transducer circuitry that performs the mapping between the two interfaces. Its layout can be combined with the custom circuit in the same chip [Borriello85a].

The remainder of this paper is organized into four sections. Section 2 addresses the problem of interface specification and presents an approach based on *augmented timing diagrams*. This provides an intuitive graphical language for interface specification. We have implemented *Waves*, an interactive editor for creating the waveforms and appending to them the constraints that fully specify an interface. Section 3 describes the algorithms used in *Janus*, an interface transducer generator. In Section 4, we compare Janus's output to a human-generated design for an actual transducer between a commercial system bus and a microprocessor. Section 5 concludes with some remarks about other tools that are made possible by explicit interface specifications.

2. Specification of Interfaces

An interface is the boundary across which a circuit communicates with its surroundings. Designers commonly use timing diagrams to describe interfaces, both to communicate interface designs among themselves and to document them. These portray the signal waveforms, basic event sequencing, and timing constraints between events. Accompanying text describes the semantic operations supported by the interface and various properties of the signals. These properties describe whether a signal is synchronous to a clock, setup and hold time requirements, rise and fall times of transitions, electrical requirements, etc..

Timing diagrams are the basis for our specification of interfaces. All interface details can be represented in timing diagrams if the diagrams are augmented with some simple procedural extensions. We do this by representing conditional and looping sequences using a graphical regular expression syntax. Arbitrary combinational and sequential logic can be described through Boolean expressions and latching conditions attached to the timing diagram. This is a much more natural and concise way of describing the interface than with a programming language, because it focuses on the interface's constraints rather than the logic circuitry that operates on its signals.

The *Waves* editor supports interactive specification of timing diagrams. A specification consists of a diagram that describes the constraints on the signals during each interface operation. We classify these constraints into six categories: logical, sequencing, simultaneity, synchronicity, timing, and electrical. The categories are not independent but rather correspond to the type of constraints to which designers are accustomed.

Logical constraints determine the logic levels along the signal waveform and when the signal is to be treated as an input, an output, or both. The levels include a *tri-state* and *don't care* state, as well as *low* and *high* levels. A *valid* logic level implies either a 0 or a 1 (see Figure 2). Some signals may be specified as periodic, and have certain phase and duty cycle relationships. The most interesting parts of the waveforms are their edges, where changes in logic levels occur. The remaining constraints deal with relationships between these *events*.

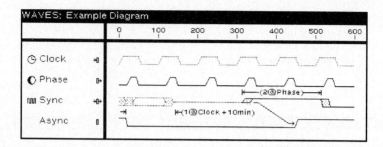

Figure 2. An example of a timing diagram generated with *Waves*. On the left are the signal names with small icons to indicate some signal properties. The icons on the left are symbols for a clock, a phase of a clock, a synchronous signal, or if none, an asynchronous signal. The icons on the right are symbols for an input, output, bidirectional, or internal signal. An internal signal is used when an interface has some internal state that is maintained across operations (e.g., arbitration priority code). The largest window contains the signal waveforms and constraints. Gray waveforms represent input levels and dark ones for output levels. Timing constraints and ordering arcs are visible, simultaneity relations are not. The "@" is to be read as "cycles of". The time line is used only for relative placement and does not imply absolute positions for the events.

Sequencing information represents either causality or simple ordering among the events. Events that occur on the same signal are implicitly ordered in time. The designer explicitly provides *ordering arcs* to order events among different signals. Timing, synchronicity, and simultaneity constraints all deal with relative positioning of events. The *timing constraint* is the most general, specifying a minimum and/or maximum separation between two events. *Synchronicity constraints* relate a signal edge to the edge of the edges of a periodic waveform. The relationship is represented by a min/max timing constraint that corresponds to setup and hold times. *Simultaneity constraints* state that two events occur at the same time, within some tolerance.

Electrical constraints specify whether the signal should be tri-statable or open-collector, its termination resistance, the values of input and output currents and capacitances, and the required voltage levels and noise margins. These details are entered into a table with an entry for each signal. We will not discuss the design issues for this class of constraints as they are orthogonal to the algorithms presented in this paper.

Of course, there are aspects of an interface that cannot be specified solely in terms of logic, sequencing, timing, and electrical constraints. Among these are conditionals, loops, Boolean relations, etc. Two extensions are necessary. The first is to provide a procedural escape so that information most easily expressed as a Boolean expression or latching condition can be entered directly. The second is a means of specifying conditional behavior or repeating sequences of events in a diagram, and the ability to compose diagrams hierarchically.

A regular expression syntax is used to describe looping and conditional sequences. Segments of the drawing are specified to appear an arbitrary number of times or to be selected by some condition (see Figure 3). Events follow a specific path through the diagram depending on which conditions are true. A different event, timing constraint, or Boolean condition selects the diagram segment that is followed.

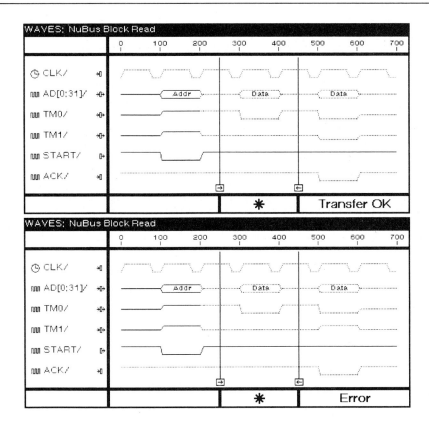

Figure 3. An example of a timing diagram with multiple segments. This is a description of the Texas Instrument NuBus's read operation [TexasInstruments85]. The number of words of data transferred is a function of some control signals. The transaction can either end properly or with an error. The diagram is broken up into three segments: the first is always used, the second can be repeated as required to transfer the complete block of data (not the Kleene star), and the third shows the ending sequence of events. In the two cases above, the second pulse on TM1/ indicates whether the transfer completed or an error occured. An identifying text string is assigned by the user to each conditional portion.

To make sure that a sequence of events can be repeated (i.e., the operation started again without concern for reinitialization), signal waveforms must have the same logic value at the beginning and end of a diagram. Levels must also be compatible at the boundaries between diagram segments.

Internally, timing diagrams are represented as event graphs. Each event is analogous to a statement in a programming language co-routine. This view is useful because co-routines are a familiar way to think about parallel execution. At any event in a diagram a *call* may be made to another diagram, causing the *start* node of the graph of the called diagram to be superimposed. A *rendezvous* in the calling diagram will superimpose the *end* node of the diagram being inserted (see Figures 4 and 5). These four types markers are attached directly to the edges of the waveforms using the editor.

3. Synthesis of Transducers

A transducer is a collection of logic circuitry that connects two compatible circuit interfaces. In general, it includes both synchronous and asynchronous components and must satisfy the timing constraints of both interfaces. Transducers are control-intensive, with modest datapaths. Their synthesis is, therefore, a special case of general circuit synthesis [Thomas83]. Our approach is to generate hardware elements and their interconnections by identifying sub-graphs within the event graphs derived from the interface timing diagrams. The example we use throughout this section, a transducer that connects a synchronous microprocessor to an asynchronous system bus, is based on Figure 4.

The synthesis algorithm involves five basic steps:

(1)   generate an event graph for each of the timing diagrams,
(2)   add arcs to interconnect the graphs whenever data must pass through the transducer,
(3)   use the configurations of nodes and arcs to choose idealized templates of logic and wires,
(4)   verify that the generated circuitry meets the timing constraints, and modifying the circuit to resolve violations, and
(5)   make adjustments to correct for the idealized circuitry in the final logic implementation.

We will discuss each of these steps in turn and use a small example to demonstrate the result. On one side of the transducer will be a simple microprocessor memory read interface, and on the other a commercial system bus, in this case the Intel Multibus [Intel82] (see Figure 4). For brevity, we are only considering the memory read operation.

Generating an event graph from a timing diagram is straight-forward. Each event (or edge) in the diagram corresponds to a node in the graph. A simple graph transformation is used to convert signals that have a tri-state output into two signals, one for enabling the output drive and another for the logic value. The nodes are divided into four types: asynchronous input, asynchronous output, synchronous input, and synchronous output. The arcs in the graph are of two types: sequencing arcs and min/max timing constraint arcs. Simultaneous events are grouped in super-nodes. Setup/hold and rise/fall times are not considered at this stage.

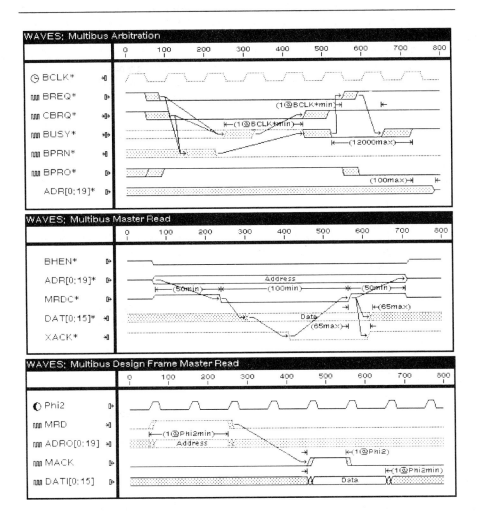

Figure 4. Waves timing diagrams describing the bus arbitration sequence used at the beginning of a read operation across the Intel Multibus, the basic read transaction on the bus, and at the bottom the read operation for a simple microprocessor. The first diagram calles the second as a co-routine. It is called from the falling edge of BUSY* and returns at the rising edge of the same signal. There is one signal in the first diagram that is constrained by a Boolean expression, BPRO* is set to (OR BPRN* (NOT BREQ*)). It is not represented in the graph. The ADR* lines in the first diagram are not part of the sequence of events. They are only present to express a constraint between this diagram and the one called as a co-routine. The event will be merged with the identical event in the second diagram. The first and second diagrams consistute one side of the transducer to be generated and the third is the other. The three diagrams are the input to Janus.

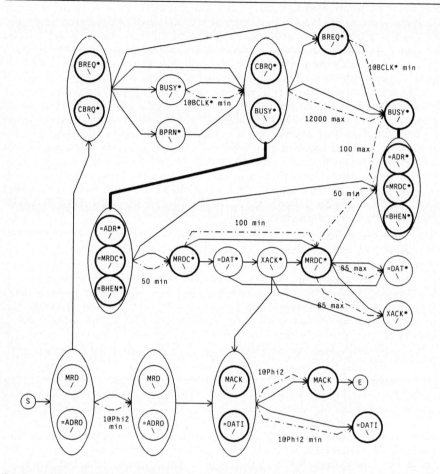

Figure 5. The combined graph to be implemented by Janus. There are three types of arcs: ordering constraints (solid), timing constraints (dashed), and co-routine calls and returns (bold). Darker nodes are outputs of the transducer (those to be implemented), lighter one are inputs (generated by the environment). Simultaneity relations are represented by ellipses combining nodes into super-nodes. Signal names prefixed with an "=" sign enable a tri-state output with the same name. The bold undirected arcs show the superposition of nodes caused by the co-routine call from the first to the second diagram in Figure 4. Also, the ADR* events are combined.

The graphs of the two interfaces are interconnected by generating additional arcs based on where data is moved across the interface. Data is identified in the diagrams by a common label in both interface specifications. In this case, the data are the identically labelled *Data* and *Address* signals in both diagrams. To insert the arcs, we must determine the *duration* and *controllability* of the data signals. The duration of data is defined by the portion of the graph over which the data has a valid logic level. Data is controllable if there is an output signal from the transducer that can be used to extend its duration. If the duration cannot be extended for the period over which the data is needed for transfer, then we must select a latching event that occurs within the data's duration. The value held in the latch will then be transferred across the other interface when appropriate. The graphs are interconnected by ordering arcs to ensure the proper sequencing of events to transfer data. In this example, the *Address* lines are the first data transferred; they can be latched on the microprocessor side as soon as MRD rises so there is an arc added from the bottom graph to the top graph (see Figure 5). The second data are the *Data* lines, and here we use the first event after the lines have been asserted to form an ordering arc with the first node where the data is required on the other side.

Once the graphs are interconnected, we use the complete graph to guide the selection of a set of building blocks. The primary building block is an idealized storage element. It is similar to an S-R latch and is ideal because its state changes on rising input edges rather than input levels. The output is set high on the first rising edge on S, and is reset on the first rising edge on R. This simple assumption makes it much easier to use the event graph (already based on edges) to generate state changes. Later analysis of the the inputs will determine if this flip-flop can be implemented as just two cross-coupled NOR gates or if extra circuitry will be needed to correct for inconsistencies with the idealized behavior.

An idealized flip-flop is assigned to each control signal (i.e., those signals that are not periodic and do not carry data) with polarity based on the initial level of the signal. Each flip-flop will have an extra input that forces its output to the level of the control signal at the beginning of the operation. This ensures that the level does not change except when a specific operation is in progress. A flip-flop will be assigned to enable each operation and will be set and reset by the first and last events in that operation. The other building blocks available include: complex logic gates, counters, multiplexors, delay lines [Bell85], latches, synchronizers, and standard D flip-flops.

Each node and its incident arcs is then used to select a particular connection between the flip-flops. The connection may involve some other circuitry, such as logic gates or synchronizers. Templates are selected based on the nodes from which the arcs eminate (see Figure 6). Some nodes do not require attention because they are implemented outside the transducer. Optimizations can be made when a familiar pattern is present in the graph. Particular patterns of nodes and arcs may have a simpler implementation than would be generated by the general method. For example, we can detect two events on a synchronous signal that are separated by one cycle and use a D flip-flop and NOR gate for their realization (see the *MACK* signal in Figure 8). Simple procedures are used to   check for the applicability of these optimizations from most specific to most general as the algorithm progresses through the graph.

Arc Types	Circuitry and/or Connections

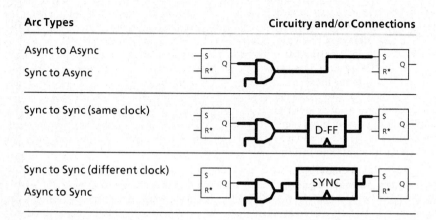

Figure 6. Templates for the implementations of each of the different types of ordering arcs in the graphs. More logic gates may be generated when boolean constraints are attached to some of the nodes.

The graph is traversed beginning with the start node. The only arcs used at this stage of the algorithm are the ordering arcs. The arcs leaving the start node are placed on an ordered queue and grouped together if they point to the same node (or *incident* node). Arc groups are ordered on the queue by increasing depth of their incident node from the start node of the graph. The first group on the queue is removed and used to generate some connections between control signal flip-flops. A node is considered to be implemented when its arc group (containing all arcs pointing to it) is taken off the queue and used to generate the circuitry that will cause the event represented by the node. *Joins* in the graph (i.e. nodes with more than one incident ordering arc) generate an extra logic gate before making a connection to an input of the control signal flip-flop. The gate ensures that all the preceding events have occured before the incident event is allowed to occur. *Forks* are easily implemented by a single event causing multiple following events through fan-out of its flip-flop output. When a node has been implemented, the arcs leaving that node are added to the queue, possibly being merged into already existing arc groups. This process continues until all ordering arcs are removed from the queue. There are two ways an arc is processed: as part of a group of arcs taken from the queue, or by never entering the queue because of being implemented by a sub-graph optimization.

After the entire graph is traversed and all events have been implemented, the next step is to check min/max timing constraints. The *paths* in the event graphs spanned by each constraint are identified. The path is broken down to all its component *simple paths*, those that have a single path from first to last nodes. A *circuit path* is the series of connections and logic used to implement the nodes between the first and last nodes on the path in the event graph. These are found by keeping back pointers to all generated circuitry during the template selection process.

Minimum timing constraints are considered first. In general, the problem is handled by adding delay to circuit paths. The minimum amount of delay needed to meet the constraints is used. All circuit paths are evaluated for their duration based on the typical delays of the logic circuitry (each module has associated input to output delays). Paths not meeting the minimum delay are identified. A wire is then selected to have extra delay since it is generating an event too quickly. We use a heuristic that first adds delay to the most common connection in all the paths. The delay added is the minimum necessary to make one path meets its constraint. We expect that this will reduce the number of delays that must be introduced. A delay element consists of a simple clocked flip-flop whenever possible. High-level policies discussed in the next section determine when a more costly delay line is to be used. The process continues until all paths meet their minimum constraints.

Violations of maximum timing constraints are handled differently. A path that does not meet its maximum constraint cannot be implemented by the fastest available circuit blocks within the allotted time. To give the circuit more time to generate the event, a transitive operation is performed on the incident arcs to the node. The tails of the arcs are moved back to a previous node. The node is then reimplemented with circutry that takes advantage of the earlier event.

Conditional paths through a diagram are handled implicitly by having the event that occurs first determine which part of the graph will actually fire next. Boolean constraints attached to a signal edge are easily incorporated into the synthesis scheme by generating a complex gate at the end of the connections being used to generate the event.

The last issue to consider is repeating events. These occur when either a signal rises or falls more than once during the course of the operation, or if there is a looping construct in the timing diagram. In these cases, some storage elements must be introduced to maintain information about which transition is currently active. For a loop this is a counter, and for multiple transitions it can be a simple set of flip-flops. Additional inputs to logic gates are generated to trigger events based on the state of these flip-flops.

In the final step, we must adjust for our assumptions about idealized flip-flops that are actually implemented by cross-coupled NOR gates. The waveforms of the flip-flop inputs must be analyzed to determine whether they are consistent with the assumption that S in never high once R has gone low. These analyses can be performed directly on the graph by checking for transitions preceding and/or succeeding the one in question. We want to make sure that each flip-flop sets and resets only once per operation for each of its pairs of S and R connections. The fix is to use another flip-flop to prolong the duration of the R input being high (since the flip-flop is reset-dominant this will keep the output low). This extra flip-flop can then be cleared by any signal that occurs after the S input has gone low (see Figure 7) or by an event generated at the end of the operation.

4. An Example

There are three goals that a designer strives to achieve in the design of an interface transducer. The first and most important is to maximize the data communication bandwidth. Every interface has a theoretical limit of data transfer determined by the interface specification, including sequences of events and timing

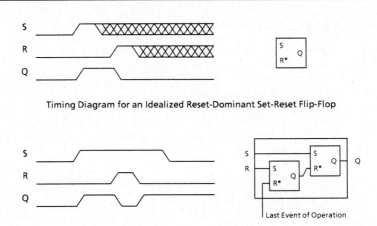

Timing Diagram for an Idealized Reset-Dominant Set-Reset Flip-Flop

Problem with Assumption and Corrective Circuitry

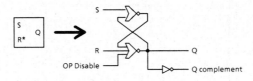

Actual Implementation

Figure 7. The timing diagram for an idealized reset-dominant set-reset flip-flop. Also shown is the additional circuitry required to correct the behavior when the idealizing assumption, that S is never high after R has gone low, is not met. The actual implementation shows the "OP Disable" signal used to initialize the flip-flop.

constraints. Transducer circuitry should generate events as fast as possible while still satisfying all timing constraints. The second goal is circuit robustness, the ability of the circuitry to catch all events and not reach an inconsistent or deadlocked state. Lastly, there is circuit size and complexity, which should be minimized.

There are important tradeoffs among these three goals. Optimal designs in terms of low overhead and high robustness tend to be costly in circuit complexity and design time. However, since transducer circuitry appears once per system, a somewhat larger circuit can be accomodated. The synthesis algorithm is driven by designer specified policies, quantifying the tradeoffs between speed and complexity. For example, designers tell the system how much of a delay penalty to accept before using a more costly delay line (in size and complexity), instead of clocked flip-flops, to meet minimum timing constraints.

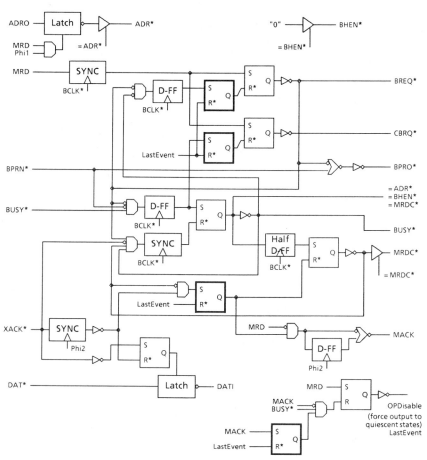

Figure 8. The circuitry generated by Janus from the interface specifications given in the diagrams and graphs of Figures 4 and 5. The S-R* flip-flops outlined with a darker line are those added to correct for the non-ideal behavior of the actual implementation. Signal flow is left to right, inputs are on the left, output on the right. Some circuitry near the bottom of the schematics is used to generate the "OP Disable" and "Last Event" signals. A half flip-flop is one half of a master-slave and provides a half-cycle delay. The "MACK" signal is generated by optimized circuitry for creating one-cycle pulses.

Assumptions regarding the response time of external circuitry can decrease the effort required in making the circuit robust. If constraints on external signals can be more precisely defined, then some circuitry can be eliminated. For example, if the minimum response time of an external circuit is greater than the minimum constraint between two transducer outputs, then a delay may not have to be added to meet that constraint. The timing diagram model allows these types of assumptions to be entered on the waveforms.

We have chosen for our example an application for which we have human-designed circuitry. The Multibus Design Frame (MDF) [Borriello85b] is an instance of an interface transducer between the Intel Multibus and a synchronous custom MOS internal circuit. Although the MDF includes circuitry for more operations than a data read, we have concentrated on the read operation to explain the entire synthesis process for this example in the space available. Figure 8 shows the circuitry generated by Janus from the graph of Figure 5.

Table 1 compares the synthesized transducer with the human-designed circuit. There is an entry for each of the different part types used with a gate count for that part. For this example, Janus's output has only 11% more gates. The average fan-in/fan-out of the gates is equal.

Transducer Circuitry Gate Count			
Part Type	Janus	Human	Difference
Latch	36@4 = 144	36@4 = 144	0
Synchronizer	3@10 = 30	3@10 = 30	0
Logic Gates	23@1 = 23	23@1 = 23	0
S-R* FFs	10@2 = 20	3@2 = 6	7@2 = 14
D FFs	3@10 = 30	2@10 = 20	1@10 = 10
Half D FFs	1@5 = 5	1@5 = 5	0
Total	262	228	24 (11%)

Table 1. A gate count comparison of the Janus generated circuitry and that done by a human designer. The table includes an entry for each building block type with the equivalent number of gates.

For other design metrics, however, Janus' circuit is superior. In bus efficiency, it uses 5% less time to perform a read (assuming a typical memory access time over the bus). This is because Janus uses a high level on the MRD signal to start an operation, while the human-generated circuit waits for the falling transition of MRD. This is due to the unspecified duration of the MRD pulse. Janus did not make the simplifying assumption that it will probably last only one cycle. This assumption makes the design simpler, since there is less graph parallelism to implement. For the case when MRD is only one-cycle long then Janus is 5% better, if it lasts longer however, Janus does not pay the penalty of waiting for its falling transition. This difference accounts for most of the extra gates.

5. Conclusions

Traditional hardware description languages do not provide an easy way to represent interface specifications. Extensions have been made to handle interface constraints [Nestor86], but they do not address the fundamental problem of having interface constraints embedded in the logic description. Programming languages that support communicating sequential processes have been modified to describe hardware constructs providing an easy path to interface simulation [Altman80, Parker81, Martin86]. However, these require the designer to learn another programming language and its associated debugging methods. We have developed an interface specification method based on timing diagrams. Timing diagrams can describe all interface details, when extended with simple procedural escapes to handle conditionals and loops. They are familiar to designers and can be used for interactive error-reporting and prompting of the designer.

An interface specification independent of the surrounding circuitry forms a basis for CAD tools that address circuit interface issues. We have described a new kind of CAD tool that would have been impossible without this abstraction, an interface transducer generator. We are developing another application for generating parameterized input vectors for simulators and testers. Output vectors can then be compared against a specification of the interface behavior rather than a single set of fixed result vectors [Arnold85]. Tools that check the compatibility of two interfaces are also possible. This is especially useful in large evolving design projects where consistency checking early in the design process is crucial [Katz83]. Analysis applications include evaluating the efficiency of an interface for data transmission and critiquing interface designs.

Previous work has used graphs to guide the synthesis of asynchronous circuits. The existing techniques fall into two categories. The first deals with asynchronous circuit synthesis [Hollaar82]. In real applications, however, constraints on the waveforms eliminate many concerns with unrestricted input changes that can cause these circuits to be quite complex. More efficient designs can be generated if these constraints are taken into account. The second category is self-timed control circuit synthesis [Chu86a, Chu86b]. This approach assumes that all circuit elements follow the same request-acknowledge four-cycle communication protocol, thus many simplifications can be made. This assumption is only appropriate when all circuit components are under the designer's control, which is not the case when interfacing a custom chip to a commerical system bus.

In summary, we have factored out interfaces as an independent specification, expressed through timing diagrams. A new tool, Janus, has been described which can synthesize transducers from interface specifications, making it possible to embed custom VLSI within a system context more rapidly. The tool generates circuitry comparable in both performance and size to human-designed transducers.

6. References

[Altman80] A. Altman, A. Parker, The Slide Simulator: A Facility for the Design and Analysis of Computer Interconnections, ACM, 1980.

[Arnold85] J. Arnold, The Knowledge-Based Test Assistant's Wave/Signal Editor: An Interface for the Management of Timing Constraints, Proceedings of the Second Conference on Artificial Intelligence Applications, December 1985.

[Bell85] A. Bell, R. Lyon, G. Borriello, Self-Calibrated Clock and Timing Signal Generator for MOS/VLSI Circuitry, U.S. Patent 4,494,021, January 1985.

[Borriello85a] G. Borriello, R. Katz, A. Bell, L. Conway, VLSI Design by the Numbers, IEEE Spectrum, February 1985.

[Borriello85b] G. Borriello, R. Katz, Design Frames: A New System Integration Methodology, 1985 Chapel Hill Conference on VLSI, 1985.

[Chu86a] T. Chu, On the Models for Designing VLSI Asynchronous Digital Systems, Integration, the VLSI journal, Vol. 4, August 1986.

[Chu86b] T. Chu, L. Glasser, Synthesis of Self-Timed Control Circuits from Graphs: An Example, Proceedings of the IEEE International Conference on Computer Design, October 1986.

[Hollaar82] L. Hollaar, Direct Implementation of Asynchronous Control Units, IEEE Transactions on Computers, Vol. C-31, No. 12, December 1982.

[Intel82] Intel Multibus Specification, Intel Corporation, 1982.

[Katz83] R. Katz, S. Weiss, Chip Assemblers: Concepts and Capabilities, 20th Design Automation Conference, 1983.

[Martin86] A. Martin, Compiling Communicating Sequential Processes into Delay-Insensitive VLSI Circuits, Journal of Distributed Computing, Vol. 1, No. 3, 1986.

[Nestor86] J. Nestor, D. Thomas, Behavioral Synthesis with Interfaces, International Conference on Computer-Aided Design, November 1986.

[Parker81] A. Parker, J. Wallace, SLIDE: An I/O Hardware Descriptive Language, IEEE Transactions on Computers, Vol. C-30, No. 6, June 1981.

[TexasInstruments85] NuBus Specification, Texas Instruments, 1985.

[Thomas83] D. Thomas, et al., Automatic Data Path Synthesis, IEEE Computer, December 1983.

AUTHOR INDEX

DATE